Applying Critical Mathematics Education

New Directions in Mathematics and Science Education

Series Editors

Wolff-Michael Roth (*University of Victoria, Canada*)
Lieven Verschaffel (*University of Leuven, Belgium*)

Editorial Board

Angie Calabrese-Barton (*Michigan State University, USA*)
Pauline Chinn (*University of Hawaii, USA*)
Brian Greer (*Portland State University, USA*)
Lyn English (*Queensland University of Technology*)
Terezinha Nunes (*University of Oxford, UK*)
Peter Taylor (*Curtin University, Perth, Australia*)
Dina Tirosh (*Tel Aviv University, Israel*)
Manuela Welzel (*University of Education, Heidelberg, Germany*)
Qiaoping Zhang (*The Chinese University of Hong Kong*)

VOLUME 35

The titles published in this series are listed at *brill.com/ndms*

Applying Critical Mathematics Education

Edited by

Annica Andersson and Richard Barwell

BRILL

LEIDEN | BOSTON

Cover illustration: Artwork by Liza Maxe

All chapters in this book have undergone peer review.

Library of Congress Cataloging-in-Publication Data

Names: Andersson, Annica, editor. | Barwell, Richard, 1969- editor.
Title: Applying critical mathematics education / edited by Annica Andersson and Richard Barwell.
Description: Leiden ; Boston : Brill, [2021] | Series: New directions in mathematics and science education, 2352-7234 ; volume 35 | Includes bibliographical references and index.
Identifiers: LCCN 2021020406 (print) | LCCN 2021020407 (ebook) | ISBN 9789004465411 (paperback) | ISBN 9789004465428 (hardback) | ISBN 9789004465800 (ebook)
Subjects: LCSH: Mathematics--Study and teaching. | Educational sociology.
Classification: LCC QA11.2 .A635 2021 (print) | LCC QA11.2 (ebook) | DDC 510.71--dc23
LC record available at https://lccn.loc.gov/2021020406
LC ebook record available at https://lccn.loc.gov/2021020407

Typeface for the Latin, Greek, and Cyrillic scripts: "Brill". See and download: brill.com/brill-typeface.

ISSN 2352-7234
ISBN 978-90-04-46541-1 (paperback)
ISBN 978-90-04-46542-8 (hardback)
ISBN 978-90-04-46580-0 (e-book)

Copyright 2021 by Koninklijke Brill NV, Leiden, The Netherlands, except where stated otherwise. Koninklijke Brill NV incorporates the imprints Brill, Brill Nijhoff, Brill Hotei, Brill Schöningh, Brill Fink, Brill mentis, Vandenhoeck & Ruprecht, Böhlau Verlag and V&R Unipress.
All rights reserved. No part of this publication may be reproduced, translated, stored in a retrieval system, or transmitted in any form or by any means, electronic, mechanical, photocopying, recording or otherwise, without prior written permission from the publisher. Requests for re-use and/or translations must be addressed to Koninklijke Brill NV via brill.com or copyright.com.

This book is printed on acid-free paper and produced in a sustainable manner.

Contents

Foreword   VII
   Ole Skovsmose
List of Figures and Tables   X
Notes on Contributors   XI

1 Applying Critical Mathematics Education: An Introduction   1
   Annica Andersson and Richard Barwell

2 Culturally Situated Critical Mathematics Education   24
   Annica Andersson and David Wagner

3 Decolonising Mathematics Education in a Time of Reconciliation   47
   Lisa Lunney Borden

4 *Propio* as a Decolonising Tool for Mathematics Education   71
   Aldo Parra and Paola Valero

5 The Potential of an Africa-Centred Approach to Theory-Use in Critical Mathematics Education   100
   Kate le Roux and Sheena Rughubar-Reddy

6 Tensions and Failures in an Analysis of Whiteness among a Racially and Socially Diverse Group of Mathematics Teacher Educators   123
   Victoria Hand, Beth Herbel-Eisenmann, Sunghwan Byun, Courtney Koestler and Tonya Bartell

7 "Mathematics Is Bad for Society": Reasoning about Mathematics as Part of Society in a Language Diverse Middle School Classroom   144
   Ulrika Ryan, Annica Andersson and Anna Chronaki

8 A Critical Mathematics Education for Climate Change: A Post-Normal Approach   166
   Richard Barwell and Kjellrun Hiis Hauge

9 The Mathematical Formatting of How Climate Change Is Perceived: Teachers' Reflection and Practice   185
   Lisa Steffensen, Rune Herheim and Toril Eskeland Rangnes

10   The Mathematical Formatting of Obesity in Public Health Discourse   210
      Jennifer Hall and Richard Barwell

Epilogues

11   From the Present Towards Hope for the Future   231
      Ulrika Ryan and Lisa Steffensen

12   Critical Mathematics Education Imaginaries: Culturally Situated, Situating, Transformative, Decolonising, and More   240
      Anita Rampal

13   Pessimism of the Intellect, Optimism of the Will   248
      Swapna Mukhopadhyay and Brian Greer

     Index   265

Foreword

Mathematics education can be a place where students address oppression and exploitation taking place in communities and societies. It can be a place where political visions for the future become formulated, and where students' aspirations, hopes, and dreams get articulated and find resources.

It can be a place where students at social risk come to understand the nature of the oppression to which they are subjected. These students might establish a basic political awareness for a critical citizenship. They might achieve new opportunities in life and get the means to move on in the educational system. They might come to see that further studies can also be for them.

It can be a place where students in comfortable social positions become aware of the many cases of social injustices that take place within the present social order. These students might come to acknowledge that individual welfare is different from social welfare, and that the economic dynamics that produce inequalities in society can be critically explored. Some of the students' taken-for-granted assumptions and preconceptions might be challenged.

It can be a place where mathematics comes to be used to identify cases of social oppression, such as in terms of racism and sexism. This identification can be in terms of numbers revealing biases with respect to jobs and salaries. Numbers might also demonstrate ethnic biases with respect to poverty and wealth. It might show biases with respect to how the police treats different groups of people. Mathematics might help to uncover and identify a range of cases of social injustice.

It can be a place where students experience that the very rationality of mathematics can be questioned. The use of mathematics can be problematic, and conclusions based on calculations might be doubtful. The "divinity" of mathematics can be challenged. At all levels of the educational system—primary school, secondary school, university—mathematics can be critically addressed.

It can be a place where students with different abilities can come to work and learn together. Mathematics education might become inclusive. The very conceptions of being normal and not being normal can be put aside, and turn mathematics education into a place where no "normalisations" are in operation. Mathematics education can become a place for everybody.

It can be a place where students with different cultural, economic, social, religious and ethnic backgrounds can meet each other. People get moved around due to war, violence, poverty, hunger, displacements, immigration and deportation. This makes it important to create communication across differences and mathematics education might form such communicative bridges.

It can be a place where students and teachers engage in dialogue. Teaching and learning can turn into processes of exploration, where suggestions, hypotheses and reasoning guide what is taking place. Different landscapes can be investigated and students can experience what it could mean to reach an insight through self-guided activities.

It can be a place where students find possibilities for relaxing, playing and enjoying themselves. Mathematics education is not only composed of content-focused teaching-learning processes. This education is part of life. It can be part of both the students' and the teachers' lifeworlds. It can be a place where everybody would like to stay.

Could mathematics education be such a place?

Maybe not.

Maybe what I have presented is not realistic. Maybe it is a pedagogical illusion of the kind of place that mathematics education could be. All the same, the aspiration of critical mathematics education is to turn mathematics education into just such a place.

We are living in a world where the dynamics of globalisation incorporate the extensive formation of ghettos. Dominant economic structures cause social exclusion. The global market is not for everybody. An ever-growing group of people are disposable according to the capitalist order of things. The world will experience new tensions and maybe wars due to the scarcity of resources. Hunger problems haunt the world today and we can expect them to escalate. Pollution appears to be a direct consequence of the acceleration of production. Clean drinking water will be in short supply and the ocean is turning into a soup of plastic. The production of food reaches new degrees of technical efficiency, for instance due to genetic manipulation and the extensive use of pesticides. The long-term consequences of this efficiency will only appear later. We might come to experience new types of diseases and new patterns of epidemics.

The present state of global development brings us to new complexities of conflicts and crises. Like during the period between the First and the Second World Wars, we see a growth of undemocratic movements. However, contrary to previously, the political extreme right now works in combination with neoliberal economic priorities. This creates deep controversies in the way conflicts and crises are handled. We are living through a period of profound uncertainties.

The socio-political and economic situation makes it difficult for critical mathematics education to pursue its aspirations. In countries where the extreme right is in power, as in Brazil at the moment, an intense preoccupation with what takes place in education can be observed. What can be printed and not printed in textbooks is brought under government control. What the teachers are doing starts to be observed. Recommendations for denouncing teachers addressing "political" issues are brought into circulation. The extreme right tries to keep strict control of what is taking place in school. This means that critical mathematics education faces severe obstacles.

On the one hand, patterns of oppression, exploitation and social exclusion combined with the dominance of extreme right-wing political priorities tend to make it impossible to pursue the aspirations of critical mathematics education. On the other hand, the very patterns of oppression, exploitation, social exclusion and extreme right-wing dominance makes it necessary to pursue the aspirations of critical mathematics education.

How can we respond to such a dilemma?

One way of finding out if something is possible or not, is to try to do it. This book provides an important demonstration of the richness of initiatives that it is possible to take in critical mathematics education. It has been a great pleasure for me to read the chapters and experience the powerful dynamics emerging from educational practice. The examples show that critical mathematics education can make a difference for many students.

The book makes an important contribution to critical mathematics education. It brings about hopes, aspirations and imaginations in a period where social, political and economic crises form our lifeworlds.

Ole Skovsmose

Figures and Tables

Figures

4.1 Geopolitical division of Colombia. The State of Cauca is shown in dark grey. (Image created by Milenioscuro, CC BY-SA 4.0, https://commons.wikimedia.org/w/index.php?curid=6031789). 73
4.2 Inzá seen from the school at Lomitas. 76
7.1 Flow chart of lesson orchestration. 151
7.2 Image of the concept map showing the inferential interconnections that the students made. 153
8.1 Temperature and rain in Bergen, Norway, August 31st since 1920 (www.yr.no). 180
8.2 Temperature in Bergen, Norway, August 31st since 1920 (www.yr.no) together with moving average of 5 years and a linear regression. 180
9.1 The picture on Max's first slide (photograph by Arne Naevra). 195
9.2 Kim's measurement table and four of the questions. 198
9.3 Kim's quiz. 201
9.4 Schmidt's graph (2020, personal communication) – climate model projections versus satellite observation (for an older version of this graph, see Schmidt, 2016). 202
9.5 The temperature graph from the quiz, recreated from a graph in Watts (2017) (Source: Met Office). 203
9.6 The two questions Max used to replace two of Kim's questions (a normal level is the arithmetic average of recorded levels from 1961–1990). 203
9.7 The graph to the left shows data from satellites with an annual increase of 3.2 mm, while the graph on the right shows coastal tide records with an annual increase of 1.8 mm (Source: NASA, https://climate.nasa.gov/vital-signs/sea-level/, accessed 2018). 204

Tables

2.1 Comparison of concerns. 34
8.1 Principles for teaching mathematics in the context of climate change. 177

Notes on Contributors

Annica Andersson
is a Professor of Mathematics Education at the University of South-Eastern Norway (USN). She is the leader of the Norwegian Research Council-funded project MIM: Mathematics Education in Indigenous and Migrational Contexts: Storylines, Cultures and Strength-Based Pedagogies. Annica's research is located at the intersections of mathematics education, language and cultural responsiveness and with a particular focus on equity, authority, discourses and human relationships in school mathematics education contexts.

Tonya Gau Bartell
is an Associate Professor of Mathematics Education at Michigan State University, USA. Her research focuses on teachers' development of equitable teaching practices with specific attention to issues of culture, race, and power. She is a co-editor of the *Journal for Teacher Education* and editor of the monograph *Toward Equity and Social Justice in Mathematics Education* (Springer, 2018).

Richard Barwell
is a Professor of Mathematics Education and Dean at the Faculty of Education, University of Ottawa, Canada. His research interests include language and discourse in mathematics classrooms, language diversity in mathematics education and critical mathematics education in relation to sustainability and ecosystem collapse. He is a former editor of the journal *For the Learning of Mathematics*. Prior to his academic career, he taught mathematics in the United Kingdom and Pakistan.

Lisa Lunney Borden
is a Professor of Mathematics Education at St. Francis Xavier University in Canada and holds the John Jerome Paul Chair for Equity in Mathematics Education. Having taught 7–12 mathematics in a Mi'kmaw community, she credits her students and the community for helping her to think differently about mathematics teaching and learning. She is committed to research and outreach that focuses on decolonising mathematics education through culturally based practices and experiences that are rooted in Indigenous languages and knowledge systems. Lisa teaches courses at the undergraduate and graduate level in mathematics education and Indigenous education. She is a sought-after speaker on Indigenous mathematics education, working with mathematics educators across Canada as well as internationally.

Sunghwan Byun

is a doctoral candidate at Michigan State University, USA. He is a former high school teacher and beginning teacher educator passionate about ensuring minoritised youths' access to the conversational floor in mathematics classrooms. His research focuses on social interaction in both mathematics classrooms and teacher education settings with the aim of equitable participation of mathematics learners. He uses conversation analytic approaches to explore pragmatic actions of teachers and teacher educators to achieve the ideals of equity and social justice in everyday practice.

Anna Chronaki

focuses on the socio-political and cultural-historical dimensions of mathematics education. Her work is based on contemporary anthropological and new materialist perspectives of mathematics education trying to create pedagogic experimentations and to theorise with a caring concern for potentially minor democratic renewals in curricular context and pedagogic praxis. She co-edited the volume *Challenging Perspectives on Mathematics Classroom Communication* (IAP, 2005) and edited the book *Mathematics, Technology and the "Body" of Education: Gendered perspectives* (UTH Press, 2009). In addition, she has edited the translation from English to Greek of Valerie Walkerdine's and Rik Pinxten's work. More recently, she has contributed papers to three special issues of the journal *ZDM*, concerning language research (2018), identity research (2019) and body studies (2019).

Brian Greer

worked for most of his career in the School of Psychology, Queen's University of Belfast, before undergoing paradigm shifts into Critical Mathematics Education and moving to the United States where he taught briefly at San Diego State University before taking early working retirement in Portland, Oregon. He co-edited *Culturally Responsive Mathematics Education* (Routledge, 2009) and *Opening the Cage* (Sense, 2012) and worked on a professional development project in schools in North Portland on Culturally Responsive Elementary Mathematics Education. He was one of the organisers of the Eighth International Conference on Mathematics Education and Society, held at Portland State University in 2015. He is currently working on the relationships between mathematics-as-discipline and mathematics-as-school-subject.

Jennifer Hall

is a Lecturer in Mathematics Education at Monash University in Melbourne, Australia. She has experience teaching and conducting research in Canada and Australia. In her research, she focuses on the relationships that students form with mathematics, studying how their in- and out-of-school experiences influence their views. She has a particular interest in exploring students' gendered relationships with mathematics and the ways in which gender-related research in mathematics education is conducted. Additionally, she researches representations of mathematics, mathematicians, and gender in popular culture; pre-service teachers' experiences with and views of numeracy; and students' experiences in university mathematics degree programs.

Victoria Hand

is an Associate Professor of Mathematics Education at the University of Colorado Boulder, USA. Hand's research interests revolve around opportunities to learn in mathematics classrooms in relation to issues of power, identity and race. She has often approached these topics from the perspective of students, and their experiences in different kinds of mathematical learning environments and systems. Hand is currently focused on broadening research efforts in mathematics education through participatory and community-based approaches.

Kjellrun Hiis Hauge

is an Associate Professor and a mathematics educator at the Faculty of Education, Arts and Sports, Western Norway University of Applied Sciences (HVL), Norway. She is the head of the strategic research programme Sustainability, Participation and Diversity. Her research is on democratic practices in teaching and learning, critical citizenship and students' capacity to engage critically with mathematics based information. In particular, her research is related to uncertainty and risk associated with contemporary and controversial societal issues, including oil exploitation, climate change and fake news. Related to this, she develops ideas for teaching and learning that challenge the idea that quantified information is either correct or wrong.

Beth Herbel-Eisenmann

is a Professor of Mathematics Education at Michigan State University, USA. Much of Herbel-Eisenmann's research draws on positioning theory and critical discourse theories to understand issues of authority and voice in mathematics classrooms and professional development contexts. Recently, Herbel-Eisenmann has partnered with colleagues to understand how using ideas from positioning theory might support mathematics teacher-researchers to understand and incorporate students' perspectives as they make changes to their classroom discourse and how implicit bias related to race and gender shapes mathematics teachers' facilitation of classroom discourse and talk about their students.

Rune Herheim

is an Associate Professor at the Faculty of Education, Western Norway University of Applied Sciences (HVL), Norway. Herheim is also chief editor of *Tangenten*, a national journal for mathematics teaching. His research interests concern the teaching and learning of mathematics with digital tools, students' mathematical argumentation and agency when issues from society are present, and the use of authentic data in mathematics teaching.

Courtney Koestler

is an Associate Professor of Instruction and Director of the OHIO Center for Equity in Mathematics and Science at Ohio University in Athens, Ohio, USA. Their scholarly interests and expertise centre on diversity, justice, critical literacy, and critical pedagogies in early and elementary education, teacher education, and mathematics education. Koestler is also a proud, former public school teacher and spends time each week working with youth and teacher-colleagues in classrooms.

Kate le Roux

is an Associate Professor in Language Development in the Academic Development Programme at the University of Cape Town, South Africa. Her research and teaching is located at the intersection of language, mathematics and the learning of disciplinary knowledge in science and engineering. This work has a particular focus on equity issues related to access, identity and power in multilingual higher education contexts. Theoretically, she draws on critical linguistics, critical mathematics education, multilingualism and multimodality for learning, and Southern theory.

Swapna Mukhopadhyay

is Professor Emerita in Curriculum and Instruction in the Graduate School of Education at Portland State University in Oregon, USA. Heavily influenced by Ethnomathematics, she taught future elementary teachers (and now mathematics students) about mathematics education with an emphasis on mathematics as a cultural construction. Recently, she has co-edited *Culturally Responsive Mathematics Education* (Routledge, 2009) and *Alternative Forms of Knowing (in) Mathematics* (Sense, 2012). Her current work includes a study of boat-builders on the Bay of Bengal, and leading a professional development project in schools in North Portland on Culturally Responsive Elementary Mathematics Education. She was one of the organisers of the Eighth International Conference on Mathematics Education and Society, held at Portland State University in 2015.

Aldo Parra

is an Associate Professor at the Universidad del Cauca, Colombia. He holds a PhD from Aalborg University, Denmark, with a thesis on a decolonial theory for ethnomathematics. He has worked in initial and continuing teacher training in Bogotá, Cauca, Nariño and Putumayo. He has also worked with indigenous communities in the Amazonian region and Cauca state. His research interests are related to indigenous education, linguistic diversity, critical mathematics education, ethnomathematics, epistemology and network theory. He is an active member of the International Network of Ethnomathematics, and was a member of its steering committee and part of the International Program Committee of the 6th International Congress of Ethnomathematics. He has also worked at the Columbian National Institute of Health in the development of mathematical models and knowledge management in public health. He is editor-in-chief of the *Latin American Journal of Ethnomathematics* and chair of the Topic Study Group 51 "Mathematics education for ethnic minorities" of the ICME-14 congress.

Anita Rampal

was formerly Dean, Faculty of Education, Delhi University, India. She has been Executive Committee member of the International Commission on Mathematics Instruction, and of Mathematics Education and Society (MES). She was also the Chairperson of the Primary Textbook Committees of India's National Council of Educational Research and Training (NCERT), which in 2006 developed innovative primary mathematics textbooks based on a critical pedagogy and a social constructivist approach. She was associated with policy-making, state educational initiatives, the Right to Education, the people's science movement, and the National Literacy Campaigns. She works in the areas of Policy Analysis, Curriculum Studies, Critical Mathematics Education, Science-Technology-Society Studies, Education for Sustainable Development and Teacher Education.

Toril Eskeland Rangnes

is Associate Professor at the Faculty of Education, Western Norway University of Applied Sciences (HVL), Norway. Rangnes has a background as a teacher in primary, lower secondary school, and teacher education. Her research interests concern exploring students' agency in mathematical conversations when issues from society are present, and studying how preservice teachers can facilitate students' multimodal argumentation and participation in multilingual classrooms.

Sheena Rughubar-Reddy

is a Senior Lecturer in the Numeracy Centre in the Academic Development Programme at the University of Cape Town, South Africa. She teaches quantitative literacy in interventions for students in the Faculties of Health Science and Humanities, where students' ability to apply numerical reasoning in context is developed. Her research interests deal with the theoretical basis of quantitative literacy in higher education, critical mathematics education and issues of social justice.

Ulrika Ryan
presently holds a postdoctoral position within the MIM (Mathematics education in Indigenous and Migrational contexts) project. Her research interests concern social epistemological dimensions of mathematics education. From perspectives of cognitive and social justice, her research focuses on language, social and discursive diversity in mathematical practices. She is particularly interested in how students in heterogeneous classrooms inhabit the learning space together as they encounter school mathematics. Her work is inspired by contemporary pragmatic philosophical perspectives and postcolonial ideas.

Lisa Steffensen
is an Assistant Professor at the Department of Language, Literature, Mathematics and Interpreting, at the Faculty of Education, Western Norway University of Applied Sciences (HVL). Her PhD involved a teaching and research partnership in a lower-secondary school mathematics classroom focused on critical mathematics education and climate change. Steffensen has a background as a mathematics and natural science teacher in lower secondary school. Her research interests concern how mathematic education can contribute to developing students' critical competencies by working with socio-political topics in the mathematics classroom.

Paola Valero
is a Professor of Mathematics Education at the Department of Mathematics and Science Education, Faculty of Science, Stockholm University, Sweden. Her research interests are mathematics education at all levels; in particular policy enactment processes, curricular development, multiculturalism and multilingualism in mathematics education, and diversity in mathematics teacher education. Currently, her research explores the significance of mathematics and science education as fields where power relations are actualised in producing subjectivities and generating in(ex)clusion of different types of students. She is currently the leader of the Swedish Research Council funded national Graduate school "Relevancing mathematics and Science Education (RelMaS)". Her research has been part of the Nordic Center of Excellence "Justice through education in the Nordic Countries".

David Wagner
is a Professor of Mathematics Education at the University of New Brunswick, Canada, and an Adjunct Professor (Professor II) at the University of South-Eastern Norway. He is most interested in human interaction in mathematics and mathematics learning and the relationship between such interaction and social justice. This inspires his research which has focused on identifying positioning structures in mathematics classrooms by analysing language practice, on teaching approaches that support sustainability, on ethnomathematical conversations in Indigenous communities, and on working with teachers to interrogate authority structures in their classrooms. He serves as co-editor of *Educational Studies in Mathematics* and on editorial boards of other journals. He has taught grades 7–12 mathematics in Canada and eSwatini.

CHAPTER 1

Applying Critical Mathematics Education: An Introduction

Annica Andersson and Richard Barwell

Abstract

In this introductory chapter, we first set out our broad characterisation of critical mathematics education, drawing on contemporary issues including, for example, global climate change and rapid societal challenges. Critical mathematics education is driven by urgent, complex questions; is interdisciplinary; is politically active and engaged; is democratic; involves critique; and is reflexive and self-aware. This perspective leads us to argue for the necessity of critical mathematics education, for which we summarise three significant traditions derived from Freire, Foucault, and the Nordic School. Finally, we provide an overview and discussion of the contributions to this volume, and show how they apply critical mathematics education in unique ways that relate to the six previously described features of this approach. We conclude by reiterating the urgent necessity of applying critical mathematics education.

Keywords

critical mathematics education – Freire – Foucault – Skovsmose – mathematics – climate change – race and racism – ethnomathematics – Indigenous perspectives

∙∙∙

> This is all wrong. I shouldn't be up here. I should be back in school on the other side of the ocean. Yet you all come to us young people for hope. How dare you! You have stolen my dreams and my childhood with your empty words. And yet I'm one of the lucky ones. People are suffering. People are dying. Entire ecosystems are collapsing. We are in the beginning of a mass extinction, and all you can talk about is money and fairy tales of eternal economic growth. How dare you!
> […]

The popular idea of cutting our emissions in half in 10 years only gives us a 50% chance of staying below 1.5 degrees [Celsius], and the risk of setting off irreversible chain reactions beyond human control. Fifty percent may be acceptable to you. But those numbers do not include tipping points, most feedback loops, additional warming hidden by toxic air pollution or the aspects of equity and climate justice. They also rely on my generation sucking hundreds of billions of tons of your CO_2 out of the air with technologies that barely exist.

So, a 50% risk is simply not acceptable to us—we who have to live with the consequences. To have a 67% chance of staying below a 1.5 degrees global temperature rise—the best odds given by the [Intergovernmental Panel on Climate Change]—the world had 420 gigatons of CO_2 left to emit back on January 1st, 2018. Today that figure is already down to less than 350 gigatons. How dare you pretend that this can be solved with just "business as usual" and some technical solutions? With today's emissions levels, that remaining CO_2 budget will be entirely gone within less than 8½ years.

There will not be any solutions or plans presented in line with these figures here today, because these numbers are too uncomfortable. And you are still not mature enough to tell it like it is. You are failing us. (Greta Thunberg's address at the United Nations Climate Action Summit in New York City, 23 September 2019)[1]

We wrote the first draft of this introduction in the same week that Greta Thunberg made her speech at the UN Climate Action meeting in New York in the autumn of 2019. Millions of young people worldwide were demonstrating with the goal of making our state leaders take action and follow the Paris Agreement on climate change. Thunberg's speech, partly quoted above, is a powerful call for change. It also involves a lot of applied mathematics. She refers to probabilities describing future global temperature change, as well as notions like tipping points and feedback loops. She refers to carbon budgets and projections for the likely timelines for humans to burn through that budget. Thunberg relates this mathematics to her values and her rage; she connects the mathematics of climate change to the responsibilities of leaders.

Greta Thunberg began her climate activism as a secondary school student when, instead of attending classes, she sat outside the Swedish parliament to protest at government inaction on climate change. Since that time, she has become the figurehead of worldwide youth-led demonstrations calling for stronger, faster action on climate change. As such, she is seen as a remarkable individual—a student who skipped school to change the world.

What would or could mathematics education be like if we took Greta Thunberg as its inspiration? It would be driven by urgent, complex questions that connect mathematics with science, geography, languages, and other curriculum subjects. It would be politically active and engaged, involving direct interaction with political leaders and institutions. It would be democratic in its orientation, promoting access to significant current information, debate about possible responses, and participation. This mathematics education would involve critique, using mathematics to interrogate complex problems, to question and to challenge. It would also be reflexive and self-aware, critiquing the role of education and of mathematics itself in contributing to problems like climate change. Thunberg, it should be noted, did not neglect her school assignments. It's just that school work was insufficient to change the world.

This vision of mathematics education is, broadly, a good example of what we mean by *critical mathematics education*. Over the past decades, different versions of critical mathematics education have emerged, drawing on different theoretical sources and traditions. While these different versions each have their distinctive aspects, they generally all share these common underlying features: in summary, critical mathematics education is *driven by urgent, complex questions*; is *interdisciplinary*; is *politically active and engaged*; is *democratic*; *involves critique*; and is *reflexive and self-aware*.

There is no shortage of urgent, critical problems that mathematics education can and should engage with. During the time it has taken to complete this book, we have seen the COVID-19 pandemic, widespread forest fires in many parts of the world, more evidence of how plastic particles have contaminated every part of the web of life, Black Lives Matter protests, and several election campaigns notable for "fake news." These phenomena are all a matter of life and death, all have a clear political dimension, all are interdisciplinary in nature, and all involve mathematics in different ways. There is plenty to be done with critical mathematics education.

There is now a well-established critical mathematics education research literature, as well as a growing popular literature. In the next part of this introductory chapter, we provide an overview of this work, first highlighting recent trends in the public understanding of mathematics, before offering an overview of significant early contributions, key concepts and principles in critical mathematics education. These contributions explore how mathematics teaching, curriculum and assessment is often implicated in social, economic and environmental injustice, either through the inequities of schooling, or through the content and nature of the mathematics curriculum.

Schooling is, of course, a central organising institution in the structuring of contemporary society. How does mathematics in school contribute to social-economic, racial or gender inequities? The mathematics curriculum, as proposed, taught and lived, paints a particular portrait of mathematics and of society. Does this curriculum prepare docile workers for an increasingly polarised economic system, or does it prepare future citizens who are able to critique the conditions of their lives and work for change? More broadly, how do popular discourses about mathematics contribute to problematic features of the organisation of our society? And how does our own activity as mathematics education researchers maintain or dismantle inequitable or problematic structures?

Research in critical mathematics education has sought to address these kinds of questions. We argue that much of this work is theoretical in nature, doing the important intellectual work of shaping the terrain, through the elaboration of concepts, principles and ideas. One of our motivations for proposing this book was to offer a collection of writing that shows how these concepts, principles and ideas can be *applied*, in school classrooms, teacher education classrooms, in curriculum development or in research projects. In so doing, we wanted to extend the nature and scope of what applying critical mathematics education can do; and we also sought to include scholars applying ideas from critical mathematics education in contexts that have rarely appeared under this heading in the past. In the last part of this chapter, we discuss some different forms of *applying* critical mathematics education and explain how they are illustrated by the chapters of this book.

1 The Growing Relevance of Critical Mathematics Education

Before examining the scholarly literature falling under the general heading of critical mathematics education, we first draw attention to the increasing popular awareness of how mathematics sometimes contributes to inequality or social injustice. More and more books and articles are appearing that draw attention to the role of mathematics in our society. These are not simply popular mathematics texts, designed to explain how probability or geometry are applied in contemporary society. A book like Nate Silver's *The Signal and the Noise* (2012), for example, makes a valuable contribution to explaining the application of probability in topics as diverse as baseball, the weather, political polling and election predictions. This book is critical in the sense that it contributes to an understanding of the application of Bayesian statistics in commonly consumed information. However, it is not critical in our stronger sense of critiquing the implicit biases and assumptions embedded in this mathematics.

Several other recent popular books offer examples of this more critical take on the role of mathematics in society. The central argument of Caroline Criado Perez's *Invisible Women* (2019), for example, is that a lack of gender-specific data in many aspects of society, including the economy, healthcare, design and architecture, employment practices, and government welfare programmes, results in systemic biases against women. To give one example, car safety standards are, according to Criado Perez, almost entirely based on a standard male norm, including a standard crash test dummy modelled on a "typical" 70 kg man. As a result, the majority of car safety data is not valid for women drivers. And it turns out that car safety features are not as effective for women, resulting in a higher proportion of injuries and deaths when women drivers are involved in road traffic accidents. Another example of this male bias has recently been highlighted in the UK, where the personal protective equipment necessary for healthcare workers fighting the COVID-19 pandemic was reportedly "designed for a 6 foot 3 inch bloke built like a rugby player."[2] Since approximately 80% of healthcare workers are women, the equipment was, incomprehensibly, designed for a male minority. For women healthcare workers, this equipment would often not fit correctly, thereby putting their own health and lives at risk. Criado Perez's book is an excellent resource for critical mathematics education. It is driven by a complex and persistent problem—that of a structural male bias in much economic and scientific activity. It challenges leaders and organisations to make structural changes, and clearly highlights how mathematics and science do not magically ensure an objective gender-aware approach to problem-solving.

In *Weapons of Math Destruction,* Cathy O'Neil (2017), writes about the inequity built into numerous socially significant algorithms, in relation to domains like crime prevention, insurance, and healthcare. In one chapter, for example, she shows how algorithms designed to make policing more efficient in some cities in the United States predict crime hotspots and so determine where police resources are allocated. These hotspots coincide with low-income (which in the US are often majority Black) neighbourhoods which are then subject to intensive policing methods. These methods in turn can result in a higher than average proportion of arrests for low-level infractions, so that residents in these neighbourhoods are more likely to have criminal records. Part of the bias comes from the fact that low-level infractions also occur in affluent neighbourhoods (including so-called "white collar" crime), but since police are not deployed in these neighbourhoods, criminal records are not built up. This chain of circumstances is driven by mathematics but results in the perpetuation of a form of inequality and, indeed, deadly structural racism, in urban policing.

In *Algorithms of Oppression,* Safiya Umoja Noble (2018) investigates structural biases in internet search algorithms with respect to race. She shows, for example, how entering into Google "why are black women so ..." results in words like angry, loud and mean, while similar searches for white women result in the words pretty and beautiful. Again, this bias is a result of complex mathematical algorithms, is, one assumes, not deliberate, but nevertheless perpetuates problematic racial and gender stereotypes. Both O'Neil's and Noble's books are resources for critical mathematics education. They make visible and critique how mathematics is part of the fabric of society, through the use of algorithms that encode human biases, blind spots and prejudices.

Hans Rosling, through his posthumous book *Factfulness: Ten Reasons We're Wrong About the World and Why Things Are Better Than You Think*, challenges our preconceptions and misconceptions (Rosling, Rosling Rönnlund, & Rosling, 2018). He asks why so many people, including Nobel laureates and other researchers, journalists, politicians and "ordinary" people, get some numbers so wrong on pressing issues such as poverty, pandemics and climate change. He shows how divisive ideas (separating *us* from *them*), the huge influence of the media and social media (telling us what to fear), and our perception of progress (seeing how things are getting worse rather than better) may hinder clear conversations and knowledge development. He invites us to think about, for example, the "gap instinct" (p. 31), or what we understand as "gap mathematics": the tendency to divide everything into two opposites, or dichotomies, or binary thinking. For example, consider comparisons of mean values, and the impact such comparisons might have on our worldview, when not also analysing the equally important distribution of data. Only looking at mean values gives very different results from analysing the distribution of women's and men's results in mathematical SAT-tests, for example. Rosling's point is that this "us and them" construct, or the "gap instinct," is not borne out by facts. It usually originates in large comparisons where the differences of the means and averages between compared labelled groups might not be as big as these means or averages indicate when distribution is also analysed.

There is a powerful political rhetoric around the "gap instinct" which we believe clearly connects with critical mathematics education. For example, the phrase "the growing gap," so frequently used by journalists in the media and by political leaders in their rhetoric, is an example of "gap" language where mean and average numbers are used for comparisons instead of measures of distribution, such as standard deviation or variance. We believe it is important to talk about and teach about these consequences and other mathematically oriented rhetorical language, such as the "generalisation instinct" (Rosling, Rosling Rönnlund, & Rosling, 2018, p. 173), the "perspective instinct" (p. 221) and the "urgency instinct" (p. 265). This is an important conversation to have specifically in mathematics education, since arguments with numbers are rhetorically powerful.

The fact that books like these have appeared in recent years is a positive development. There seems to be a greater awareness in society and in popular culture that mathematics, and in particular, the use of algorithms, are not simply neutral tools for enhancing efficiency in information systems. Mathematics, the communication of mathematics, and mathematics education can have unintended but very real consequences for people's lives. The question that follows for educators from this awareness is what, if anything, should mathematics teachers do about it? Should we, as teachers of mathematics, or educators of teachers of mathematics, address this dimension of mathematics in our work? This is precisely where critical mathematics education has something to offer.

2 Three Traditions of Critical Mathematics Education

Most research in mathematics education is concerned with questions of teaching, learning, assessment, curriculum, teacher education, and so on: practical problems arising from mathematics education in classrooms. It seeks to answer questions about how children or adults learn mathematics, how best to teach mathematics, how to prepare teachers to teach mathematics and how to assess what students have learned. This work is, of course, entirely reasonable and important. Nevertheless, there is a danger that this kind of focus is too narrow. For most mathematics educators, mathematics is not simply a set of procedures to be applied, or a set of facts to be memorised. Mathematics is a way of thinking and understanding the world. More particularly, mathematics is a human activity and reflects human concerns. It also, therefore, reflects human biases, blind spots and structures of dominance and oppression. A long-standing strand of research has adopted socio-cultural, socio-political and critical perspectives (for example, Atweh, Forgasz, & Nebres, 2001; Gutiérrez, 2013; Valero & Zevenbergen, 2004). This work has often been focused on the "hidden curriculum" of mathematics classes, the role of mathematics in the creation of a particular kind of social and economic organisation, such as that which has resulted in the climate crisis, and the need for students to learn about the role of mathematics in structuring their society and their lives.

In this section, we restrict ourselves to reviewing work that fits our characterisation of critical mathematics education research—that is, research that examines ways in which mathematics education can be driven by urgent, complex questions; is interdisciplinary; is politically active and engaged; is democratic; involves critique; and is reflexive and self-aware. We introduce three broad critical mathematics education traditions: Freirean, Foucauldian and the Nordic School. This characterisation is, of course, a simplification and the different traditions (and others besides) have certainly influenced each other in important ways, sometimes explicitly, but often implicitly. These different traditions share similar objectives but draw on different theoretical ancestors. This organisation is helpful for making sense of the different strands of thought influencing the field of critical mathematics education, but should definitely not be seen as creating discrete silos of work.

The first tradition we will describe is inspired by the work of Freire, focused on the value of mathematics for "reading the world." Freire's work was itself directly inspired by Marx's analysis of the structural basis within capitalism of the oppression of the working class and can be understood as an extension of Marx's ideas into the realm of pedagogy. In particular, Freire's emphasis on the importance of consciousness can be traced to Marx so that for Freire, a critical, transformative education must be designed around consciousness raising, with a particular focus on literacy (Lake & Kress, 2013). If, with Marx, Freire believed that only the oppressed can break the bonds of their oppression, then literacy was the key and the focus of his *Pedagogy of the Oppressed* (Freire, 2007).

Freire's ideas have particularly influenced North American approaches to research in critical mathematics education. In this tradition, mathematics is understood as being used not only for doing commerce, engineering, science, and so on, but also for conducting critical analyses of society, as a way of reading and transforming the world. The role of mathematics education is, therefore, to enable students, and particularly students who are marginalised by society in different ways, to use mathematics as a tool for their own empowerment. Marilyn Frankenstein was an early proponent of Freire's work in mathematics, publishing an article in 1983 with the title "Critical mathematics education: an application of Paulo Freire's epistemology." In this work, she draws out the important link between epistemology and emancipation or social transformation in relation to mathematics teaching:

> Freire's theory compels mathematics teachers to probe the nonpositivist meaning of mathematical knowledge, the importance of quantitative reasoning in the development of critical consciousness, the ways in which math anxiety helps sustain hegemonic ideologies, and the connections between our specific curriculum and the development of critical consciousness. In addition, his theory can strengthen our energy in the struggle for humanization by focusing our attention on the interrelationships between our concrete daily teaching practice and the broader ideological and structural context. (Frankenstein, 1983, p. 324)

The key point here is that it is insufficient to think of mathematics as a tool for understanding the world and therefore potentially as a tool for understanding inequality or oppression. Drawing on Freire's ideas, Frankenstein argues that we need to change how we think about the nature of mathematical knowing. Mathematics is a human activity and as such reflects human relations, including oppressive or hegemonic relations embedded in our social structures. Mathematics teaching must therefore address the social basis of mathematical knowledge and its implication in the structure of society, in order to empower students to challenge oppression.

This kind of approach has slowly been taken up around the world, but particularly in the Americas. Most notably, Gutstein's *Reading and Writing the World With Mathematics: Toward a Pedagogy for Social Justice* (2006) describes his work as a high school mathematics teacher in Chicago in the 1990s and into the 2000s. The Freirean influence is clear from the beginning:

> Students need to be prepared through their mathematics education to investigate and critique injustice, and to challenge, in words and actions, oppressive structures and acts—that is, to "read and write the world" with mathematics ... to read the world is to understand the socio-political cultural-historical conditions of one's life, community, society, and world; and to write the world is to effect change in it. (p. 4)

As an illustration of this approach, the book begins with Gutstein's account of teaching mathematics in September 2002, one year after the 9/11 attacks on New York. He describes how, over the course of the following days, he explores students' questions about the attacks and constructs mathematics problems, such as one about the number of full four-year university scholarships that could be paid for with the cost of one B2 stealth bomber. This example illustrates how students can use mathematics to read the world, and potentially, like Greta Thunberg, to effect change in it. More implicit is the epistemological status of mathematics highlighted by Frankenstein: mathematics teaching in this way also challenges students' relationship with mathematics. Students are not passive consumers of mathematical information and methods; they are active in seeking, interpreting and critiquing mathematical information and its application.

The second tradition of critical mathematics education research we describe draws on the work of Foucault. In this tradition, the focus is on mathematics as a discourse that plays a role in the organisation of human affairs. That is, the uses of mathematics, or references to mathematics, have various effects, many of which may be largely unnoticed or even invisible. From this perspective, the teaching and learning of mathematics is not simply a process of transmitting facts and procedures from teachers to students. Underlying the teaching and learning process are assumptions about the nature of rationality, of students, of teachers and of society, assumptions that may not be apparent to any of the participants. Mathematical discourses, for example, can construct particular kinds of categories in particular orders. To give one example, the idea of "normal," such as normal height, normal personality or normal behaviour, only arose with the emergence of modern statistics in the nineteenth century (Hacking, 1990). In similar vein, discourses of mathematics education construct learners and teachers in particular ways, as having particular roles and as performing particular functions, such as, for instance, the idea that mathematics is an innate talent seen in a few socially awkward boys and men.

Walkerdine's (1988) critical analyses of the mathematics education of young children is an important early example of a Foucauldian critical mathematics education study. Walkerdine's wide-ranging work drew explicitly on Foucault's ideas to show how ideas about learning and about mathematics produced particular kinds of children and particular kinds of rationality. In particular, she critiqued the then popular Piagetian perspective on children's mathematical learning and development, showing how it depended on particular assumptions about children and about mathematics that, in fact, reflected discourses of modernity, rationality and what it means to be human. Such theories, she argued, assume development to be a progressive, natural process that would, in "normal" children, result in a developed rationality of deductive reasoning and control of one's world. A key point here is that there is nothing "natural" about these assumptions or about this kind of rationality. Walkerdine also showed how the discourses of early childhood mathematics classrooms were strongly gendered, producing differences in the construction of girls and boys in relation to mathematics.

We call the third tradition of critical mathematics education the Nordic School as it was initiated by Scandinavian researchers. An early contribution to this strand of thinking came from Stig Mellin-Olson's (1987) book *The Politics of Mathematics Education*, in which he made two important points still relevant today. First, he noted that the diverse cultural practices in which different forms of mathematics arise (e.g., housebuilding, playground games) imply a political dimension to mathematics education. This political dimension is related to the relationships of dominance and resistance between the various cultures in which these cultural practices are embedded. Second, Mellin-Olsen highlighted the "the ideological content of mathematical models: what is being left out in the mathematical model, and which economic, physical or social theory leads to the relationships which are mathematised?" (p. 203).

These ideas were taken up and developed by Ole Skovsmose. In *Towards a Philosophy of Critical Mathematics Education*, Skovsmose (1994) sets out a detailed argument about how mathematics shapes modern society, often through technology, in often invisible ways. As a result, Skovsmose argues that it is not sufficient for children to only learn about how to do or use mathematics. They also need to learn about, and how to critique, the role of mathematics in their lives, in society and not the least, as a crucial part of the technology of economic development.

The Nordic School has developed ideas from within mathematics education, with a particular focus on how to change "traditional" mathematics classroom teaching towards a more student-centred environment in which societal challenges can be addressed, in which the role of mathematics in society can be pin-pointed, and in which critique of mathematics and its applications is allowed and even expected. This shift is accompanied by a reconceptualisation of the role of students in mathematics classrooms from a place of silence, individual calculations and mathematical exercises to a space of dialogue, reflection and critique (see Skovsmose, 2001a, 2009, 2012; Skovsmose & Nielsen, 1996).

These three broad traditions of critical mathematics education have different theoretical sources and slightly different foci. The Freirian tradition draws on Marxian theory and focuses on reading and writing the world with mathematics. The second tradition draws on Foucault's post-structuralist theory and focuses on mathematics in relation to discourses. The third tradition focuses more clearly on mathematics and mathematics learning, as developed most notably by Skovsmose. Despite their differences, all three seek to interrogate the world with mathematics, and mathematics with the world, through focusing on significant issues, often relating to injustice, oppression and critiques of contemporary society. All three traditions lend themselves to democratic values and political participation. And all three subscribe to a more expansive, and hence interdisciplinary, view of mathematics as being about more than a collection of facts, concepts and procedures.

In recent years, research in critical mathematics education has diversified and has made connections and synergies with other critical traditions in mathematics education or in educational research more broadly. Critical mathematics education researchers have engaged, for example, with ethnomathematics (Knijnik, 2007; Powell & Frankenstein, 1997), with Indigenous and decolonising perspectives (e.g., Gutiérrez, 2017; Parra-Sanchez, 2017), with critical pedagogy (Appelbaum, 2008), with the politics of post-colonial contexts (Vithal, 2003) or with gender studies (see Mendick, 2006). These different theoretical and methodological traditions have been developed extensively in mathematics education research and classrooms, and there are currently examples of how these theories can be applied in classrooms to better understand the role and power of mathematics in society and in education.

3   Applying Critical Mathematics Education: The Contribution of This Book

We see this book as distinct from previous collections of writing about critical mathematics education due to its focus on *applying* critical mathematics education. By "applying," we do not simply mean a teaching activity or programme. We seek to illustrate and explain how critical mathematics education can be used to understand the role of mathematics in mathematics classrooms, teacher education programmes or in critical analyses of specific issues. The book therefore extends the ways in which ideas in critical mathematics education have been applied. It shows how critical mathematics education can be applied to a wide range of topics, including topics not previously addressed (e.g., environmental sustainability, obesity). Our aim was to collect examples of applying the theoretical apparatus of critical mathematics education to understand a wide range of contemporary social phenomena in new ways. Chapters apply critical mathematics education to contemporary social challenges that have been under-examined in mathematics education, such as the global economy, peace, racial justice, decolonisation and migration.

The chapters showcase work conducted in different parts of our world, written by researchers with a diversity of mother tongues and cultural backgrounds, conducting their teaching, research and writing in their specific local contexts, but with global relevance and importance. The authors all share a profound belief that mathematics education can make a change in and for the world, through changing children's, students', teachers' and researchers' perceptions of mathematics, mathematics learning and the role of mathematics in society. We wish we could add that we share this belief with politicians, policymakers and curriculum designers, but we fear that this goal has yet to be reached.

We have organised the book in three informal parts. The chapters in the first part address questions about relationships between critical mathematics education, ethnomathematics and mathematics education research as a form of culturally situated research. Hence these chapters interrogate intersections of ethnomathematics, decolonisation and Indigenous ways of knowing. In these chapters, critical mathematics education is applied as dialogue between researchers and community members, between different ways of knowing mathematics, and between different theories. The second part comprises two chapters that focus on the importance of the theoretical and epistemological choices we make in the conduct of our research with respect to the dynamics of race and the necessity of researcher reflexivity. In these chapters, critical mathematics education is applied to an understanding of the research process. The third part focuses on research that seeks to understand the role of mathematics in organising society, and that works to include this focus in mathematics classrooms. In these chapters, critical mathematics education is applied in critical analyses of the social relevance of mathematics, as well as in mathematics classroom pedagogy. Of course, the chapters in the book could have been organised in many different ways and some chapters would fit well into more than one part, and the themes are interwoven. Nevertheless, they provide some structure for the book and support the reader in navigating between the chapters.

3.1 *Intersections of Critical Mathematics Education, Ethnomathematics, Decolonisation and Indigenous Ways of Knowing*

If critical mathematics education is politically engaged, democratic and reflexive, then its researchers must critically examine the role of their work in perpetuating structures of injustice and oppression, and must ask how their work can contribute to dismantling such structures. This kind of critical reflexivity is hard to do: as Foucault showed, these structures are embedded in our ways of knowing and interacting, and are therefore difficult to dismantle. What is known as mathematics comes from a specific Indo-European tradition that encodes a particular set of habits of mind. The challenge of how to see beyond our particular ways of knowing is particularly apparent in work that seeks to critically engage with ways of knowing that fall outside of this tradition and to do so in ways that are respectful, reciprocal and empowering. Critical mathematics education has perhaps not always put such concerns in the foreground.

Researchers working within ethnomathematics have grappled with some of these challenges for some time (see, for example, Barton, 2008; Pinxten & François, 2011). There has been little work, however, that applies ideas from critical mathematics education to ethnomathematics. The first contribution to this book, by Annica Andersson and David Wagner, explores possibilities for synthesising critical mathematics education and ethnomathematical concerns for teaching and research. Through a discussion of the history of ethnomathematics and of critical mathematics education, they tease out and discuss the intersections between these two areas, and develop a theoretical framework building on these common concerns. The framework is then used to analyse two empirical articles: one by Nutti (2013), who accounts for ethnomathematical research and teaching in an Indigenous Sápmi context; and one by Rubel et al. (2016) who give an account of critical mathematics education in a disadvantaged North American context. With this analysis, the authors demonstrate how the application of ideas from critical mathematics education to ethnomathematics is productive for both approaches. In particular, critical mathematics education gains a stronger sense of the situatedness of mathematical knowing.

In the chapter by Lisa Lunney Borden, a critical mathematics perspective is explored in relation with Indigenous mathematics education in Atlantic Canada. Using examples from her own 22-year learning journey together with a Mi'kmaw First Nation's community, she shows powerfully that moving towards decolonising mathematics and mathematics education comprises much more than applying mathematics to culturally relevant contexts or artefacts. Lunney Borden situates her text in the stories witnesses have shared about their experiences in Indian Residential Schools,[3] now published in reports arising from Canada's Truth and Reconciliation Commission. Hence, we are now starting to understand the impact these schools have had on over 150,000 Indigenous children, spanning over 100 years, and the inter-generational trauma that continues to this day. Lunney Borden lays out the role education has played in "creating inequity, perpetuating stereotypes and silencing Indigenous voices," and makes the clear claim that education is also the vehicle for addressing these wrongs and finding a new way forward. Her examples of critical mathematics education projects include examining diabetes rates in Indigenous communities, language revitalisation, persistent problems with unsafe drinking water and social justice issues. The projects described by Lunney Borden are contextually grounded as they emerged from specific Indigenous communities and were rooted in the stories shared by both Indigenous school teachers and Elders. Her chapter is an example of how critical mathematics education can contribute to the dismantling of oppressive social and economic structures by engaging with critique and decolonisation of mathematics, of education and of mathematics education research.

The third chapter in this part also engages with decolonisation through an Indigenous Colombian perspective on critical mathematics education. Aldo Parra and Paola Valero invite us to the Lomitas community in the Andes mountains, in the region of Tierrradentro in Colombia, a village that is only accessible on foot. There, through Parra's field work, they explore the thought-provoking conceptualisation of *propio*. Propio is a notion that emerged in Colombian Indigenous education to "think about, characterise and purposefully manage the relationship between community, knowledge and action in face of the life and political struggles of an Indigenous group." *Propio* may be acknowledged as an educational project, revealing decolonising standpoints and aiming to endorse a critical understanding of, for example, both intra- and extra-cultural conflicts and possibilities for a cultural diversity. Parra and Valero are applying critical mathematics education through democratic, participatory, and reflexive methods.

These three chapters are examples of applying critical mathematics education in ways that reflect all three traditions we described above. We see traces of the Freirean tradition, for example, in Parra and Valero's account of how the mathematics is driven by critical issues identified and developed by the people of Lomitas. We see traces of the Foucauldian tradition in the recurring attention to language and to the ordering of language and ways of knowing. In her work, Lunney Borden and her collaborators, for example, seek to re-order both language and ways of knowing through a repositioning of Mi'kmaw language in mathematics. And all three chapters examine how mathematics contributes to social reality in ways that extend beyond the technological contexts often considered in the Nordic tradition.

3.2   *The Dynamics of Race in Critical Mathematics Education Research*

In the second informal part of the book, the critical, reflexive, politically engaged commitments of critical mathematics education are applied to questions of race and racism. It is a matter of serious concern that critical mathematics education researchers do not seem to have engaged deeply with this topic, despite some clear connections. Critical race theory has had a growing influence within mathematics education (e.g., Davis & Jett, 2019; Martin, 2013) and has highlighted structurally racist assumptions within the organisation of mathematics curriculum, schooling and in mathematics education research, particularly in the United States (e.g., Martin, 2013), but critical mathematics education researchers have been slow to extend their work in this direction.[4] The two chapters in this part invite us to do just that.

Kate le Roux and Sheena Rughubar-Reddy situate their chapter theoretically, socially, culturally and historically in the complex context of South Africa. More specifically, they examine mathematics education in an access programme for prospective medical doctors at the University of Cape Town, in which its racial history impacts what happens today. In particular, the programme is designed to correct the overwhelming disadvantage Black students have had in being admitted to medicine programmes. The authors guide us through the voices of the university's historical structures, the experiences of Matla, a student in the programme, and through voices from student protests and strikes for racial justice. Building on the South African academic Hilary Janks's critical literacy framework and the concepts of access, domination, diversity and design, the authors tease out complex relationships between mathematics, mathematics education and power. Through using southern African theories, they challenge our "northern" epistemologies and theories, and respond to the question, in the place and context of South Africa: "What might a critical mathematics education look like in this extremely complex context at this moment in time?"

The second chapter in this part, by Victoria Hand, Beth Herbel-Eisenmann, Sunghwan Byun, Courtney Koestler and Tonya Bartell, is written in the context of an educational research project on the development of equitable mathematics education systems in the United States. This group of authors share their collaborative encounters, experiences and tensions that arose during a critical reflexive study of Whiteness within the research group, exploring how the collaborative project maintained White institutional space. The analysis phase of the overall project resulted in "insights that came at significant cost to scholars of Colour involved in the analysis" and that hence threatened the project as a whole. They describe the tensions and perpetuation of patterns of racial privilege and dominance that occurred when White scholars in the team pushed the project forward, without taking time to hear and discuss moments of "confusion, doubt or other emotionally-led stopping-points." The group utilises the notion of "failure" to describe the "systematic ways that 'best intentions' become a means for further oppression."

These two chapters show how critical mathematics education can be applied to questions of racial justice, although both are clearly first steps. Le Roux and Rughubar-Reddy's chapter shows how mathematics education can act as a racially organised and organising gate-keeper, something that is apparent in many other parts of the world. Similarly to the chapters in the previous part, they question the ordering of ways of knowing about mathematics and mathematics education and seek to invert that ordering by bringing locally relevant perspectives to their analysis. In Hand et al.'s chapter, this ordering extends to the social practices within the research group. Their chapter demonstrates how applying critical mathematics education means reflexively paying attention to the conduct of critical mathematics education research.

3.3   *Understanding the Role of Mathematics in Organising Society*

The last set of chapters focus squarely on the organising role played by mathematics in contemporary society, a role particularly highlighted by Skovsmose (e.g., 1994). Indeed, Skovsmose has provided several specific examples in his writing, including that of airline seat reservation systems that rely (or did so pre-pandemic) on algorithms and overbooking to ensure full flights, with the result that occasionally some passengers would be "bumped" because too many seats had been sold (Skovsmose, 2001b). This idea, and the explanatory concept of "formatting," in which mathematical models become prescriptive of reality, has an analytic potential that has only recently started to be realised. Indeed, O'Neil's (2017) book, in effect, sets out a series of examples. The chapters in this part, then, extend these ideas into new areas.

The chapter by Ulrika Ryan, Annica Andersson and Anna Chronaki, describes a multilingual and multicultural school context in Sweden where a 10-year-old student argued that "Mathematics is bad for society." Inspired by this statement, a small-scale project was created to explore this idea in his exceptionally language diverse, but unilingual (Swedish only) middle school classroom. The young students were challenged to make value-laden critical interconnections between mathematics and society, because in such a language diverse classroom "embracing students' personal ways of knowing is intertwined with the socially and culturally normative inferences inherent in language(s)." Theoretically, the authors mainly frame their analysis with Wittgensteinian ideas, such as language games and, specifically, the *language game of giving and asking for reasons* (GoGAR) (Brandom, 1998, 2001). The authors argue that the conversations about the idea that "mathematics is bad for society" allowed the young students to see mathematics and society as interconnected and to grasp the political role of mathematics in society, and hence to become critically mathematical literate. The students had to shift from accepting to questioning the strong prevailing discourses about mathematics as neutral or beneficial. This chapter illustrates how critical mathematics education can be applied in a classroom setting.

The second and third chapters in this part look at the connection of mathematics to climate change. Richard Barwell and Kjellrun Hiis Hauge's chapter draws our attention to important questions of how mathematics educators can prepare teachers to teach critically and mathematically in an intertwined manner. The authors offer a set of principles based on critical mathematics education, as well as the theory of post-normal science, that are designed to inform classroom practice. Post-normal science reconceptualises the relationship between science, policy and democracy in the context of global challenges featuring high levels of conflict, uncertainty, and urgent risks. Barwell and Hauge prompt us to consider what a mathematics pedagogy for the climate might look like, a question we could purposefully ask in each of our specific contexts. They present three groups of principles relating to forms of authenticity, forms of participation, and reflecting on and with mathematics. These principles are a starting point for thinking and teaching about mathematics teaching in relation to climate change specifically, but are also helpful for planning critical mathematics tasks, problems and teachings in relation to other (post-normal) topics.

From Bergen, following in the tradition of Stieg Mellin Olsen, Lisa Steffensen, Rune Herheim and Toril Eskeland Rangnes write about bringing climate change into the mathematics classroom. Their starting point is the idea that students' and citizens' understanding of climate change depends on deep critical mathematical understandings, such as knowledge about how mathematical models work to predict future climate changes. With this in mind, they initiated a research project with three lower secondary school teachers and analysed the teachers' choices and arguments for when they included climate change examples in their mathematics classes. In particular, the research focused on "identifying the potential for facilitating students' awareness and understanding of the formatting power of mathematics." They show how these three teachers emphasise the importance of being critical and mathematically literate with the purpose of both understanding and influencing society in their classroom teachings. They close by highlighting the central role teachers have in this way of teaching. They also reveal how they needed to develop further awareness both about mathematical argumentation and "of how they themselves make use of the formatting power of mathematics in their teaching and facilitation for critical learning."

The final chapter in this part, by Jennifer Hall and Richard Barwell, presents a critical mathematics education analysis of the mathematical formatting of the body mass index (BMI) and the societal power that it has. They examine the history and recent use of this measure to show mathematics affects our view of weight, obesity, and body image. They argue that mathematics contributes "to the creation of obesity as a concept and as a problem, and thus shapes people's experiences of obesity and of themselves." They systematically guide us through the history of the BMI formula and show examples of its construction of "obesity discourses" and how these are used in, for example, news media, schools, and insurance companies. In this chapter, a critical mathematical analysis is used to draw attention to the way that the discursive power of mathematics transforms the rich diversity of human life—in this case, human bodies—into "a normative, prescriptive, and ideological abstraction." This transformation then supports forms of intervention and control, and problematic normative discourses of body image, gender, and race.

The four chapters in this part illustrate different ways of applying critical mathematics education to urgent issues in order to promote democratic citizenship and political engagement. These chapters extend previous work in critical mathematics education, for example by focusing on environmental and health issues. They illustrate how democratic citizenship can be fostered in mathematics classrooms by exploring landscapes of investigation with schoolchildren and their teachers. Democratic citizenship also needs detailed analyses of particular mathematical interventions in society, with particular attention to their historical dimension. As Foucault demonstrated, to understand the contemporary organisation of knowing, it helps to trace a historical trajectory. This kind of critical mathematics analysis offers great potential for researchers to challenge public discourses around phenomena like obesity and climate change, and other post-normal challenges.

3.4 Epilogues

The book ends with three Epilogues, with the purpose of inviting scholars with a range of voices and experiences to reflect on applying critical mathematics education, as presented in the preceding chapters. The first is by Ulrika Ryan and Lisa Steffensen, contributors to some of the chapters in the book, who represent up-and-coming voices in this field. The second is by Anita Rampal, whose critical reflections, deeply embedded in the Indian context, with social justice issues like poverty, inequity and caste, challenge our thinking about applying critical mathematics education in contexts very different from Eurocentric ways of thinking and knowing. The final epilogue is by Swapna Mukhopadhyay and Brian Greer, both of whom would, in Swedish metaphor and with great respect, be called "old foxes" of critical mathematics education research. All three epilogues are extended reflections on implicit and explicit themes that appear in the main chapters of the book and prompt new directions for the future. The three epilogues draw out the contemporary relevance of the contributions to this book, clearly influenced by the events of a particularly tumultuous 2020.

4 Concluding Remarks

Greta Thunberg is right. She and her friends should not have needed to be present at the United Nations Climate Action Summit in New York City in 2019, demonstrating and taking action for climate change. She should have been in school, as should all her demonstrating friends and young activists. The irony is that Greta Thunberg and all the other activists probably learned a great deal more about applied mathematics, science, social studies, and so on, and about the critical use of mathematics, when demonstrating in city centres and talking at meetings of world leaders, than if they had been back in school, solving simultaneous equations in their regular mathematics classes.

Does this really have to be the case? What is our role as teachers of mathematics, or educators of teachers of mathematics? Should we address this dimension of mathematics in our work? We believe that we should. If anything, all the chapters in this book have taught us the need for a more societally important, politically relevant, democratic mathematics teaching at all levels of the education system. Climate change is an urgent global topic, as is the aftermath of the COVID-19 pandemic in which we find ourselves. Invisible women in technological development and the impact of big data where the use of mathematics contributes to inequality or social injustice are other examples of the global use of mathematics that impact us as individuals and in our personal lives. However, applying critical mathematics education is equally important in local contexts. Examples like drinking water challenges in Indigenous communities, BMI-measures that affect healthcare decisions, a young boy in a rural school questioning if mathematics is good for society, post-colonial documents with powerful numbers, or the complexity of teaching post-apartheid university mathematics courses in South Africa are all local contexts where applying critical mathematics education can make a difference.

In this book, the contributors show how some version of critical mathematics education can be applied in many different ways and in a wide variety of contexts to offer alternative ways of thinking about mathematics in schools, in universities, in research and in society. Critical mathematics education can be applied to projects of decolonisation, of ethnomathematics, and empowerment. It can be applied to questions of race, racism, obesity or climate change. It can be applied in classrooms or in communities. It can be applied as theory, as a form of analysis or as a way to think about pedagogy. Critical mathematics education has developed many principles and concepts. How else can they be applied?

We find ourselves finishing this introduction during a peak of the COVID-19 pandemic. Thunberg's *cri de coeur* about not being in school, is now, more than a year later, the reality for many children and youth in the world during the widespread lockdowns. The pandemic is a time when we see mathematical models, diagrams and graphs from all over the world, perhaps more than ever before. We notice them every day, in all kinds of media. As noted by a friend on Annica's Facebook wall, the number of exponential graphs on Facebook is increasing exponentially. To the questions posed above, we now also ask how this COVID-mathematics will influence our future teaching or our students' interest in societal mathematics, when schools and universities open again.

Our hope is that the tremendous value of applying critical mathematics education, in all the different ways shown in this book, will open up the range of possibilities for research and practice in mathematics education in order to focus on local and global challenges in local contexts. It has been a privilege to work with the texts for this volume. We hope that this work will inspire new creativity in mathematics learning, teaching and curriculum, so that all children can become as critically mathematically literate as Greta Thunberg and all her activist friends around the world. We should not fail them in any mathematics classroom.

Notes

1 https://news.un.org/en/story/2019/09/1047052
2 https://www.theguardian.com/world/2020/apr/24/sexism-on-the-covid-19-frontline-ppe-is-made-for-a-6ft-3in-rugby-player
3 Indian Residential Schools were state-sponsored schools to which Indigenous children were forcibly sent from the nineteenth century onwards, with the explicit goal of erasing their Indigenous cultures and languages. Children were sent hundreds of kilometres away from home from the age of five. The last such school closed in 1996.
4 This observation raises the uncomfortable possibility that the loose coalition of researchers we identify as critical mathematics educators needs to question its own biases and that we need to consider the biases in our characterisation of this coalition.

References

Appelbaum, P. (2008). *Embracing mathematics: On becoming a teacher and changing with mathematics.* Routledge. https://doi.org/10.4324/9780203930243

Atweh, B., Forgasz, H., & Nebres, B. (Eds.). (2001). *Sociocultural research on mathematics education: An international perspective.* Lawrence Erlbaum. https://doi.org/10.4324/9781410600042

Barton, B. (2008). *The language of mathematics: Telling mathematical tales.* Springer. https://doi.org/10.1007/978-0-387-72859-9

Brandom, R. B. (1998). *Making it explicit: Reasoning, representing, and discursive commitment.* Harvard University Press.

Brandom, R. B. (2001). *Articulating reasons: An introduction to inferentialism.* Harvard University Press. https://doi.org/10.2307/j.ctvjghvzo

Criado Perez, C. (2019). *Invisible women: Data bias in a world designed for men.* Adams.

Davis, J., & Jett, C. C. (Eds.). (2019). *Critical race theory in mathematics education.* Routledge. https://doi.org/10.4324/9781315121192

Frankenstein, M. (1983). Critical mathematics education: An application of Paulo Freire's epistemology. *Journal of Education, 165*(4), 315–339. https://doi.org/10.1177/002205748316500403

Freire, P. (2007). *Pedagogy of the oppressed.* Continuum.

Gutiérrez, R. (2013). The sociopolitical turn in mathematics education. *Journal for Research in Mathematics Education, 44*(1), 37–68. https://doi.org/10.5951/jresematheduc.44.1.0037

Gutiérrez, R. (2017). Living mathematx: Towards a vision for the future. In E. Galindo & J. Newton (Eds.), *Proceedings of the 39th annual meeting of the North American Chapter of the International Group for the Psychology of Mathematics Education* (pp. 2–26). Hoosier Association of Mathematics Teacher Educators.

Gutstein, E. (2006). *Reading and writing the world with mathematics: Toward a pedagogy for social justice.* Taylor & Francis. https://doi.org/10.4324/9780203112946

Hacking, I. (1990). *The taming of chance.* Cambridge University Press. https://doi.org/10.1017/cbo9780511819766

Knijnik, G. (2007). Mathematics education and the Brazilian Landless Movement: Three different mathematics in the context of the struggle for social justice. *Philosophy of Mathematics Education Journal, 21*(1), 1–18.

Lake, T., & Kress, R. (2013). Freire and Marx in dialogue. In R. Kress & T. Lake (Eds.), *Paulo Freire's intellectual roots: Toward historicity in praxis* (pp. 29–52). Bloomsbury. https://doi.org/10.5040/9781472553164.ch-002

Martin, D. B. (2013). Race, racial projects, and mathematics education. *Journal for Research in Mathematics Education, 44*(1), 316–333. https://doi.org/10.5951/jresematheduc.44.1.0316

Mellin-Olsen, S. (1987). *The politics of mathematics education.* Reidel.

Mendick, H. (2006). *Masculinities in mathematics.* McGraw-Hill Education.

Noble, S. U. (2018). *Algorithms of oppression: How search engines reinforce racism.* New York University Press.

Nutti, Y. J. (2013). Indigenous teachers' experiences of the implementation of culture-based mathematics activities in Sámi school. *Mathematics Education Research Journal, 25*(1), 57–72. https://doi.org/10.1007/s13394-013-0067-6

O'Neil, C. (2017). *Weapons of math destruction: How big data increases inequality and threatens democracy.* Broadway Books.

Parra-Sanchez, A. (2017). Ethnomathematical barters. In H. Straehler-Pohl, N. Bohlmann, & A. Pais (Eds.), *The disorder of mathematics education* (pp. 89–105). Springer. https://doi.org/10.1007/978-3-319-34006-7_6

Pinxten, R., & François, K. (2011). Politics in an Indian canyon? Some thoughts on the implications of ethnomathematics. *Educational Studies in Mathematics, 78*(2), 261–273. https://doi.org/10.1007/s10649-011-9328-z

Powell, A. B., & Frankenstein, M. (Eds.). (1997). *Ethnomathematics: Challenging Eurocentrism in mathematics education.* State University of New York Press.

Rosling, H., Rosling Rönnlund, A., & Rosling, O. (2018). *Factfulness. Tio knep som hjälper dig att förstå världen* [*Factfulness: Ten reasons we're wrong about the world—and why things are better than you think*]. Natur & Kultur.

Rubel, L. H., Lim, V. Y., Hall-Wieckert, M., & Sullivan, M. (2016). Teaching mathematics for spatial justice: An investigation of the lottery. *Cognition and Instruction, 34*(1), 1–26. https://doi.org/10.1080/07370008.2015.1118691

Silver, N. (2012). *The signal and the noise: The art and science of prediction.* Penguin.

Skovsmose, O. (1994). *Towards a philosophy of critical mathematics education.* Kluwer. https://doi.org/10.1007/978-94-017-3556-8

Skovsmose, O. (2001a). Landscapes of investigation. *Zentralblatt für Didaktik der Mathematik, 33*(4), 123–132. https://doi.org/10.1007/BF02652747

Skovsmose, O. (2001b). Mathematics in action: A challenge for social theorising. In E. Simmt & B. Davis (Eds.), *Proceedings of the 2001 Annual meeting of the Canadian Mathematics Education Study Group* (pp. 3–17). CMESG.

Skovsmose, O. (2009). *In doubt: About language, mathematics, knowledge and lifeworlds*. Sense. https://doi.org/10.1163/9789460910289

Skovsmose, O. (2012). *An invitation to critical mathematics education*. Sense. https://doi.org/10.1007/978-94-6091-442-3

Skovsmose, O., & Nielsen, L. (1996). Critical mathematics education. In A. J. Bishop, K. Clements, C. Keitel, J. Kilpatrick, & C. Laborde (Eds.), *International handbook of mathematics education* (pp. 1257–1288). Kluwer. https://doi.org/10.1007/978-94-009-1465-0_36

Valero, P., & Zevenbergen, R. (Eds.). (2004). *Researching the socio-political dimensions of mathematics education: Issues of power in theory and methodology*. Springer. https://doi.org/10.1007/b120597

Vithal, R. (2003). *In search of a pedagogy of conflict and dialogue for mathematics education*. Springer. https://doi.org/10.1007/978-94-010-0086-4

Walkerdine, V. (1988). *The mastery of reason: Cognitive development and the production of rationality*. Routledge.

CHAPTER 2

Culturally Situated Critical Mathematics Education

Annica Andersson and David Wagner

Abstract

Based on a synthesis of connections between ethnomathematics and critical mathematics education, we present a set of four "concerns," framing what we call culturally situated critical mathematics education. We see any ethnomathematics or critical mathematics education work as fitting within this framing. We illustrate the framework with an analysis of two empirical articles, one reporting an ethnomathematical teaching and research project in a Sámi context, and one reporting on a critical mathematics education teaching and research project in an underprivileged context in the USA. Our analysis shows how the concerns bring the strengths of ethnomathematics to critical mathematics education and vice versa.

Keywords

critical mathematics education – ethnomathematics – cultural situatedness

∴

For several years, we have engaged in conversations about ethnomathematics and critical mathematics education. These are labels that may be identified as theoretical research areas, research methodologies and/or pedagogies. We have asked ourselves questions about the relationship between ethnomathematics and critical mathematics education and about how these differences are connected to theory and practice. We have also asked ourselves in what geographical spaces each of these approaches is used. Who in our field applies ethnomathematical theories or critical mathematics education theories in their research work and who critiques it?

In this chapter, we explore the possibility of synthesising critical mathematics education and ethnomathematics. Through our previous work, which we see as located within both fields, we see each approach informing the other. Through a discussion of ethnomathematics and critical mathematics education, we tease out and discuss the intersections between them. We address the question about differences by first focusing on commonalities, and come to see that the differences may be seen as variations of similar orientations. In this vein, we propose a synthesised *culturally situated critical mathematics education* as a framework, structured around a set of guiding analytical "concerns." This framework encompasses both ethnomathematics and critical mathematics education in a way that brings the strengths of each to the other. We apply this framework to analyse two empirical articles: one by Nutti (2013), who accounts for ethnomathematical research and teaching in Indigenous Sápmi context; and one by Rubel et al. (2016) who give an account of critical mathematics education in a disadvantaged North American context. With this analysis, we demonstrate how the framework can help researchers using critical mathematics education and/or ethnomathematics reflect on their work.

1 Locating Ethnomathematics

We begin with an overview of our prior work in which we mapped the trajectory of ethnomathematics and asked what could be counted as ethnomathematical research within the Mathematics Education and Society (MES) conference proceedings (Andersson & Wagner, 2015). For this analysis, we searched for *ethnomathematics* (and other forms of the word by searching on *ethnomathematic**) in all accepted symposia and papers in the proceedings. We found some interesting numbers to unpack further. For example, for a high number of the papers in which we found the word *ethnomathematics,* the word was only used once or twice; these papers were not focusing on ethnomathematical research in particular. In an even higher number of papers, the word or a form of it was present only in the reference list. In contrast to the word *ethnomathematics,* the word *culture* (or its variant, *cultural*) was present in almost all accepted MES papers. The word *culture* was used in a variety of contexts, usually in a nominal way, with no theorisation of culture or the place of culture in mathematics. The word *anthropology* was rare.

As an example of *potential* ethnomathematical work, we decided that it could make sense to place any work on language register as ethnomathematical because it focuses on an artefact (mathematics language) of a specific culture (a language register). For example, Zolkower and de Freitas (2010) "guided [teachers in the] deconstruction of whole-group interaction texts selected as paradigmatic instantiations of this genre" (p. 509). Their attention to a genre, which is a part of the mathematics classroom register, would seem to place the work in a culture, but their reporting does not connect the language practice to the culture. Their investigation of linguistic patterns is not uncommon in the field, including some of our own work (e.g., Herbel-Eisenmann & Wagner, 2010). We find that such work is not identified as ethnomathematical, though we see that it could be designated as such.

Our closer look at the MES papers in which *ethnomathematics* appeared more than once in the body of the text found that the largest number of these papers used ethnomathematical research to justify and/or position their own research, and/or, in a few sentences, show awareness that ethnomathematics exists. Fewer papers specifically situated the research in ethnomathematical theories. There were also papers that talked about ethnomathematical research: such papers may argue that ethnomathematical research is important, should be done with care and awareness, or raise concerns—for example concerns about exoticism or, as in the papers from South Africa, about ghettoisation.

Almost all papers in the MES proceedings raise concerns about cultural aspects and/or particular cultural groups. However, the number of papers explicitly addressing, critiquing, or discussing ethnomathematical research is low. This finding highlights the significance of culture to sociocultural and sociopolitical research even when it is not explicitly ethnomathematical. We also found interesting the demographics of who does ethnomathematics and who critiques it. In general, we found that explicitly ethnomathematical work has been done in colonised settings, and critiques of ethnomathematics have been done by people of coloniser cultures, with the exception of researchers from South Africa, whose experiences with Apartheid motivated concerns about the ghettoisation of groups of people.

2   Locating the Myth of Culture-Free Mathematics

Critiques of ethnomathematics and the relative paucity of explicitly ethnomathematical work (even at MES conferences) point to a general avoidance of ethnomathematics in our field. We also have anecdotal evidence of a general rejection of ethnomathematics; each of us has written about our early interest in ethnomathematics and the lack of encouragement we received in the field (Andersson & Wagner, 2015). We think that the myth that mathematics is free of culture is part of the reason for this rejection. But this does not explain the rejection of ethnomathematics from scholars who acknowledge the cultural nature of mathematics. Hence, we consider it necessary to elaborate the basic myth of a non-cultural mathematics, which we consider to be the most significant myth related to mathematics, most certainly to ethnomathematics but maybe also in relation to critical mathematics education.

The word *myth* is used generally to describe something that is not true. However, we see myths as the stories people use to interpret their experience—and they can go beyond stories, to include any texts (words, images, memes, etc.). These stories are common expressions of widespread belief. In this way, myth may also be regarded as formative. What makes something a myth is not its falseness but rather its pervasiveness in a discourse and/or a culture. We have elaborated this view of myth elsewhere (Andersson & Wagner, 2018; Wagner, 2019), a view that follows Barthes (1957/2009) and connects with anthropological perspectives on myth (e.g., Geertz, 1974).

The view that mathematics is free of culture is a myth because it is a widespread belief. The view is also mythic because it is a view that is generally unfounded, which is not to say that it is (completely) untrue—it is what Barthes (1972/2009) calls a tautology, one of the rhetorical tools of myth he identified. The myth about mathematics being free of culture is not completely untrue because mathematics characteristically aims for abstraction and generalisation. In other words, it generally steps away from particularities, context, and thus culture. However, we see such moves for abstraction as human moves, and they are thus situated. The move for abstraction is a move within culture, so we do not see abstraction as culture-free. Jurdak's (2016) conclusions in his article about ethnomathematics and real-world problem solving in schools resonate with our view:

> The contribution of ethnomathematics to mathematics education is vital as far as its illumination of the cultural value of linking mathematics to culture and of the educational value of ethnomathematical practices in the learning and teaching of mathematics. (p. 131)

Related to the myth of culture-free mathematics, scholarship has a range of perspectives of how to think of academic mathematics as a culture. We identify three different scholarly positions on the relationship between ethnomathematics and academic mathematics. We notice that they each verify the significance of the myth that math is culture-free.

In 1996, in his early work on defining ethnomathematics as a research program (building on the work by Ubiritan D'Ambrosio, Marcia Ascher and Paulus Gerdes), Barton (1996) stated that:

> Ethnomathematics is a research programme of the way in which cultural groups understand, articulate and use the concepts and practices which we describe as mathematical, whether or not the cultural group has a concept of mathematics. (p. 214)

In other words, the 'we' indicates that what 'we' (as academic mathematicians, outside of culture) define as mathematics is the norm to which ethnomathematics is to be explored and explained. At the same point in time, Borba (1997) viewed ethnomathematics as an (kind of) academic mathematics and argued that:

> The accepted mathematics ... ranges from ones developed by students to the one accepted/developed/intended by the teacher. In the classroom dialogue, the teacher can learn from the ethnomathematics "spoken" by the students, just as the students are learning from the academic ethnomathematics of the teacher. (p. 268)

However, this quotation still positions academic mathematics as the norm – as the mathematics stated in school jurisdiction steering/curriculum documents and hence to be distributed by the teacher. Academic mathematics is the mathematics that is acceptable to teach and to explore. This alienates students who come to class with other mathematics—ethnomathematics.

Some years later, Rowlands and Carson (2002) firmly asserted in a critical, and critiqued, article about ethnomathematics that:

> The goal of ethnomathematics should be to examine human mathematical thinking in tribal cultures in order to help students recognise both the universal nature of human ingenuity and the remarkable diversity of its many forms of expression. As an introduction to the historical origins of mathematical thought worldwide, it is a potentially useful practice. However, to substitute a curriculum of ethnomathematics for instruction in formalised, modern mathematics may become a form of cultural disenfranchisement. (p. 92)

They concluded by stating that:

> Mathematics is universal because, although aspects of culture do influence mathematics, nevertheless, these cultural aspects do not determine the truth content of mathematics: Pythagoras' theorem was developed by the Greeks and independently by the Chinese a century and a half later and 'Pascal's triangle' was developed by the Chinese centuries before Pascal. Mathematics transcends the civilisations of ancient Greece and China and the France of Pascal and it is this universalism that has to be emphasised in the classroom—rather than the geometrical patterns in traditional crafts. (p. 98)

Hence, there is a tension in our field about how to position ethnomathematics and academic (western) mathematics in relation to each other, both in research and in school mathematics. Most mathematics education scholars position academic mathematics as the norm, and as we have shown above, even ethnomathematicians often position academic mathematics as the norm. Others see academic mathematics and ethnomathematics either as complementary or as informing each other.

Parra (2018) has confronted the tension between these positionings by seeing mathematics as performative. Mathematics is done in different cultures. If someone from one culture encounters mathematics being done in another culture, it is necessary for them to interpret that mathematics through their own cultural lens. Parra encouraged a focus on the interactions between the people in a culture and the ethnomathematician. Parra's approach sidesteps the myth of culture-free mathematics (probably intentionally).

We consider the myth of a culture-free mathematics through the different tensions that we identify in relation to ethnomathematics with the purpose of considering possible reasons for avoiding ethnomathematics. First, a tension between structuralism and functionalism are central to the myth of culture-free mathematics. Structuralism takes commonalities as evidence of a human essence on which language is structured. Functionalism takes these commonalities as evidence that people in different cultures are responding to similar challenges and thus invent similar ways of responding to these challenges. Applying this idea to ethnomathematics, we can distinguish between people who see a mathematical essence (mathematical truth) that manifests in different cultures and people who see mathematics as situated (as human responses to particular situations). We think that most ethnomathematics researchers have the functionalist perspective: mathematics arises out of particular contexts (and these contexts may have similarities resulting in some similar mathematics), but Rowlands and Carson (2002) take a structuralist perspective.

The "truth" in the myth described above relates to the characteristic move to or for abstraction in mathematics. From a functionalist perspective, humans in many cultures have found it helpful to make such moves for abstraction—to look for patterns and commonalities across particular contexts and to try to think about these things separate from the contexts. From a structuralist perspective, abstraction would be seen as a set of pre-existing truths that humans can work at uncovering, and different cultural mathematics are therefore seen as multiple perspectives on the same thing. We see elements of both approaches within ethnomathematics scholarship. For example, Borba (1997) could be seen to value understanding different perspectives as a way of getting a better picture of the truth (that is structuralism) or to value mathematics as a medium through which to understand better the contexts of different people (that is functionalism).

Second, ethnomathematics may be seen as a form of colonialism. There might be a view that ethnomathematics is just another instance of taking riches from other cultures. Colonialists first took (and continue to take) the resources from other people's land and from the land itself. This extraction is a form of abstraction. We sell them a 'better life' (our culture, our languages), leaving behind only remnants of their culture and language. And now, with ethnomathematics we aim to take their ideas (their mathematics) and maybe make them ours. This could be a structuralist perspective in which we see ethnomathematics as mining for new perspectives so that we can understand better the things we are all trying to understand. If we accept this structuralist view, then we might feel that it is warranted to dig together with diverse people to find the treasure and share it, but to do this with cultural sensitivity.

Third, we reflect on what Dowling (1998) called the "myth of emancipation." In response to the work of Paulus Gerdes, Dowling noted that the "difficulty is that it appears that a European is needed to reveal to the African students the value inherent in their own culture" (p. 12) and that this revelation is done in European terms. This criticism is problematic because Gerdes became a citizen of Mozambique and renounced his Dutch citizenship. We do not see abstraction from culture as particularly relevant to Dowling's challenge of ethnomathematics. Nevertheless, Dowling's criticism addresses a motive that is commonly expressed by people who do ethnomathematics—for example, Gerdes (1997) wrote that ethnomathematics has emancipatory power because uncovered mathematical practices can inspire confidence in students who may assume that they cannot do mathematics. We would argue along the lines of Borba (1997) and Parra (2018) that the judging can go both ways—academic mathematics may be used to evaluate (consider the benefits of) another culture's mathematics and vice-versa.

Fourth, a wariness of colonialism and ethnomathematics may be an expression of fear of addressing thorny issues. This fear may be stronger amongst people of privilege, perhaps because we are less motivated to change the structures that have brought us privilege. Our counting of MES papers showed the tendency for ethnomathematics to be taken up in colonised settings, although we could not determine the motive for the tendency.

3 Locating Critical Mathematics Education

In the previous section, we examined the cultural situatedness of ethnomathematics by considering the locations from which it is done and critiqued. In this section, we do something similar with critical mathematics education, which is the focus of this book. Critical mathematics education has developed in two geographically different contexts: a Scandinavian tradition and a North American tradition.

The Scandinavian tradition started in Norway with Stieg Mellin-Olsen's (1987) sociopolitical work, and was followed in Denmark by the rich production of Ole Skovsmose (e.g., 1994, 2001) and others. In this tradition, Skovsmose formulated critical mathematics education as addressing a range of "concerns" which Skovsmose and Nielsen (1996) articulated as follows:

a. Citizenship identifies schooling as including the preparation of students to be an active part of political life.
b. Mathematics may serve as a tool for identifying and analysing critical features of society, which may be global as well as having to do with the local environment of students.
c. The students' interest emphasises that the main focus of education cannot be the transformation of (pure) knowledge; instead educational practice must be understood in terms of acting persons.
d. Culture and conflicts raise basic questions about discrimination. Does mathematics education reproduce inequalities which might be established by factors outside education but, nevertheless, are reinforced by educational practice?
e. Mathematics itself might be problematic because of the function of mathematics as part of modern technology, which no longer can be reviewed with optimism. Mathematics is not only a tool for critique but also an object of critique.
f. Critical mathematics education concentrates on life in the classroom to the extent that the communication between teacher and students can reflect power relations. (p. 1257)

The first of these concerns covers the whole of critical mathematics education, constructing a concept of citizenship that assumes an active political life. We emphasise that political activity requires engagement with local contexts, which include both environmental and cultural considerations. In other words, political activity is by nature situated. This situated aspect of critical mathematics education connects with traditional definitions of ethnomathematics, such as Barton's (1996) characterisation of it as being interested in how "cultural groups understand, articulate and use the concepts and practices which we describe as mathematical" (p. 214). A significant difference is that critical mathematics education engages students in doing mathematics in a cultural situation, while traditional ethnomathematics studies, observes and documents the mathematics done in a cultural situation.

In addition to the Scandinavian branch of critical mathematics education, we recognise the branch of critical mathematics education developed by

North American researchers such as Gutstein (e.g., 2006), Frankenstein (e.g., 2001), Brantlinger (2013) and others, mainly based on Freire's (1968/1996) fundamental theoretical ideas concerning literacy, oppression and human rights in schooling in South American contexts. Critical mathematics education from this perspective is also ethnomathematical in several aspects. For example, Gutstein (2010) reported on his action research in a classroom in which "reading and writing the world—with mathematics—were very much the agenda" (p. 272). He carefully described cultural aspects of the classroom and thus exercised a particular form of ethnomathematics in his reporting, in addition to leading his students in cultural situated work (Andersson & Wagner, 2015). This may be different from analysing ethnomathematics in a culture in which the researcher is not actively taking part.

The way that we have described critical mathematics education might be regarded as a kind of mathematics arising in specific cultural contexts. The mathematics is different in the different contexts but of course they have similarities as they represent people responding to similar problems—in this case they are responding to inequities in their societies. Similarly, our analysis of the MES proceedings (Andersson & Wagner, 2015) considered the demographic and geographic contexts of ethnomathematical work. We did not describe ethnomathematics as abstracted knowledge, but rather we situated it in the cultural context of mathematics education research. This was an ethnomathematical move. But it was also a critical mathematics education move, because the move was motivated by the kinds of concerns that drive critical mathematics education.

We note that in this book, with its strong focus on critical mathematics education, there are two chapters that focus on ethnomathematics and how ethnomathematical teaching and research may be addressed as critical mathematics education. Like Lunney Borden, and Parra and Valero (both this volume), we are motivated to connect the two. Both Lunney Borden and Parra have written about their research in Indigenous settings and have raised political, decolonising questions. We note that these researchers have conducted their research in the Americas—in Colombia and Canada—where the critical mathematics education tradition usually explicitly or implicitly is informed by the theoretical ideas developed by Freire (i.e. 1968/1996).

4   The Concerns of Culturally Situated Critical Mathematics Education

Given the connections between ethnomathematics and critical mathematics education, we present a set of concerns focusing on a synthesis of the two. We call these the concerns of *culturally situated critical mathematics education*. With this adjusted list of concerns (adjusted from the list from Skovsmose and Nielsen, 1996), we would see any ethnomathematics or critical mathematics education work as fitting. The importance of this unified set of concerns is that critical mathematics education work can benefit from attending to the ethnomathematical concerns that are added into the framework, and vice versa. We acknowledge that there are examples of scholarship that already straddle the line between these two traditions. Parra and Valero (this volume) and Lunney Borden (this volume) are examples of this. For another example, we point to the work by Knijnik (2012) who introduced power concerns into her ethnomathematical work:

> Introducing power into the ethnomathematical discussions avoided a naïve understanding of the mathematical diversity. Making power explicit in ethnomathematics could allow us to analyse how the politics of knowledge operates in schooling processes and, in particular, in the mathematics curricula. (p. 89)

Our list of concerns, given below as the things we pay attention to in culturally situated critical mathematics education, borrows heavily from Skovsmose and Nielsen's (1996, p. 1257) list, and has been developed in our process of reading and writing about ethnomathematics and critical mathematics education over time.

1. *Analysing community features*: Mathematics may serve as a tool for identifying and analysing critical features of a community, which may include its global context but must focus on the local context of students.
2. *Focusing on acting persons*: Educational practice must be understood in terms of acting persons. This means that pure, abstracted knowledge is not sufficient. Instead, the focus is on mathematical practices of people in the community, including students as active citizens.
3. *Reflecting on mathematics*: Mathematics is not only a tool for critique but also an object of critique. Educational practice must reflect on the role of mathematics in relation to inequities. It asks how the mathematical and mathematics education practices in the community, initiate, reproduce, sustain, or transform inequalities. Whose needs are favoured?
4. *Reflecting on education*: Culturally situated critical mathematics education is attentive to life in the classroom. It recognises that communication among teachers, students and others in the school milieu can reflect, create and sustain power relations.

We compare our list of concerns with the list from Skovsmose and Nielsen (1996) in Table 2.1. The first concern identified by them—promoting "preparation of students to be an active part of political life" (p. 1257)—encompasses all

TABLE 2.1 Comparison of concerns

Skovsmose & Nielsen (1996, p. 1257)	Andersson & Wagner
(a) Citizenship identifies schooling as including the preparation of students to be an active part of political life.	1. *Analysing community features*: Mathematics may serve as a tool for identifying and analysing critical features of a community, which may include its global context but must focus on the local context of students.
(b) Mathematics may serve as a tool for identifying and analysing critical features of society, which may be global as well as having to do with the local environment of students.	
(c) The students' interest emphasises that the main focus of education cannot be the transformation of (pure) knowledge; instead educational practice must be understood in terms of acting persons.	2. *Focusing on acting persons*: Educational practice must be understood in terms of acting persons. This means that pure, abstracted knowledge is not sufficient. Instead, the focus is on mathematical practices of people in the community, including students as active citizens.
(e) Mathematics itself might be problematic because of the function of mathematics as part of modern technology, which no longer can be reviewed with optimism. Mathematics is not only a tool for critique but also an object of critique.	3. *Reflecting on mathematics*: Mathematics is not only a tool for critique but also an object of critique. Educational practice must reflect on the role of mathematics in relation to inequities. It asks how the mathematical and mathematics education practices in the community, initiate, reproduce, sustain, or transform inequalities. Whose needs are favoured?
(d) Culture and conflicts raise basic questions about discrimination. Does mathematics education reproduce inequalities which might be established by factors outside education but, nevertheless, are reinforced by educational practice?	4. *Reflecting on education*: Culturally situated critical mathematics education is attentive to life in the classroom. It recognises that communication among teachers, students and others in the school milieu can reflect, create and sustain power relations.
(f) Critical mathematics education concentrates on life in the classroom to the extent that the communication between teacher and students can reflect power relations.	

concerns, in our view and is thus not represented separately in our list. The second concern in our list emphasises the active aspect of the concern expressed by Skovsmose and Nielsen, but our articulation differs in that we want to see the students already active politically, not only preparing to be active later. Following this orientation to action, our labels for each concern focus on action.

Our *first concern* is very similar to the second concern identified by Skovsmose and Nielsen. We have emphasised the need to address local contexts, which was not a requirement in the way they articulated the concern. This local emphasis is something we think ethnomathematics contributes to critically minded mathematics educators. Our *second concern* is a rewrite of the third concern identified by Skovsmose and Nielsen. We turned it around to start with the positive statement—what mathematics should do, instead of what it should not do. The focus on the actions of people in the community is clearly an ethnomathematical concern. Connecting the students' actions to the actions of community members brings critical mathematics education and ethnomathematics together. Our *third concern* is a rewrite of the fifth concern identified by Skovsmose and Nielsen. Our *fourth concern* brings together the fourth and sixth concerns identified by Skovsmose and Nielsen, which are closely related to each other.

We will illustrate our four concerns by using them to analyse two articles, one that would normally be seen as ethnomathematical and one that would normally be seen as an example of critical mathematics education. This analysis aims to show how the concerns bring the strengths of ethnomathematics to critical mathematics education and vice versa.

5   Exemplars: Two Articles

For the purpose of this chapter, we analysed two published journal articles: one representing ethnomathematical research and teaching by Nutti (2013) with the title "Indigenous Teachers' Experiences of the Implementation of Culture-based Mathematics Activities in Sámi School"; and another representing critical mathematics education research and teaching by Rubel et al. (2016) entitled "Teaching Mathematics for Spatial Justice: An Investigation of the Lottery." Nutti's research presents teachers' reflections on a cultural based mathematics teaching during an ethnomathematical teaching sequence in a Scandinavian Indigenous setting with the intention to recreate a Sámi cultural activity in a mathematical school context. Rubel et al.'s work is situated in a disadvantaged community school in northern America, a school where all students are identified as having relatively low socioeconomic status (they qualify for free or reduced lunches) and all are identified as Hispanic (75%) or Black (25%). The research focuses on students and their mathematical learning during a teaching sequence based on place-based pedagogies. The teachers in their study led students in using digital technologies to map the location of money spent on government-sponsored lotteries in their city and the location of distributed profits from these lotteries. Their work identified which neighbourhoods gained money from the lottery system and which neighbourhoods lost money.

We chose these two articles with the following criteria in mind. First, we wanted articles that described exemplary practices. Second, we wanted articles by scholars who are not the most commonly cited authors in relation to critical mathematics education and ethnomathematics. In other words, these are scholars who are drawing on powerful traditions of mathematics education to impact their practices locally. We also wanted a geographical difference—hence research conducted on different continents.

Methodologically, the two research projects show similarities. Nutti labeled her methodology as action research, conducted in teaching circles with evaluations after each sequence. Rubel et al. identified their work as grounded theory research, conducted in iterations with evaluations in between the iterations. Both used data collected from observations, interviews and field notes. In other words, both these articles represent research and teaching sequences with teachers collaborating with researchers, on an action research/iterative/emancipatory basis.

There are similarities and differences in the results presented by these researchers. Nutti's research addresses social justice concerns: Indigenous teachers are not using mathematics textbooks in Sámi because they have found that the textbooks did not lead to Sámi culture-based teaching, as the textbooks were translated. During the research period, a lack of suitable teaching materials— culturally relevant textbooks, national curricula, and tests— forced the teachers to become creative in order to implement culture-based teaching. Teachers "began to act as potential agents of Indigenous school transformation by starting to work with Sámi culture-based mathematics activities" (Nutti, 2013, p. 69). In addition, her research confirms prior research findings in other contexts[1]: Indigenous knowledge was seen by textbooks as less important than western school mathematics and thus teachers chose not to implement a culture-based teaching approach, due to "their wish to prepare the pupils in 'the best possible way'" (p. 70). Despite these concerns and challenges, the teachers became self-empowered by the work and teaching experiences, became "agents for school-change" (p. 71) and engaged further in the design of a Sámi culture-based mathematics education syllabus.

Rubel et al. reported higher student engagement and improved mathematical learning during teaching sequences on spatial justice. They stressed that students' interest in the digital and mobile technologies increased their activities in the classrooms compared with their usual mathematics teaching. The article is rich in students' voices (with extensive quotations) on mathematics, mathematical findings and problems, and complex reflections on social justice. However, the different approach to teaching also "introduced an element of challenge to their mathematics class" (Rubel et al., 2016, p. 12), according to the collaborating teachers.

We synthesise our findings from these two articles to say that when teaching becomes contextualised into cultural or familiar out-of-school contexts, and connects to experiences of social injustice, students' engagement in mathematical learning increases. However, teachers need support during implementation phases of new or different ways of acting and teaching in the classroom. This observation confirms prior findings by, for example, Andersson (2015), Lasky (2005), and Clarke (2007).

We now analyse these two articles in relation to the four concerns of culturally situated critical mathematics education. In this analysis, we emphasise how the concerns bring ethnomathematical concerns to critical mathematics education and vice versa.

5.1 *Analysing Community Features*

Both articles detail the local contexts and environments of the students and their families. These environments are also related to the global context, such as, for example, the impact of colonisation and boarding schools in the Indigenous context, or growing up as a Black or Hispanic student in disadvantaged circumstances. The importance of knowing (western) mathematics (also a global context) or following a national syllabus in mathematics is problematised in both cases. Both articles then describe challenges faced by mathematics teachers who want to acknowledge students' cultural and societal backgrounds. For example, Nutti states that "The goal of Indigenous education is that it should be approached on the basis of the Indigenous language and culture; this is also the case with Sámi education" (p. 57).

Nutti described how participant "teachers' work with culture-based mathematics activities took the form of Sámi cultural thematic work with ethnomathematical content, multicultural school mathematics with Sámi cultural elements, and Sámi intercultural mathematics teaching" (p. 63). She emphasised how the widespread failure to implement culturally relevant teaching was a result of teachers having responsibility without resources, and thus connected local challenges to national policies (not quite global, but at least beyond the local): "It is therefore up to each teacher to design and develop a culture-based Sámi education by transforming cultural knowledge into teaching, with the result that no cultural implementation usually takes place in mathematics" (p. 58).

Rubel et al. used a place-based education framework and noted that it "is less frequently described with respect to mathematics in the literature and is another approach to context-based learning that centers on phenomena in students' local, physical environments" (p. 1). Place-based education emphasises local issues, which is a departure from Skovsmose and Nielsen's critical mathematics education concerns, but is not unlike some USA-based versions of critical mathematics education. Rubel et al. referred to critical mathematics research developed in the Americas, stating that "Learning more mathematics enables students to access a range of opportunities beyond the gate usually outside of the neighborhood" (p. 2). They quoted Frankenstein and Gutstein, both situated in the USA, to identify how they "view mathematics as an agentive tool that can support students from within their neighborhoods to fight *for* the neighborhood and demand justice and equity on its behalf" (p. 2). In a similar way, Nutti wrote that the "key to Sámi up-bringing was for children to become *iešbirgejeaddji*, independent, and to *birget*, manage" (p. 61). This empowerment both for teachers and their students was situated in their respective local contexts. Nutti concluded that "in order to support the teachers to become agents for school change, they need Indigenous knowledge, mathematics knowledge, and mathematics education knowledge, followed by the possibility to integrate the Indigenous culture into mathematics teaching" (p. 70). Similarly, Rubel et al. described how they supported teachers' interest in using mathematics for empowering their students: "The research questions consider how the spatial focus supported the learning of mathematics and provided opportunities for students to think critically about the lottery using that mathematics" (p. 1).

We note that despite the geographically, culturally and socially contextual differences between the research settings, there are similarities in how the research and ethics were addressed, how well the context is described and how the local school contexts have an impact on the teaching and research. The empowerment apparent in both research projects identifies them as emancipatory research. Both critical mathematics education and ethnomathematical research and teaching have strong potential to use mathematics as a tool for identifying and analysing critical features in both the local and global contexts that impact what happens in mathematics classrooms. These articles show how mathematics may better serve both students and teachers in a particular community.

5.2 Focusing on Acting Persons

Following the first concern about the importance of how mathematics plays out in local and wider contexts, this second concern focuses on actions by people in the different mathematics (education) practices. These people can be students, teachers and researchers as featured in the two articles here, but may include other actors, including most importantly (from an ethnomathematics perspective) members of the community doing mathematics (or not doing it when they could be). As shown in both articles, but more explicitly in Nutti's work, other actors may include textbook authors and curriculum writers and politicians, all of whom impact from a distance action, decision-making and changing practice locally in schools.

Nutti described changes in teacher actions during the study: "the teachers changed from a problem-focused perspective to a possibility-focused culture-based teaching perspective characterised by a self-empowered Indigenous teacher role, as a result of which they started to act as agents for Indigenous school change" (p. 69). To give two examples, Nutti stated that a "central factor in the teachers' work with Sámi culture-based mathematics activities was the ethnomathematics research field" (p. 69) which justified both a more culture-based mathematics education "as well as legitimising school transformation and enabling the teachers to overcome the limitations imposed by textbooks, national curricula, and tests" (p. 69).

Rubel et al. also described how their project engaged students in action to analyse and understand better significant aspects of their community, namely the publicly organised lottery and its effects on the community: "Findings include student interest in and engagement with the theme of the lottery familiar from outside of school with associated social justice implications" (p. 20). They concluded that "youth can traverse urban spaces on foot with mobile technologies to learn in place and mapping technologies can be used in the classroom as a way to study about place" (pp. 2–3).

Neither of the papers explicitly addressed relationships of power between the actors in the classrooms and the research group. We think it is likely that these relationships were addressed in the research—for example, we see that Rubel et al. showed awareness of possibilities for agency in the relationship: "the topic of the lottery as a spatial justice issue was not co-constructed with students [...] but selected by a design team comprised of individuals neither demographically similar to the students nor local to their neighborhoods" (p. 21). We are told that students developed critical stances about the lottery, which addressed power relations outside the classroom. Implicitly, we can read into the research texts concerns for the teachers' work situations, time and space issues and empowerment of teachers while moving into new ways of teaching. There is also evidence of care taken for students and their cultural and societal situation.

5.3 Reflecting on Mathematics and on Education

Our analysis of the articles shows that it is difficult to separate reflection on mathematics in society from reflection on school practices. However, we think that both are important forms of reflection and thus deserve to be separate concerns. Here we analyse the two articles on these two concerns together because the authors wrote about them in conflated ways—for example, Nutti (2013) wrote about reflection as follows:

> The teachers' self-critical examination can be viewed in the light of Laenui's (2000) decolonisation concepts: "rediscovery," "mourning," "dreaming," "commitment," and "action." The teachers' active engagement, and visions of culture-based teaching and its implementation were central. They tried to rediscover or reinvent Sámi culture in a mathematics school context. (p. 69)

This concern moves from specific actions in a context towards general practices in mathematics education. In the Indigenous context, two main concerns regarding discrimination and its impact were addressed. Both related to aspects of colonisation and its impact on the communities, families, language and relationships, historically and currently. Nutti recognised that the "concept of 'decolonisation' was visible in the teachers' narratives" and that the teachers' theme work in their teaching "had a decolonisation perspective, as the teachers wished to provide the pupils with an opportunity to learn Sámi traditional knowledge such as reindeer counting terms, Sámi traditional body measurements, and the way of measuring snow depth" (p. 64). Rubel et al. also moved to generalise in their conclusions: their pedagogical focus (critical mathematics education) "encourages students to 'decolonise' place by recognising and repudiating the unjust forces that intersect it and to "reinhabit" place by engaging its local features in spite of negative, impactful external forces" (p. 3).

Nutti "detected a conflict between Indigenous teachers' wish to give the pupils an education equal to the teaching in the national school and culture-based teaching, [...] there was a conflict between preparing the pupils for education in the national school and providing them with specific Sámi culture-based knowledge" (p. 67). In contrast, Rubel et al.'s article showed rich examples that the critical mathematics education and place-based teaching approaches enriched the students' (western) mathematical and social justice knowledge. The teachers' narratives and experiences reported by Nutti in addition addressed obstacles, including "shortage of time, restrictions due to national syllabuses and tests, disinterested parents, limited resources, and lack of knowledge of Sámi culture-based mathematics teaching" (pp. 67–68). She concluded that if "teaching materials based on Sámi culture [had] been available, the teachers might have been able to work with further implementation work" (p. 68) and she asked for the development of an Indigenous mathematics curriculum. By contrast, Rubel et al. found that through using the available curriculum, teachers could develop tasks that required students to learn the expected mathematics, as well as opening up "the power of maps toward redefining place to people" (p. 5).

This concern demands reflection on how mathematics and mathematics education practices reproduce, initiate and/or sustain inequalities. To implement Indigenous curriculum in a respectful and peaceful decolonising way, conceptions of mathematics itself seem to present significant problems related to the myth of culture-free mathematics. This concern extends to mathematics education research, as we have noted in our previous work that critiques of ethnomathematics seem to be raised mostly by western scholars, while Indigenous researchers use ethnomathematical research to raise social justice concerns in their communities.

The use of mathematics as a tool for critique, which is part of this concern, is well-developed in Rubel et al.'s teaching and research. Part of their article's aim was to show how "mathematics can be used to analyze, critique, and respond to issues of social as well as spatial justice" (p. 1):

> A word wall activity revealed an array of associations with places in their neighborhoods ("cornerstore," "gas station," "supermarket," and "vending machines") and with their families ("grandfather," "grandmothers (Doreen)," and "uncle"). Students named specific groups of people; the descriptors mostly aligned with demographics of people in their neighborhoods ("Puerto Ricans" and "poor people"). Despite some positive associations with the lottery ("fun to do," "happy," and "hope"), students expressed a sense that winning the lottery is a matter of low probability ("one-in-a-million") and high-lighted darker connotations ("broke," "sad," "so pissed," "addiction," and "drug"). Some students expressed indignation at what they sensed was an unfair outcome of the lottery ("they take half your money") perhaps affecting specific groups of people differently, such as by race ("black people don't win"). (p. 10)

Neither of the articles addressed the complementary concern—mathematics as an object of critique. However, we find implicit critiques in both of them:

mathematics is used to maintain colonisation practices through the western textbooks not recognising Sápmi language or specific Sámi ways of counting, and the lotteries are developed to take "half your money." Nutti found that the main motive for teachers' choices "appeared to be the teachers' desire to prepare the pupils in 'the best possible way' for further studies in the municipal compulsory school system" (p. 67). The teachers' concern suggests the question: What if they had a Sámi culture-based mathematics teaching instead, with Sámi cultural thematic work with ethnomathematical content based on Sámi ontology and epistemology, with a decolonisation perspective? A more explicit critique would lead to further questions, including: Who decides, and where is the power of western mathematics located? The subtle authority of the curriculum discourse dismisses ethnomathematics as a teaching and research subject as we have shown above. This dismissal may also be the case with critical mathematics education teaching and research, which is more commonly described as possible (and fruitful) specifically in disempowered, poor and disadvantaged contexts. However, it could be used in all contexts to address, understand and impact, for example, environmental issues (as illustrated by some of the other chapters in this volume). In other words, dominant European and western mathematics teaching might also find more motivated students (Andersson et al., 2015), benefit from cross-subject activities (Andersson, 2011) or empower students to act and critique with mathematics and to critique mathematics itself.

There was opportunity for the students in Rubel et al.'s work to analyse and critique both mathematics and technologies, but this opportunity was not taken up. The case is rather the opposite as mathematical and technological discourses were honoured as tools of critique:

> Students were supported to learn mathematics and to build on that mathematics to develop critical opinions, with greater success at narrower levels of spatial scale. New possibilities generated by using mobile technologies toward participatory mapping were demonstrated with respect to teaching mathematics for spatial justice. The design process and its associated technological tools are adaptable to new themes and places. (p. 21)

As with explicit reflection on mathematics, neither of the papers explicitly addressed concerns of power and authority, or the relationships between the actors in the classrooms and research. If awareness of these concerns was addressed during the research phase we do not know, but the adopted emancipatory research methodologies lead us to believe that authority, agency, and positions would have been carefully and ethically taken into account. We have addressed the possibility for reflecting on power and authority in the previous section.

We know that students developed critical stances about the lottery. In other words, the students were presented with (mathematical) tasks and expected to develop certain kinds of mathematical and social justice knowledge while solving the problems: "Engaging with the *Local Lotto* maps provides opportunities for statistical analysis and critical orientations toward the represented statistics" (p. 5). What if the students had been part of the designing, or if possibilities for students' agency had been opened up? What knowledge would they have developed? A similar question could be asked of Nutti's work: How could the students have been part of the decision making around the development of Samí-based content? What would they have learned?

6 Discussion

We have presented a framework for *culturally situated critical mathematics education*, where the similarities and intersections between ethnomathematics and critical mathematics education bring the values and significance of each to the other. We have developed this less dense framework, while recognising Skovsmose and Nielsen's (1996) framework and others' critical stance towards ethnomathematics. We argue that the similarities and intersections imply a rethinking of how we can analyse and write up research that is recognised as cultural, contextual and political as we find both approaches emancipatory and decolonising.

To close, we return to questions about who does ethnomathematics and the related question about who does critical mathematics education. We wonder if our synthesised concerns would help mitigate the avoidance of ethnomathematics we have identified. Using the concerns to analyse the articles may present opportunities for a deficit assessment of either critical mathematics education or ethnomathematics. However, the concerns helped us to identify aspects that often are missing in critical mathematics education—things that ethnomathematics usually does—and vice versa. Instead, our use of the concerns to analyse the articles actually helped us appreciate the research even more, because the framework drew our attention to the power of and care taken in the research. In other words, the analysis also highlighted opportunities.

The reasons for avoidance, building on Barthes' (1972/2009) arguments about myths, all relate to the fear of engaging in morally and ethically challenging terrain. Our list of concerns is unlikely to ease this fear. Engagement in and experiences from critical, ethnomathematical or *culturally situated critical mathematics education* is probably the only realistic way to mitigate this fear. Our list of concerns may highlight how close the two approaches to mathematics education are, and how attention to the foci of both approaches can improve the practice of the both. We hope that these guiding analytical concerns will open up critical questions for researchers within both these paradigms and inform spaces to develop and discuss the cultural, contextual and political concerns in our research fields. We also hope that the concerns will guide scholars researching with critical mathematics education and ethnomathematical orientations. The four concerns—analysing community features; focusing on acting persons; reflecting on mathematics and reflecting on education—each focus on different aspects or levels of mathematical education research. This list of concerns, expressed in this way, can support research writing in both ethnomathematics and critical mathematics education contexts, creating opportunities to learn from the sensibilities of the other, and vice-versa.

Note

1   See for example Balto (2008) and Meaney (2001), but also Skovsmose for a critical discussion of ethnomathematics in relation to western academic mathematics as a gatekeeper.

References

Andersson, A. (2011). A "curling teacher" in mathematics education: Teacher identities and pedagogy development. *Mathematics Education Research Journal, 23*(4), 437–454. https://doi.org/10.1007/s13394-011-0025-0

Andersson, A., Valero, P., & Meaney, T. (2015). "I am [not always] a maths hater": Shifting students' identity narratives in context. *Educational Studies in Mathematics, 90*(2), 143–161. https://doi.org/10.1007/s10649-015-9617-z

Andersson, A., & Wagner, D. (2015). Questions from ethnomathematics trajectories. In S. Mukhopadhyay & B. Greer (Eds.), *Proceedings of the Eighth International Mathematics Education and Society Conference* (pp. 270–283). Portland State University, Ooligan Press. https://www.mescommunity.info/MES8ProceedingsVol2.pdf

Andersson, A., & Wagner, D. (2018). Re-mythologizing mystery in mathematics: Teaching for open landscapes versus concealment. *Education Sciences, 8*(2). https://doi.org/10.3390/educsci8020041

Balto, A. M. (2008). Sámi oahpaheaddjit sirdet árbevirolaš kultuvrra boahttevaš buolvvaide: Dekoloniserema akšuvdnadutkamuš Ruoŧa beale Sámis [Sámi teachers transfer traditional culture to next generations: Decolonizing action research in the Swedish part of Sápmi]. *Diedut, 4*, 7–125. https://samas.brage.unit.no/samas-xmlui/bitstream/handle/11250/177109/Diedut-2008-4-BOKBLOKKA.pdf?sequence=3

Barthes, R. (2009). *Mythologies*. Vintage Classics. (Original work published 1957)

Barton, B. (1996). Making sense of ethnomathematics: Ethnomathematics is making sense. *Educational Studies in Mathematics, 31*(1), 201–233. https://doi.org/10.1007/BF00143932

Borba, M. (1997). Ethnomathematics and education. In A. B. Powell & M. Frankenstein (Eds.), *Ethnomathematics: Challenging Eurocentrism in mathematics education* (pp. 261–272). SUNY Press.

Brantlinger, A. (2013). Between politics and equations: Teaching critical mathematics in a remedial secondary classroom. *American Educational Research Journal, 50*(5), 1050–1080. https://doi.org/10.3102/0002831213487195

Clarke, D. (2007). Ten key principles from research for the professional development of mathematics teachers. In G. C. Leder & H. J. Forgasz (Eds.), *Stepping stones for the 21st century. Australasian mathematics education research* (pp. 27–39). Sense. https://doi.org/10.1163/9789087901509_004

Dowling, P. (1998). *The sociology of mathematics education: Mathematical myths/pedagogic texts*. Falmer Press. https://doi.org/10.4324/9780203486870

Frankenstein, M. (2001). Reading the world with math: Goals for a critical mathematical literacy curriculum. In *Mathematics: Shaping Australia: Proceedings of the eighteenth biennial conference of the Australian Association of Mathematics Teachers Inc.* (pp. 53–64). https://www.aamt.edu.au/Library/Conference-proceedings/Mathematics-Shaping-Australia/(language)/eng-AU

Freire, P. (1996). *Pedagogy of the oppressed* (20th ed. rev., M. Bergman Ramos, Trans.). Penguin. (Original work published 1968)

Geertz, C. (1974). *Myth, symbol and culture*. Norton.

Gerdes, P. (1997). Survey of current work on ethnomathematics. In A. B. Powell & M. Frankenstein (Eds.), *Ethnomathematics: Challenging Eurocentrism in mathematics education* (pp. 331–372). SUNY Press.

Gutstein, E. (2006). *Reading and writing the world with mathematics: Toward a pedagogy for social justice*. Routledge. https://doi.org/10.4324/9780203112946

Gutstein, E. (2010). Our issues, our people: Mathematics as our weapon. In U. Gellert, E. Jablonka, & C. Morgan (Eds.), *Proceedings of the Sixth International Mathematics Education and Society Conference* (pp. 270–279). Freie Universität Berlin. https://www.mescommunity.info/mes6b.pdf

Herbel-Eisenmann, B., & Wagner, D. (2010). Appraising lexical bundles in mathematics classroom discourse: Obligation and choice. *Educational Studies in Mathematics, 75*(1), 43–63. https://doi.org/10.1007/s10649-010-9240-y

Jurdak, M. (2016). *Learning and teaching real world problem solving in school mathematics: A multiple-perspective framework for crossing the boundary*. Springer. https://doi.org/10.1007/978-3-319-08204-2

Knijnik, G. (2012). Differentially positioned language games: Ethnomathematics from a philosophical perspective. *Educational Studies in Mathematics, 80*(1), 87–100. https://doi.org/10.1007/s10649-012-9396-8

Laenui, P. (2000). Processes of decolonization. In M. Battiste (Ed.), *Reclaiming Indigenous voice and vision* (pp. 150–160). UBC Press.

Lasky, S. (2005). A sociocultural approach to understanding teacher identity, agency and professional vulnerability in a context of secondary school reform. *Teaching and Teacher Education, 21*(8), 899–916. https://doi.org/10.1016/j.tate.2005.06.003

Meaney, T. (2001). An indigenous community doing mathematics curriculum development. *Mathematics Education Research Journal, 13*(1), 3–14. https://doi.org/10.1007/BF03217095

Mellin-Olsen, S. (1987). *The politics of mathematics education*. Reidel.

Nutti, Y. J. (2013). Indigenous teachers' experiences of the implementation of culture-based mathematics activities in Sámi school. *Mathematics Education Research Journal, 25*(1), 57–72. https://doi.org/10.1007/s13394-013-0067-6

Parra, A. (2018). *Curupira's walk: Prowling ethnomathematics theory through decoloniality* (Doctoral dissertation). Aalborg Universitet. https://doi.org/10.5278/vbn.phd.eng.00050

Rowlands, S., & Carson, R. (2002). Where would formal, academic mathematics stand in a curriculum informed by ethnomathematics? A critical review of ethnomathematics. *Educational Studies in Mathematics, 50*(1), 79–102. https://doi.org/10.1023/A:1020532926983

Rubel, L. H., Lim, V. Y., Hall-Wieckert, M., & Sullivan, M. (2016). Teaching mathematics for spatial justice: An investigation of the lottery. *Cognition and Instruction, 34*(1), 1–26. https://doi.org/10.1080/07370008.2015.1118691

Skovsmose, O. (1994). *Towards a philosophy of critical mathematics education*. Kluwer. https://doi.org/10.1007/978-94-017-3556-8

Skovsmose, O. (2001). Landscapes of investigation. *Zentralblatt für Didaktik der Mathematik, 33*(4), 123–132. https://doi.org/10.1007/BF02652747

Skovsmose, O. (2010). Critical mathematics education: In terms of concerns. In B. Sriraman, C. Bergsten, S. Goodchild, G. Palsdottir, B. Dahl Søndergaard, & L. Haapasalo (Eds.), *The first sourcebook on Nordic research in mathematics education* (pp. 671–682). Information Age.

Skovsmose, O., & Nielsen, L. (1996). Critical mathematics education. In A. J. Bishop, K. Clements, C. Keitel, J. Kilpatrick, & C. Laborde (Eds.), *International handbook of mathematics education* (pp. 1257–1288). Kluwer. https://doi.org/10.1007/978-94-009-1465-0_36

Wagner, D. (2019). Changing storylines in public perceptions of mathematics education. *Canadian Journal of Science, Mathematics and Technology Education, 19*, 61–72. https://doi.org/10.1007/s42330-018-00039-1

Zolkower, B., & de Freitas, E. (2010). What's in a text: Engaging mathematics teachers in the study of whole-class conversations. In U. Gellert, E. Jablonka, & C. Morgan (Eds.), *Proceedings of the Sixth International Mathematics Education and Society Conference* (pp. 508–517). Freie Universität Berlin. https://www.mescommunity.info/mes6b.pdf

CHAPTER 3

Decolonising Mathematics Education in a Time of Reconciliation

Lisa Lunney Borden

Abstract

Canada's Truth and Reconciliation Commission (TRC) lays out the role education has played in creating inequity, perpetuating stereotypes and silencing Indigenous voices, and makes the clear claim that education is also the vehicle for addressing these wrongs and finding a new way forward. In light of the TRC'S calls to action, in this chapter I consider what it means to decolonise mathematics education. To that end, I review literature relating to decolonising education, critical mathematics education, and ethnomathematics to explore what it might mean to decolonise mathematics education. Drawing upon examples from empirical research, I then consider what decolonisation could look like in mathematics teaching and learning focusing on beginning with different stories, centring community knowledge, and moving beyond material culture to ensuring Indigenous ways of knowing being and doing are central to the practice of teaching and learning. I conclude that when students can learn mathematics in ways that align with their community worldview, then they are likely to have more success while acknowledging that the process of decolonising is one that is ongoing and ever evolving.

Keywords

decolonising – Mi'kmaw – verbification – L'nui'ta'simk – mathematics education

∙ ∙ ∙

"You better be good or they'll send you to Shubie school!" One student was teasing another in my 7th grade math class. It was 1995, I was 24 years old with my first full-time teaching job in We'koqma'q First Nation, a Mi'kmaw[1] community in Nova Scotia, Canada. I didn't know what "Shubie school" meant at the time, so I naively asked. The response: "You know Miss, where they send kids and they get beaten by the nuns and priests."

Shubie school was the Indian Residential School in Shubenacadie, Nova Scotia operating between 1929 and 1967, where hundreds of Mi'kmaw children, including many from the community of We'koqma'q, were sent by Indian agents acting on behalf of the Government of Canada. As the Truth and Reconciliation Commission of Canada (2015) would show:

> These residential schools were created for the purpose of separating Aboriginal children from their families, in order to minimize and weaken family ties and cultural linkages, and to indoctrinate children into a new culture—the culture of the legally dominant Euro-Christian Canadian society, led by Canada's first prime minister, Sir John A. Macdonald. (p. v)

Much of the history of the Indian Residential School system remained unknown to the majority of Canadians until residential school survivors began to speak out about the horrors they had experienced. In 1995, when I began teaching in We'koqma'q, survivors were just beginning to share their experiences publicly. These disclosures led to the largest class-action lawsuit against the Canadian government in history. This lawsuit was settled by the government in 2005. The Truth and Reconciliation Commission was a direct result of this settlement.

Throughout the ten years I taught in We'koqma'q, and the nearly 13 years I have been continuing to work alongside this community in my academic role, I have come to understand much more deeply the very personal impact that residential schools had on the community I would come to call home. By 2015, over 6,000 witnesses from across Canada had told their stories of residential school to the Truth and Reconciliation Commission and all Canadians have begun to understand the impact these schools had on over 150,000 Indigenous children, spanning over 100 years, and the inter-generational effects that continue today.

The Indian Residential School was just one of many colonial practices designed to force assimilation of Indigenous Peoples in Canada and to destroy Indigenous language, cultural practices, and relationships with the natural world. As Tuck and Yang (2012) have stated:

> Settler colonialism is different from other forms of colonialism in that settlers come with the intention of making a new home on the land, a homemaking that insists on settler sovereignty over all things in their new domain. ... In order for the settlers to make a place their home, they must destroy and disappear the Indigenous peoples that live there. (pp. 5–6)

Canada's residential school system was designed to do just that, to erase Indigenous Peoples from the Canadian landscape and destroy their relationship to the land. The Truth and Reconciliation Commission (2015) referred to these practices as cultural genocide, explaining:

> Cultural genocide is the destruction of those structures and practices that allow the group to continue as a group. States that engage in cultural genocide set out to destroy the political and social institutions of the targeted group. Land is seized, and populations are forcibly transferred and their movement is restricted. Languages are banned. Spiritual leaders are persecuted, spiritual practices are forbidden, and objects of spiritual value are confiscated and destroyed. And, most significantly to the issue at hand, families are disrupted to prevent the transmission of cultural values and identity from one generation to the next. (p. 1)

The Truth and Reconciliation Commission (2015) has clearly stated that the Indian Residential School system perpetuated an act of cultural genocide on Indigenous peoples, the effects of which are still significantly impacting these communities today. The final report includes 94 calls to action in response to the horrors of residential schools that are focused on establishing a renewed relationship between Indigenous and non-Indigenous Canadians to "restore what must be restored, repair what must be repaired, and return what must be returned" (Truth and Reconciliation Commission of Canada, 2015, p. 6). The ultimate goal of reconciliation is "to transform Canadian society so that our children and grandchildren can live together in dignity, peace, and prosperity on these lands we now share" (p. 8). The Truth and Reconciliation Commission names the education system as having an essential role in repairing the damages caused by residential schools. In particular, call to action 10 focuses on the need to develop an Education Act for and with Indigenous peoples in Canada to ensure greater educational outcomes but also the revitalisation of culture and language. The Truth and Reconciliation Commission (2015) has stated:

> Based on all that it has heard from thousands of former students and family members throughout the country, the Commission is convinced that such an Act must recognize the importance of education in strengthening the cultural identity of Aboriginal people and providing a better basis for success. (p. 149)

The Truth and Reconciliation Commission lays out the role education has played in creating inequity, perpetuating stereotypes and silencing Indigenous voices, and makes the clear claim that education is also the vehicle for addressing these wrongs and finding a new way forward. It is perhaps a common expectation that matters of colonialism and reconciliation are best left to the history or social studies classroom, but mathematics too has a role to play in helping students to understand this colonial history and mathematics can play a role in addressing the inequities that are a direct result of colonisation. In fact, I argue that mathematics has served as a vehicle for perpetuating the myth of cultural superiority that the Truth and Reconciliation Commission (2015) has pointed out was a central focus of the Indian Residential School system and the Canadian colonial system of education in general.

Mi'kmaw scholar, Marie Battiste (2013) has argued for transformation rather than integration of Indigenous knowledges to work toward decolonisation and reconciliation. I have long believed that to achieve reconciliation settlers must work to recognise the colonial legacy inherent in our education system and to engage in processes that aim to disrupt and dismantle this colonial system. Mathematics education is no exception. To this end, I question what it means to decolonise mathematics education. What role can mathematics education play in addressing the Truth and Reconciliation Commission calls to action to bring about reconciliation? What does such a mathematics programme look like?

1   Decolonising Mathematics Education

I struggle when I use the word decolonisation for a multitude of reasons. The fact that this word is a noun raises issues for me as I truly believe words like decolonisation – and reconciliation – need to be replaced with verbs to highlight the reality that these are ongoing processes that should aim to regularly confront and challenge colonial processes. Many critical mathematics education scholars talk of colonialism as a thing that has happened (see Joseph, 2011; Skovsmose, 2016), yet Indigenous scholars like Smith (1999) and Kovach (2009) remind us that in settler states there is nothing post about colonialism. Additionally, I am keenly aware the scholars like Tuck and Yang (2012) would argue that decolonisation and reconciliation are incommensurable notions. These tensions are important to consider and I continue to grapple with them, yet I also feel a sense of urgency to do something.

Battiste (2013) has explained that Eurocentric control over what is legitimated as knowledge results in cognitive imperialism, which positions some knowledges as superior and others as inferior. Gutiérrez (2017a) has provided an example of how such cognitive imperialism plays out in mathematics arguing that "School mathematics curricula emphasising terms like Pythagorean theorem and pi perpetuate a perception that mathematics was largely developed by the Greeks and other Europeans" (p. 17), and that despite this obvious Eurocentric focus, mathematics educators often claim that mathematics is culturally neutral and value free. Aikenhead (2017) has referred to this phenomenon as "mathematics myth blindness" (p. 121) and pointed out that mathematics' "privileged status rests on the myth that its Platonist content is acultural, universalist, value free, objective in its use, and nonideological" (p. 121). In drawing attention to the non-European roots of mathematics, Joseph (2011) has argued that ideological beliefs about European superiority meant that "The contributions of the colonised peoples were ignored or devalued as part of the rationale for subjugation and dominance" (p. 4), echoing ideas of settler colonialism as described above. Thus, to decolonise mathematics we need to challenge these myths and tell a different story.

To challenge colonial narratives, I have often drawn upon ideas in the field of ethnomathematics in my own work (Lunney Borden et al., 2019; Lunney Borden & Wiseman, 2016; Wagner & Lunney Borden, 2015). I have particularly drawn inspiration from those who suggest that ethnomathematics is political in nature and serves to challenge the hegemonic thinking of school-based mathematics (D'Ambrosio, 2006; Powell & Frankenstein, 1997). I see power in the way that "Ethnomathematics problematises the 'great narrative' which modernity considers to be academic mathematics" (Knijnik, 2002, p. 13). According to Adam et al. (2003), ethnomathematics has particularly supported Indigenous mathematicians by giving them an avenue to critically explore the role of mathematics in colonisation and find new ways to "engage with the discipline constructively" (p. 329). They have suggested that "decolonisation involves reclaiming, protecting, and valuing the unique ways of Indigenous knowing and doing" (p. 328). Thus, I value the aspects of ethnomathematics that have made space to think critically about what mathematical knowledge is centred, and what mathematical knowledge is othered, in school mathematics. Such an approach allows one to see how mathematics has played a role in the erasure of Indigenous ways of knowing, being, and doing that align with what we call mathematics today in school.

An ethnomathematical approach has supported the development of practices that strive to restore, repair, and return (Truth and Reconciliation Commission, 2015) aspects of culture, language, and identity within the Mi'kmaw communities in which I work (Lunney Borden et al., 2019; Lunney Borden & Wiseman, 2016; Wagner & Lunney Borden, 2015). These practices work to elevate community voices, centre community stories, and draw upon community ways of knowing, being, and doing. This approach aligns with ideas put forth by Smith (1999), a Maori scholar, who stated that decolonisation is not about rejecting outright all Western knowledge but rather she argued, "it is about centring our concerns and world views and then coming to know and understand theory and research from our own perspectives and for our own purposes" (p. 39). If a colonial system of education is all about eradicating Indigenous voices, practices, ideologies, relationships to land and so on, then decolonisation is about elevating and centring these things.

One common criticism of ethnomathematics is that it focuses too much on cultural artefacts or uncovering hidden mathematics as a way to link to Western mathematics and risks further marginalising these ideas (Doolittle, 2006; Rowlands & Carson, 2002; Vithal & Skovsmose, 1997). I acknowledge there is a real danger of trivialising local knowledge and making it seem inferior to Western mathematics if the inclusion is done in such a way as to make it merely an add-on or an example of the application of Western mathematics. As Lipka (2002) stated, "The connection of local knowledge to schooling is not an easy process, however. The challenge is to adapt local culture and knowledge to Western schooling without trivializing and stereotyping" (p. 3). Elsewhere, I have described how such trivialisation can be mitigated by beginning in community contexts and allowing knowledge to emerge in meaningful ways (Lunney Borden & Wiseman, 2016). Such an approach works toward decolonisation by centring community ways of knowing, being and doing which begins a shift to address questions not only focused on content but also on the epistemological notions that underpin pedagogical approaches.

Battiste (2013) has argued that "educators must help students understand the Eurocentric assumptions of superiority within the context of history and to recognize the continued dominance of these assumptions in all forms of contemporary knowledge" (p. 186) in order to decolonise the education system. We must also confront head on the impact of colonial systems that have, for far too long, made Indigenous students feel excluded from the field of mathematics. As Battiste (2013) has argued:

> As educators and teachers begin to confront new schemes of Indigenous knowledge and learning in reconciliation that create ethical, trans-systemic educational systems, they will need to identify new processes. These include raising the collective voice of Indigenous peoples, exposing the injustices in our colonial history, deconstructing the past by critically examining the social, political, economic, and emotional reasons for silencing Aboriginal voices and experiences of Aboriginal people in the curriculum, recognizing it as a dynamic context of knowledge and knowing, and communicating the emotional journey that such explorations will generate. (p. 167)

Such an approach requires a critical examination of mathematics more broadly drawing from the field of critical mathematics education:

> The critique of mathematics education has emerged from the restraint of being directed *internally*, that is to say concerned primarily with how mathematics is learned and taught, to being also *external*, concerned with the embeddedness of mathematics education and mathematics within historical, cultural, social, and political contexts, and the implications and ramifications thereof. (Skovsmose & Greer, 2012, p. 3)

While in various aspects of my mathematics education work, I concern myself with both ideas of how mathematics is taught and learned, and how it is used to "read and write the world" (Gutstein, 2006), I also seek to go beyond these internal and external contexts to consider how mathematics works to reinforce myths of cultural superiority. While there is some emergent work that is beginning to address the ways in which whiteness is normalised within mathematics education research (Battey & Leyva, 2016; Martin, 2011; Stinson, 2017), I believe more needs to be done. I connect then to Gutiérrez (2017b) who has challenged that "Within mathematics education, we have convinced ourselves that 'equity' is a strong enough agenda when maybe revolution should be the goal" (p. 11). I am reminded of Tuck and Yang's (2012) caution that decolonisation is not to be used in a metaphorical sense.

As such, I continue to be uncertain what decolonisation really looks like and I recognise that that is part of this unlearning process. Tuck and Yang (2012) draw upon Fanon (1963) to remind us that the process will be messy and difficult, it may at times feel dangerous and unfriendly, but that we will get there "in the exact measure that we can discern the movements which give [decolonisation] historical form and content" (Fanon, 1963, p. 36). So, I attend to the movements of my own journey alongside Mi'kmaw communities, and will use the remainder of this chapter to share what I have learned and how it may be moving us in the direction of decolonisation.

In the remaining parts of this chapter, I will describe aspects of my learning from and with Mi'kmaw people as I began to transform my own practices with respect to mathematics education. I outline ways I believe provide insight into the process of decolonising mathematics. I will show how I began with engaging differently in research through using a process rooted in the community. I will share how initial ethnomathematical conversations brought me to deeper insights about the mathematical knowledge that has always been a part of Mi'kmaw practices, and how this understanding generated the Show Me Your

Math programme that encouraged students to have similar conversations with Elders and knowledge keepers. I will argue that while ethnomathematical conversations enabled students to make greater connections between their own cultural identity and the mathematics they were learning in school, these practices were simply not enough to truly decolonise mathematics. I will then share how conversations with teachers and Elders in local Mi'kmaw communities have led to a greater focus on teaching mathematics through Mi'kmaw ways of knowing that are embedded in the language and values of the community.

2   Decolonising Methodology

Smith (1999) has claimed that for much Indigenous research, what is most important—even more important than outcomes—is the process: "Processes are expected to be respectful, to enable people, to heal and to educate. They are expected to lead one small step further towards self-determination" (p. 128). When I began my doctoral studies, and took on this academic role, I worked with community members to ensure that I was doing this work in a good way. The questions I was hoping to explore had emerged collaboratively in working with Elders and teachers in numerous Mi'kmaw communities during my years as a teacher. It seemed only appropriate, then, that the community would also guide me in determining a process for investigating these questions. I sought a process that would be appropriate for entering into learning conversations in a more formal way.

In my years teaching in We'koqma'q, I had come to learn that often such a search could involve exploring words in the language itself. Blackfoot scholar, Little Bear (2000) has explained, "Language embodies the way a society thinks" (p. 78), an idea echoed by Inglis (2004) who similarly argued that "The Mi'kmaw language grammatically encodes details concerning how speakers experience the world and how a speaker and the person spoken to connect with and evidence this experience" (p. 400). Thus, I went about finding an appropriate word to guide my research by engaging in conversations with community Elders. While many words were suggested, the word that seemed most appropriate and had the most agreement from Elders was *mawikinutimatimk*, meaning coming together to learn together. This is a word that was shared with me by the late Grand Chief, Ben Sylliboy.[2] *Mawikinutimatimk* is a way of engaging with one another to discuss an issue or solve a problem. It includes the idea that everyone who comes together in the discussions has things to share and things to learn.

Inspired by Smith's (1999) call to decolonise research in a way that draws upon the interrelated principles of resistance, political integrity, and privileging

Indigenous voices (Rigney, 1999), I used this approach to ensure the work would be done in relationship. As Kovach (2009) has argued:

> Indigenous methodologies, by their nature, evoke collective responsibility ... Specific responsibilities will depend upon the particular relationship. They may include guidance, direction, and evaluation. They may include conversation, support, and collegiality. Responsibility implies knowledge and action. It seeks to genuinely serve others, and is inseparable from respect and reciprocity. (p. 178)

Mawikinutimatimk is this type of relational process. Through *mawikinutimatimk*, I am able to come into conversation with community members bringing what I have to offer, honouring the knowledge they bring, and working together to make change for students.

Working alongside community members, teachers and Elders, to engage in regular conversations about the complexities and challenges they were seeing with respect to students learning mathematics in school, as well as the ideas from community that might support mathematics learning, we were able to develop ideas about how to transform mathematics education for Mi'kmaw students (Lunney Borden, 2010). This was possible because of the trust and respect I had gained living and learning in community. While I was technically the researcher, I was also a long-term partner in the journey of improving education. I continue to work in this way in all that I do.

These reciprocal and respectful relationships have enabled me to come to learn new stories, be inspired by new ideas, and change my own understandings of mathematics teaching and learning. The stories I have learned have helped me to understand how to elevate voices and centre community knowledges to decolonise mathematics education. Yet, I am also bound to respect the sacredness of these relationships and to ensure I protect the knowledge from appropriation. As such, I have made clear in my writing about my methodological approach (Lunney Borden, 2010; Lunney Borden & Wagner, 2013) that *mawikinutimatimk* should not be co-opted by researchers outside of the Mi'kmaw community. Rather, what others might do is take the time to build relationships and learn appropriate processes within their own context.

3 Beginning with a Different Story

Elevating voices requires the telling of different stories. Recalling Gutiérrez's comments above about the privileging of Greek terms like pi; I begin with a story of this relationship within the Mi'kmaw context.

As a doctoral student, I had the opportunity to work on an ethnomathematics research project (see Wagner & Lunney Borden, 2015) which allowed me to formalise many of the informal conversations I had with community Elders as a teacher. To begin these conversations, we drew upon the work of Bishop (1991) to invite a broader understanding of how mathematics might play out in various cultural practices. Using the list of activities Bishop had developed – counting, measuring, locating, designing, playing, and explaining – we invited Elders to share examples of how they might engage in these practices. While this approach may be rooted in a more Eurocentric view of mathematics, the focus on verbs that described processes resonated with the Elders and provided a way to talk about processes within the community that might align with what we call mathematics in school. It was during one of these conversations that the late Dianne Toney, a quill box maker, shared knowledge that had been passed down to her from other basket makers. She explained that to make a ring from a wood strip for a circular box top, she would measure three times across the circle with the wood strip and add a thumb width more to make a circular ring that would fit perfectly. Dianne did not call this relationship pi, but stated that this was knowledge that had been passed to her from previous generations of basket makers (Wagner & Lunney Borden, 2015).

As I shared this story with other Mi'kmaw people, it was not at all a surprise. This was common knowledge not only amongst basket makers but others as well. One day, at a Show Me Your Math fair, Mi'kmaw Elder, Ernest Johnson demonstrated how to make a ring for a hand drum from wood by measuring across an existing drum three times and adding "a little bit more" which he demonstrated with his hand. These examples show that Mi'kmaw people have known about the relationship between the circumference and the diameter of a circle likely before they knew about Greece.

A Eurocentric approach to teaching mathematics treats pi as the official mathematical knowledge and this knowledge known by Mi'kmaw people as other. Such practices reinforce the myth of cultural superiority outlined in the Truth and Reconciliation Commission and the critiques of Eurocentric mathematics (Aikenhead, 2017; Gutiérrez, 2017a; Joseph, 2011). But, we can tell a different story.

4 Centring Community Knowledge: Show Me Your Math

David Wagner and I were inspired by the stories that Dianne and other Mi'kmaw Elders told us, but we were also uncomfortable with being the intermediaries transferring these Elder stories to teachers and students in the same communities (see Wagner & Lunney Borden, 2011). It was this discontent that led us to work with teachers and Elders in Mi'kmaw communities to develop the Show Me Your Math programme (Lunney Borden et al., 2019) as a way to encourage students to have conversations with community members like the conversations we had been experiencing with Elders.

Between 2007 and 2017, thousands of Mi'kmaw children have engaged in both individual and group projects where they have learned mathematics in the context of some aspect of community knowledge. Over the years, projects have focused on the mathematics related to Mi'kmaw technologies and innovations such as canoes and canoe paddles, snowshoes and toboggans, wi'kwams and sweat lodges, bows and eel spears. Projects have also examined sports and games of Mi'kmaw peoples such as lacrosse, waltes (a dice and bowl game), hockey (there is a Mi'kmaw claim to the game's origins) and the numerous card games that are very much a part of modern Mi'kmaw culture. Traditional crafts such as basket making, quillwork, leatherwork, and birch bark biting have also been topics of investigations, as have practices associated with making clothing such as regalia and shawls, moccasins and beadwork designs. These are just a few of the many projects students have explored, and with each project there is a sense that the ways of reasoning often attributed to the domain of mathematics are highly evident in many community practices. This insight allows Mi'kmaw students to see that their Elders were mathematicians too and this changes their relationship with mathematics. These community stories provide counter narratives to the stories in their textbooks imply that mathematics has been developed only by those of European descent.

Perhaps because Show Me Your Math was developed with teachers (mostly Mi'kmaw teachers) and Elders, we found that teachers immediately began to take ownership over the programme ensuring widespread participation. Each year, as students would come together to share their work at the annual math fair, more ideas would be shared, more Elders would get involved, more parents and community members would come out to celebrate the work students had done. Over time, we also began to see that these projects created space for learning far beyond the mathematics involved (Lunney Borden & Wagner, 2011). Projects have examined high rates of diabetes in communities, challenges with language revitalisation, and social justice issues. One recent project involved student inquiry into the ongoing problem of unsafe drinking water in their community, something that is an epidemic in First Nations communities in Canada (Government of Canada, 2018). These projects have allowed students to explore issues relevant to their lives and communities, and to understand better the role mathematics plays in these explorations.

Recently, while attending a conference in Toronto,[3] I was a member of a panel with Aaron Prosper, a Mi'kmaw university student who had attended high school in Eskasoni First Nation. Aaron talked about his own experience of doing Show Me Your Math in high school. He recalled doing a project on waltes, a game played with a wooden bowl and six dice, traditionally made from caribou bones. The object of the game is to score points and collect sticks by getting five or six of the six dice face up or face down. This mathematically rich game predates European contact, involves probability, and varies the counting in different rounds. In his exploration, Aaron learned so much more than just the math. The project provided him with an opportunity to talk with his grandmother about waltes and learn more about the history of colonisation and its impacts upon their community.

While examining his grandmother's waltes game he noticed a hole had been drilled through the centre of the bowl. His grandmother explained to him that these holes had been drilled in waltes bowls by the government agents to prevent Mi'kmaw people from putting water in the bowls to use for divination as cultural practices were forbidden in Indigenous communities until the 1950s (Manuel & Derrickson, 2015). Aaron's project helped him see mathematical knowledge that was present in his community pre-contact, but it also helped him learn about the history of oppression and colonisation that was imposed upon his community. Such learning is more holistic and more relevant to the lives of students.

The holistic nature of Indigenous knowledge systems and the need for such a holistic approach to education has been well documented in the literature (Battiste & Henderson, 2009; Kirkness, 1999; Kovach, 2009). Cree scholar, Dwayne Donald (2009) has argued that Indigenous knowledges compel one to "look at the world holistically and search for regular observable patterns in nature as a way to make sense of the world and our place in it" (p. 13). Indigenous education must centre on the belief that learning is holistic, lifelong, experiential, rooted in Indigenous languages and cultures, and spiritually oriented (Cappon, 2008). Battiste and Henderson (2009) have argued that:

> The task for Indigenous scholars and educators has been to affirm and activate holistic paradigms of Indigenous knowledge to reveal the wealth and richness of Indigenous languages, world views, teachings, and experiences, all of which have been systematically excluded from history, from contemporary educational institutions, and from Eurocentric knowledge (EK) systems. (p. 5)

We found that the ethnomathematical approach for Show Me Your Math created space for such holistic learning to take place. Through our conversations with teachers and students, we saw that Show Me Your Math was helping to develop a sense of wholeness for students which we saw as one of the factors contributing to the quality of this programme: "Wholeness resists fragmentation, thus quality mathematics experiences require *cultural synthesis* bringing together cultures and values from mathematics and the community, *personal holism* including the child's experiential, conceptual, and spiritual development, and *intergenerational interaction*" (Lunney Borden & Wagner, 2011, p. 379). This sense of wholeness ensures that learning is not fragmented, is consistent with community ways of knowing, and supports students to learn mathematics from who they are rather than having to change their worldview to learn mathematics.

Over time, teachers became more interested in integrating Show Me Your Math into their daily teaching practices, rather than viewing it as a special project. While there is not enough space here to go into depth about these projects, it is worth noting that many of the teachers who have participated in these inquiry projects now feel comfortable engaging in this type of learning and are doing it more often. Such practices allow Mi'kmaw knowledge to be a starting point for learning rather than an add-on, which helps to avoid the tendency to privilege Western knowledge. These projects provided opportunities to reclaim Indigenous knowledges nearly erased by colonial practices, thus returning, repairing, and restoring that which has been taken as per the Truth and Reconciliation Commission. Although this has been successful in changing the relationship many students have with mathematics, it is still not enough.

5 It's Not Enough!

Wiseman (2016) writes of the discomfort that comes from having integrated Indigenous knowledges in some ways but still feeling as if it is not quite enough. This discomfort brings educators to act in new ways and to seek new knowledge. When I talk about Show Me Your Math and share examples of the ethnomathematical projects students have done, I am often concerned that educators will think this is enough. I worry they will make a canoe paddle, do some birch bark biting, make a basket, or do some beadwork, and check off the box that says they have integrated Indigenous knowledge. There are many reasons why this is not enough.

First, the projects we have done in Mi'kmaw communities, emerged from those communities. They are rooted in the stories of teachers and Elders from these communities and are relevant to the lives of these students. Transplanting Mi'kmaw practices to another Indigenous context may be completely inappropriate. It is important for educators to come to know the community in which they are working, to work with community members to determine the contexts that are appropriate to explore, and to work with Elders and knowledge keepers to ensure any work is done in a good way.

Secondly, while Show Me Your Math has provided students with many opportunities to explore the innovations of their ancestors and reclaim the knowledge that has been systematically erased by colonial practices, many projects have been situated more historically. We believe these historical examinations provide students an opportunity to learn about the strength of their ancestors and find that strength within themselves. This shifts the story from a thing of the past to a story for the present. Many teachers who have implemented Show Me Your Math projects use them as a way to honour not only the knowledge of the past but the resilience and strength of Mi'kmaw people in the present. Linking back and bringing forward is an important aspect of this work, yet it remains only an historical lens. I am reminded of Skovsmose's (1994) caution that we must also look to students' foreground – a perceived set of opportunities that students believe will emerge as possibilities for the future based on social context.

Thirdly, infusing Indigenous knowledges is more than just using an Indigenous artefact or context as an example of a mathematical practice. Too many times, I have witnessed a view that integrating Indigenous knowledge means finding a community context for an outcome. I recall one time being asked by a workshop participant what a cultural connection might be for numbers to 1,000, an outcome she needed to address. This is not what it means to integrate Indigenous knowledges or to decolonise mathematics. Decolonising mathematics is more than just applying mathematics to culturally relevant contexts or making connections to artefacts.

6 Beyond Baskets and Beadwork: Doing Math through/with L'nui'ta'simk

As Show Me Your Math was taking off in the early years, I was also engaged with teachers and Elders in two community schools while I was doing my doctoral research through *mawikinutimatimk* (Lunney Borden, 2010). When I first began my doctoral programme, I had visions of creating resources similar to those that had been developed amongst the Yup'ik for the Math in a Cultural Context programme (Lipka & Topkok, n.d.), drawing from the work I had begun with the conversations with Elders. However, as I stated above, I quickly realised that this would not be enough. It was apparent to me that I needed to have a greater understanding of where the conflicts were arising for Mi'kmaw students and this led to conversations with Elders and teachers that raised new ideas about language, values, ways of knowing, being, and doing that would help to decolonise mathematics. These ways of knowing, being, and doing were described as *L'nui'ta'simk* (our people's ways of thinking or worldview) and were contrasted from *Aklasiewita'simk* (Anglophone or European ways of thinking or worldview). In order to understand *L'nui'ta'simk*, it was essential to understand the Mi'kmaw language, not just speaking the language but learning about how the language is structured and how that structuring helps one to understand the embedded worldview.

As Little Bear (2000) has stated "Aboriginal Languages are, for the most part verb-rich languages that are process- or action-oriented" (p. 78). Mi'kmaq is one of the many verb-based Aboriginal languages spoken in Canada. The verb-based nature of Mi'kmaq implies a worldview that is more focused on active relationships that are constantly in flux. As Henderson (2000) has described:

> speakers build up verb phrases from what we could call implicate roots, containing the action or motion of the flux, and have hundreds of prefixes or suffixes to choose from to express an entire panorama of energy and motion. The use of verbs rather than a plethora of noun subjects and objects is important: it means that very few fixed and rigid separate objects exist in the Mi'kmaq worldview (or landscape). What they consider instead is great flux, eternal transformation and interconnected space. (p. 264)

This attention to action and flux means that concepts typically described in static ways in English would instead be quite dynamic and relational in Mi'kmaq. How one sees the world also defines how one reasons about the world including reasoning about mathematical concepts and ideas. As such:

> A proper understanding of the link between language and mathematics may be the key to finally throwing off the shadow of imperialism and colonisation that continues to haunt education for Indigenous groups in a modern world of international languages and global curricula. (Barton, 2008, p. 9)

I have described elsewhere (see Lunney Borden, 2010, 2012) that even when Mi'kmaw children do not speak their Indigenous language, it is highly likely they are still using the ways of thinking and grammar structures of that language; speaking English does not mean thinking English. When teachers learn about ways of thinking embedded in Indigenous languages, it can provide them with new ways to think about teaching mathematics.

Mathematics as taught in schools, however, tends towards nominalisation where processes are turned into nouns (Schleppegrell, 2007). While operations in mathematics might be about combining, separating, comparing, fair sharing, grouping, and so on, we have turned these into nouns like addition, subtraction, multiplication, and division, and we talk of sums and differences, products and quotients, rather than processes or actions. Functions are models that describe patterns and change, yet we treat them as objects with roots, intercepts, maxima, minima, and so on. One of my favourite examples of nominalisation is transformations of quadratic functions where we talk of horizontal and vertical translations, reflections and stretches, yet this is fundamentally about moving a graph around on a grid. Dynamic graphing software has enabled the study of this concept to be much more active, yet there still is an emphasis on the nouns. If students progress far enough in mathematics they may get to talk about functions that are increasing and decreasing, concepts of change and flux, and more verb-based ideas related to mathematics. However, for many students, the earlier dense noun work may prevent them from reaching these levels of mathematics. This awareness of the dominance of nominalisation, in direct contrast to the verb-based nature of the Mi'kmaw language, led me to the idea of verbifying mathematics (Lunney Borden, 2011) by focusing more on actions and changes to help students focus on processes rather than things.

The effectiveness of making greater use of verbs became apparent to me when working with a group of Grade 3 students (eight- and nine-year-olds) exploring prisms and pyramids. The expectation for this grade, according to the approved curriculum, was that students would count edges, faces, and vertices, and name the shapes of the sides. In this class, they instead spoke about how the shapes were forming and what the shapes could do. For example, one student stated that a cube could "sit still" rather than stating it had a flat face. Several students talked about how pyramids were forming into a triangle and gestured with their hands to show how the sides were coming to a point. There is a word in Mi'kmaq, *kiniskwikiaq,* which means forming into a point, which is used to describe this very process. While it was likely that many of these students did not know that word, they almost all were using this idea to describe the pyramid. This is an example of how students are using *L'nui'ta'simk* even if they are speaking English. These students were using many verbs to describe the shapes they were exploring and by being attentive to these verbs, I saw how much they understood about shapes in a very holistic way. Additionally, their teacher and I were able to build from what they knew to what the curriculum expected by connecting the verbs to the nouns once the students understood the concepts.

I have written more extensively about what verbifying can look like for teachers but I will give some examples here (see Lunney Borden, 2018). Verbifying mathematics might look like asking students how a graph is changing rather than asking what the slope is. It might involve younger students engaging with storyboards to tell joining and separating stories about quantities. It might involve asking how a pattern is formed or how to make the next element of a pattern rather than asking for the pattern rule. These subtle shifts can bring attention to the process associated with a concept more than the definition of a concept. I am not arguing that students should never learn the nouns but rather that educators should help students focus on the processes until a concept is understood and once it is understood, as mathematicians do, we name it.

A second important idea that I learned from my *mawikinutimatimk* conversations was the important role of spatial reasoning within the Mi'kmaw community. Whenever I would ask an Elder a question about how much or how many, the answer was always *tepiaq* and was accompanied by a spatial gesture to show the size of *tepiaq*. *Tepiaq* means enough. When I asked about this, I was told that space matters for survival. As Richard, an Elder who participated in my study, explained, "The native way of life is you have just enough and to share" (Lunney Borden, 2010, p. 175). Ma'li, another Elder, built upon Richard's comment and connected this with a need for survival explaining that enough really means "enough for survival, and that's *L'nu* (our people)" (p. 175). If it is about surviving the winter or feeding your family, what matters is enough. Enough is also a foundational value in the Mi'kmaq community because it is about taking only what you need and ensuring the survival for generations to come.

Although there are complex counting ideas within the Mi'kmaq language as evidenced by games like waltes, these are more for play, and space is the heart of mathematical reasoning – the stuff that is about survival. However, in school we act as though number and counting are about survival, and space tends to be treated like play. Again, this learning helped me to think more critically about what and how I was teaching. Building mathematical understanding through spatial reasoning was always something I had found helpful in supporting my students, but this learning helped me realise how vital it was. Thus, I now strive to help teachers understand how concepts of quantity, operations, patterns, and relations, and so on can be taught through spatial approaches. For example, I use Cuisenaire rods to show that a length of 5 units and 8 units together creates the same length as 6 units and 7 units, thus showing that 5 + 8 = 6 + 7. Students might also use ten frames to examine their 7s facts for multiplication since placing 7 counters on a ten frame clearly shows that 5 and 2 are partitions of 7. Thus building 6 sets of 7 on a ten frame helps students to see that an easy way to calculate this is to count by 5s and count by 2s. So, 6 × 7 = 6 × 5 + 6 × 2. The ten frame allows students to understand the distributive property in a very concrete way. I have also used area models with students for everything from finding the factors of 12 to completing the square. Spatial approaches to mathematics help students to think about mathematical concepts in hands-on and concrete ways and a spatial approach is culturally rooted in *L'nui'ta'simk*.

While the model I developed in my doctoral work extends beyond the verbifying and spatialising that I have described here, these are two very specific practices that stem from the worldview of the Mi'kmaw people. These examples provide insight into how decolonising mathematics must go beyond ethnomathematical investigations and move toward a deeper focus on the integration of worldview, ways of knowing, being, and doing, that help students to understand mathematics in ways that are culturally rooted.

7   Conclusion

In this chapter, I have used examples from my own learning journey over the past nearly 22 years, to show how we might move toward decolonising mathematics education. I have shared processes that I believe have helped me, and those I work with, to decolonise mathematics for Mi'kmaw children. These have included ethnomathematical investigations and activities, but have extended beyond that as well. I have shown that elevating community voices and centring community stories can be a starting point for decolonising mathematics, but more so, that there needs to be a focus on the centring of the ways of knowing, being, and doing that are embedded in community languages and cultures. When students can learn mathematics in ways that align with their community worldview, then they are likely to have more success.

I continue to implement the lessons learned from my doctoral work in Mi'kmaw schools today by working alongside teachers and students to build engaging tasks that focus on verbifying and spatialising mathematics. While we are still in the early stages of this work, the enthusiasm from students and teachers leads me to believe that we are definitely moving in the right direction. For example, in a series of lessons for Grade 3 students, we began with a set of centres inviting students to roll dice and use the numbers to build sets of counters with and without ten frames, take jumps on a number line, or make rows of square colour tiles. We did not talk about multiplication, yet this is what was being modelled. The students shared strategies for determining the total amount and articulated their observations about ideas relating to commutativity. When they were introduced to a series of word problems involving these types of models, they easily were able to use concrete models and pictures to solve the problems. It was only after these lessons that students realised they were doing multiplication. One student, after explaining to me how she did something a certain number of "times", declared to the class: "Hey this sets of, rows of, jumps of stuff is just times!" Focusing on actions (verbifying) and using concrete models (spatialising) of the concept of multiplication allowed these students to develop strategies for solving multiplicative problems in more culturally inclusive ways.

I am still not confident that I know what decolonisation means, but I do think that some of these processes and practices that I have described above might help others to think about how they might engage in learning together with the communities they serve and thinking of ways to challenge the colonial discourse in school mathematics by beginning in community. I believe that the process of decolonising is one that is ongoing and ever evolving and will no doubt continue far into the future. Certainly, 500 years of colonialism in Canada will not be addressed in a brief amount of time, yet, I argue, we must continue the work of confronting colonialism as we encounter it and finding new ways to move forward together.

I began with wondering how mathematics education might address the calls to action of the Truth and Reconciliation Commission and take a role in working toward reconciliation. As I reflect upon my experiences, I turn often to the call to return, repair, and restore, and these words stick with me as ways to guide the work I do in mathematics education. I believe decolonising mathematics teaching and learning in the ways I have described above can help to address the Truth and Reconciliation Commission. By centring community knowledge, we can return ways of knowing, being, and doing that have been nearly erased by colonial efforts. We can repair the relationship many Indigenous youth and educators have with mathematics by honouring those ways of knowing that have supported Indigenous innovations and technologies and align with what we now call mathematics in schools. We can work collaboratively with community knowledge keepers to restore these knowledges and bring them alongside and into conversation with Western knowledges so that all students, Indigenous and non-Indigenous, see that Indigenous peoples were problem solvers and innovators. We can restore the ways of knowing, being, and doing that are a central part of community languages and worldviews and use these to engage in learning mathematics in new ways. It is my hope and belief that all of these processes will lead to experiences that are more equitable for Indigenous students in mathematics classrooms and will transform the field of mathematics itself. This will be a step toward reconciliation.

8 A Postscript

In front of the new We'koqma'q School today stands a monument dedicated to the residential school survivors from that community. It bears the names of every community member who went to "Shubie school" and declares *"Ma'tlipia'tiwkw App"* meaning it will never happen again, words carefully chosen by members of the Indian Residential Schools survivors group. It was the first such monument constructed in Canada. Beside the monument is a bench where visitors can sit and where you often find one of the classes from the school learning together. Inside the school, biographies of these survivors hang along the hallway where students, staff, and visitors can read their stories and remember. Some of the survivors continue to work in the school as teachers and support staff, alongside the descendants of other survivors who have also taken up the call to be educators who help to transform the system. Students no longer make jokes about being sent to "Shubie school" for they have come to understand in very real ways the impact these schools had on their community and their families. Survivors' stories are documented through school projects[4] that focus not only on what happened but also on the resilience of the Mi'kmaw people that has helped them to survive. The school commits itself every day to ensuring that Mi'kmaw children receive an education that is about them and for them, where they gain the knowledge and confidence to continue the work of decolonisation and ensure it never happens again.

Notes

1 Mi'kmaw is used as an adjective; Mi'kmaq is used as a noun. The traditional territory of the Mi'kmaq, known as Mi'kma'ki, contains all of Nova Scotia, Prince Edward Island, parts of New Brunswick, Quebec in the Gaspé Region, and Maine. There are also many Mi'kmaw people living in Newfoundland and Labrador.
2 Mi'kmaw Grand Chief, Ben Sylliboy, passed away on November 30, 2017 and was buried on December 9, 2017. This death occurred during the time I was preparing this manuscript. As a child, Ben attended residential school. As a residential school survivor, he played an important role in the survivors group in We'komqa'q. He was an important leader to the entire Mi'kmaq nation and an important influence on my work. I dedicate this piece to his memory.
3 People for Education Conference, November 11, 2017.
4 See for example, https://vimeo.com/143251875

References

Adam, S., Alangui, W., & Barton, B. (2003). A comment on: Rowlands & Carson "Where would formal, academic mathematics stand in a curriculum informed by ethnomathematics? A critical review". *Educational Studies in Mathematics, 52,* 327–335. https://doi.org/10.1023/A:1024308220169

Aikenhead, G. S. (2017). Enhancing school mathematics culturally: A path of reconciliation. *Canadian Journal of Science, Mathematics and Technology Education, 17*(2), 73–140. https://doi.org/10.1080/14926156.2017.1308043

Barton, B. (2008). *The language of mathematics: Telling mathematical tales.* Springer. https://doi.org/10.1007/978-0-387-72859-9

Battey, D., & Leyva, L. A. (2016). A framework for understanding whiteness in mathematics education. *Journal of Urban Mathematics Education, 9*(2), 49–80. https://doi.org/10.21423/jume-v9i2a294

Battiste, M. (2013). *Decolonizing education: Nourishing the learning spirit.* UBC Press.

Battiste, M., & Henderson, J. Y. (2009). Naturalizing Indigenous knowledge in Eurocentric education. *Canadian Journal of Native Education, 32*(1), 5–18.

Bishop, A. J. (1991). *Mathematical enculturation: A cultural perspective on mathematics education.* Kluwer. https://doi.org/10.1007/978-94-009-2657-8

Cappon, P. (2008). Measuring success in First Nations, Inuit and Métis learning. *Policy Options, 29*(5), 60–66. https://policyoptions.irpp.org/magazines/whither-the-liberals/measuring-success-in-first-nations-inuit-and-metis-learning/

D'Ambrosio, U. (2006). *Ethnomathematics: Link between traditions and modernity.* Sense. https://doi.org/10.1163/9789460911415

Donald, D. (2009). Forts, curriculum, and Indigenous Métissage: Imagining decolonization of Aboriginal-Canadian relations in educational contexts. *First Nations Perspectives, 2*(1), 1–24. https://www.mfnerc.org/wp-content/uploads/2012/11/004_Donald.pdf

Doolittle, E. (2006). Mathematics as medicine. In P. Liljedahl (Ed.), *Proceedings of the 2006 Canadian Mathematics Education Study Group Conference* (pp. 17–25). Edmonton, AB, Canada.

Fanon, F. (1963). *The wretched of the Earth.* Grove Press.

Government of Canada. (2017, June 23). Safe drinking water for First Nations Act. https://www.sac-isc.gc.ca/eng/1330528512623/1533729830801

Gutiérrez, R. (2017a). Political conocimiento for teaching mathematics: Why teachers need it and how to develop it. In S. E. Kastberg, A. M. Tyminski, A. E. Lischka, & W. B. Sanchez (Eds.), *Building supports for scholarly practices in mathematics methods* (pp. 11–37). Information Age.

Gutiérrez, R. (2017b). Why mathematics (education) was late to the backlash party: The need for a revolution. *Journal of Urban Mathematics Education, 10*(2), 8–24. https://doi.org/2151-2651

Gutstein, E. (2006). *Reading and writing the world with mathematics: Toward a pedagogy for social justice.* Routledge. https://doi.org/10.4324/9780203112946

Henderson, J. Y. (2000). Ayukpachi: Empowering Aboriginal thought. In M. Battiste (Ed.), *Reclaiming Indigenous voice and vision* (pp. 248–278). UBC Press.

Inglis, S. (2004). 400 years of linguistic contact between the Mi'kmaq and the English and the interchange of two world views. *The Canadian Journal of Native Studies, 24*(2), 389–402.

Joseph, G. G. (2011). *The crest of the peacock: Non-European roots of mathematics* (3rd edition). Princeton University Press. https://doi.org/10.1515/9781400836369

Kirkness, V. J. (1999). Aboriginal education in Canada: A retrospective and prospective. *Journal of American Indian Education, 39*(1), 14–30.

Knijnik, G. (2002). Ethnomathematics: Culture and politics of knowledge in mathematics education. *For the Learning of Mathematics, 22*(1), 11–14.

Kovach, M. (2009). *Indigenous methodologies: Characteristics, conversations and contexts.* University of Toronto Press.

Lipka, J. (2002). *Schooling for self-determination: Research on the effects of including native language and culture in the schools.* ERIC Clearinghouse on Rural Education and Small Schools. ERIC Identifier ED459989.

Lipka, J., & Topkok, A. (n.d.). *Math in a cultural context: Lessons learned from Yup'ik Eskimo Elders project.* University of Alaska Fairbanks, School of Education. Retrieved July 6, 2009, from http://www.uaf.edu/mcc/

Little Bear, L. (2000). Jagged worldviews colliding. In M. Battiste (Ed.), *Reclaiming Indigenous voice and vision* (pp. 77–85). UBC Press.

Lunney Borden, L. (2010). *Transforming mathematics education for Mi'kmaw students through mawikinutimatimk* (Doctoral dissertation). University of New Brunswick. https://www.collectionscanada.gc.ca/obj/thesescanada/vol2/002/NR82763.PDF

Lunney Borden, L. (2011). The "verbification" of mathematics: Using the grammatical structures of Mi'kmaq to support student learning. *For the Learning of Mathematics, 31*(3), 8–13.

Lunney Borden, L. (2012). What's the word for …? Is there a word for …? How understanding Mi'kmaw language can help support Mi'kmaw learners in mathematics. *Mathematics Education Research Journal, 25*(1), 5–22. https://doi.org/10.1007/s13394-012-0042-7

Lunney Borden, L. (2018). Drawing upon Indigenous knowledges to transform the secondary mathematics classroom. In A. Kajander, J. Holm, & E. Chernoff (Eds.), *Teaching and learning secondary school mathematics: Canadian perspectives in an international context* (pp. 61–72). Springer. https://doi.org/10.1007/978-3-319-92390-1_7

Lunney Borden, L., & Wagner, D. (2011). Show me your math. *CMS Notes, 43*(2), 10–11.

Lunney Borden, L., & Wagner, D. (2013). Naming method: "This is it, maybe, but you should talk to …". In R. Jorgensen, P. Sullivan, & P. Grootenboer (Eds.), *Pedagogies to enhance learning for Indigenous students* (pp. 105–122). Springer. https://doi.org/10.1007/978-981-4021-84-5_7

Lunney Borden, L., Wagner, D., & Johnson, N. (2019). Show me your math: Mi'kmaw community members explore mathematics. In C. Nicol, S. Dawson, J. Archibald Q'um Q'um Xiiem, F. Glanfield, & A. J. Dawson (Eds.), *Living culturally responsive mathematics curriculum and pedagogy: Making a difference with/in Indigenous communities* (pp. 91–112). Brill Sense. https://doi.org/10.1163/9789004415768_005

Lunney Borden, L., & Wiseman, D. (2016). Considerations from places where Indigenous and Western ways of knowing, being, and doing circulate together: STEM as artifact of teaching and learning. *Canadian Journal of Science, Mathematics and Technology Education, 16*(2), 140–152. https://doi.org/10.1080/14926156.2016.1166292

Manuel, A., & Derrickson, G. C. R. M. (2015). *Unsettling Canada: A national wake-up call*. Between the Lines.

Martin, D. B. (2011). What does quality mean in the context of White institutional spaces? In B. Atweh, M. Graven, W. Secada, & P. Valero (Eds.), *Mapping equity and quality in mathematics education* (pp. 437–450). Springer. https://doi.org/10.1007/978-90-481-9803-0_31

Powell, A. B., & Frankenstein, M. (Eds.). (1997). *Ethnomathematics: Challenging eurocentrism in mathematics education*. State University of New York Press.

Rigney, L. I. (1999). Internationalization of an Indigenous anticolonial cultural critique of research methodologies: A guide to Indigenist research methodology and its principles. *Wicazo sa review, 14*(2), 109–121. https://doi.org/10.2307/1409555

Rowlands, S., & Carson, R. (2002). Where would formal, academic mathematics stand in a curriculum informed by ethnomathematics? A critical review of ethnomathematics. *Educational Studies in Mathematics, 50*(1), 79–102. https://doi.org/10.1023/A:1020532926983

Schleppegrell, M. J. (2007). The linguistic challenges of mathematics teaching and learning: A research review. *Reading & Writing Quarterly, 23*(2), 139–159. https://doi.org/10.1080/10573560601158461

Skovsmose, O. (1994). *Towards a philosophy of critical mathematics education*. Kluwer. https://doi.org/10.1007/978-94-017-3556-8

Skovsmose, O. (2016). What could critical mathematics education mean for different groups of students? *For the Learning of Mathematics, 36*(1), 2–7.

Skovsmose, O., & Greer, B. (Eds.). (2012). *Opening the cage: Critique and politics of mathematics education*. Sense. https://doi.org/10.1007/978-94-6091-808-7

Smith, L. T. (1999). *Decolonizing methodologies: Research and Indigenous peoples*. Zed Books.

Stinson, D. (2017). Beyond White privilege: Toward White supremacy and settler colonialism in mathematics education [Editorial]. *Journal of Urban Mathematics Education, 10*(2), 1–7. http://ed-osprey.gsu.edu/ojs/index.php/JUME/article/view/348/225

Truth and Reconciliation Commission of Canada. (2015). *Honouring the truth, reconciling for the future: Summary of the final report of the Truth and Reconciliation Commission of Canada*. Truth and Reconciliation Commission of Canada. http://www.trc.ca/assets/pdf/Honouring_the_Truth_Reconciling_for_the_Future_July_23_2015.pdf

Tuck, E., & Yang, K. W. (2012). Decolonization is not a metaphor. *Decolonization: Indigeneity, Education and Society, 1*(1), 1–40.

Vithal, R., & Skovsmose, O. (1997). The end of innocence: A critique of 'ethnomathematics'. *Educational Studies in Mathematics, 34*(2), 131–157. https://doi.org/10.1023/A:1002971922833

Wagner, D., & Lunney Borden, L. (2011). Qualities of respectful positioning and their connections to quality mathematics. In B. Atweh, M. Graven, W. Secada, & P. Valero (Eds.), *Mapping equity and quality in mathematics education* (pp. 379–391). Springer. https://doi.org/10.1007/978-90-481-9803-0_27

Wagner, D., & Lunney Borden, L. (2015). Common sense and necessity in (ethno)mathematics. In K. Sullenger & S. Turner (Eds.), *New ground* (pp. 113–127). Sense. https://doi.org/10.1007/978-94-6300-022-2_7

Wiseman, D. (2016). *Acts of living with: Being, doing, and coming to understand Indigenous perspectives alongside science curricula* (Doctoral dissertation). University of Alberta. https://doi.org/10.7939/R3ST7F75V

CHAPTER 4

Propio as a Decolonising Tool for Mathematics Education

Aldo Parra and Paola Valero

Abstract

The concept of *propio*, used in Indigenous *educación propia*, has a triple meaning: *propio* as pertinence/utility, as property/belonging, and as appropriation/transformation. This conceptualisation results from a decolonial stance towards education as a central element in the political struggle for Indigenous identity affirmation and self-determination. We examine the concept of *propio* through an example of an educational experience with the Nasa Indigenous people in Colombia, exploring the three meanings of *propio* and distinguishing it from existing approaches to differentiated Indigenous education. We also address the question of whether *propio* can be of relevance in non-Indigenous contexts and its potential contribution to political approaches in mathematics education.

Keywords

Indigenous education – Nasa People – decoloniality – ethnomathematics – critical mathematics education

∙ ∙ ∙

As education has increasingly become a key mechanism of social, economic and political in(ex)clusion, the predicaments of education for Indigenous populations have been intensely debated in both Indigenous communities and in communities of scholars who work for and with the struggle for Indigenous self-determination (Dei & Kempf, 2006; Tattay, 2011). As a result, different proposals for Indigenous education and Indigenous mathematics education have emerged to challenge the colonial desire of states to assimilate Indigenous peoples. What is common to many of these proposals is a political reading of the effects of knowledge, school knowledge and school pedagogies in generating in(ex)clusion, assimilation or possible routes to identity affirmation and self-determination.

In this paper, we explore the conceptualisation of *propio*,[1] a notion that emerged in Colombian Indigenous education to think about, characterise and purposefully manage the relationship between community, knowledge and action in face of the life and political struggles of an Indigenous group. The instantiation of *propio* in an educational project, *educación propia*, is explored as a tool that unfolds decolonising standpoints in and for education. In particular, we focus on what such an idea may mean in the realm of mathematics education. We argue that *propio* and *educación propia* resonates with the political turn in mathematics education (Gutiérrez, 2013; Valero, 2004). It allows us to sharpen the critique of the epistemic superiority of dominant Western mathematics and, at the same time, offers a performative capacity for transforming educational practices.

We start by providing an account of the emergence of the concept of *propio*, as part of the political struggle of the Nasa Indigenous people in Colombia. We then illustrate the main features of *propio* as it unfolded in a concrete educational practice involving mathematics. Resemblances and differences with other proposals of Indigenous mathematics education are discussed. Finally, we reflect on the ways in which and the extent to which the concept of *propio* could be unfolded in non-Indigenous settings, thus constituting a useful political tool for mathematics educators.

1   Traces of One Colombian Indigenous Education

The Andes mountains, in what today is known as South America, is the land called *Abya-yala*, "the land in full maturity." This was the name that several Indigenous peoples had for their territory when the Spanish colonisers declared it to be the "the new world of the Americas." Abya-yala in its contemporary use signals the political resistance of Indigenous peoples in the face of the now national—still colonising—government forces. In particular, several Indigenous peoples have, since 1971, raised their voices against the ethnocide that they were suffering in the state of Cauca, a predominantly rural area in the south west of Colombia (see Figure 4.1). They created the Regional Indigenous Council of Cauca [in Spanish, *Consejo Regional Indígena del Cauca* (CRIC)] to represent their people's interests to the national government. In 1971, the council presented a seven-point agenda for negotiation with the Colombian authorities, one of these points being the "defense of Indigenous history, language, culture and traditions," and another being the "training of Indigenous

FIGURE 4.1 Geopolitical division of Colombia. The State of Cauca is shown in dark grey. (Image created by Milenioscuro, CC BY-SA 4.0, https://commons.wikimedia.org/w/index.php?curid=6031789)

teachers to educate according to the Indigenous situation and in their mother tongue" (Consejo Regional Indígena del Cauca, 2004, p. 28, our translation).

From the beginning of the struggle, education has been at the center of the resistance and Indigenous peoples have tried to consolidate a specific, differentiated educational model. Over the past 40 years, they have forged the right to have Indigenous teachers, to teach bilingually, to introduce culturally relevant content into the curriculum, and to create Indigenous teacher education programmes. These changes have been the product of long debates with, protests against and proposals to the regional and national authorities, always aimed at obtaining greater autonomy in the processes of schooling. Nowadays, Colombian national educational policy acknowledges the right of each Indigenous nation to have a "Differentiated Indigenous Educational System" (in Spanish, *Sistema Educativo Indígena Propio*, from now on SEIP). More recently, the Indigenous educational model has been called *educación propia*, as a result of a long process of refinement, rearrangement, and differentiation of several earlier models, such as ethno-education in the 1970s–1980s, and bilingual intercultural education in the 1990s–2000s.[2] *Educación propia* can therefore be understood as one stage in a continuous quest for autonomy, now guided and structured by the notion of *propio*.

Throughout this process of negotiation, internal debates have arisen concerning the very existence of the *school* as an institution and the accompanying subjectivation of children through the processes of individualisation and universalisation of the self, and detachment from community and home. These processes are effects of power which alter the fundamental inseparability of person, community and territory in the Indigenous worldview. These debates have resulted in an educational model that goes beyond the boundaries of any particular school, aiming to cover the whole community and its inhabited territory. *Educación propia* addressed the demand for school-based education imposed by the Colombian government. By re-structuring the "guidelines, foundations, approaches, methods, contents, styles of administration, assessment and control" (Consejo Regional Indígena del Cauca, 2015, our translation), the organisation of the curriculum allowed schools to structure their space in continuity and interrelationship with family and community spaces. The aims of *educación propia* are "strengthening authority, autonomy, territory, self-esteem and cultural identity, to promote the knowing and valorisation of knowledge and practices that can be owned or appropriated, and to promote a critical understanding of intra- and extra-cultural conflicts, as well as a positive interpretation of cultural diversity" (CONTCEPI, 2013, p. 20, our translation).

These ideas were realised in schools that project community interests, founded on culturally rooted forms of identity expression and ancestral ways of teaching and learning. Such an approach makes it possible to transcend the focus on individuality and universality, and to conceive of the educational process as a collective and openly political engagement. The organisation and functioning of *educación propia*, as expressed in a Communitarian Educational Project (in Spanish, *Proyecto Educativo Comunitario*, from now on PEC), covers not only teachers and children within the school building, but also all community members along with their territory. In other words, *educación propia* expresses an understanding and commitment to education as a process of teaching-learning acquired "before birth and even after death" (Sichra, 2004, p. 65, our translation). PECs promote awareness of the educational subjectivation processes that shape and consolidate Indigenous identities. Furthermore, PECs are defined by each community in a *resguardo*,[3] according to the community's traditions, capacities, interests and concerns. It is the responsibility of the *cabildo*[4] to guide the formulation and implementation of the PEC. Research and the production of knowledge are considered connatural activities in the PEC, that are devoted to face the predicaments that *resguardos* have to deal with. Teachers are often selected among community members, privileging political, linguistic, and cultural capacities over pedagogical or academic skills (Guido Guevara et al., 2013; Ministerio de Educación Nacional de Colombia, 2010). Finally, a PEC is continuously assessed and refined by the community through a communication process that transforms "the very notion of school, the ways in which community appropriates it, the teacher's roles within the community, and the role of education in an Indigenous society" (Tattay, 2011, pp. 39–40, our translation).

In the next section, we provide an example of the principles of *educación propia* in action. We illustrate some of the characteristics mentioned above and connect them with mathematics education. It is important to note that this experience is just one among many other enactments of *educación propia*, and for that reason the case cannot be considered as a guide to what should or must be done. However, this example serves to highlight the connections that the notion of *propio* articulates.

2   Recognising Lomitas: A Fieldwork Experience

This educational experience was conducted in 2011 (Parra, 2011) in the Village of Lomitas, belonging to the Resguardo of San Andres de Pisimbalá, in the region of Tierradentro, the sacred land of the Nasa people. Lomitas is a village located at the top of a mountain, bordering with the urban settlement of the municipality of Inzá, a town located in a valley. The village enjoys an excellent view over Inzá (see Figure 4.2), but the village and the town are separated by a river and two steeply sloping mountains, so that the two places are separated by a journey of more than one hour. Lomitas is only accessible on foot. This geographical setting of isolation and proximity made the village a strategic point in the military confrontation that Colombia suffered for 60 years. In 2010, the school building in the village was (ab)used by guerrilla troops to attack, from a distance, the police station at Inzá. This is just one example of the serious threats to sovereignty and self-determination that the Nasa people in Lomitas face.

FIGURE 4.2   Inzá seen from the school at Lomitas

Lomitas school offers pre-school and primary school for students from 4 to 10 years old. In 2011, it had three teachers in charge of two grades each. The teachers had different backgrounds: one had no prior experience or teacher education and was in his first year of teaching. A second teacher had completed secondary school and had had some brief training as a teacher. The last teacher had a university degree in ethno-education, which is a bachelor's programme for Indigenous teachers. The latter two teachers had been working in Lomitas for 7 years and had been re-elected by the community.

When Aldo arrived in the community to learn about mathematics education as part of *educación propia*, one of the teachers, Diego Guegia, explained an idea that he had been considering with the aim of rescuing the memory of the community. The elders in the community had told him stories about some of the special places in the territory, involving mythical and cultural aspects. He noticed that his students were referring to some of these places using names in Spanish because they did not know the names in Nasayuwe, the Nasa language. He realised that the children did not know the stories either. He considered this to be an educational problem.

Diego began to explore ways to integrate such stories and the knowledge involved in them with school activities. He, the other two teachers and Aldo exchanged ideas and decided to create a toponymy project involving seven distinctive places of Lomitas. The project consisted of conducting collective research about the seven places, such as by identifying their stories and installing informative plaques for visitors and locals. Each plaque would contain the name in Nasayuwe, history and other relevant information. The goal was to demarcate and reaffirm the community's territory and sovereignty.

In the following days, Diego explained the idea to the community and invited elders to tell the stories and assess the project. They arranged to make a journey to visit the places with the students. One week after the first meeting, elders and authorities went to the school and guided a 4-hour walk through the village, telling the stories of the places which were important for diverse reasons: because there is a special plant used for cleaning and health, or a special historical event happened there, or the place is of spiritual and sacred significance. Stories were told in Nasayuwe; children also asked questions in Nasayuwe. At the end of the journey, everybody ate together, with a lunch prepared by some of the parents who were waiting for the group to return to the school.

The next days in school were used to organise the information. Children wrote and drew each story. If further clarification was needed, the teacher provided additional information. Diego proposed the creation of a kind of footpath for visitors that connected the places and where information was provided about each place, the route and the *resguardo*. The children recalled plaques that they had seen at the nearby Tierradentro archeological park, and wanted to do something similar. A new task emerged: the children had to establish what kind of information an informative plaque should contain. They identified the altitude, the distance to other places, a map and stories about the place. They also decided that there should be a red point indicating where the reader is located. The children had to obtain data, establish a design for the plaque, and decide which information they wanted to put on each one of them along the path. Therefore, for example, students needed to measure the distance between the places.

How to measure distance was a challenge, because the path is full of slopes and curves. It was not clear what measuring instruments students could use. Diego and Aldo proposed to combine and contrast several measures. Students in groups should measure how much time it takes to go from one place to the next. One group proposed to measure the number of steps that a person takes. They realised that such a unit is relative to each person, so they established a sort of protocol for the measurement by selecting the smaller children and asking them to walk slowly and with regular steps. Diego suggested to use another instrument, a *guasca* that is a rope made of natural fiber, used by almost all Nasa people for different purposes. We prepared ropes of the same length (7 meters). To measure time, we had borrowed five mobile phones and used their chronometers. Children learned how to use mobile phones on the same day, as these artefacts were not very common at that time because they were expensive and there is no good signal in the mountains where Lomitas is located.

Diego devoted one entire day to do the first measurements. Each team had 5 children with different roles: one was the walker, one counted the steps of the first one, two measured the walking path with guascas, and the last one recorded the time spent by the walker. Conflicts soon emerged: the number of steps quickly got quite high, and the child counting the steps spent a lot of time saying the number and asking the walker to slow down so that he could count. The children recording the time then protested because slowing down the pace affected their measure. The children took the measures several times, going back and forth, and found them similar in guascas, but very different in time. Many groups explained the differences, saying, for example, that it is not the same when a person goes down-hill than when climbing up. Some children believed that the distance is not the same, while others realised that speed could explain the differences. When converting the number of steps into the amount of guascas, teachers perceived a problem in the accuracy and asked the children to explain how they had obtained the measurements. Some children revealed that they had lost count of the steps and were guessing. One group created a strategy to count the number of steps: for each 10 steps they took, they put a small rock in their pocket and started counting again. When they arrived at the endpoint, they multiplied the number of rocks by ten, and added the final steps. It became evident that a new day of measurement would be necessary to resolve the issues that had appeared during the first day.

Once the data had been obtained in homogeneous ways, all groups gathered and explained their results. Diego made a table with the results and a drawing of the situation. Questions arose about time and distance: Which is the longest section of the route? Which are the closest places? Which segment is steeper? How much time does it take to walk the entire footpath? How long is the proposed route? To address these questions, students needed to add seconds and minutes which are not in a decimal system. Diego also requested answers in metres, so they needed to convert their measures of guascas. To do this, we measured the length of a guasca (7 meters) and the length of a student's step (0.5 metres). They then had to multiply numbers with decimals and round up. They converted the informal measures of each section of the route into meters and added them. They checked that the total was equal to the conversion of the sum of the whole route, obtained by adding the informal measures. Diego explained that the results must be the same, exemplifying the distributive property of addition and multiplication. Much of the standard content of the non-Indigenous mainstream mathematics curriculum gained meaning and utility within the framework of this project.

With the numerical data analysed, the next task was to trace a proper map for Lomitas. Students consulted some geography books to see the usual conventions of representation, but they did not find anything specific about Lomitas. Aldo suggested the use of Google Maps and explained to Diego how to use it. While he was showing the tool to the children, explaining that a satellite can take pictures of the Earth, one student replied that such system is a threat to the territory, because many people can obtain information about them without Indigenous permission and without any control of the use of such information. Diego extended this reflection, saying that Indigenous people need to be aware of the possibilities of these technologies. Students used the views that Google Maps offered—at that time it was two-dimensional and not very detailed—as a reference to create on paper their own representations of Lomitas. When working on drawing their maps, children located the different special places that they had previously identified, in such a way that the data obtained could be represented.

A new stage of the project was to define a plaque for each place. Students watched a video that Aldo had recorded during the first work session with the elders, and they remembered important details of the stories. Groups were responsible for proposing a draft of the final plaques. They had to display on a blank page all the information collected. Groups were also asked to create small verses about the particular story of each place. Part of the plaque needed to be written in Nasayuwe, other parts in Spanish, and others with numerical information. Teachers gave feedback about the drafts, until they were approved. For the next stage, teachers invested part of their salary in paint, brushes, wood and sandpaper so that students could prepare the final plaques. Colours, texts, and proportions were defined. They needed to know how to create some colours, how to prepare a wooden surface, which type of painting they would use, and how to paint. The school turned into a small carpentry workshop for a week.

In parallel, Diego was coordinating a final event in the form of a traditional *minga*.[5] The community cut wooden poles to hang the plaques, and the school prepared special food for the day. Elders, parents and authorities were invited. It was now the turn of the children to retell the stories to the community. They recited the verses they had created and explained how to read the information contained in the plaque. The children signed the back of each plaque and the adults installed them. When the journey ended back at the school, parents expressed their approval and assessed the work, stressing the importance of knowing the history of Lomitas and the Nasa tradition.

3 Delineating the Notion of *Propio*

The fieldwork experience we have described helps us to characterise the notion of *propio*. The educational activity was not created to improve students' performance in a pre-stablished curricular topic. The overall aim was to address concerns within the community about the territory, concerns that are necessarily cultural and political. This aspect illustrates the role of school envisioned in *educación propia*. This role is not about the improvement of teaching, using the customary focus on disciplinary content, in order to improve individual results. Rather, schools and educational activity respond to an agenda of relevance for the community. Thus, a first connotation of *propio* connects with *proper, adequate, pertinent* and *useful*. A proper education for the student and the community fosters knowledge and values needed to address the demands of their life in a political struggle for identity and territory. It also legitimates local forms of organisation and communication, and nurtures leaders who can address the perceived educational problems of the community. It can be said that educational practices in the communities are *made for* Indigenous communities and are therefore attuned to Indigenous interests.

We can see similarities between this approach and other experiences in ethnomathematics and in critical mathematics education. For example, in the work on mathematics education the Landless People's Movement in Brazil, principles like "learning in the process" and "knowledge is political" are developed to "allow articulating the local world of each settlement and the immediate demands of the struggle with educational processes" (Knijnik, 2004, p. 128). This articulation resulted in new pedagogies of mathematics that responded to the needs of peasants in their struggle, and at the same time gave opportunities for children and youth to continue their studies. Meanwhile, in Skovsmose's (2009, 2011) conceptualisation of mathematics in action, a critical distance from diverse uses of mathematics favours the recognition of the intentions, motivations, consequences, and risks that each mathematical object or technique comprises. This critical distance makes possible a critique of the modernist conception of (mathematical) knowledge in which objectivity, certainty, transparency, progress, and neutrality are naturalised values (Skovsmose, 2009).

The experience of Lomitas also allows us to problematise the traditional sources and places of knowledge. Who decides what is true or false or what deserves to be learned and problematised in the educational process? The answer is clear in this case: the community and the territory. In the PEC, the community defines what is important to be discussed in schools. It is important to mention that the SEIP grants communities the power of hiring and assessing teachers according to their own criteria. For instance, teachers can be selected by a spiritual test of their energies, made by a *Kiwethê*, a traditional healer of the community, who establishes which candidate is best aligned to the desires of the community. This form of selection is reasonable since the teachers' role is to facilitate or catalyse, rather than to transmit previously determined knowledge. Knowledge is held and created by community members.

As our example illustrated, elders and children were the main actors. They exchanged the role of source and target of knowledge at different points in the process. They recovered and actualised their knowledge about the community and the territory and made it available. This entails a second sense of the term *propio*: Nasa are the *owners* of this education, and values like *property* and *belonging* are fundamental in the relation between the community and the content of education. As stated by its Intercultural and Bilingual Educational Programme [in Spanish, *Programa de Educación Bilingüe Intercultural*, from now on PEBI], education is their own because the Nasa have "the faculty to orient, direct, organise and construct educational processes and proposals with a critical and purposeful positioning towards the education that we want" (PEBI, 2010, p. 7, our translation). We can summarise that characteristic as an education *made by* Indigenous people.

The third sense of *propio* that we want to explore became evident in the experience when students proposed to make the plaques and used new ICT devices to obtain and analyse information. *Propio* then takes the sense of *appropriated*, or something foreign, not belonging to one's culture, that is taken on board because it is functional with respect to one's needs. Neither teachers nor parents took issue with using and taking advantage of foreign technologies such as mobile phones or computers. They considered it important to take advantage of non-Indigenous tools, as far as they contributed to their autonomy. The possibility of appropriation of technologies or the knowledge of others moves away from essentialist views of Indigenous education that argue for a purity of traditional community knowledge (Scandiuzzi, 2009). Rather, this view of appropriation constitutes a political conception of interculturality where "based on our own knowledge, we move to integrate knowledge from the outside" (Consejo Regional Indígena del Cauca, 2004, p. 115, our translation). Tattay (2011) explains that interculturality is conceived as:

> Horizontality within the frame of a political relationship [...] Interculturality implies a relation among diverse agents, conceptions, strategies and tools; it also implies contact among diverse cultural expressions, considering relations of power and domination. And because of that, the permanent effort to create situations of equity among knowledge(s) of diverse natures becomes necessary. (p. 91, our translation)

The comment of the 9-year-old child about the information on the community's territory available to other people through geographic information systems such as Google Maps being a threat is framed within such horizontality. This approach supports the use of such tools while maintaining a critical sense of the developments of other cultures.

Finally, it is important to comment on the role of research in education and how it is understood by the Nasa people. Research is central to *educación propia* since it has become a strategy to create and re-create knowledge in relation to their culture, and to circulate the knowledge in the community. In this sense, research is also a pedagogical strategy. Research unfolds "a process of self-re-cognition, because it allows us to discover how much we know ourselves about our culture, our territory and about different ways to communicate in the family, in the community and in other spaces" (Caicedo et al., 2009, p. 131, our translation). Research is understood to be a tool for strengthening (Indigenous) identity, appropriating the territory, and producing collective knowledge. Research is, therefore, "a strategy of hope, dignity and freedom" (Caicedo et al., 2009, p. 131, our translation).

The participatory and intercultural way in which the experience in Lomitas combined diverse types of sources (e.g., oral tradition, the internet, the territory) and procedures (e.g., information sharing in the community, data collection, conceptualisation in mother tongue, space intervention, minga) allows us to see an intentional re-signification of notions such as research, knowledge and learning. The third meaning of *propio* and the role of research highlighted above are the conditions that transform, adapt and condense external elements in such way that they can be taken on board according to Nasa cultural and political conceptions. In short, Nasa people appropriate non-Indigenous concepts and procedures, when trying to do education *à la* Indigenous Nasa.

4 Walls and Bridges between Other Educational Proposals

In this section we analyse similarities and differences between *educación propia* and other approaches in Indigenous and in mainstream education that seems to be in line with the characteristics of *educación propia*. Our argument may seem less specific to mathematics education because alternative educational proposals are usually designed and conducted within holistic frameworks that do not follow disciplinary scientific divisions. To balance this situation, we discuss a few (but growing) experiences that have tried to bring Indigenous or community-based education to mathematics education.

Educación propia shares characteristics with place-based or land-based education in its deep interest for the local environment as source of knowledge

(Sobel, 2004), with inquiry-based or problem-based education for their research-driven methods (Nicol et al., 2013), and with Freirean popular education and participatory action research for their interest in critique and attempting to change reality through collaborative action (Zavala, 2013). The centrality of community and the collective construction of meaning relates *educación propia* with the African philosophical humanist notion of Ubuntu that is a key component of African Indigenous ways of knowing and being (e.g., Swanson, 2015). Meanings of *propio* like belonging and transformation resonate with the decolonising methodologies proposed by Smith (2013). However, we claim that the notion of *propio* marks out a different problematisation that generates new insights for (mathematics) education.

To frame the differences between *educación propia* and other proposals, we follow Rojas and Castillo (2005) in their study of how educational policies have dealt with cultural diversity in Colombia. They claim that the recognition of cultural diversity during the late twentieth century is a double edged sword. While it is true that the acknowledgement of cultural diversity is the result of the demands of social movements—and it can be considered an achievement—at the same time, it can be seen as the state co-opting those demands. Until the middle of the twentieth century most nation-states subscribed to an image of a homogeneous, monocultural society, in which ethnic minorities were positioned as inferior, and even as less than human; their existence was denied and they were treated as the savage "Other" in need of being civilised through education. By the end of the twentieth century, there had been a substantial change in social representations of minorities such that "cultural difference" was promoted to the level of a human right, and many nations were reframed as multicultural and pluriethnic. Therefore, discourses, as ways of enunciation and representation, were modified. However:

> new representations are still controlled by dominant places and discourses, subjected to their forms and processed in their space space ... For the state, constitutional recognition of ethnic diversity constitutes an opportunity to consolidate a development and action model for the state in territories (and populations) previously marginalised or towards populations upon which it had been unable to exercise effective action. (Rojas & Castillo, 2005, p. 54, our translation)

Rojas and Castillo argue that the right to be diverse may also constitute a re-arrangement of the hegemonic discourses that maintain the subaltern and *minoritarian* condition of diversity, where ethnic groups and cultures are presented as special groups full of particularities and localities, while the *majoritarian* society is depicted as not particular, but universal. Accordingly, education for these minorities is defined as one that respects and recognises their localities while at the same time giving access to the "real deal" of universal knowledge. Evidence of this type of re-arrangement is that educational proposals for differentiated education make room for inclusion of cultural content in the curricula, but do not give leadership, control of assessment processes or of economic resources to Indigenous populations or grass-roots movements. As a result we face what Walsh has called "neoliberal multiculturalism" (Walsh, 2007). In this frame, the provision of Indigenous education is a right "that the dominant sectors have considered as their own and a way of making the minorities part of (in-corporated into) the project of society" (Rojas & Castillo, 2005, p. 138, our translation).

We contend that *educación propia* attempts to contest this subaltern condition in different ways with respect to other types of differentiated education. For instance, the role of school is different. Makoni and Pennycook (2007) rightly stress that:

> While indigenous communities regard schools as sites of contact between indigenous communities and the 'white-man's world,' education being understood as taking place at home, Western scholarship takes the opposite view, defining what indigenous communities regard as education to the relegated status of socialization. (p. 30)

Although in *education propia* school is useful in the process of acquiring non-Indigenous tools needed to improve the ways in which communities interact with the state, that is not the main role attributed to the school. Tattay (2011) pointed out that "[since the early years, the CRIC] designed school to catalyse communitarian processes, understanding by communitarian not only something only needing tools from "inside"; but also something that strengthens culture and the organisation with a kind of toolbox from various sources" (p. 43, our translation).

Educational models and associated educational research on Indigenous education, such as ethno-education (Blanco-Álvarez, 2008), bilingual intercultural education (Santibañez, 2016), culturally responsive/relevant education (Lipka, Sharp, Adams, & Sharp, 2007) and place-based/land-based education (Boyer, 2006) propose to implement changes in the curriculum or in pedagogical styles, without doubting or fundamentally questioning the structure and purpose of the school itself. Almost no attention is paid to the integrationist principle that subsumes the diversity of Indigenous knowledge and practices into the traditional hegemonic educational models managed and normalised by the state (Parra et al., 2016). For instance, when trying to link school and culture, some of these proposals include cultural knowledge as part of the curriculum subjects to be taught (e.g., bilingual intercultural education in Perú), while others take advantage of cultural heritage to facilitate the learning of disciplinary subject-matter (e.g., culturally responsive education).

In mathematics education, such proposals are illustrated in the following two approaches. Nicol et al. (2013) observed that "[t]eachers generally did not consider Indigenous knowledge, culture, or the community as resources for mathematics problems, however they did speak to the need to draw upon students' prior knowledge in designing mathematics lessons" (p. 79). They developed a model of culturally responsive mathematics in which traditional Indigenous stories can be re-worked to achieve the learning of the disciplinary knowledge prescribed in the mainstream curriculum. In the same way, Sobel (2004) noted that "[p]lace-based education is the process of using the local community and environment as a starting point to teach concepts in language arts, mathematics, social studies, science and other subjects across the curriculum" (p. 6).

We can see in these proposals how the school intervenes in the communitarian space: first school and its agents—teachers and/or researchers—find objects in the community, like social or environmental problems, oral stories, traditional forms of knowing, etc. These objects are then treated, studied and problematised in school ways to obtain individual learning in students. In brief, the school intervenes in the community to achieve its own aims. Conversely, the ideas of *educación propia* explore the relationship between school and community the other way around. It is the community that intervenes in the school space, finding some objects in it—such as the curriculum, assessment techniques, teacher education, etc.—that the community treats, studies and problematises in communitarian ways, to obtain collective learning in the community. Individual benefit results from the achievement of collective goals. In brief, the community enters the school to achieve the community's aims—not the aims of the school.

At first glance this difference may seem a mere change of order because the educational models use similar means (inquiry-based and participatory methodologies), and because *educación propia* does not refuse academic (disciplinary subject-matter) achievement. Also, each one of the models mentioned have clearly stressed that they aim to "develop and/or maintain cultural competence" (Ladson-Billings, 1995), or to "help students develop stronger ties to their community" (Sobel, 2004). However, they are not pursuing the same aims as *educación propia*. Making school more context-aware generates the risk of scholasticising the culture. Instead, by trying to make the community more school-aware, *educación propia* may communitarise the school. These trends therefore face the cooptive force of (neoliberal) multiculturalism in very different ways.

Proposals that move from school towards the community are often instrumentalised and in the long run are reduced to styles of teaching that end up being assessed in terms of how efficient they are in increasing school performance and reducing, for example, the achievement gap in mathematics (Santibañez, 2016; Warren & DeVries, 2009). This point indirectly reinforces the idea that there is certain type of knowledge and way of life that deserve to be pursued. In their strong critique of some North American attempts to incorporate Indigenous perspectives in mathematics education, Stavrou and Miller (2017) pointed out that:

> A decolonizing and anti-oppressive education mean much more than the common understanding of promoting cultural diversity and non-Western perspectives. It requires identifying and challenging the root causes of oppression, how inequality is reproduced in the classroom, and finding strategies to counter educational discourses that position Western knowledge as superior and other knowledge (such as Indigenous knowledge) as inferior. (p. 99)

Furthermore, Molina Bedoya and Tabares Fernández (2014) argued that although the concept of "dialogue of knowledge(s)" permeates almost any current proposal of Indigenous education, it falls short in recognising that "more than the convergence of knowledge(s) of diverse types, what is needed for an effective interculturality is dialogue among human beings, coming from different spaces, with cultural practices and diverse historic experiences" (p. 13, our translation). In the same vein, Grosfoguel (2012) has clearly pointed out how the logic of neoliberal multiculturalism does not entail any change in the *locus of enunciation*[6] established by colonial hierarchisations:

> Hegemonic liberal multiculturalism allows each racialized group to have its space and celebrate its identity/culture, as long as they do not question the ethnic/racial hierarchies of white supremacist power and as long as they leave the status quo intact. This privileges certain elites within the racialized/inferiorized groups, granting them a space and resources as "tokens," "model minority," or "symbolic showcases," thereby giving a cosmetic multicultural tinge to white power, while the majority of these populations victimized by this rampant racism experience the coloniality of power on a daily basis. (p. 87)

It is precisely to this point that the triple meaning of *propio* (pertinent, owned, and appropriated) becomes relevant as it enacts a radical displacement in the locus of enunciation and locates the discussions of Indigenous education on a different plane. Through the notion of *propio*, Nasa people are not just claiming that their knowledge deserves to be called knowledge instead of beliefs. They also reject the subaltern position that denies them the intellectual status of knower and condemns them to the role of the known. The problem in the midst of education is therefore no longer a struggle for recognition, but a fight for autonomy and self-determination.

5   *Propio*, a Decolonising Tool

The Nasa people conceive of autonomy in relation to the construction of their own thinking (Levalle, 2017). This became evident in their re-definition of education, research, school, and knowledge. Such redefinitions counteract an epistemic violence that hierarchises and classifies knowledges through dichotomies such as theoretical/practical, local/universal, scientific/vernacular, and that operates in the intertwining of knowledge and power, (dis)abling entire populations as ignorant or trustable. The deliberate creation and use of such re-definitions allows us to recognise the potential of the notion of *propio* as a de-colonising tool for thought.

It is a matter of consensus in the community of researchers and activists in decolonising processes that coloniality is not only a matter of political dominance, but is always accompanied by the establishment of a matrix of diverse hierarchisations: religious, linguistic, ethnic, economical and, of course, epistemic. Colonisation simultaneously ran military invasions in the territories that today constitute Latin America and enthroned a geopolitics of knowledge (Mignolo, 2002). The latter vindicated a universal, objective character for Euro-centered knowledge and labelled the knowledge developed in colonised territories as localised and subjective. Such assemblages of hierarchisations and dichotomies were fertile soil for the consolidation of the project of modernity. The regimes of truth that sustain modernity proscribe any doubt about such dichotomies as a threat to development and as an anchor to an obscure and esoteric past. The decolonial project and Indigenous resistance converge in their rejection of this "God's eye-view" epistemology and share a disdain to replace one hegemony with another. This point is relevant when it comes to mathematics, given its centrality in Western modernity and in its entanglement with political power in the assimilation of Indigenous populations in Latin America (Valero & García, 2014). As Stavrou and Miller (2017) pointed out: "Applying decolonizing strategies to mathematics will make visible that it is a subject developed in time and place, and will expose the imperialistic operation that deprives mathematics of its historical roots and human construction" (p. 106).

This decolonial response to an imposed modernist universality is particularly important in the conceptualisation of *propio*. Thus, *propio* is not proposing an essentialist account that would impose a different centre; neither is it a relativist proposal that would deny the advances and achievements of modernist science. Instead, the idea of *propio* assumes the lack of a unified global epistemic center, and is interested in the processes of appropriation and creation of knowledge that each culture and community can develop. Thus, the notion of *propio* refers to a complex interplay of the categories inside/outside (of Indigenous social, cultural and political spaces), that are not conceived of as mutually excluding but as nested and implicated in a continuous, mutual reshaping. Rappaport (2008), an anthropologist who has studied the political and cultural resistance of the Nasa people for more than 30 years, reflected about this issue:

> [for indigenous activists], culture is not an existing constellation of practices and meanings located on the "inside" but a projection of how future lifeways should look, driven by a process in which elements of the inside are revitalized through the incorporation of ideas from outside; that is, culture necessarily straddles the frontier. This is not a strategic deployment of essentializing discourses to describe what exists "out there" but a model of what "should be," a blueprint for the future … While ethnographers engage in cultural description with an eye to analyzing it, indigenous autoethnographers study culture to act upon it. (pp. 20–21)

Rappaport calls our attention to the ways in which "inside" is conceived by Nasa people as *process*, instead of *condition*. While the latter prefigures an immanent and already existing identity that deserves to be preserved, the former is appealing to the journey that communities are doing when interacting with other groups, aiming to transcend and survive without cooptation. Thus, identity is in permanent construction. As Tattay (2011) explains, "the notion of *propio* underscores that the appropriation, adjustment and reorientation of external knowledge(s) are not the exclusive privilege of the others. Internal adjustment and orientation make those elements belong to current indigenous identities. In that sense, *educación propia* does not only deal with the inside" (p. 34, our translation, emphasis added). As illustrated by the project in Lomitas, Nasa people do not refuse knowledge and technologies (such as digital geographic information systems) produced by others; instead, they are trying to appropriate them.

With these insights, we locate the notion of *propio* beyond short-sighted identity politics and multicultural approaches, and move it closer to Harding's (2008) standpoint epistemologies and decolonial stances. *Propio* escapes a modernist, "God's eyes-view" perspective. Instead it situates its approach to knowledge geographically, historically, linguistically, and culturally. In *educación propia*, the notion of *propio* expresses an epistemological conceptualisation made by Indigenous people in Cauca. Levalle (2017) reported that for the Nasa people every process of knowing is at the same time a process of feeling. Indigenous researchers talk about "feeling the messages of the territory" or "getting reconnected with the origin's history." This has the aim of re-harmonising with the territory. In that sense, *propio* knowledge is a knowledge that is felt, mainly bodily. The Nasa educational leader Inocencio Ramos explained how the Nasa people understood "to know" as related to the capacity of feeling and dreaming, and this relation is expressed in the Nasayuwe language. The words for reflect, think, analyse and plan are all related with the heart and the spirits. For those reasons, Inocencio Ramos stated that to know is to "think with the heart" or "corazonar"[7] (Levalle, 2017, p. 132, our translation). *Propio* knowledge is also collective, because "it is re-created in the memory of the people and also in the set of presences that inhabit the territory. It is a deeply relational and intersubjective knowledge" (Levalle, 2017, p. 141, our translation).

6   How Global Is the Local?

In this final section we address how the political, cultural and epistemological insights gathered in the notion of *propio* and its unfolding in *educación propia* resonate with concerns and questions raised in other contexts, Indigenous or not. Although *propio* is a result of the Nasa strategy of cultural resistance, it allows us to think about other experiences in mathematics education and propose directions for action. In this way, *propio* may also help us to address the tendency in some sociopolitical research towards critical contemplation and turn critique into a performative force.

The development of a differentiated education (*Te Aho Matua*) in Aotearoa/New Zealand by Māori people has been another long process characterised by a quest for autonomy and self-determination, accomplished by the community and invited researchers. The process was acknowledged by the state after years of negotiation and legitimation of educational initiatives. The work to decolonise methodologies and pedagogies and reconstruct them from a Māori perspective suggests that *propio* is a construct that can be applied beyond the specificity of Nasa people.

When examining the role of the language *Te Reo Māori* in the teaching and learning of mathematics, Meaney, Trinick, et al. (2012) described a variety of experiences in which Indigenous identities became strengthened in the complex linking of past with future. Such experiences deployed a series of techniques and strategies in which we can recognise the same intention to appropriate, and to make mathematics education pertinent and relevant, that we have highlighted here in the case of the Nasa.

Barton et al. (1998) described how Māori people created their own mathematical registers in *Te Reo*, including for Western mathematical concepts, through an ongoing process of appropriation (one sense of *propio*). Meaney, Trinick, et al. (2012) reported the historical development of *Te Kura o Te Koutu* school, a grassroots educational initiative in Rotorua, where Māori communities define and manage their own education (the sense of *propio* as property/belonging is evident). McMurchy-Pilkington et al. (2013) and Meaney, McMurchy-Pilkington, et al. (2012) have discussed the evolving political controversies associated with curriculum development in Aotearoa/New Zealand in the last 20 years and the views that academic research promoted or neglected within such development (making visible a third sense of *propio*: pertinence). Direct resemblances between the Māori and Nasa experiences were explored by Parra and Trinick (2018).

It is relatively easy to establish connections among educational initiatives in Indigenous nations because the shared history of colonisation makes evident the desire to displace the locus of enunciation that *propio* proposes. Certainly, it is more difficult to argue for decolonisation in groups and communities that do not recognise themselves as formerly colonised. The relevance of the concept of *propio* for mathematics education more broadly resides in the possibility of using it as a tool to think and act in non-Indigenous contexts. We acknowledge that the cultural dimension of Indigeneity provides a space for reflection, struggle and action different from the one that non-Indigenous contexts have.

Some non-Indigenous experiences in mathematics education can resemble the conceptualisation of *propio*. The case of Brazilian rural communities in the struggle for land ownership is such a context. Knijnik (1996, 2002, 2004, 2007), Knijnik and Wanderer (2010), and Knijnik et al. (2012) have reported how peasant work techniques of importance for material and economic survival—such as measuring land and agricultural production—were described, used and contrasted with techniques accepted by the state. These mathematical techniques were also used strategically to defend the peasants' interests.

They were also modified by the appropriation of other techniques that allowed them to resist and find new ways of working. These communities were part of the Landless Movement, a large NGO with the political project of land ownership for dispossessed peasants. Education in the landless settlements was the context in which the mathematical activities were inscribed. Although here there is no ethnic condition involved in cultural struggle, this case has a similar political condition of resistance and communitarian re-affirmation that the CRIC provided for the Nasa's education project.

Could other contexts of tension, such as the education of refugee or immigrant minorities in Europe, the education of underprivileged, Black urban populations in the USA, or the education of large impoverished population in Latin America, be examined with the lenses of *propio* and *educación propia*? Rather than a new model or trend within political approaches of mathematics education, we propose *propio* as a useful theoretical concept to activate the specificity of each context. To be faithful to the meaning of property and pertinence, *propio* is not a concept to be applied but rather to be interpreted and rooted in new situations.

Nowadays there is a growing tendency of tight political governance of (mathematics) education for the satisfaction of the macro-economic interests of the state or of private capital. Indeed, in a post-political time where government is organised to serve not the interests of the public common good, but the interests of private corporations, the character of education has been transformed into an arena for making economically-oriented subjectivities (Valero, 2017). Given the articulation between mathematics, science and technology with the production of new forms of capital, mathematics education features strongly in the project of transforming the population into the rational, numerically equipped, economically aware and entrepreneurial subjects that are necessary for economic production. The notion of *human capitals* is provocatively proposed by Brown (2015) to capture the tendency to reduce humanity to economic relations of capital generation. In this scenario, education operates classifications and orderings of people according to their mathematical performance; and it does so not only through assessment systems, but also through keeping its distance from peoples' lives and experiences.

This tendency not only impacts the educational practices of mathematics, but also affects theorisation of mathematics education as a field of research and practice. The urge to increase achievement promotes an understanding of the field being about the education needed to obtain mathematical knowledge: in other words, education *for* mathematics. This understanding installs a regime of truth that operates by naturalising epistemological and political assumptions, and by recognising some research questions and methods as possible and desirable, while deeming some others as irrelevant or deviant. For instance, the current interest in "best practices" or in reducing "the gap" are examples of what is taken as desirable, shaping the field as a quest for *efficiency* in teaching and research practices that should have a direct impact on students' achievement. Within this understanding, a problematisation of the type of society being reified and reproduced through school mathematics practices does not seem to belong to research in mathematics education. Such an endeavor is seen as a task for sociology or cultural studies.

Sociocultural and sociopolitical approaches in mathematics education are pushing the limits of what mathematics education could be, by presenting experiences that call into question this desire of achievement and its associated regime of truths, even taking the risk of being labelled as ill-founded or primitive. Ethnomathematics targeted the epistemological nature of mathematics, problematising the story of a universal and culture-free mathematics that schooling has fostered for decades. Studies of subjectivity in mathematics classrooms focus on how students are subjectified and disciplined in certain ways (Valero & García, 2014; Valero, 2017). This kind of research analyses the ways in which humans are mathematically enculturated, understanding that mathematics education should also study the education that is being done *through* mathematics.

When *educación propia* problematises daily life and brings knowledge closer to people's experience, it is not falling into naive empiricism or an activism that may ultimately contribute to discourses that capitalise on the subjectivation of the person. Instead, *educación propia* may allow "the recovery of the conditions of a self-determined existence based on the recognition of the complex relations of domination and resistance that occur between certain class sectors" (Molina Bedoya & Tabares Fernández, 2014, p. 7, our translation).

The concept of *propio* embodies a critical standpoint towards mathematics education, for it raises awareness of the sociopolitical constrains on the constitution of mathematical knowledge and the power effects associated with this constitution. As Tattay (2011) pointed out, the interculturality promoted by the notion of *propio* "does not address a merely pedagogic issue, it is also a political issue on the dispute of imaginaries about what is the knowledge that matters, the knowledge that has the magic to be recognised inside and outside" (p. 91, our translation). The aim of expanding the history and epistemology of mathematics also makes it possible to trace connections between *propio* and ethnomathematics as far as the conceptions of knowledge as collective, attached to bodily perception and with nature as its source, are used to contrast and contest the distinctive Western, rationalist narrative of mathematical knowledge. For these reasons, we think that that *propio* escapes the locality of the Nasa people and meets and enhances global developments in mathematics education.

While we propose the mobilisation of the concept from their Nasa cradle to other spaces, we foresee some critical issues that may arise in non-Indigenous contexts. All the experiences that we have referred to as enactments of *propio* share the condition of being conducted within the frame of a pre-existing organisational process that makes the experience possible. Such processes provide a social bond that is not always present in all school contexts or situations. Another critical issue is the reference to a cultural heritage as a base on which new possibilities can be built, as a response to the hegemonic ones. Economic, cultural and linguistic dispossession may deny even the chance to remember a different past and imagine a different future. In that matter, we acknowledge that many issues surrounding the concept of *propio* cannot cross the boundary of Indigeneity. However, there are situations where the need for pertinence, relevance and belonging of education are highly important. In these contexts, the idea of mathematics education as a technical matter of improving "how to teach mathematics" calls for a political position that questions "what and why to teach mathematics."

When contrasting *educación propia* with other educational models (Indigenous or not), we can call into question the widespread and normalised definition of mathematics education in general as the education needed for (the sake of) mathematics. We can also formulate an alternative definition of an education that is done through (the support of) mathematics. The former locates the student as a cognitive subject, determined by the (dis)possession of certain knowledge that matches the expectations of a curriculum; the latter understands the student as a human subject, being and becoming part of a culture and society. *Educación propia* therefore entails a radically different comprehension of what mathematics education is, both as a field of practice and as a field of research.

The main contribution of *educación propia* and *propio* to mathematics education in non-Indigenous environments is to explore the ongoing enactment of this different comprehension. The Nasa educational developments are useful because "they are not only ways to experiment, but above all expressions which show not merely how 'things can be otherwise' but that they indeed are in other ways" (Quijano Valencia, 2016, p. 302, our translation). Our claim is that by paying attention to the possibilities of the appropriation processes that every local community can undertake, mathematics education can develop rooted and meaningful alternatives to the omnipresent economisation that homogenises and standardises mathematics education worldwide. Through the notion of *propio*, we can articulate local responses at a global scale that, paraphrasing Harding (2008), conceive of mathematics education from below. Emulating the Nasa assumptions about culture as an operative space in which communities build their future, mathematics education based on *propio* does seem possible as an analytical option. We contend that communities *can make it* possible as a political challenge.

Finally, the shift of attention towards action and performativity battles sociopolitical and critical mathematics education (research) that has avoided formulating explicit ways in which such understanding can be deployed to conduct education. Although this reluctance can be considered as a coherent effort—not to replace one hegemony with another and falling into a new quest for efficiency—it can also be seen as a reductive and immobilising choice. The critical contemplation enhances the field with frameworks with which to analyse educational practices, but not with a framework with which to perform or transform them. *Educación propia* and *propio* are useful tools for mathematics education that offer a performative capacity because the political question of pertinence in practice is foregrounded.

Notes

1 *Propio* in Spanish is an adjective that is mainly used in the sense of belonging to someone, or owned. When qualifying the noun *educación* [education], the adjective changes to *propia* for grammatical reasons of agreement between noun and adjective. *Educación propia* mean literally "own education."
2 For a short overview of Indigenous education in Latin America with respect to mathematics education see Parra et al. (2016).
3 *Resguardo* is an indigenous reservation area created by the Spanish Crown in the 16th century as the basic unit of Indigenous territory. It has been acknowledged by the republican governments of Colombia, and remains as a constitutional right of Indigenous peoples.
4 *Cabildo* is the political and organisational council that governs the *resguardo*. This political and administrative organisation allows some degree of autonomy and self-determination.
5 *Minga* comes from the Quechuan *minka*, and refers to a collective work of common utility, usually agricultural work, but it also can be the building of bridges, roads or even an intellectual work. Minga is the form of work organisation most used by Nasa people (Bolaños et al., 2012).
6 Mignolo (2000) introduced this concept first, but we take it here as "the geo-political and body-political location of the subject that speaks" (Grosfoguel, 2011, p. 5). This notion is crucial to understand not only the epistemic and political struggles of Indigenous nations, but also why well-intended discourses of inclusion are structurally constrained.
7 *Corazonar* is a metaphoric word game in Spanish, that mixes *corazón* (the heart) with *razonar* (to reason).

References

Barton, B., Fairhall, U., & Trinick, T. (1998). Tikanga Reo Tātai: Issues in the development of a Māori mathematics register. *For the Learning of Mathematics, 18*(1), 3–9.

Blanco-Álvarez, H. (2008). La Educación Matemática desde un punto de vista sociocultural y la formación de Licenciados en Matemáticas y Etnoeducadores con énfasis en matemáticas [Mathematics Education from a sociocultural point of view and the education for mathematics teachers and Ethnoeducators with an emphasis on mathematics]. *Boletín de La Asociación Colombiana de Matemática Educativa, 1*(1), 4–6.

Bolaños, G., Bonilla, V. D., Caballero Fula, J., Espinoza, M. A., García, V. J., Hernández Lara, J., Peñaranda, D. R., Tattay, P., & Tattay Bolaños, L. (2012). *Nuestra vida ha sido nuestra lucha: resistencia y memoria en el Cauca indígena* [*Our life has been our struggle: resistance and memory in the indigenous Cauca*]. Organización Internacional para las Migraciones (OIM-Misión Colombia). http://hdl.handle.net/20.500.11788/1037

Boyer, P. (2006). *Building community: Reforming math and science education in rural schools*. Alaska Native Knowledge Network.

Brown, W. (2015). *Undoing the demos: Neoliberalism's stealth revolution*. The MIT Press.

Caicedo, N., Guegia, G., Parra, A., Guegia, A., Guegia, C., Calambas, L., Castro, H., Pacho, C., & Diaz, E. (2009). *Matemáticas en el mundo Nasa* [*Mathematics in the Nasa world*]. (2nd ed., N. Caicedo & A. Parra, Eds.). CIIIT.

Consejo Regional Indígena del Cauca. (2004). *¿Qué pasaría si la escuela...? Treinta años de construcción de una educación propia* [*What would happen if school...., 30 years of making a propio education*]. Popayán.

Consejo Regional Indígena del Cauca. (2015, June 10). *Programa de educación* [*Education programme*]. https://www.cric-colombia.org/portal/proyecto-cultural/programa-de-educacion/

CONTCEPI. (2013). *Perfil del Sistema Educativo Indígena Propio, SEIP* [*Profile of owned Indigenous educational system*]. ONIC – OPIAC – CIT – CRIC.

Dei, G. J. S., & Kempf, A. (2006). *Anti-colonialism and education: The politics of resistance*. Brill. https://doi.org/10.1163/9789087901110

Grosfoguel, R. (2011). Decolonizing post-colonial studies and paradigms of political-economy: Transmodernity, decolonial thinking, and global coloniality. *Transmodernity: Journal of Peripheral Cultural Production of the Luso-Hispanic World, 1*(1), 1–38.

Grosfoguel, R. (2012). The dilemmas of ethnic studies in the United States: Between liberal multiculturalism, identity politics, disciplinary colonization, and decolonial epistemologies. *Human Architecture: Journal of the Sociology of Self-Knowledge, 10*(1), 81–90.

Guido Guevara, S. P., García Ríos, D. P., Lara Guzmán, G., Jutinico Fernández, M. del S., Benavides Cortés, A. L., Delgadillo Cely, I., ... Bonilla García, H. (2013). *Experiencias* de educación indígena en Colombia: entre prácticas pedagógicas y políticas para la educación de grupos étnicos [Indigenous education experiences in Colombia: Between pedagogical practices and policies for the education of ethnic groups]. Universidad Pedagógica Nacional.

Gutiérrez, R. (2013). The sociopolitical turn in mathematics education. *Journal for Research in Mathematics Education, 44*(1), 37–68. https://doi.org/10.5951/jresematheduc.44.1.0037

Harding, S. (2008). *Sciences from below: Feminisms, postcolonialities, and modernities.* Duke University Press. https://doi.org/10.1215/9780822381181

Knijnik, G. (1996). *Exclusão e resistência: Educação matemática e legitimidade cultural* [Exclusion and resistance: Mathematical education and cultural legitimacy]. Artes Médicas.

Knijnik, G. (2002). Curriculum, culture and ethnomathematics: The practices of 'cubagem of wood' in the Brazilian Landless Movement. *Journal of Intercultural Studies, 23*(2), 149–165. https://doi.org/10.1080/07256860220151050

Knijnik, G. (2004). Lessons from research with a social movement: A voice from the south. In P. Valero & R. Zevenbergen (Eds.), *Researching the socio-political dimensions of mathematics education: Issues of power in theory and methodology* (pp. 125–141). Springer. https://doi.org/10.1007/1-4020-7914-1_11

Knijnik, G. (2007). Mathematics education and the Brazilian Landless Movement: Three different mathematics in the context of the struggle for social justice. *Philosophy of Mathematics Education Journal, 21*(1), 1–18.

Knijnik, G., & Wanderer, F. (2010). Mathematics education and differential inclusion: A study about two Brazilian time–space forms of life. *ZDM Mathematics Education, 42*(3–4), 349–360. https://doi.org/10.1007/s11858-010-0247-8

Knijnik, G., Wanderer, F., Giongo, I. M., & Duarte, C. G. (2012). *Etnomatemática em movimento* [Ethnomathematics in motion]. Autêntica.

Ladson-Billings, G. (1995). But that's just good teaching! The case for culturally relevant pedagogy. *Theory into Practice, 34*(3), 159–165. https://doi.org/10.1080/00405849509543675

Levalle, S. (2017). *Investigacion comunitaria intercultural y resistencia a la violencia política en el Consejo Regional Indígena del Cauca – CRIC – Tierradentro, Colombia (1994–2016)* [Intercultural communitarian research and resistance to political violence at the Cauca Regional Indigenous Council – CRIC – Tierradentro, Colombia (1994–2016)] (Unpublished master's thesis). Universidad de Buenos Aires.

Lipka, J., Sharp, N., Adams, B., & Sharp, F. (2007). Creating a third space for authentic biculturalism: Examples from math in a cultural context. *Journal of American Indian Education, 46*(3), 94–115.

Makoni, S., & Pennycook, A. (2007). *Disinventing and reconstituting languages.* Multilingual Matters. https://doi.org/10.21832/9781853599255

McMurchy-Pilkington, C., Trinick, T., & Meaney, T. (2013). Mathematics curriculum development and Indigenous language revitalisation: Contested spaces. *Mathematics Education Research Journal, 25*(3), 341–360. https://doi.org/10.1007/s13394-013-0074-7

Meaney, T., McMurchy-Pilkington, C., & Trinick, T. (2012). Indigenous students and the learning of mathematics. In B. Perry, T. Lowrie, T. Logan, A. MacDonald, & J. Greenlees (Eds.), *Research in mathematics education in Australasia 2008–2011* (pp. 67–87). Sense. https://doi.org/10.1007/978-94-6091-970-1_5

Meaney, T., Trinick, T., & Fairhall, U. (2012). *Collaborating to meet language challenges in Indigenous mathematics classrooms.* Springer. https://doi.org/10.1007/978-94-007-1994-1

Mignolo, W. D. (2000). *Local histories/global designs: Coloniality, subaltern knowledges, and border thinking.* Princeton University Press. https://doi.org/10.1515/9781400845064

Mignolo, W. D. (2002). The geopolitics of knowledge and the colonial difference. *The South Atlantic Quarterly, 101*(1), 57–96. https://doi.org/10.1215/00382876-101-1-57

Ministerio de Educacion Nacional de Colombia. (2010). *Decreto 2500 de 2010* [Decree 2500 of 2010]. Colombia.

Molina Bedoya, V. A., & Tabares Fernández, J. F. (2014). Educación Propia: Resistencia al modelo de homogeneización de los pueblos indígenas de Colombia [Propio education: Resistance to the homogenisation model for Indigenous peoples of Colombia]. *Polis: Revista Latinoamericana, 13*(38), 149–172.

Nicol, C., Archibald, J., & Baker, J. (2013). Designing a model of culturally responsive mathematics education: Place, relationships and storywork. *Mathematics Education Research Journal, 25*(1), 73–89. https://doi.org/10.1007/s13394-012-0062-3

Parra, A. (2011). *Etnomatemática e educação própria* [Ethnomathematics and propio education] (Master's thesis). São Paulo State University at Rio Claro. http://hdl.handle.net/11449/90222

Parra, A., Mendes, J. R., Valero, P., & Villavicencio Ubillús, M. (2016). Mathematics education in multilingual contexts for the Indigenous population in Latin America. In R. Barwell, P. Clarkson, A. Halai, M. Kazima, J. Moschkovich, N. Planas, M. Setati-Phakeng, P. Valero, & M. Villavicencio Ubillús (Eds.), *Mathematics education and language diversity: The 21st ICMI study* (pp. 67–84). Springer. https://doi.org/10.1007/978-3-319-14511-2_4

Parra, A., & Trinick, T. (2018). Multilingualism in indigenous mathematics education: An epistemic matter. *Mathematics Education Research Journal, 30*(3), 233–253. https://doi.org/10.1007/s13394-017-0231-5

PEBI. (2010). Construyendo el Sistema Educativo Indígena Propio [Building an owned Indigenous educational system. *Çxayu'çe, 14,* 4–10.

Quijano Valencia, O. (2016). *EcoSimías: Visiones y prácticas de diferencia económico cultural en contextos de multiplicidad* [EcoSimías: Visions and practices of cultural economic difference in contexts of multiplicity]. Universidad del Cauca.

Rappaport, J. (2008). Beyond participant observation: Collaborative ethnography as theoretical innovation. *Collaborative Anthropologies, 1,* 1–31. https://doi.org/10.1353/cla.0.0014

Rojas, A., & Castillo, E. (2005). *Educar a los otros: Estado, políticas educativas y diferencia cultural en Colombia* [Educating the others: State, educational policies, and cultural difference in Colombia]. Universidad del Cauca.

Santibañez, L. (2016). The indigenous achievement gap in Mexico: The role of teacher policy under intercultural bilingual education. *International Journal of Educational Development, 47,* 63–75. https://doi.org/10.1016/j.ijedudev.2015.11.015

Scandiuzzi, P. P. (2009). *Educação indígena X educação escolar indígena: Uma relação etnocida em uma pesquisa etnomatemática* [Indigenous education vs. indigenous school education: An ethnocidal relationship in an ethnomathematical research]. UNESP.

Sichra, I. (2004). *Género, etnicidad y educación en América Latina* [Gender, ethnicity, and education in Latin America]. Morata.

Skovsmose, O. (2009). *In doubt: About language, mathematics, knowledge and lifeworlds.* Sense. https://doi.org/10.1163/9789460910289

Skovsmose, O. (2011). *An invitation to critical mathematics education.* Sense. https://doi.org/10.1007/978-94-6091-442-3

Smith, L. T. (2013). *Decolonizing methodologies: Research and Indigenous peoples* (2nd ed.). Zed Books.

Sobel, D. (2004). *Place-based education: Connecting classroom and communities.* Orion Society.

Stavrou, S. G., & Miller, D. (2017). Miscalculations: Decolonizing and anti-oppressive discourses in Indigenous mathematics education. *Canadian Journal of Education/Revue canadienne de l'éducation, 40*(3), 92–122.

Swanson, D. M. (2015). Ubuntu, radical hope, and an onto-epistemology of conscience. *Journal of Critical Southern Studies, 3,* 96–118.

Tattay, L. (2011). *La "educación propia" en territorios indígenas caucanos: Escenarios de hegemonía y resistencia* ["Own education" in Cauca indigenous territories: Scenarios of hegemony and resistance] (Master's thesis). Flacso at Quito, Ecuador. http://hdl.handle.net/10469/6800

Valero, P. (2004). Socio-political perspectives on mathematics education. In P. Valero & R. Zevenbergen (Eds.), *Researching the socio-political dimensions of mathematics education: Issues of power in theory and methodology* (pp. 5–23). Springer. https://doi.org/10.1007/1-4020-7914-1_2

Valero, P. (2017). Mathematics for all, economic growth, and the making of the citizen-worker. In T. S. Popkewitz, J. Diaz, & C. Kirchgasler (Eds.), *A political sociology of educational knowledge: Studies of exclusions and difference* (pp. 117–132). Routledge. https://doi.org/10.4324/9781315528533-8

Valero, P., & García, G. (2014). El currículo de las matemáticas escolares y el gobierno del sujeto moderno [School mathematics and the governing of the Modern subject]. *Bolema, 28*(49), 491–515. https://doi.org/10.1590/1980-4415v28n49a02

Walsh, C. (2007). Interculturalidad colonialidad y educación [Interculturality, coloniality, and education]. *Revista Educación y Pedagogía, 19*(48), 25–35. https://revistas.udea.edu.co/index.php/revistaeyp/article/view/6652/6095

Warren, E., & DeVries, E. (2009). Young Australian Indigenous students' engagement with numeracy: Actions that assist to bridge the gap. *Australian Journal of Education, 53*(2), 159–175. https://doi.org/10.1177/000494410905300205

Zavala, M. (2013). What do we mean by decolonizing research strategies? Lessons from decolonizing, Indigenous research projects in New Zealand and Latin America. *Decolonization: Indigeneity, Education, & Society, 2*(1), 55–71.

CHAPTER 5

The Potential of an Africa-Centred Approach to Theory-Use in Critical Mathematics Education

Kate le Roux and Sheena Rughubar-Reddy

Abstract

Critical mathematics education has been described as a developing and contextual approach to the relations between mathematics, mathematics education and power. Writing from the context of a South African university, in this conceptual chapter we demonstrate the potential of Africa-centred theory-use in critical mathematics education. We draw on Hilary Janks's four interrelated concepts for critical literacy, namely, access, domination, diversity and design. These concepts are put to work—they become Africa-centred critical mathematics education—when we analyse the case of mathematics education in a professional programme for prospective medical doctors. Our theory-use at multiple levels of the context—from the mathematics classroom, to the medical programme, university and societal contexts—surfaces that access to dominant knowledge involves physical, financial, academic, and social access. Access is structured by institutional practices, both mathematical and non-mathematical, with students acting agentically beyond the classroom to challenge dominant practices. We identify in this contested space some, but also many unrealised, opportunities both for the recognition of diverse knowledges, values, social relations, positionings, and ways of using language, and for generating new meanings. Crucially, our analysis shows some aspects of knowing, acting, being and interrelating in the current context of university education in South Africa that cannot be quantified. We argue that other scholars can entangle Janks's four concepts in their contexts to ask, "What might critical mathematics education look like in my context at this moment?"

Keywords

critical mathematics education – Africa-centred theory-use – access – domination – diversity – power

∙ ∙ ∙

Recent publications on critical mathematics education (CME), such as the edited volumes by Alrø et al. (2010a) and Ernest et al. (2016), offer critical reflection on the past, present and future of ideas that have developed over four decades. These debates on the nature and scope of CME suggest that it is not a homogeneous "already formulated theoretical position" (Skovsmose, cited in Alrø et al., 2010b, p. 3). Rather, CME is a critical "approach to" or critical "concerns about" the relations between mathematics, mathematics education, and power in society, based on values of democracy, social justice and freedom (Ernest, 2016; Skovsmose, 2011). CME has been used as a lens in research on these relations, and to inform curriculum and pedagogy in mathematics classrooms.

As mathematics education scholars at a university in South Africa at this time, we identify in these recent debates three key features of CME that underpin the contribution in this chapter. The first of these features is the view of mathematics and mathematics education as historical, social, and political practices that can be variously "disempowering" (Skovsmose, 2011, p. 7) and/or "empowering" (p. 10). The second, following Ernest (2016, pp. 100–101), is that we consider the "critical" in CME to refer to a "crisis" situation that requires action in the form of analysis or "critique." We are, however, challenged by Ernest's (2016) call for a reflexive use of the notion of "critical" by considering how it might be not an end in itself, but rather the means "of moving toward better theories and a better and more just society" (p. 107). D'Ambrosio (2015) consistently reminds us that this society needs to include dignity for all. Ernest (2016) suggests that to achieve a more just society, critique needs to be supplemented by creativity. Indeed, Ernest's call for reflexivity can be located in broader concerns about the practice of mathematics education research such as, for example, how the choice of theory constructs the world of mathematics education (Pais & Valero, 2014; Atweh & Clarkson, 2001). The third key feature we take forward in this chapter is the notion of CME as developing and contextual. Skovsmose notes that, "CME, with its European roots, can be transposed to a South African context, or to any other context for that matter. A critical approach is always in need of being reworked and changed" (cited in Alrø et al., 2010, p. 2).

Chronologically, the development of CME internationally coincided with momentous events in South Africa: first, a growing opposition to the geographical, social, economic, educational and psychological divisions entrenched during the colonial and apartheid eras; and then second, the transition to democracy during the 1990s. Critical approaches to mathematics education, such as the notion of *People's Maths for People's Power* (Bopape, 1998), were used in South Africa to understand how our thinking had been structured by the related Western institutions of economics, government and education, including mathematics education (e.g., Khuzwayo, 1998; Vithal & Skovsmose, 1997). For many mathematics teachers and mathematics education researchers who were educated under apartheid, including ourselves, CME offered an attractive set of ideas for the "rebuilding project" (Vithal & Volmink, 2005, p. 12) of re-imagining mathematics and mathematics education from a democratic perspective.

Twenty-five years into the democratic South Africa, progress has been made on this rebuilding, but pre-democracy divisions continue to be (re)produced in educational institutions and in society. Stark evidence for these divisions includes inequities in access to quality housing, education and healthcare, an increasingly racialised and xenophobic public discourse, and a government that is perceived as out of touch with its citizens. Participation in what have become regular civil protests has extended from the urban poor and workers to include university students and middle class professionals. In such a context, values of freedom, democracy, equity, social justice, human dignity and care are under threat (Cross & Ndofirepi, 2017; Pithouse, 2016). These events require that public universities in South Africa ask pressing questions about what it means to be a university in and for Africa today.

At this critical moment in the history of our country and universities, we act reflexively in this conceptual chapter to demonstrate the potential of Africa-centred theory-use in CME. We act creatively by recruiting a framework for critical literacy conceptualised by South African scholar Hilary Janks. This framework is then "reworked" (Skovsmose, cited by Alrø et al., 2010, p. 2)— it becomes *Africa-centred CME*—when we put it to work to understand the relations between mathematics, mathematics education and power in the description of a particular case. The case concerns mathematics education in a professional programme for prospective medical doctors at the South African university where we are located. The description addresses various levels of context; the mathematics classroom, the professional programme, and more broadly the university and national contexts. The resulting version of an Africa-centred CME offers one response to the question: "What might CME look like in this context at this moment?"

We begin by explaining an Africa-centred approach to theory, before describing the case focusing on four aspects. We then describe Janks's (2010) critical literacy framework, and while it is fresh for the reader, put the key concepts to work in the description of the case.

1 An Africa-Centred Approach to Using Theory

An Africa-centred approach to theory, like the broader Southern Theory (e.g., Connell, 2007) from which it draws, is a developing area of scholarship underpinned by a critical engagement with the geopolitics of knowledge production and inequities in this regard between the "North" and related "South", terms which we explain next. "Place", both geographic and socio-political, is a necessary concern in this scholarship, as suggested by the naming. For although theory may appear neutral and universal (Connell, 2007), it is actually about "history, culture and for most of us, modernity itself" (Ashcroft, 2014, p. 65), and the dominance of theory from the Western episteme makes it difficult to think outside of this theory (Mbembe, 2016). Thus for scholars in South Africa at this critical moment, the choice of theory has to take into consideration what theory is appropriate for this context, the historical and socio-political roots of a theory, and the individual scholar's positioning in the context.

Yet, an Africa-centred approach seeks to avoid simply labelling theories and the related positionings of scholars who use them with simple "place"-based binaries such as "Eurocentric" vs. "Afrocentric", "global North" vs. "global South", or "traditional" vs. "modern" (Cooper & Morrell, 2014, p. 3).[1] Rather, Bhan (2019, p. 643) argues that the "South" is identifiable by empirical similarities in "the ways of moving and practices" where "the majority holds political, economic, spatial and ecological vulnerability" made so by the geohistorical processes of colonialism, Euromodernity, and neoliberal globalisation. Crucially, the notion of "place" suggested by this naming is flexible, dialectical (Morrell, 2016) and relational, relations that may be of "authority, exclusion and inclusion, hegemony, partnership, sponsorship, appropriation" (Connell, 2007, p. ix).

To illustrate this approach we turn briefly to recent discussions of three areas of research conducted in southern Africa; social HIV research (see Hodes & Morrell, 2018), gender studies (see Morrell, 2016), and mathematics education (see le Roux, 2019). These three discussions describe how researchers working in these areas in this context act agentively and reflexively with theory; theory becomes Africa-centred as it is "entangled" in African contexts (Cooper & Morrell, 2014, p. 3). The research discussed was conducted by researchers with varied lived experiences of a very complex local context, but with a common commitment to solving a local problem. This research approach does not involve applying what is presented as a universal theory, developed in the "North", in a unique context, a practice that potentially essentialises and others "South" contexts. Rather, Africa-centred theory-use is dialectical; contexts have "power and meaning" (Hodes & Morrell, 2018, p. 24) and their complexity, such as the scale of the HIV pandemic, or the prevalence of multilingual classrooms, surfaces new questions and theoretical developments. "Place" is thus "visible" (Cooper & Thesen, 2014, p. 188) in "new" theory which might be in the form of new perspectives on "North" concepts such as *agency, risk, otherness* and language as a *resource*, or the use of "South" concepts from African philosophy. This engagement with context produces research that contributes locally to policy and practice, but the researchers have acted agentively and strategically to make a global knowledge contribution through offering context, local theoretical concepts, new ways of using "North" concepts, and particular research methods.

The conceptualisation in this chapter offers a version of Africa-centred CME by putting a critical literacy framework to work in the context of a professional programme for medical doctors (henceforth the *medical programme*) at a South African university. Since context is important in our approach, we describe the case next.

2 A Description of the Case of Mathematics Education in a Professional Programme for Prospective Medical Doctors in South Africa

It is not possible in this chapter to describe the vastness and complexity of this case. Our intention is to offer Africa-centred theory-use as an approach, and to demonstrate, in the version of Africa-centred CME produced here, the potential of this approach. Our choice of what to describe is also not neutral. It is shaped by our interest in the relations between mathematics, mathematics education and power in society, and our positioning as CME scholars scholar in this context. Our choice also shapes what it is possible to say in this chapter. With this in mind, our selection of sources—policy, academic literature, opinion pieces, research data, and classroom experience—aims to include the diversity of voices present in the context. The case is presented in the form of four vignettes.

2.1 Vignette 1: A Professional Undergraduate Programme for Prospective Medical Doctors

The university is an historically-white, English-medium, public university in South Africa. It aspires to be an "inclusive, engaged and research-intensive African university" and a global leader in higher education. It wishes to improve the lives of students and "advance a more equitable and sustainable social order" (University of Cape Town, 2016, p. 4). A "locally relevant" (Faculty of Health Sciences, 2015, p. 6) medical programme at this university means educating graduates to work in a national health system that promotes a primary healthcare approach in a diverse, multilingual country.[2] This approach views healthcare as a fundamental human right and aims to provide for all the essential and quality healthcare necessary for being productive socially and economically (Public Health Care Directorate, 2018). Thus graduates need basic science knowledge, "biopsychosocial and cultural competence" (Hartman et al., 2012, p. 478), evidence-based reasoning and problem solving skills, and various literacies (including mathematics).

Selection for one of the 225 places each year in the highly competitive medical programme uses a numerical score constituted mainly by school leaving and university entrance test marks, and to a lesser extent a score for a written personal report. For "redress" purposes, the selection of South African students also takes into account "diversity" (demographics) and "disadvantage" (home and school background) (University of Cape Town, 2017a). Given the national interest in promoting quality healthcare for all, the programme also seeks to attract students from rural areas. The application process is increasingly conducted online. Students who meet a "means test" of their family finances qualify for government- or university-funded financial aid for fees and basic subsistence costs.

Students enrolled in the programme are assessed formatively and summatively through portfolios and written, clinical, and oral tests (University of Cape Town, 2017b). First-year students identified in mid-year assessments as not coping with the demands of their courses are placed in a one year programme—the "intervention programme"—where they receive intensive support in a small group before rejoining the "mainstream programme" (Alexander et al., 2005).[3]

2.2   Vignette 2: Mathematics in the First Year of the Medical Programme

The first-year core medical course in the programme includes an assessed mathematics component (named *Quantitative Literacy*) designed to help students meet the quantitative demands of their initial medical studies. The design considers the varied mathematical resources students bring from school, and also that school mathematics itself is not necessarily sufficient preparation for medical studies (Frith & Prince, 2009). Thus, the component consists of written materials for all students, as well as compulsory weekly classes for students who perform below a cut-off mark on the quantitative literacy component of the university entrance test. In the "intervention programme" all students attend a weekly mathematics class that uses an additional set of written materials. This first-year level mathematics component does not take a CME approach; it has an explicit agenda of socialisation into medical studies, but the design has a largely implicit social justice agenda. We elaborate on this component by focusing on a module—named *Prison Overcrowding and Health* (or *Prisons*)—in the "intervention programme."

The *Prisons* module aims to develop students' understanding of mathematical concepts, such as ratio, proportion, percentage, other rates, and absolute and relative number and change, to explore the prison population in South

Africa, and the implications for individual and public health, and human rights. Each activity consists of an extract (possibly edited) from a research or media article, followed by a set of questions about the extract. Answering the questions involves reading quantitative information in text, tables and charts, doing calculations, explaining the meaning of numerical information, and writing descriptions, for example of trends. Weekly classes are a mix of direct teaching by the lecturer, small group work, and plenary discussions.

To explore the prison population and prison overcrowding in South Africa students use rates of change, proportion and absolute numbers represented in line and bar charts, together with classroom discussions about the functioning of the criminal justice system, to investigate the growth in the South African prison population over time. Students compare the South African prison population rate to that of other countries, and investigate how South African crime rates are calculated. Taken together, the questions are designed to build an understanding of why certain South African prisons are "400 percent overcrowded" (Ngcukana et al., 2008) and the effective floor space per prisoner is 1.91m^2. These numbers are illustrated with a photograph showing men crammed into a prison cell. This information leads to consideration of health implications. For example, students read of an almost six-fold increase in the mortality rate of prisoners from 1995 to 2005, an increase that is generally attributed to the AIDS pandemic (Muntingh, 2008), and that 300,000 prisoners are released into society each year (Goyer, 2002).

2.3 Vignette 3: The Student Voice

The following description is based on the transcript of an interview with the student Matla (a pseudonym meaning "strength" in the Sotho group of languages) enrolled in the medical programme. The interview was conducted at the end of his first year and formed part of a longitudinal study of undergraduate students' experiences of university.[4] We selected this interview since Matla performed well at school, he viewed his future career as a medical doctor as a public good, and given his background, he may have been considered in the university "redress" categories on admission. This interview took place prior to the student protests described in vignette 4, but Matla's university experiences resonate in many ways with the issues made visible in the protests.

Matla spent most of his childhood living with his grandparents in various "rural" (the quote signals Matla's talk) areas of South Africa. He attended a private, church-run high school with "very high" discipline, "dedicated" teachers, and a "small library." He said the new computers and science laboratory equipment were seldom used as "no one was able to teach us." He said his school was populated with "black" students and teachers. The official medium of instruction was English, but teachers used his "home language", Sepedi, as a "compromise" to help the students "understand."

Matla was recognised as one of the "top" and "best" students in the district, and he applied to the medical programme at "Africa's leading university." He aimed to "help" and "work with people" where he lived who "need medical attention" and "don't have that privilege to be in hospitals."

During the university application process Matla corresponded with the university by post and telephone. He arrived at the start of the new academic year thinking he had been selected, but was told he was on the waiting list. He appealed this decision and, after many visits to the management office, was admitted. He said his father was funding his studies.

Matla did not, however, secure a place in a university residence. For the first semester he rented private, off-campus accommodation where he was the only first-year and the only medical student. He described this time as "traumatising." The "dangerous" environment—Matla was robbed during his commute and one of his classmates was shot near campus—meant he had to leave campus before sunset thus missing out on academic and non-academic activities. After one month he was "privileged" to move closer to campus, but security remained a concern and cooking for himself took up study time. Indeed, he said "top" students did not stay off campus, and that "this thing of exclusion [from the university]" is "real" for those not in residence.

Matla said he did not have "the privilege of using a computer" before coming to university. On account of lacking confidence, "being ashamed of my English", and "struggling to construct" what he wanted to say, he did not ask questions in the first-year class or contribute to the small group learning spaces used extensively in the programme.

Since his school was not "multiracial", Matla looked forward to being part of a racially diverse class at university. He was thus "surprised" to find that "we are mixed in a class but during discussions you just find groups of specific races." His university experience made him think for the first time that race "does really exist", but in a "subtle" way. While in some interactions "you almost [...] forget that you are black, they are white", at other times he was reminded of his difference and felt invisible; on one occasion he had asked for directions, but the person "just looked at me, he didn't say a word and then he continued." Asked whether he felt he fitted in at the university, Matla responded emphatically "No, no, I never did that"; he had not met anyone who shared his "background", "principles", "interests", "work ethic", and "dreams."

On the basis of his performance in the first semester of his first year—he "ran short of only two marks"—Matla was placed in the "intervention programme." Since he was seen as a "role model" in his home community, he was "ashamed" of this placement and initially felt "divided from the mainstream." After six months Matla felt "much better" about this move and he had "a little bit of confidence" to ask questions in the smaller class. However his enduring sense that his classmates led "different lifestyles" meant that "sometimes maybe I just think maybe I'm not meant to be here."

Matla described school mathematics as "just calculations" and "you didn't have to like conclude, like there was not a lot of writing." But at university he had to do "a lot of writing" about "figures" for "different diseases and their prevalence rates." This involved "like writing sentences and paragraphs […] we are given statistics of a particular population and now you have to compare." He felt this mathematics was useful for his studies and his medical career as he needed to "get used to the language that is used in medical journals", and he would "hopefully" publish one day.

2.4 Vignette 4: Student Protest

University student protest is not unique to South Africa, but takes on particular meaning in this context. Since 1994 universities have experienced scattered protests, but from March 2015 these developed into a national movement (Pithouse, 2016) collectively known as "Fallism" (as for #RhodesMustFall and #FeesMustFall). In a call for "free, decolonised" university education Fallism highlights the lived, intersectional experience of students who face socio-economic exclusion from and feel they do not belong in post-1994 South African universities, question the relevance of their university knowledge for this lived experience (Booysen, 2016), and champion the rights of campus workers. The movement draws variously on discourses of decolonialism, black consciousness, radical feminism, and pan-Africanism (Mpofu-Walsh, 2016). It problematises university structures and government funding priorities in an unequal society, but also the underlying dominant patriarchal, racial, imperialist, liberal, and marketisation ideologies informing these structures (Booysen, 2016; McKenna, 2015; Pithouse, 2016).

At our university the Fallist movement problematised treatment of student protesters, admissions and academic exclusion policies, stigmatisation associated with being a student in an "intervention programme", residence culture, and campus workers' conditions of service (Omar, 2016). Students in the Health Sciences Faculty tabled a specific list of demands that related to student fees, assessment practices and teaching and learning issues (Shackville TRC, 2016).[5] These students requested transparency in the calculation of their declared fees (for example, costing for each course) and also in additional hidden costs (for example, their vaccines and transport to off-campus clinics). They raised numerous issues related to the settling of university fee accounts such as payment deadlines, the use of compound interest calculations on overdue accounts, and access to accommodation and learning materials for students who had overdue accounts but had been granted a a period of grace to raise outstanding fees. Students also wanted an opportunity to appeal financial exclusions (not just academic exclusions) and were concerned about the working conditions (financial and security related) of bus drivers who transport them on clinic visits.

Health Sciences students also raised concerns about the fairness of clinical examinations in which each student is assessed on an assessment of a different patient, in some cases by only one assessor. Students felt "judged on the basis of their appearance or the accent with which they spoke English" (Behari-Leak et al., 2016). Students wanted standardisation of follow-up questions and transparency in how marks are arrived at. They also demanded free access to all written examination scripts post assessment. They requested that lecture slides be made available prior to classes, that all lectures be recorded, and that "sensitization education" be provided for staff in relation to "race, gender, sexuality, transphobia, class and ability" (Shackville TRC, 2016). In the context of the robbing of students on an off-campus clinic visit, students wanted safe transport.

Negotiations between these Health Sciences students and management were facilitated by a mediator and a working group composed of black scholars at the university. According to Behari-Leak et al. (2016), discussions were inclusive in nature, and aimed to "create a space in which students' demands were thoroughly analysed and deeply understood." They argue that "students seemed visibly encouraged by the alignment between their own ways of understanding the issues and what the analysis allowed those "in power" to see about hierarchies of power and patterns of inclusion and exclusion that self-perpetuate within faculties and departments" (Behari-Leak et al., 2016). Following this facilitation, management, staff and students continued to work towards achieving the targets set during these initial negotiations.

Yet on the whole, the protests left the university community, including the Fallism movement itself, "deeply divided" (Ndelu, 2017, p. 58) along lines of race, class, gender, age, experience and profession. The effects of the trauma (Pityana, 2016), a result of both the verbal and physical violence generated in the context, on individuals' personal and professional lives continue to be felt and seen years on.

3 A Critical Literacy Framework for Understanding the Relations between Literacy and Power in South Africa

In this section, we describe the theory we have used to understand these vignettes describing the case of the medical programme. We summarise its history and resonance with the concerns of CME scholars. The South African academic Hilary Janks's (2010) *critical literacy framework* offers four interrelated concepts—*access*, *domination*, *diversity* and *design*—to understand the relations between literacy and power. Like CME, this framework is underpinned by a social justice agenda and commitment to social action (Janks, 2010). While Janks draws more broadly on, amongst others Paulo Freire, Norman Fairclough, and Brian Street, her contribution is shaped by "place", that is, her positioning as a scholar in South Africa. We describe the four concepts with respect to the relations between mathematics and mathematics education, and power in society.

The concept of *access* is about successfully participating in dominant mathematics and mathematics education practices. Janks (2010), drawing on Bourdieu (1991, p. 55), argues that access is not just about being "understood" in the dominant practices, but also about being "listened to", and hence having access to influential audiences, networks and forms of distribution. In mathematics education, Gutiérrez (2012) identifies a view of access as the resources available for learning, such as, good teachers, adequate classroom materials, quality curriculum, and support outside of class.

Domination is the view that mathematics and mathematics education are not neutral in society but are historically, socially and politically constituted and (re)produce asymmetrical power relations. Building on the seminal work of Skovsmose (1994), Yasukawa et al. (2012) offer a three-part concept of *mathematics-based human action* which is productive for understanding how mathematics works ideologically to shape our views of the world, how we act, and who we can be.

Diversity recognises that different mathematics practices may be characterised by different knowledges, values, social relations, positionings, ways of using language, and so on (Janks, 2010). Hence there are different ways of, in Gutstein's (2012) terms, writing and reading the world with mathematics. These differences may lead to hierarchical power relations and to domination. However, diversity can be productive and a resource for change, such as when, for example, it promotes reflection on taken-for-granted ways and seeing one another as productive resources for meaning making (Janks, 2010). In her related concept of *identity*, Gutiérrez (2012) argues for balance between the self and other. She suggests that the mathematics curriculum should be a "mirror" (p. 19) in the sense that a student sees the self and the community in which they identify in the past, present and future, and has opportunities to draw on their cultural and linguistic resources. The curriculum should also be a "window" as the student sees others and other views of the world (p. 20).

Janks's (2010) fourth concept, *design*, recognises student agency and creativity to draw on their resources to generate new meanings and hence challenge and change existing practices. In Janks's framework, this is about the redesign of texts and hence writing new meanings in the world. With common roots in the work of Freire, this notion can be linked to Gutstein's (2012) notion of *"writing* [acting on and changing] *the world"* (p. 23, emphasis in original) with mathematics.

Janks's central argument is that these four concepts are "equally important", and *"crucially interdependent"* (Janks, 2010, p. 26, emphasis in original). To help understand this interdependency, Janks (2010) considers what an absence of each orientantion might mean (see Janks, 2010, p. 26, for the full matrix). We explore these interrelations in our analysis and discussion of the medical programme case.

4   Entangling the Concepts in the Case of Medical Education

In this section, we put to work the four concepts—access, domination, diversity and design—to understand the relationship between mathematics and mathematics education, and power in the context described in the four vignettes.

4.1   *Access*

Institutional decisions about whether a student gains admission, or physical access, to the medical programme are based on an admissions score that quantifies the student's prior academic performance, potential to cope with the medical studies, and personal report. The additional "disadvantage" and "diversity" categories for South African students recognise dominance, that is, the historical and enduring inequities by race, class, geography and language in opportunities for quality schooling in South Africa, and hence the need for redress. They also recognise the need for the university student population and the medical profession to reflect the demographic diversity of the country. The provision of financial aid, based on a measure of a student's family finances, recognises that taking up a place in the programme also requires financial access.

A range of assessments—of the dominant knowledge, skills, literacies (including mathematics), and ways of acting and interacting professionally—used throughout the programme measure whether a student is participating successfully in or demonstrating academic access to the dominant practices.[6] Indeed, the "intervention programme" is a response to the "diversity" of the intake (Alexander et al., 2005, p. 66), and exists for students whose marks identify them as needing additional opportunities to learn how to "becom[e] an effective learner" (p. 67) at university. The first-year mathematics component, including the "intervention programme" mathematics, aims to cater for the diversity of students' mathematical resources and to facilitate academic access to the quantitative aspects of initial medical studies.

Matla's admissions score did not give him automatic physical access to the medical programme. Not having physical access to a computer constrained his communication with the university about this outcome. As discussed in relation to the concept of *design*, he exercised agency by visiting management offices regularly and was admitted. Having gained physical access, Matla's first semester assessment scores identified him, by only two marks in his view, as needing additional support to gain academic access and he was placed in the "intervention programme." In his view, his lack of digital literacies constrained his academic access. His fear of speaking English meant he did not seek help and constrained the extent to which he was understood and listened to in peer learning spaces. Being in the smaller "intervention programme" class helped him to develop some voice, and he felt that the mathematics classes facilitated academic access to the discipline. Yet the "two marks" that saw him placed in the "intervention programme" came at a personal cost in terms of how he positioned himself in his home community and relative to other medical students.

Matla did not gain physical access to a university residence. During his commute from his off-campus accommodation he was the victim of the crimes quantified in his "intervention programme" mathematics module, *Prisons*. He felt his accommodation situation constrainted his access to academic resources. This situation also heightened his sense of not belonging on campus—his absence of social access—on account of not being a "top" student admitted to university residence, his race, and the lack of opportunities to make friends with students who shared his lifestyle.

Many of Matla's concerns about his physical, academic and social access to university were raised by the Fallist movement, which used protest action to get an audience in institutional transformation debates. Calls for "free" higher education highlight relations between funding, physical access to universities, and ultimately academic access, even for those who do qualify for financial aid. Calls for "decolonisation" point to a sense of not belonging socially in physical, human and knowledge spaces that are seen as white, English, colonial and middle class. Health Sciences students highlighted constraints on academic access by calling for better access to learning materials (including for students struggling to pay outstanding fees), fairer assessment practices for measuring academic access, and safe physical access to off-campus learning sites. The student action also looked beyond student access to campus workers' access to better working conditions and rights to human dignity.

4.2   Domination

The first-year mathematics component in the medical programme provides opportunities for students to strengthen their understanding of mathematics for "*reading* [understanding] *the world*" (Gutstein, 2012, p. 23, italics in the original).

In this case the "world" is a primary healthcare approach to medical provision in a diverse and inequitable country. In *Prisons,* students have some opportunity, for example when studying different ways that national crime rates can be calculated, to explore the mathematics-based human action underpinning the numbers. Matla suggested that his mathematics classes supported his "reading" of his medical studies, and offered the possibility for *"writing* [acting on and changing] *the world"* (Gutstein, 2012, p. 3) through his future medical research.

This analysis points to limitations in the extent to which the formal mathematics component provides opportunities for students to demonstrate how mathematics might (re)produce relations of power in the university or wider context. However, we do see the student protestors communicating that mathematics is not neutral in their experiences of university. For example at our university, students challenged how placement in "intervention programmes", based on quantitative assessments, positions certain students as different by race and thus reinforces stereotypes of the "normal" university student. Students actively worked in various forums, in some cases in collaboration with staff, to identify alternative funding models for universities (e.g., Bassier et al., n.d.). The Health Sciences students challenged the fairness of numerical clinical assessment scores and how these numbers quantify their appearance and language use. These students highlighted the extent to which they themselves figure in national crime statistics. They appealed to management to unpack the mathematics-based human action behind fee calculations, and challenged how the mathematics of finance acts to further indebt students with outstanding fees, to control who has physical access to marked assessment scripts, and to deny physical access to university residence and learning materials for students who have committed to settling outstanding fees. The mediation process between students and management on these issues aimed to make explicit the power relations at work at the university.

In addition, students at the university challenged longstanding management claims, based on financial calculations, that changes to the working conditions of campus workers are unaffordable. Thus, they highlighted that decision-making on this issue should not be based on mathematics alone, but consider ethical, social justice and educational issues (McKenna, 2015). Indeed, when using the *Prisons* materials in the classroom, we have learnt that the numbers themselves are not enough to "read" the world of prisons; students need to physically occupy a space of $1.91m^2$ to start to understand the health and human rights implications of prison overcrowding. This action points to ways of knowing and being that are part of living that are not easily objectified quantitatively (Green, 2014). The period of student protest at the university also points to the trauma that results when power struggles take place through verbal and physical violence.

4.3 Diversity

The "intervention programme" historically represents the university's attempts to facilitate academic access to university disciplines for a diverse student intake. Certainly, in terms of academic access, the programme is alert to Janks's (2010) point that without access to the dominant discipline, a celebration of a diverse intake may "ghettoise" (p. 26) students who have historically not had access to university. Yet the students' concerns expressed during the protests point to how the "intervention programme" may work against social access, for example, by reinforcing stereotypes about who requires additional support. In addition, although Matla saw the diversity of his class and the campus as potentially a productive resource, he was disappointed by what he experienced as "subtle" racism and a lack of integration in the classroom. In Gutiérrez's (2012) terms, to Matla the campus was not a window on a multiracial society as expected. Yet Matla also struggled to see the campus as a mirror on his own life; he could not identify classmates who shared his background and lifestyle, and since the diversity of language resources brought to the classroom were not recognised, he lacked a voice in classes conducted in English.

The medical programme aims to prepare graduates who can respond to the healthcare needs of all in a diverse South Africa. Matla was motivated to study medicine when he saw the needs of people near his home who, twenty years into democracy, could not access quality healthcare. The mathematics component in this programme aims to use mathematics and the diversity of the class as a window onto the context in which students will practice. As noted, Matla saw this mathematics as equipping him to understand the disciplinary context and to read related medical journals. The *Prisons* module provides a window on the health and human rights issues related to prison overcrowding, and the implications for society. It is also a mirror on the lives of the students, including Matla, many of whom figure personally in the crime statistics as victims of the prisoners they read about.

The student protests inserted the voices of some students into debates about university transformation, offering staff and the public a window onto the experiences of students who traditionally have not had access to university and onto the lives of campus workers. For Health Sciences students this insertion included how these experiences are structured in relations of dominance and the accompanying numerical discourses of fees and assessment (Behari-Leak et al., 2016). The mediation of discussions between Health Sciences students and management aimed to be inclusive. However, at the university more broadly, the interactions within and between student, staff and management groups during the protests did not always recognise the diverse histories present on campus. Experiences and voices were thus silenced, resulting in widespread and enduring trauma.

4.4 Design

The analysis of the mathematics materials in *Prisons* suggests that the focus is on "reading" the health context in South Africa, and offers only the potential for design or "writing" the world. The latter action might be triggered, for example, by the opportunities for students to question taken-for granted assumptions about prisons and prisoners, and to understand how different calculations, for example of crime statistics, may result in different action. This possibility of design is also suggested by Matla's statement that he might use mathematics as a researcher in the future.

Looking beyond the classroom we see some possibilities for design and for writing new meanings using mathematics and other means. By personally appealing his unsuccessful application for a place in the medical programme, Matla exercised agency and was granted physical access to the programme. The students used protest action to get an audience and hence offered a challenge, not just to university structures, but also to the underpinning ideologies of these institutions. They challenged the university to consider what knowledges, activities, literacies, ways of interacting and being should be valued in a university in and for Africa. By questioning how mathematics-based human action shapes their university experiences, students opened possibilities for design of new fee structures, pedagogical spaces and assessment practices. The recent changes to employment conditions for campus workers show how relations can be structured on principles other than those of marketisation and mathematical calculations of affordability. The student action in relation to student and worker experience signals an opportunity to put this understanding to work beyond university campus boundaries in relation to the experiences of the urban poor and mineworkers in South Africa (Pithouse, 2016).

The mediation process between Health Science students and management points to the possibility of design in relations between university participants at different levels of the institutional hierarchy. On the other hand, the divisions that emerged across the university during this time and the resulting personal trauma suggest that this relational design has yet to be realised.

5 Discussion and Conclusions: An Africa-Centred Critical Mathematics Education

At this critical moment in the history of our university and country, we have acted agentively and creatively to entangle four related concepts from critical literacy in the description of a case of mathematics education at a South African university. From an Africa-centred perspective, this context has "power and meaning" (Hodes & Morrell, 2018, p. 24). In this closing section, we discuss how the concepts are "reworked and changed" (Skovsmose, cited in Alrø et al., 2010, p. 2) as they are entangled in "place", and how these Africa-centred concepts bring into view the complexity of the relations between mathematics, mathematics education and power in this description.

Our analysis surfaces the multi-faceted nature of student access to the medical programme in this context, comprising the related notions of physical, financial, academic, and social access, which may or may not be structured mathematically. Physical access, for example, is not limited to a numerical score that says who gets admitted, but crucially has to include access to material resources such as online communication, university residence, and safe movement on and off campus. Academic access is not just about demonstrating participation in scored assessments, but having a space (along with the necessary linguistic reources) to be heard and listened to by others. While the "intervention programme" might promote academic access, it may work against social access by reinforcing historical stereotypes. Financial access is not just about being able to afford fees and basic subsistence, but paying for hidden costs. Indeed physical access may be lost on account of poor academic performance or lack of finance.

This multifaceted concept of access needs to be recognised for, as Janks (2010) suggests, without access for all in a diverse intake of students, dominant institutional and societal practices will simply be (re)produced without critique. In addition, without this recognition, the marginalisation of precisely those whom university redress policies seek to benefit will continue, and what this diverse intake offers the university and society in terms of design will remain on the periphery.

We have also surfaced how, in its admissions practice, the university uses mathematics to recognise historical inequities in access to quality education and to identify who requires additional support to gain academic access. We have identified limitations in the extent to which the mathematics component of the programme provides opportunities for students to explore how mathematics writes the world. However, the student protestors surfaced how university practices that shape their own lives and the lives of workers are underpinned by, for example, colonial and capitalist ideologies and related numerical discourses. The concept of domination thus shows that there are some aspects of knowing, acting, being and interrelating in the current context of university education in South Africa that cannot be quantified.

This notion of domination is necessary alongside access, diversity and design, Janks (2010) argues. Attention to access without recognising domination simply naturalises how the dominant practices, including mathematics, are used. Not recognising how the experiences of students such as Matla are structured by dominant practices, including mathematics, risks simply celebrating the diversity suggested by the intake into the medical programme. While the "intervention programme" exists to respond to diversity and has some success regarding academic access (Alexander et al., 2005), domination brings into view unintended consequences such as racial stereotyping. Crucially, without recognition of practices as historical, social and political, the roots of different participants' perspectives on the world remain opaque. Without an understanding of these diverse ideas we close the possibility of designing the world.

Institutional admissions practices mean that the student cohort looks more racially diverse than in the past, the "intervention programme" supports this diversity with respect to academic access, and the mathematics curriculum has the potential to provide for students both a window and mirror on the healthcare context. These practices recognise how difference in South Africa is structured in dominance. Yet the student voice highlights that this recognition needs to include how students feel and experience their difference on campus, on account of their race but also their class, not as productive but as a sense of not belonging. While the student protestors provide a window on their lives and the lives of the workers, it has been argued that the divisions experienced by all participants in the institution since the start of the 2015 protests is itself a mirror on current society in South Africa (Pityana, 2016).

We have identified, particularly in the agency of students, possibilities for the design of ways of knowing, acting, interacting and being at the university and beyond in society. This includes, but is not restricted to, how mathematics might be used in this design. As Janks (2010) notes, design can only be achieved with recognition of dominance and the use of the design resources provided by the diversity of participants. The mediation attempts during the protests hint at this possibility. However, in the years since the start of the protests it has become clear that considerable work needs to be done regarding the design of relations between participants both in terms of the recognised power hierarchies and the diverse histories of participants.

In conclusion, as mathematics education scholars at a South African university, the context and time has warranted that we explore the question, "What might CME look like in this context at this moment?" We have thus worked creatively with key concepts that are of concern in CME, namely access, domination, diversity and design, to explore in our context relations between mathematics, mathematics education and power in a description of a case. This description of the case of mathematics education in a professional programme for medical doctors is necessarily selective. However, our theory-context work has surfaced the multifaceted nature of each of these concepts, their interrelated nature, and the challenges of ensuring that all four are accounted for in practice. The resulting conceptualisation thus demonstrates the potential of the approach used in this chapter.

The particular version of Africa-centred CME offered here can, in itself, be used locally by participants at the university, as they work to reinsert the primacy of democracy, social justice, freedom, equity, dignity and care at the university and in society. Crucial to this complex work are relational conversations in which all four multi-faceted concepts are recognised as equally important and in which all voices are listened to. This requires the creation of spaces where participants feel they belong, relations of dominance are understood, diversity is recognised and viewed as productive, and opportunities for design are created. Further theory-context work can be done to develop the version of Africa-centred CME offered here. Finally, scholars in other contexts can engage in the theory-context work demonstrated here to explore what happens to these or other CME concepts in their "places."

Notes

1 Binary classifications such as this have tended to dominate key debates in South Africa, for example, how health services might respond to the HIV-AIDS pandemic (Green, 2014) and about how universities might be decolonised.
2 After successfully completing this six-year programme, two years' internship and a year's community service, an individual can register and practise as a medical doctor in South Africa.
3 Our use of quotes signals our recognition of how such commonly used institutional terms themselves (re)produce difference.
4 The study was funded by the Andrew W. Mellon Foundation.
5 The medical programme is located in this faculty, along with professional programmes in health and rehabilitation and postgraduate programmes. So the student protesters described here included, but were not restricted to, medical programme students.
6 Following Morrow (2007), this notion of "access" is often referred to as *epistemological access* in this context.

References

Alexander, R., Badenhorst, E., & Gibbs, T. (2005). Intervention programme: A supported learning programme for educationally disadvantaged students. *Medical Teacher*, 27(1), 66–70. https://doi.org/10.1080/01421590400016472

Alrø, H., Ravn, O., & Valero, P. (Eds.). (2010a). *Critical mathematics education—Past, present and future: Festschrift for Ole Skovsmose*. Sense. https://doi.org/10.1163/9789460911644

Alrø, H., Ravn, O., & Valero, P. (2010b). Inter-viewing critical mathematics education. In H. Alrø, O. Ravn, & P. Valero (Eds.), *Critical mathematics education: Past, present and future: Festschrift for Ole Skovsmose* (pp. 1–9). Sense. https://doi.org/10.1163/9789087907174_003

Ashcroft, B. (2014). Knowing time: Temporal epistemology and the African novel. In B. Cooper & R. Morrell (Eds.), *Africa-centred knowledges: Crossing fields and worlds* (pp. 64–77). James Currey.

Atweh, B., & Clarkson, P. (2001). Internationalization and globalization of mathematics education: Towards an agenda for research/action. In B. Atweh, H. Forgasz, & B. Nebres (Eds.), *Sociocultural research on mathematics education: An international perspective* (pp. 77–94). Erlbaum.

Bassier, I., Velelo, L., Coenraad, S., Chikte, A., Wenana, C., Murithi, G., Dhlamini, W., & Mtsweni, N. (n.d.). Protesting policy: Interrogating free decolonised higher education funding. *University of Cape Town News*. http://www.news.uct.ac.za/images/userfiles/files/downloads/fepg/FundingFreeDecolonisedEducation_Long.pdf

Behari-Leak, K., Ramugondo, E., & Kathard, H. (2016, October 11). Students in South Africa feel unheard. Here's one way to listen. *University of Cape Town News*. https://www.news.uct.ac.za/article/-2016-10-11-students-in-south-africa-feel-unheard-heres-one-way-to-listen

Bhan, G. (2019). Notes on a Southern urban practice. *Environment and Urbanization, 31*(2), 639–654. https://doi.org/10.1177/0956247818815792

Booysen, S. (2016). Two weeks in October: Changing governance in South Africa. In S. Booysen (Ed.), *FeesMustFall: Student revolt, decolonisation and governance in South Africa* (pp. 22–52). Wits University Press.

Bopape, M. (1998). The South African new mathematics curriculum: People's mathematics for people's power? In P. Gates (Ed.), *Proceedings of the First Mathematics Education and Society Conference* (pp. 97–116). Centre for the Study of Mathematics Education, Nottingham University. https://www.mescommunity.info/

Bourdieu, P. (1991). *Language and symbolic power*. Harvard University Press.

Connell, R. (2007). *Southern theory: The global dynamics of knowledge in social science*. Polity.

Cooper, B., & Morrell, R. (2014). Introduction: The possibility of Africa-centred knowledges. In B. Cooper & R. Morrell (Eds.), *Africa-centred knowledges: Crossing fields and worlds* (pp. 1–20). James Currey.

Cooper, B., & Thesen, L. (2014). Retrieving the traces of knowledge-making while editing a book on postgraduate writing. In B. Cooper & R. Morrell (Eds.), *Africa-centred knowledges: Crossing fields and worlds* (pp. 178–190). James Currey.

Cross, M., & Ndofirepi, A. (Eds.). (2017). *Knowledge and change in African universities: Re-imagining the terrain* (Vol. 2). Sense. https://doi.org/10.1007/978-94-6300-845-7

D'Ambrosio, U. (2015). From mathematics education and society to mathematics education and a sustainable civilization: A threat, an appeal, and a proposal. In S. Mukhopadhyay & B. Greer (Eds.), *Proceedings of the Eighth International Mathematics Education and Society Conference (MES8)* (Vol. 1, pp. 19–30). MES 8. https://www.mescommunity.info/MES8ProceedingsVol1.pdf

Ernest, P. (2016). The scope and limits of critical mathematics education. In P. Ernest, B. Sriraman, & N. Ernest (Eds.), *Critical mathematics education—Theory, praxis and reality* (pp. 99–126). Information Age.

Ernest, P., Sriraman, B., & Ernest, N. (Eds.). (2016). *Critical mathematics education: Theory, praxis and reality*. Information Age.

Faculty of Health Sciences. (2015). *Strategic plan: Vision 2030*. Faculty of Health Sciences, University of Cape Town. http://www.health.uct.ac.za/sites/default/files/image_tool/images/116/aboutus/Vision%202030%20January%202015%20website.pdf

Frith, V., & Prince, R. (2009). A framework for understanding the quantitative literacy demands of higher education. *South African Journal of Higher Education*, 23(1), 83–97. https://doi.org/10.4314/sajhe.v23i1.44804

Goyer, K. C. (2002, November). Prison health is public health: HIV/AIDS and the case for prison reform. *SA Crime Quarterly*, 2. https://issafrica.org/01-nov-2002-sacq-no-2/prison-health-is-public-health

Green, L. (2014). Re-theorizing the indigenous knowledge debate. In B. Cooper & R. Morrell (Eds.), *Africa-centred knowledges: Crossing fields and worlds* (pp. 36–50). James Currey.

Gutiérrez, R. (2012). Context matters: How should we conceptualize equity in mathematics education? In B. Herbel-Eisenmann, J. Choppin, D. Wagner, & D. Pimm (Eds.), *Equity in discourse for mathematics education: Theories, practices, and policies* (pp.17–33). Springer. https://doi.org/10.1007/978-94-007-2813-4_2

Gutstein, E. (2012). Mathematics as a weapon in the struggle. In O. Skovsmose & B. Greer (Eds.), *Opening the cage: Critique and politics of mathematics education* (pp. 23–48). Springer. https://doi.org/10.1007/978-94-6091-808-7_2

Hartman, N., Kathard, H., Perez, G., Reid, S., Irlam, J., Gunston, G., Janse van Rensburg, V., Burch, V., Duncan, M., Hellenberg, D., Van Rooyen, I., Smouse, M., Sikakane, C., Badenhorst, E., & Ige, B. (2012). Health sciences undergraduate education at the University of Cape Town: A story of transformation. *South African Medical Journal*, 102(6), 477–480. https://doi.org/10.7196/samj.5680

Hodes, R., & Morrell, R. (2018). Incursions from the epicentre: Southern theory, social science and the global HIV research domain. *African Journal of AIDS Research*, 17(1), 22–31. https://doi.org/10.2989/16085906.2017.1377267

Janks, H. (2010). *Literacy and power*. Routledge. https://doi.org/10.4324/9780203869956

Khuzwayo, H. (1998). "Occupation of our minds": A dominant feature in mathematics education in South Africa. In P. Gates (Ed.), *Proceedings of the First Mathematics*

Education and Society Conference (pp. 244–266). Centre for the Study of Mathematics Education, Nottingham University. https://www.mescommunity.info/

le Roux, K. (2019). An Africa-centred knowledges approach to theory use in research about mathematics education and society. In J. Subramanian (Ed.), *Proceedings of the Tenth International Mathematics Education and Society Conference (MES10)* (pp. 730–739). https://www.mescommunity.info/proceedings/MES10.pdf

Mbembe, A. J. (2016). Decolonizing the university: New directions. *Arts & Humanities in Higher Education, 15*(1), 29–45. https://doi.org/10.1177%2F1474022215618513

McKenna, S. (2015, October 20). Five trends South Africa's universities must reject if they really want change. *The Conversation*. https://theconversation.com/five-trends-south-africas-universities-must-reject-if-they-really-want-change-49452

Morrell, R. (2016). Making Southern theory? Gender researchers in South Africa. *Feminist Theory, 17*(2), 191–209. https://doi.org/10.1177%2F1464700116645877

Morrow, W. (2007). *Learning to teach in South Africa*. HSRC Press.

Mpofu-Walsh, S. (2016). The game's the same: 'MustFall' moves to Euro-America. In S. Booysen (Ed.), *FeesMustFall: Student revolt, decolonisation and governance in South Africa* (pp. 74–86). Wits University Press.

Muntingh, L. (2008, May 26). The prevalence of HIV in South Africa's prison system: Some, but not all the facts, at last. *CSPRI Newsletter*. http://acjr.org.za/resource-centre/26%20-%20May%202008.pdf

Ndelu, S. (2017). 'Liberation is a falsehood': Fallism at the University of Cape Town. In M. Langa (Ed.), *#Hashtag: An anlaysis of the #FeesMustFall movement at South African universities* (pp. 58–82). The Centre for the Study of Violence and Reconciliation. https://www.csvr.org.za/pdf/An-analysis-of-the-FeesMustFall-Movement-at-South-African-universities.pdf

Ngcukana, L., Jika, T., & Jeptha, T. (2008, July 30). *Inside prison hellhole—"Help us, we are going to die in here"*. The Centre for the Study of Violence and Reconciliation. https://csvr.org.za/media-articles/latest-csvr-in-the-media/1966-inside-prison-hellhole-300708

Omar, Y. (2016, September 21). Students present demands at mass meeting. *University of Cape Town News*. https://www.news.uct.ac.za/article/-2016-09-21-students-present-demands-at-mass-meeting

Pais, A., & Valero, P. (2014). Whither social theory? *Educational Studies in Mathematics, 87*, 241–248. https://doi.org/10.1007/s10649-014-9573-z

Pithouse, R. (2016). *Writing the decline: On the struggle for South Africa's democracy*. Jacana.

Pityana, B. (2016, December 21). Education 'an area of government failure'. *News 24*. https://www.news24.com/Columnists/GuestColumn/education-an-area-of-government-failure-20161221

Public Health Care Directorate. (n.d.). *What is primary health care?* http://www.primaryhealthcare.uct.ac.za/phcd/approach

Shackville TRC. (2016, September 22). *List of demands tabled by students of the Faculty of Health Sciences*. https://web.facebook.com/shackvilleTRC/posts/318738471813532?_rdc=1&_rdr

Skovsmose, O. (1994). *Towards a philosophy of mathematics education*. Kluwer. https://doi.org/10.1007/978-94-017-3556-8

Skovsmose, O. (2011). *An invitation to critical mathematics education*. Springer. https://doi.org/10.1007/978-94-6091-442-3

University of Cape Town. (2016). *Strategic planning framework*. https://www.paperturn-view.com/newsroom-and-publications/strategic-plan-digimag-v2?pid=MjA20459

University of Cape Town. (2017a). *2018 Undergraduate Prospectus*. https://www.uct.ac.za/downloads/uct.ac.za/apply/prospectus/uctugprospectus.pdf

University of Cape Town. (2017b). *Faculty of Health Sciences (undergraduate) 2017*. http://www.students.uct.ac.za/sites/default/files/image_tool/images/434/study/handbooks/2017/HS_UG_2017.pdf

Vithal, R., & Skovsmose, O. (1997). The end of innocence: A critique of 'ethnomathematics'. *Educational Studies in Mathematics, 34*, 131–157. https://doi.org/10.1023/A:1002971922833

Vithal, R., & Volmink, J. (2005). Mathematics curriculum research: Roots, reforms, reconciliation and relevance. In R. Vithal, J. Adler, & C. Keitel (Eds.), *Researching mathematics education in South Africa: Perspectives, practices and possibilities* (pp. 3–27). HSRC Press.

Yasukawa, K., Skovsmose, O., & Ravn, O. (2012). Shaping and being shaped by mathematics: Examining a technology of rationality. In O. Skovsmose & B. Greer (Eds.), *Opening the cage: Critique and politics of mathematics education* (pp. 265–283). Sense. https://doi.org/10.1007/978-94-6091-808-7_14

CHAPTER 6

Tensions and Failures in an Analysis of Whiteness among a Racially and Socially Diverse Group of Mathematics Teacher Educators

Victoria Hand, Beth Herbel-Eisenmann, Sunghwan Byun, Courtney Koestler and Tonya Bartell

Abstract

In this chapter, we describe and critically examine the tensions and failures that emerged around a study of Whiteness among a racially diverse research team and the harm this caused to colleagues of Colour. Following Martin (2008), Whiteness is examined as a series of discursive moves that frame and guide activity among interlocutors. Analysis of the mechanisms through which the White researchers instantiated an institutional space of Whiteness on the research project unearthed significant discomfort among the authors along the lines of race and status. We draw on the concept of tensions and Pais's notion of failure to discuss the difficulty of balancing discussions of ideologies versus individuals, racialisation versus intersectionality, agency and power, and academic versus practical change.

Keywords

Whiteness – equity – justice – mathematics education

•••

> Therefore, we argue that neither trust nor solidarity is gained (nor should it be) by the assertion of good intentions, nor is it accomplished merely once and then set aside. Instead, politicized trust calls for ongoing building and cultivation of mutual trust and racial solidarity. It is thus a trust that actively acknowledges the racialized tensions and power dynamics inherent in design partnerships. (Vakil et al., 2016, p. 199)

In this chapter, we focus on racism and critical Whiteness studies in mathematics education. We recognise that in many countries, race is perceived as less of a dividing factor than issues like class, ethnicity, or language. In contrast, in the United States, the economic system was led by a capitalist approach that drew heavily on the enslavement of African peoples, who were assigned the legal status of property of Whites (Harris, 1995). This system meant that White[1] people in the United States could accumulate their capital and build substantial social and material infrastructures (e.g., government, school system, roads, cities) through the hyper-exploitation of Black people. This history of racial exploitation has been erased and considered as "a thing of the past" over time by the dominant White narrative and is conveniently omitted from most United States history books. Despite the fact that slavery itself became illegal in 1865 and despite the civil rights movement in the 1950s and 1960s, our current social systems (e.g., economic, criminal, political and educational systems) are still organised around White supremacy (see Jung et al., 2011).

The social construction of race and racism is reproduced systematically in different contexts. Drawing from the tenets of critical race theory, many have cited the persistence of racism despite policies and practices aimed to combat it (e.g., DeCuir & Dixson, 2004; Matias, 2013; Picower, 2009). DeCuir and Dixson (2004) stated that the permanence of racism indicates that racist hierarchical structures govern all political, economic, and social domains, and these structures maintain the privileging of Whites and the subsequent Othering of people of Colour in all arenas, including education (p. 28). Given the history of slavery in the United States, it is sometimes assumed that racism is unique to the United States when, in actuality, racism spans a variety of borders. Racism is a global experience that is not exclusive to the United States context (Bullock et al., 2019; Martin, 2009b) although it may manifest in different forms throughout the world (Nicolson et al., 2016).

The field of mathematics education research has gradually begun to turn to analyses of Whiteness in order to understand not only White privilege, but also the White domination through which White privilege is sustained and justified (Battey & Leyva, 2016; Leonardo, 2004; Martin, 2009b). In order to counter the ideological workings of Whiteness that perpetuate the oppression of people of Colour, acknowledging all forms of racism is necessary (Martin, 2009a). Although racism itself is an accurate descriptor and signifier to White supremacy (Martin, 2009a), scholars need to better understand how Whiteness operates to acknowledge that racism is endemic and to enact purposeful steps against the functions of White supremacy. The intention of the critical Whiteness study we present in this chapter was to continue in this vein.

In particular, we explore the ways that our critical study of Whiteness resulted in insights that came at significant cost to scholars of Colour involved in the analysis and, more broadly, to our project. We focus on the tensions that emerged in the analysis and the discussions that took place around them within the project team, and describe the choice of the White scholars to move forward with the publication of the findings, without pausing to lean into "stuck places," or instances when confusion, doubt or other emotionally-led stopping-points are overshadowed by the busyness of the work (Patel, 2015) and without creating opportunities for dialogue, in terms of "failure" (Pais, 2012). Before moving into this discussion, we briefly describe the research project and how the study of Whiteness came to fruition.

1   Background

The work we focus on in this chapter stems from a larger grant-funded study that explored the development of equitable mathematics education systems, through the theorisation of an "equitable system" (Cobb & Jackson, 2011). By equitable system, we were referring to intersecting levels of mathematics education that function synergistically to support the fair distribution of opportunities to learn (Hand et al., 2012). The aim of the project was to design and implement professional development modelled on both action research and participatory action research for mathematics teachers in a school district with a high percentage of African American children. Research indicates that professional development that fails to approach change from a systems perspective often falls short of expected goals (Cobb et al., 2003; Coburn, 2003; Cohen & Ball, 1999).

Our project team was comprised of 20 scholars at various times, at different career stages and with multiple areas of expertise (e.g., design and study of equitable teaching practices, opportunity to learn in mathematics classrooms, classroom discourse and positioning, bilingual education, mathematical and racial identity development, action research, design and facilitation of teacher professional development). The five principal investigators (PIs) of the research project were White. The project team also included two White, one Black, and one Latinx senior personnel; one Black postdoctoral fellow; and four Black, three Asian, and three White graduate students (which included one graduate student from Nigeria and one graduate student from Turkey). Although there is a danger in focusing solely on a single dimension of team members' identities (see, for example, Bullock, 2017), we believed strongly at the time that a focus on race could help to illuminate ways that long-standing racial injustice in the United States were also playing out in our project and, in particular, in the interactions among project team members. We also acknowledge that "choosing" a racialised term to signify someone's racial identity can be problematic, in part because this identity may not be consistent across contexts, and because of the ways in which race intersects with other socially constructed concepts (e.g., ethnicity, nationality).

In this chapter, we report on the work of a subset of scholars from the larger project team, who set out to analyse part of the planning and design of the teacher professional development from the perspective of critical Whiteness studies (e.g., Giroux, 1997; Leonardo, 2002; Picower, 2009). The point was to closely examine the ways in which our project space maintained White institutional space. Leonardo (2004) argues that Whiteness saturates everyday school life (and also our project work) and that one of the first steps to articulating its features is coming to terms with its specific modes of discourse. We sought to understand whether and how Whiteness was operating in order to disrupt dominant norms and engage in explicit work to disrupt its function.

To understand how Whiteness was operating in the project team and its work, we examined a transcript of a discussion among project team members about the design of the professional development. Martin's (2009b) articulation of mathematics as White institutional space was particularly useful for examining these interactions. Haviland's (2008) framework for identifying White educational discourse was also employed to analyse discourse moves within the transcript that maintained or disrupted Whiteness. The findings from this analysis were presented in the first version of this chapter that we submitted.

The reviewer and editor feedback that we received focused on two major points. The first point was that much of the chapter was written in an academic tone that served to strip away our feelings and uncertainties about the process of analysis and findings. The reviewers suggested that we take a more narrative tone to bring the full complexity and emotionality of our conversations into view. A second point was that the focus of the chapter on the results alone masked the tensions that emerged in the process of analysing the data. Although some tensions were described in the first draft, the reviewers felt that emphasising the tensions would highlight the complicated nature of this work. These points surfaced questions such as:
- When did different kinds of tensions emerge?
- Whose tensions were they?
- How did the discussion of tensions land differently on different project team members?

The subject of tensions inherent in our analysis also emerged during preparations for various presentations for conferences in 2017 and 2018 and we began to more explicitly name tensions that occurred throughout the process of transcribing and analysing the interactions in the project meeting. As we continued to talk about the project meeting, our analysis of Whiteness, and the findings and tensions, the White scholars began to realise that the conversations were harming colleagues. We came to realise that revisiting the project meeting we had analysed, which highlighted ways scholars of Colour were being tokenised and potentially silenced, caused harm. Discussions about the silences of scholars of Colour during the meeting, the White scholars came to realise, made it seem as if scholars of Colour did not have agency in that interaction, when, in fact, scholars of Colour may have chosen to remain silent, to express disagreement or to actively resist the interactions or ideas. Through further discussion among the authors, the White scholars came to see that focusing on Whiteness was not an act of ally work nor was it anti-racist. A contrast, here, is an anti-racist approach, or one that actively seeks to dismantle systems of oppression, with a non-racist approach, or one that may make visible systems of oppression, but does little to change them (Duarte & Smith, 2000).

Doing an empirical critical Whiteness study on ourselves inevitably created tensions. Various authors felt the tensions, but ultimately they landed on the scholars of Colour in both personal and structural ways. Scholars of Colour had to relive experiences of trauma that occurred during the project meetings and during presentations of the findings of the critical Whiteness study at professional conferences, where other scholars challenged and critiqued the interpretations. Because of status differences, scholars of Colour also experienced trauma due to the professional burden involved in critiquing their mentors. This trauma was further exacerbated by the personal relationships scholars of Colour had built with PIs over time, and the recognition of the PIs in the field as "equity scholars." The laying of harm and traumatic experiences onto members of the project team who held the least power in the project and in the field of mathematics education contradicted the very aims of the work, and in the end, perpetuated racism.

As a result of this conclusion, we (as authors) grappled both intellectually and emotionally with the question of whether or not to proceed with this chapter. Although it was an easy decision to shift away from the analysis of Whiteness in the project meeting, it was more difficult to decide if the discussion of tensions was similarly going to cause harm, both to individuals working on the chapter and to others on the project team and beyond. In particular, we worried about the different audiences for the chapter, and how it would be read differently across them. For example, we considered the possibility of White readers continuing to make excuses for the White PIs, or treating the stuck places represented by the tensions as "real". We also did not want to write the chapter solely for a White audience, which again would only serve to perpetuate White supremacy. Writing on the tensions in a linear and objective format does not do justice to the dozens of discussions that we had, which were organic, intertwined, emotionally laden, and filled with stops and starts.

Where did all of these issues leave us? In an awkward and very uncomfortable place. We decided to move forward as a group because of the desires of the scholars of Colour for the perspective to be represented and for the harm to come to do some good. In the section below, we theorise the role of tensions in collaborative activity involving dominant discourses and identities and those marginalised by them. We employ the notion of "failure" (Pais, 2012) to describe the systematic ways that "best intentions" become a means for further oppression. This discussion is followed by text from discussions of tensions that took place among pairs of authors.

2 Framing Tensions and Failures

Differential power structures along the lines of race and other forms of status permeated our research project from the outset, as we have already described. The research proposal was predominantly written by White scholars and received funding as such. The majority of the graduate students and half of the junior faculty were scholars of Colour. These clear lines of power along race and academic status meant that tensions naturally emerged in the joint work. Additionally, some of the ways we addressed (or not) the tensions were failures on our part. Pais (2012), in particular, argues that we need to do more to explore failures in equity-oriented work. We describe more about these two concepts—tensions and failures—in the sections below.

Tensions are often viewed as unwanted and unproductive sources of friction and indecision that undermine goals. Tensions can also be perceived, however, as spaces in which dominant perspectives, practices, values and identities are poised to undermine those of individuals and communities that have become "problems" or have been made invisible within the system of White supremacy. In other words, tensions are fissures, fractures or eruptions in the tightly woven fabric of dominant society, and thus, are places to tug on, widen and to invite the othering, queering and perverting of discourses and practices (Britzman, 1995). They can signal opportunities for individuals to pause (Patel, 2015), to seek to understand the ways of knowing and being of the "other," to take a critical look at the history of the structures and practices through which the tension emerged (Bang, 2009; Gutiérrez & Jurow, 2016), and to seek ways to begin to transform the joint work and the positions of the participants involved (Fine, 2017).

The White scholars on our project not only failed sometimes to recognise the tensions of analysing and thus centering Whiteness in writing the original version of this chapter, despite the fact that these tensions were raised in some ways by scholars of Colour; when they were raised, they were often set aside as distractions from the critical Whiteness analysis. The fascination/obsession of White scholars with Whiteness and with their own self-reflection served only to further position scholars of Colour at the margins of the work. This marginalisation was worse than in the project itself, as the scholars of Colour were being asked to return to the initial harm, once again without acknowledgement of their agency and humanity.

We use the word "failure" deliberately, as a way to shift the focus from individuals and their "good intentions" to the "liberal-democratic capitalist view of school" (Pais, 2012, p. 84). Such a stance rejects seeing mathematics education research "as a neutral environment purged of ideology" (Pais, 2012, p. 84). We adopt this perspective of failures in equity-focused mathematics education research as a natural consequence of infinite entanglements between the systems of privilege and oppression in United States society and the inner workings of mathematics education (Martin, 2008). The admission of failings of a large and well-funded research project (may) prompt scholars to recognise that the pursuits of equity in mathematics education will be fruitless and futile without prompt and concerted attention to the stuck places in the work. We, as authors and colleagues, attempt to lean deeper into the tensions we faced in our design work, into dialogue, and towards repair and healing.

3 Exploration of Some Tensions and Failures

Although we discussed many tensions and failures within our author team and across our project team, we focus here on three emerging tensions and our failures in particular. We report on the conversations that took place among pairs of authors around each tension, while recognising and trying to note to whom "we" refers at various points in the chapter. We chose not to reveal the names, racial/ethnic identities, or institutional level of status of the particular interlocutors to protect against extremist White nationalist groups that have recently been attacking education scholars, particularly scholars of Colour, whose work challenges White supremist perspectives (e.g., Gutiérrez, 2017; MathEdCollective, 2019). We recognise the tension in appearing to "give in" to these groups, yet we recognise the realities of harm done to professional and personal lives.

3.1 Tension 1: Focusing on Ideologies and Focusing on Individual People (*Tension and Failure*)

One of the tensions that surfaced as we began to interrogate Whiteness was that in attempting to prevent the indictment of individual White project team members (whose discursive moves perpetuated Whiteness), we instead tried to frame these moves as ideological accomplishments of White supremacy. Despite our effort to separate the individual agents from the ideological analysis, the possibility of hurting our colleagues' feelings was still present when we claimed that their actions were somehow implicated in the workings of White domination. Trauma occurred both to White scholars as we engaged in the ideological critique on individuals, as well as to scholars of Colour as we critiqued the ideology and its manifestations on the project. This tension placed an undue burden on the scholars of Colour on the author team, who were graduate students when they were involved in the analysis. Throughout the analysis, we often said, "we are looking at ideologies, not individuals," with the idea that individuals would not take the analysis and subsequent remarks as a signal of disaffiliation or incompetence. This discourse was layered with one about the trust we had built with each other and how this should enable us to talk about each other as racialised and (for the White scholars) racist human beings.

The separation was indeed difficult, even though, as one White scholar expressed, the pain they experienced came more from coming to grips with themselves as oppressors, rather than feeling harmed by being called out in the analysis. Scholars of Colour also wanted the trust in the group to allow for pushback on their feelings and thoughts, instead of interpreting everything they said as an objective critique of Whiteness. Despite the fact that issues of trust among the authors and other project team members were emerging, we nonetheless pursued the separation between ideology and the speaking individuals. For instance, at one point in the analysis we removed the names from the transcript to place our focus not on the speakers, but on the discursive patterns. The White PIs even named the acts of Whiteness themselves in the process of reviewing the transcript, referring to their own moves as "perpetuating a space of Whiteness" and doing irreparable harm to their colleagues who were scholars of Colour.

Placing the analytic focus on the systemic patterns rather than individual agents in our analysis was a double-edged sword—it lowered the risk of negative interpersonal consequences, but in return, we avoided an important opportunity to learn. One of the scholars of Colour described how they appreciated hearing reflections about not doing emotional labour on the backs of scholars of Colour and about doing ideological critique that did not locate blame with individuals. At the same time, they recognised that people have felt and will feel the situation personally, and were not sure if it was actually possible (or beneficial) to separate the personal from the ideological. They argued that if we could not candidly share and reflect on what we were feeling in the process, then they were not sure what we were accomplishing through the critical work.

In our discussion of this tension, we wondered about what we achieved with the attempt to separate the individual and the ideological. We were able to frame our study to be non-confrontational to anyone in our group (both the writing group and the project group) because we could say the study was impersonal (i.e., not about you) and draw our attention to the ideology associated with individual agents. In this way, we (the White scholars) told ourselves that we were able to (successfully or not) manage the interpersonal tensions and ramifications of the study. Moving away from considering the individual agents, however, prevented us from seeing our roles as agents of change against White domination and from seeing an opportunity to actively engage in the issue. This relates to the state of "*desconocimiento*" (Anzaldúa, 1987), which Gutiérrez (2015) explained in the following way:

> On the one hand, interrogating White supremacist capitalist patriarchy requires that I am constantly reflecting on myself and the ways in which I might (unknowingly) participate in these interlocking systems of oppression. In that sense, it's all about me. Placing that responsibility elsewhere (e.g., on others who have more power, more experience, or more claim to this work) is not due to ignorance but a choice <u>not</u> to work on these issues. This choice of fleeing from Nepantla is what Gloria Anzaldúa would refer to as desconocimiento or a "refusal to know." ... I must understand not only the systems of oppression I seek to dismantle, but my place in them. (pp. 273–274)

Despite the effort to "refuse to know" the implications of individual agents, further discussion among the authors showed that the scholars of Colour still experienced this interpersonal tension. When we considered the interpersonal consequence as "managed" or "dealt with", the tension only grew and was exacerbated by feelings of mistrust and guilt among the authors without an opportunity to openly discuss them. This led to the unintended consequence of continued pain and burden on scholars of Colour who were again in a situation in which feelings and experiences were forced underground in their joint work with senior colleagues.

From our experience, we learned that applying a critical Whiteness lens to understand our own social group had an inherent risk and undue burden on scholars of Colour who were in a vulnerable position to argue for a critical view. Rather than trying to avoid the interpersonal consequence by limiting the discussion to an impersonal level, we now imagine a new beginning of this critical work. With White scholars' own understanding of their own racial position in the racial hierarchy and the associated power and privilege that are often invisible to themselves, the analysis could begin with an aim to reveal one's own implication in racial domination. When critiques are actively sought out by the White scholars, the conversation around Whiteness can position the scholars of Colour differently: they can be positioned as sighted guides for the White scholars toward racial justice, rather than a colleague with uninvited critiques. Although this will not fully remove the emotional labour of scholars of Colour for White scholars' racial learning, this change will more likely lead to opportunities to engage in racial issues that are often unnoticed and disregarded.

3.2 Tension 2: Intersectionality, Framing Agency and Power, and Relationships (Failure and Tension)

Another tension that emerged was the way that power and agency operated, were made visible or not, and were positioned through our talk. In particular, emphasising a single social identity (race) to understand how Whiteness was operating diminished our recognition of other power dynamics. We all have multiple social identities. Naming and negotiating them within collaborative work, especially when considering power and relationships, is complicated. We briefly mentioned in the Background, for example, that asking people to identify various identities like their racial identity is complicated because it is a socially constructed idea that varies by geographical location (e.g., Asian in the United States vs. Asian in the United Kingdom). When we reduced our analysis to thinking only about Whiteness, we intentionally narrowed our focus to how race and Whiteness were being perpetuated in our interactions. Yet we are not exclusively defined by one social identity.

Although there are important reasons to focus on race and racism, including that they are often avoided, other social identities like professional status, international identity, gender identity, and so on, complicated this analysis and our interpretations. Our analysis, as a process of racialisation, was harmful, but the addition of academic status and the fact that almost all of the graduate students were scholars of Colour created the potential for additional harm because of the intersection of identities. Drawing on Crenshaw (1989), Bullock (2018) points out that a key concern of intersectionality is "that racism, sexism, and other forms of oppression, when considered in parallel, appear additive, but those who experience these oppressions in combination endure multiplicative effects" (p. 126).

One of the ways we began to analyse the transcript of the project meeting was to count the number of times each person at the meeting had a turn of talk. This part of the analysis was motivated, in part, by Danny Martin's (2009b) articulation of a White institutional space. White institutional spaces are characterised, in part, by the domination of White people in conversations. When we counted up the turns of talk, we found that the turns of talk of White project members far exceeded those of scholars of Colour project members. Some of the White chapter authors concluded that the scholars of Colour, therefore, did not have the opportunity to participate in the conversation, and importantly, to have their thoughts and perspectives be taken up in any meaningful way.

An additional possible implication of this rendering of the turns of talk is that none of the project team members did anything to actively disrupt the institutional space of Whiteness. In other words, if we consider discourse to be interactionally constructed, meaning that all interlocutors are participating in the trajectory of the discourse, whether or not they are actively contributing to the turns of talk, scholars of Colour can be positioned as contributing to the space of institutional Whiteness. This interpretation frames the scholars of Colour from a deficit-oriented view without recognising their "disengagement" as an active form of resistance against White dominance, a deliberate enactment of their agency (Malagon, 2010).

This initial interpretation was challenged by one of the reviewers as well as some of the authors of this chapter, for its lack of attention to individual agency and the possibility that the scholars of Colour were electing not to participate at those times. This alternative interpretation recognises the agency that all individuals have in navigating spaces. We note that interpretation and analysis of the participation of people of Colour by White scholars have an historical basis rooted in Whiteness, through which people of Colour (often children, in mathematics education research) became tokenised, treated as unable to assert the same level of agency as White people, and ultimately erased. Despite the goal of a race-conscious study of our group, the actions of the scholars of Colour were initially interpreted through colour-blind eyes, thereby further perpetuating Whiteness. Wing (2003), a critical race feminist, stated that "[t]he reality for any group is undoubtedly much more complex, but to avoid merely talking about individuals, it is sometimes necessary to be strategically essentialist" (p. 7). In other words, strategically essentialising the research project team members as racialised human beings was necessary to understand the racial experiences of the scholars of Colour situated in the broader social context of White supremacy.

Moving away from an intersectional approach, by not looking, for example, at the intersection between racial and institutional hierarchical structures, landed more heavily on scholars of Colour, who beyond being graduate students, held other minoritised social identities. Leyva (2017) argues that intersectional analyses, or analyses of the complex ways that individuals with multiple target social identities navigate hegemonic structures (Crenshaw,

1991; hooks, 1981), can serve to enhance race-based analyses such as critical race theory by providing nuanced understandings of the layering of oppression upon individuals and the varied ways these experiences are negotiated.

3.3   Tension 3: Generating Intellectual Property Versus Changing Practice (Failure)

Our original focus on Whiteness involved marking instances of times when we noticed project team members using discursive moves that served to affirm and maintain or to disrupt Whiteness. An example of one way that White dominance was maintained in the meeting was through the discursive production of tokenised positions for scholars of Colour. In particular, "invitations" to join the conversation were extended by White scholars to other members of the project team (who were scholars of Colour) only after a topic related to Whiteness and power was introduced and not at other times, such as when feedback was solicited on particular professional development activities. For example, the simple invitation of asking "what do others think?" to scholars of Colour may have served as coded language, by positioning the scholars of Colour as "tokens." Discursive moves of this kind are often made by well-intentioned White scholars who become cognisant of the disproportionate presence of White voices. By tokenising the space through inviting scholars of Colour into conversations only when topics of race emerge, however, White people can also dehumanise their colleagues of Colour and devalue the range of their expertise, experiences, and interests.

What started out as an intellectual endeavour in which we (the authors) were simply engaging in initial passes of data analysis that we were all part of generating, we realised, became personal and painful for many of the co-authors. We (the White scholars) began to wonder about our actions, not just in the transcripts, but in our ongoing project team meetings, and to wonder whether or not we were continuing to instantiate a space of Whiteness or whether we were disrupting the oppressive structures that we had set out to disrupt.

Although the White scholars intended to be inclusive, these invitations could be, themselves, oppressive. Because a move like asking project team members to enter in the conversation can both serve to open up space and to marginalise others, there was a tension about how to respond to this in our analysis, and also in our interactions in ongoing project team meetings. It was important for us to understand the multiple roles these invitations could play (rather than simply seeing the "positive," i.e., inclusive, intention of it). Regardless of the intention, we had to consider other potential impacts.

Generally speaking, the range of ways that Whiteness was shown to be functioning in the project team meetings gave us pause, which we experienced in different ways. For example, one scholar of Colour expressed that it was difficult to know how to move forward since there was a level of care and trust among the authors, the professional development was moving forward, and individual White scholars felt remorse about what had occurred. There was a concern for further hurting White scholars in an attempt to interrogate systems. A White scholar described feeling paralysed trying to make a structural change within the entire project team because other members on the team who had not been in this conversation did not necessarily share the same desires. Another White scholar expressed feeling stuck about what to do with the information and felt complicit about not helping to change the broader group norms.

Although we ended up making some structural changes to project team meetings (e.g., project agenda items included sharing emerging analyses and discussion of the first draft of this chapter; more time for particularly sensitive items, meeting facilitators rotated through the project team, small group breakout discussions on next steps), many project team members felt that more attention was needed to fully explore the implications of these discursive moves and consider how to move forward collectively. In addition, many of the changes were made subtly by the White authors of this chapter, and the rationale for them was not made transparent to the graduate students of Colour and other project team members. The fact that these changes did not stem from a collective choice—that they were not overtly justice-oriented—did little to salve the wounds of the graduate scholars of Colour. Without a rationale, the changes felt haphazard and minimal.

Doing little to change the nature of the project work, or the social arrangements of the project team members, caused additional harm to scholars of Colour on the project. The White scholars had asked the scholars of Colour to help us examine our oppressive practices, causing one form of harm, and then did little to change the situation, layering on additional harm. This tension was noticed by our Advisory Board, who commented that they considered the work that we were engaged in, including the critical Whiteness study, to be a form of non-racist activity, rather than anti-racist activity. The White scholars were called to be accountable not only for harming fellow colleagues of Colour, but also harming the teachers who were participating in the professional development, their students, and the local community by not incorporating more attention and action to these issues.

In the subsequent year of the project, the project team decided to make a change of course and to bring in speakers on anti-racism to the professional development, both for the project team and the teachers who were involved in the grant project work. We read books and articles (e.g., Harro, 2000; Lester, 2017; Oluo, 2018; Tatum, 2000; Wolfmeyer, 2017) and the presenters led us through activities that trained our focus on racism at intrapersonal, interpersonal, institutional, and cultural levels. The need to take an anti-racist approach had been articulated by the scholars of Colour early in the grant work, but their perspectives were overridden by the White PIs, who instead employed frameworks and practices that were familiar to them.

The above tensions are not exhaustive, nor are they mutually exclusive. Many other tensions arose, some named and others yet to be named, that again are part of the failures of this project. We turn now to a discussion of the possible audiences for this chapter, and the ways that these tensions and failures could have been opportunities for growth, inspiration, and new directions for the research project.

4 Discussion

This chapter could be read in various ways by White scholars and scholars of Colour, or from another minoritised identity, and by other project team members, who have their own stories to tell. We have organised our discussion around the notion of "audience" and speak to particular groups at particular times.

We recognise (with remorse) that the primary audience for this chapter is White scholars. Even in writing about experiences of dehumanisation of ourselves and others, this chapter again positions White people (some of us) as the centre of attention. We return to this tension in the conclusion. Here, we sit with the tensions that we have described and their interactions, and consider what this means for White scholars pursuing justice in mathematics education. First, as a pair of us described when writing the first tension, the continual layering of hurt and harm on the graduate students who are scholars of Colour, coupled with the disembodiment of White scholars in order to sever bodies from racist discursive ideologies, was a White project. As DiAngelo (2011) describes, "White fragility" or the reluctance of White people to talk about race for fear of misunderstanding, blame, anger and hurt feelings, despite the desire of people of Colour to foreground these discussions and feelings, is a characteristic of White participation in racially mixed activities. As one of the scholars of Colour articulated, there was no way we could have pursued the analysis without significant trust among the group members. The level of trust among the group was exceptional. Another scholar of Colour expressed that it was because of the relationships with the White scholars that it was even possible to call out Whiteness. Yet, feelings of shock and sadness did emerge and were genuine as we found it extremely difficult to step out of ideological discourses. What sort of trust needs to be continually fostered to do this work in racially mixed groups?

Vakil et al. (2016) offer the notion of *politicised trust*, as a way to conceptualise partnerships across racial lines as necessarily mediated by "histories of race and differential power" (p. 199) that are constantly being negotiated in moments of social activity. Instead of perceiving trust as something that is achieved, Vakil et al. (2016) argue that it is constantly at play, as the "good intentions" of particular actors land on and are felt by others in ways that may cause distrust and harm. The harm caused to scholars of Colour by White scholars through the critical Whiteness study, and the lack of significant change to the project as a result of the study findings, severely damaged the trust of scholars of Colour, as the harm continued. Committing to the opening of spaces to share feelings of hurt and concern among the authors may have begun to rebuild trust and provide a stronger impetus towards change. It may also have exacerbated feelings of discomfort among the scholars of Colour as the White scholars were responsible for the progress of the research project.

An important point that we (as White scholars) take away from this experience is to learn to "pause" when there are signals from our colleagues of Colour that feelings of discomfort are emerging. These signals can be anything from a feeling shared with someone on the team, a slight hesitation or catch of breath in the midst of a discussion, silence, facial expressions, to disinterest in the work. We understand "pausing" from Patel (2015) as a way of breaking from the tendency in academia to engage in colonising practices around competition, production, and consumerisation. Instead of carrying on in a mindless way, Patel (2015) asks academics to recognise any form of knowing as "imbued with relations to social and material contexts, epistemologies, and living beings" (p. 48). This means that our analyses are not simply academic exercises. They are acts upon people, both in the immediate situation and more expansively across time and space, which have historical weight and material consequences. In our case, pausing could have entailed first having a discussion within the group about what it means to pursue a study of Whiteness with a racially mixed authoring team, and whether this enterprise was mutually beneficial.

Attending to pauses and feelings in social interaction, and their connections to power structures and histories, is often viewed as irrelevant in academia and discouraged as tangential to academic work. As the work of critical and feminist scholars is increasingly focused on discussions of equity and power, a strong emphasis on the body and its relation to space, place and history is being brought into dominant academic discourses (Anzaldúa, 1987; hooks, 1981; Greene, 1994). In this literature, feelings become an important way of interpreting and making sense of phenomena, as they can signal disconnection between dominant discourses and lived experiences and histories. We view attending to bodily sensations and feelings, as well as taking up pauses and hesitations, as a step towards politicised trust.

This chapter may also be read by scholars of Colour, who may experience a range of feelings upon reading it. Scholars of Colour may recognise their own experiences in the experiences of the graduate scholars of Colour working with a predominantly White-led research endeavour with "good intentions." It may anger scholars of Colour (and rightly so) that funding continues to flow primarily to White scholars to do this kind of work. We hope that graduate students of Colour have access to this chapter, and can think about how they can (and require faculty to) protect themselves in racially mixed research projects in mathematics education with an equity focus. As one graduate student of Colour expressed, without having a clear indication of how they were expected to participate, and the type of structural arrangements that the project team was committed to, a lot of questions came up that they were not able to ask. Graduate scholars of Colour felt tokenised and undervalued without knowing the realm of possibilities for their participation on the project. Thus, scholars of Colour reading this chapter might feel what Danny Martin, in a response to a plenary at the eighth conference for Mathematics Education and Society, has described as *righteous anger* towards the White authors of this chapter for failing on several fronts to engage in anti-racist, pro-Black activity.

5   Conclusion

We have acknowledged above that the primary audience for this chapter is White scholars, which again centres Whiteness and White logic, thus perpetuating the system of White institutional space through which our colleagues of Colour are dehumanised. So why write this chapter in the way that we did? First, our focus on tensions and stuck places resulted from deep and long conversations among the authors about the harm done to early career scholars of Colour. The White authors of this chapter asked the scholars of Colour if writing the chapter together would do further harm. The scholars of Colour said that a focus on tensions that emerged during the analysis could provide important information for future researchers. We chose to frame the situation that had occurred as a case of a failure to leave no doubt as to the outcome of the work and to signal the futility of it without "pausing" and connecting to feelings.

The graduate students of Colour were "invited" to participate in this analysis by the White PIs who received an invitation to submit a chapter for the book. The White scholars were anxious to include the perspectives of the scholars of Colour on the grant and to support them in learning about the publication process. It is clear that the White scholars were oblivious to the possible repercussions for the graduate scholars of Colour in terms of their professional careers. The White scholars were working from the "good intentions" that being involved in a publication would promote professional success. Yet, throughout the work the group kept returning to the language of "having trust with one another," which placed the analysts who were graduate students of Colour in the position of having to "hurt" people in power that were part of their mentoring team. Similarly, when the findings of the critical Whiteness study were presented at professional conferences, there was pushback and early career scholars of Colour were questioned as to whether the interpretations of Whiteness were warranted. Contrary to the hoped-for benefits, both of these effects could have negative implications for the future opportunities of early career scholars of Colour.

It is difficult to offer recommendations for studies of Whiteness among White scholars and scholars with minoritised social markers, since each reader's positionality will shape how this chapter is read. It is critical for White scholars to realise that they often serve as gatekeepers to the broader mathematics education community for graduate students and early career faculty of Colour. This means that, try as they may to break down hierarchies among personnel on a team, White scholars are necessarily perpetuating Whiteness simply through their participation. It is unfair and harmful (as we have illustrated) to expect and require scholars of Colour to make Whiteness visible to White scholars. Even if delving into the tensions ends up being and shaping the future work (as we are suggesting), it is still incumbent upon White scholars to maintain a vigilance about the various positionalities of the individuals who are part of the tensions, and what these mean for the dialogue. It is important to keep in mind the distinction between activity that simply reveals Whiteness (or a non-racist approach) with activity that interrupts and begins to dismantle it (an anti-racist approach) towards new social imaginations that transform and liberate.

We end this chapter by returning to Patel's (2015) call for researchers to pay attention to the material consequences of their activity. We have not thoroughly analysed the material outcomes of this research project, nor this chapter for the authors and project team members. One obvious result of this chapter is that the authors will be credited for having published their work formally. It is unclear as of yet what other material consequences will follow, or if social arrangements and meanings will also be reconfigured. We feel that it is important for future research project teams to consider the material consequences for different members and the costs of their participation in explicit ways in order to understand the stakes.

Acknowledgements

We thank our project team members, which includes our project team as well as the teachers and students who have graciously allowed us time with them. We recognise and thank Ashley Scroggins for her contributions, insights, and feedback on previous iterations of this chapter. Our project team includes, at various points in time, Joel Amidon, Tonya Gau Bartell, Sunghwan Byun, Missy D. Cosby, Michael Eiland, Mary Q. Foote, Victoria Hand, Frances Harper, Beth Herbel-Eisenmann, Brent Jackson, Sheeba Johnson, Durrell Jones, Courtney Koestler, Gregory Larnell, Carlos LópezLeiva, Oyemolade (Molade) Osibodu, Timothy Roberts, Ashley D. Scroggins, Anita Wager, and Ayşe Yolcu.

We also thank and acknowledge the National Science Foundation for its support of the project number DRL-1417672 entitled *Access, Agency, and Allies in Mathematical Systems* (A3IMS).

Any opinions, findings, and conclusions or recommendations expressed in this material are those of the authors and do not necessarily reflect the views of NSF.

Note

1 Following the United States census, we use White (instead of white) to refer to the historically and socially constructed notion of White race as distinguished from a colour, white.

References

Anzaldúa, G. (1987). *Borderlands/La frontera: The new mestiza*. Aunt Lute.

Bang, M. (2009). Indigenous knowledge and education: Sites of struggle, strength, and survivance. *Science Education, 93*(5), 958–959. https://doi.org/10.1002/sce.20351

Battey, D., & Leyva, L. A. (2016). A framework for understanding whiteness in mathematics education. *Journal of Urban Mathematics Education, 9*(2), 49–80.

Britzman, D. P. (1995). Is there a queer pedagogy? Or, stop reading straight. *Educational Theory, 45*(2), 151–165. https://doi.org/10.1111/j.1741-5446.1995.00151.x

Bullock, E. C. (2017). Beyond "ism" groups and figure hiding: Intersectional analysis and critical mathematics education. In A. Chronaki (Ed.), *Proceedings of the Ninth International Conference of Mathematics Education and Society* (Vol. 1, pp. 29–44). University of Thessaly Press.

Bullock, E. C. (2018). Intersectional analysis in critical mathematics education research: A response to figure hiding. *Review of Research in Education, 42*(1), 122–145. https://doi.org/10.3102%2F0091732X18759039

Bullock, E. C., Gholson, M. L., Larnell, G. V., & Martin, D. B. (2019). Race, mathematics education, and society: Toward global perspectives. In J. Subramanian (Ed.), *Proceedings of the Tenth International Mathematics Education and Society Conference* (pp. 165–170). Mathematics Education and Society. https://www.mescommunity.info/proceedings/MES10.pdf

Cobb, P., & Jackson, K. (2011). Towards an empirically grounded theory of action for improving the quality of mathematics teaching at scale. *Mathematics Teacher Education and Development, 13*(1), 6–33.

Cobb, P., McClain, K., Lamberg, T., & Dean, C. (2003). Situating teachers' instructional practices in the institutional setting of the school and school district. *Educational Researcher, 32*(6), 13–24.

Coburn, C. E. (2003). Rethinking scale: Moving beyond numbers to deep and lasting change. *Educational Researcher, 32*(6), 3–12. https://doi.org/10.3102/0013189X032006003

Cohen, D. K., & Ball, D. L. (1999). Instruction, capacity, and improvement (CPRE Research Report No. RR-043). Consortium for Policy Research in Education. https://www.cpre.org/sites/default/files/researchreport/783_rr43.pdf

Crenshaw, K. (1989). Demarginalizing the intersection of race and sex: A Black feminist critique of antidiscrimination doctrine, feminist theory and antiracist politics. *University of Chicago Legal Forum*, 139–167.

Crenshaw, K. (1991). Mapping the margins: Intersectionality, identity politics, and violence against women of color. *Stanford Law Review, 43*(6), 1241–1299. https://chicagounbound.uchicago.edu/uclf/vol1989/iss1/8

DeCuir, J. T., & Dixson, A. D. (2004). So when it comes out, they aren't that surprised that it is there: Using critical race theory as a tool of analysis of race and racism in education. *Educational Researcher, 33*(5), 26–31. https://doi.org/10.3102/0013189X033005026

DiAngelo, R. (2011). White fragility. *International Journal of Critical Pedagogy, 3*(3), 54–70.

Duarte, E. M., & Smith, S. (2000). *Foundational perspectives in multicultural education.* Longman.

Fine, M. (2017). *Just research in contentious times: Widening the methodological imagination.* Teachers College Press.

Giroux, H. (1997). Rewriting the discourse of racial identity: Towards a pedagogy and politics of Whiteness. *Harvard Educational Review, 67*(2), 285–321. https://doi.org/10.17763/haer.67.2.r4523gh4176677u8

Greene, M. (1994). Chapter 10: Epistemology and educational research: The influence of recent approaches to knowledge. *Review of Research in Education, 20*(1), 423–464. https://doi.org/10.3102/0091732X020001423

Gutiérrez, K. D., & Jurow, A. S. (2016). Social design experiments: Toward equity by design. *Journal of the Learning Sciences, 25*(4), 565–598. https://doi.org/10.1080/10508406.2016.1204548

Gutiérrez, R. (2015). Nesting in Nepantla: The importance of maintaining tensions in our work. In N. M. Joseph, C. M. Haynes, & F. Cobb (Eds.), *Interrogating Whiteness and relinquishing power: White faculty's commitment to racial consciousness in STEM classrooms* (pp. 253–281). Peter Lang.

Gutiérrez, R. (2017). Why mathematics (education) was late to the backlash party: The need for a revolution. *Journal of Urban Mathematics Education, 10*(2), 8–24.

Hand, V., Penuel, W. R., & Gutiérrez, K. D. (2012). (Re)framing educational possibility: Attending to power and equity in shaping access to and within learning opportunities. *Human Development, 55*(5–6), 250–268. https://doi.org/10.1159/000345313

Harris, C. I. (1995). Whiteness as property. In K. Crenshaw, N. Gotanda, G. Peller, & K. Thomas (Eds.), *Critical race theory: The key writings that formed the movement* (pp. 276–291). The New Press.

Harro, B. (2000). The cycle of socialization. In M. Adams, W. J. Blumenfeld, R. Castañeda, H. W. Hackman, M. L. Peters, & X. Zuniga (Eds.), *Readings for diversity and social justice* (pp. 15–20). Routledge.

Haviland, V. S. (2008). "Things get glossed over": Rearticulating the silencing power of whiteness in education. *Journal of Teacher Education, 59*(1), 40–54. https://doi.org/10.1177%2F0022487107310751

hooks, b. (1981). *Ain't I a woman: Black women and feminism*. South End Press.

Jung, M.-K., Costa Vargas, J. H., & Bonilla-Silva, E. (2011). *State of White supremacy: Racism, governance, and the United States*. Stanford University Press.

Leonardo, Z. (2002). The souls of White folk: Critical pedagogy, Whiteness studies, and globalization discourse. *Race, Ethnicity and Education, 5*(1), 29–50. https://doi.org/10.1080/1361332012011780

Leonardo, Z. (2004). The color of supremacy: Beyond the discourse of 'white privilege.' *Educational Philosophy and Theory, 36*(2), 137–152. https://doi.org/10.1111/j.1469-5812.2004.00057.x

Lester, N. A. (2017, August 29). For white allies in search of a solution to American racism/ When folks of color are exhausted. *Teaching Tolerance*. https://www.tolerance.org/magazine/for-white-allies-in-search-of-a-solution-to-american-racism-when-folks-of-color-are

Leyva, L. A. (2017). Unpacking the male superiority myth and masculinization of mathematics at the intersections: A review of research on gender in mathematics education. *Journal for Research in Mathematics Education, 48*(4), 397–433. https://doi.org/10.5951/jresematheduc.48.4.0397

Malagon, M. C. (2010). All the losers go there: Challenging the deficit educational discourse of Chicano racialized masculinity in a continuation high school. *Educational Foundations, 24*(1–2), 59–76.

Martin, D. B. (2008). E(race)ing race from a national conversation on mathematics teaching and learning: The national mathematics advisory panel as White institutional space. *The Mathematics Enthusiast, 5*(2–3), 387–398. https://scholarworks.umt.edu/tme/vol5/iss2/20

Martin, D. B. (2009a). Does race matter? *Teaching Children Mathematics, 16*(3), 134–139. www.jstor.org/stable/41199394

Martin, D. B. (2009b). Researching race in mathematics education. *Teachers College Record, 111*(2), 295–338.

MathEdCollective. (2019). The MathEdCollective: Collaborative action in an era of cyberbullying and hate. In J. Subramanian (Ed.), *Proceedings of the Tenth International Mathematics Education and Society Conference* (pp. 595–604). Mathematics Education and Society. https://www.mescommunity.info/proceedings/MES10.pdf

Matias, C. E. (2013). Tears worth telling: Urban teaching and the possibilities of racial justice. *Multicultural Perspectives, 15*(4), 187–193. https://doi.org/10.1080/15210960.2013.844603

Nicolson, M., de Oliveira Andreotti, V., & Mafi, B. F. (2016). The unstated politics of stranger making in Europe: A brutal kindness. *European Journal of Cultural Studies, 19*(4), 335–351. https://doi.org/10.1177/1367549415592896

Oluo, I. (2018). *So you want to talk about race*. Seal Press.

Pais, A. (2012). A critical approach to equity. In O. Skovsmose & B. Greer (Eds.), *Opening the cage: Critique and politics of mathematics education* (pp. 49–91). Sense. https://doi.org/10.1007/978-94-6091-808-7_3

Patel, L. (2015). *Decolonizing educational research: From ownership to answerability*. Routledge.

Picower, B. (2009). The unexamined Whiteness of teaching: How White teachers maintain and enact dominant racial ideologies. *Race Ethnicity and Education, 12*(2), 197–215. https://doi.org/10.1080/13613320902995475

Tatum, B. D. (2000). The complexity of identity: "Who am I?" In M. Adams, W. J. Blumenfeld, R. Castañeda, H. W. Hackman, M. L. Peters, & X. Zuniga (Eds.), *Readings for diversity and social justice* (pp. 15–20). Routledge.

Vakil, S., McKinney de Royston, M., Nasir, N. S., & Kirshner, B. (2016). Rethinking race and power in design-based research: Reflections from the field. *Cognition and Instruction, 34*(3), 194–209. https://doi.org/10.1080/07370008.2016.1169817

Wing, A. K. (2003). Introduction. In A. K. Wing (Ed.). *Critical race feminism: A reader* (2nd ed., pp. 1–19). New York University Press.

Wolfmeyer, M. (2017). *Mathematics education: A critical introduction*. Routledge. https://doi.org/10.4324/9781315269528

CHAPTER 7

"Mathematics Is Bad for Society"
Reasoning about Mathematics as Part of Society in a Language Diverse Middle School Classroom

Ulrika Ryan, Annica Andersson and Anna Chronaki

Abstract

In this chapter, we report on a small-scale critical mathematics education project in a Swedish classroom with students of varied language backgrounds. The project departed from the student Arvid's statement "Mathematics is bad for society." Our research interest was twofold. On the one hand, we wanted to explore what knowledge is being (re)produced by students as they try to connect and reason with a statement like "Mathematics is bad for society." And on the other hand, we were also interested in how the students in this classroom, in which they do not have shared mother tongues, can express and (dis)acknowledge knowledge when reasoning about mathematics in society. We found that when the students (and their teacher) grappled with unpacking critical aspects such as "mathematics in society," their reciprocal assessment of claims was based on their individual ways of knowing and talking, and tended to shape both their actions and the outcome of their efforts. We show that the discussion around critical aspects of mathematics in society that came to the fore was intertwined with both students' and the teacher's (lack of) meta-understanding of language diversity.

Keywords

language diversity – mathematics and society – inferentialism – knowledge bases – critical mathematics education

•••

"Mathematics is bad for society," said Arvid, a grade five (11 years old) student with Albanian background, in a somewhat challenging tone when we were awaiting the teacher for the math class to start. I, Ulrika, did not have the opportunity at that moment to reply or ask him why he claimed mathematics to be bad for society. It was one of the first days that I met the class as a participant-observer and my relations with the students had not yet developed into closer friendships. I had introduced myself as a researcher interested in reasoning in math class but had not mentioned societal aspects of mathematics. Arvid's claim got stuck in my mind and I became curious about his reasons for making the statement. I found it surprising for such a young student to say that "mathematics is bad for society," or even to position mathematics as being connected to societal matters. In my mind, Arvid's claim raised questions about middle school students' ideas on mathematics and society. (Vignette, based on Ulrika's field notes, 2017-05-08)

To the first author,[1] Arvid's statement brought forward the idea of conducting a small-scale project to explore the theme "Mathematics is bad for society" in his class. Arvid's statement seems to exemplify concerns in critical mathematics education about how societal issues of mathematics can be addressed at school, a task that remains a challenge for mathematics educators.

Critical mathematical literacy is shaped through "constructing knowledge of particular concepts, ideas, skills and facts ... to help [students] recognise oppressive aspects of society" (Gutstein, 2006, p. 6). In this line of pedagogical interventions, students often engage in discussing social issues, formulated as mathematical problems by their teachers (see for example Andersson, 2011; Barwell, 2013; Frankenstein, 1990; Gutstein, 2006, 2016). Teachers assist students in translating "real world" problems into mathematics, which in a sense creates a challenge as argued by Gutstein (2016). Drawing on the ideas of Paolo Freire, he argues that critical mathematical literacy contains knowledge of three types: classical academic, communal, and critical. However, Gutstein (2016) identifies challenges in interconnecting the different knowledge bases and asks: "How does one connect and synthesize all three knowledge bases?" (p. 458). He proposes the idea of a pedagogical "dance" that means moving between the three knowledge bases, and that "signifies the braided interconnections that people make between mathematics and socio-political reality" (p. 469). To us, embedded in the statement "Mathematics is bad for society" we see classical academic knowledge about mathematics as well as communal knowledge about society and mathematics in society. Moreover, the word *bad* opens up a value-laden space that allows for critique.

Our endeavour in this chapter is to explore how the students in Arvid's classroom struggle to make value-laden critical interconnections between mathematics and society. The classroom can be characterised as language diverse yet monolingual. It is language diverse because a third of the students belong to a wide diversity of mother-tongue backgrounds and it is also monolingual since the curriculum language is Swedish. As such, our small-scale project explored more deeply how students from diverse language backgrounds engage in making inferences and interconnections when they reason about "Mathematics is bad for society," since these inferences allow us to unpack implicit meanings in such statements (Brandom, 1994, 2000).

As we examine the outcome of this small-scale project, our interest is twofold; it is directed towards grappling with *what* knowledge the students' use, produce, and inferentially interconnect in their claims to articulate meanings of Arvid's statement, and we look at *how* that knowledge is expressed and (dis)acknowledged[2] in the language diverse yet monolingual classroom. These interests mean that we anticipate that, to achieve an understanding of knowledge, attention to its dialogical articulation is vital (Derry, 2013). Theoretically, we focus our analysis on the *language game of giving and asking for reasons* (GoGAR) (Brandom, 1994, 2000) to examine the what and the how as elements in flux in face-to-face reasoning.

The research questions explored in this chapter are:
- *What* knowledge do students use, produce, and interconnect as they reason about the statement "Mathematics is bad for society"?
- *How* do students express and (dis)acknowledge knowledge when reasoning about mathematics in society in a language diverse yet monolingual classroom?

The three knowledge bases to which Gutstein (2016) refers contain aspects of functional mathematics as well as critical knowledge about mathematics and society. Therefore, we start with some brief comments on mathematical literacy and socio-political aspects of mathematics in society. We then give a theoretical account of the GoGAR, which we use to analyse what inferential interconnections between knowledge claims about mathematics and society the students in Arvid's classroom make, as well as how they express and treat those claims as they reason about his statement "Mathematics is bad for society." Thereafter we describe the context and methodology of the present study, followed by our analysis of specific episodes and student claims. The chapter ends with some concluding remarks, which address the complexity of students' reasoning about mathematics in society in a language diverse classroom.

1   Mathematics and Society

Functional mathematical literacy refers to the capacity of creating and applying mathematical knowledge when required (Jablonka, 2003). Such conceptions of mathematical literacy are closely linked to the social and economic needs of the market, as well as the individual's participation in an advanced technologised democratic society (Jablonka, 2003; Skovsmose, 2007). At the extreme end of functional mathematical literacy, mathematics is value-free and merely technically related to societal demands (Jablonka, 2003). However, articulated in Arvid's claim "Mathematics is bad for society," mathematics is connected to society in a value-laden sense.

Critical mathematical literacy recognises mathematics as a distributor of power in society. Mathematics acts and can be made to act (Skovsmose, 2007; Chronaki, 2010). Kollosche (2014) claims mathematics to be "a body of knowledge and techniques which has served the interests of power from its very beginnings" (p. 1062), with the purpose of shaping citizens' behaviour. Being critically mathematically literate is, for instance to hold the capacity of understanding and shaping the world using mathematics to make it socially just (Frankenstein, 1990, 2014; Gutstein, 2006, 2016), environmentally sustainable (Barwell, 2013; Hauge & Barwell, 2017), or to critically understand the political role of mathematics in the world (Andersson & Wagner, 2017; Gellert & Jablonka, 2009; Kollosche, 2014; Skovsmose, 2007).

According to Skovsmose (2007), the distribution of power through the use of mathematics "refers to processes of construction, operating, consuming, marginalising which [can] be addressed functionally or critically" (p. 17). Processes of construction apply to advanced systems of knowledge and techniques used by, for example, engineers, economists, and computer scientists. Operating processes conducted by operators bring constructors' advanced use of mathematics into operation. Operators are not necessarily aware of the specific mathematics behind their performances. Citizens consume the mathematical objects, developed by constructors, which are fed mathematical information by operators. In high technological societies, mathematics has become a necessity because "if the citizens were not able to read information put into numbers, the society would not be able to operate" (Skovsmose, 2007, p. 14). However, technology blackboxes mathematics. The more technological artefacts that societal life demands, the more opaque and thus powerful the constructors' mathematics behind them becomes (Gellert & Jablonka, 2009). Hence, for citizens, mathematics in society is double-edged. On the one hand, it is a necessity or demand; on the other, mathematics is concealed by technology.

It is reasonable to problematise how students develop critical mathematical literacies as a matter of interconnecting knowledge of different kinds (Gutstein, 2016) as they reason about both mathematics per se and about how mathematics can be used. Although the perspective of critical mathematics education has much to offer in terms of reconsidering curriculum design for critical mathematical literacy (e.g., Frankenstein, 1983; Gutstein, 2006; Skovsmose, 1994; Skovsmose & Borba, 2004), particularly highlighting pedagogical moves for formatting interconnections between knowledge bases (Gutstein, 2016), our focus here will not primarily be on pedagogical issues. Nor is our focus on understanding the kinds (e.g., academic and communal, Gutstein, 2016) or funds (González, Andrade, Civil, & Moll, 2001) of knowledge that students might draw on when reasoning. Rather, our focus is on the students' articulation of the interconnections themselves and on how these suggested interconnections are treated in their reasoning, while they allow us to think about how the students in Arvid's class see mathematics and society as critically connected. To grapple with the complexity in the students' reasoning, we use the *language game of giving and asking for reasons* which is at heart of the philosophical theory of inferentialism (Brandom, 1994, 2000). Drawing on Wittgensteinian ideas, inferentialism approaches meaning and knowledge from a social pragmatic perspective emphasising that meaning has to be located in real-life practices of language use, so-called *language games*. While inferentialism attends to how people make, treat, and interconnect each other's claims in face-to-face conversations, it allows us to think about the social and epistemological complexities and dynamics in students' reasoning in a language diverse classroom. In the next section, we discuss some aspects of inferentialism in relation to the small-scale project on Arvid's statement "Mathematics is bad for society" further.

2   Reasoning as a Language Game

To grapple with how students in a language diverse yet monolingual classroom reason to interconnect claims to unpack the meaning of the statement "Mathematics is bad for society," we argue that inferentialism is fruitful because, (i) it sees reasoning as a language game in which implicit interconnections between knowledge claims can be articulated and made explicit; (ii) it argues that such articulation is first and foremost dynamic and dialogical, rather than formally logical; and that (iii) norms regulate how interconnections are made, treated and used. Conceptualising reasoning as playing the *game of giving and asking for reasons*, allows for a type of analysis that is not concerned with efficiency or correctness in students' reasoning. Analysis is not geared towards eliciting individual knowledge from social reasoning, or towards modelling individual mental representations, rather it is concerned with reasoning itself. Inferentialism asks for inferences and their origins: "An inferentialist epistemology does not prioritize students' mathematical reasoning over out-of-school reasoning; nor does it view mathematics and out-of-school reasoning as separated from one another, but rather as inferentially connected to one another" (Schindler et al., 2017, p. 7). By inferences, we do not mean formal logical ones, but inferences that are inherent in language itself. For instance, from the statement "Stockholm is north of Copenhagen" it can be inferred that Copenhagen is to the south of Stockholm provided that the social and cultural norms that regulate the concept's use allow that. Alternatively, from a person saying "I am hungry," it can be inferred that she or he wants something to eat. Hence, being hungry and eating as well as north and south are inferentially related to each other under particular socially and culturally normative circumstances that are inherent in the concept's use.

The scope of the GoGAR is not to produce "a canon or standard of right reasoning. Rather, it can help us make explicit (and hence available for criticism and transformation) the inferential commitments that govern the use of all our vocabulary, and hence articulate the contents of all our concepts" (Brandom, 2000, p. 30). That is, when we ask and give each other reasons for our claims we unpack the content of our concepts and open up a space in which concept use can be troubled, critiqued, and altered. The theory of inferentialism does not argue that the content of concepts primarily represents some object or state of affairs; rather, concepts are caught up in statements that mean something by virtue of their inferential interconnections to other statements (Bransen, 2002). Hence, Arvid's statement "Mathematics is bad for society" means something in the students' reasoning due to the inferential interconnections they make to other statements.

As Arvid and his peers ask for and give reasons for Arvid's statement (i.e. play the GoGAR), they position the statement within a network of inferential interconnections to other statements. Inferential interconnections are usually implicit, but as the GoGAR is played they are made explicit. Premises, consequences, and incompatibilities that follow from uttering a statement or making a claim come to the fore. For instance, a premise for claiming "Mathematics is bad for society" is that mathematics operates in society and that it is not value-free. A consequence is that mathematics may cause some kind of harm in society. Mathematics as disconnected from society is incompatible with the claim. This dimension of the GoGAR concerns the *what*-questions of our endeavour as presented in the introduction.

When we play the GoGAR we help each other out with discerning what follows implicitly from statements by normatively assessing and using each other's claims, which means that "playing [the GoGAR] well [is] more than a matter of an individual player's competence: to play the game of giving and asking for reasons well, one needs a team" (Bransen, 2002, p. 387). To play the GoGAR well means that the team manages to discern (at least some of) what implicitly follows from a claim and that the team has a set of reasons that could be used to back up or question other claims. For instance, if player A questions player B's claim, she might ask B for reasons for it to find out if B has good reasons for her claim. Giving reasons for a particular claim is to interconnect it to other claims or statements. If player A thinks that player B has good reasons for her claim, player A endorses it and uses it in her own reasoning. Players assess interconnections between claims according to what they find to be good, appropriate ones. Which interconnections players know of and find appropriate depends on their experiences of participating in various social practices and previously played GoGARs. This dimension of the GoGAR concerns the *how*-questions of our endeavour presented in the introduction.

Children in a language diverse classroom participate in multiple, sometimes blurred social practices, which means that "a critical perspective [on mathematics] cannot develop without espousing children's social and cultural backgrounds as well as their personal ways of knowing and learning as they develop and grow through experiencing the particular political contexts of living and work" (Chronaki et al., 2015, p. 150). The formation of students' critical reasoning about mathematics and society, in a language diverse classroom embracing students' personal ways of knowing is intertwined with the socially and culturally normative inferences inherent in language(s). Radford (2012) claims that "in the students of multicultural classrooms we ... find mathematics (as a plural noun) that speak about different worlds, even if the mathematics is expressed in the same official language. We do not produce accents when talking only. We also produce accents when thinking" (p. 341). Students' reasoning about Arvid's statement, "Mathematics is bad for society" draw on their personal ways of talking and thinking using their own particular "accents" which are influenced by the inferences they make from concepts to other concepts. As students in language diverse classrooms play the GoGAR and assess interconnections between claims, their "accents" guide their assessments as well as the interconnections they make.

3   The Present Study: Classroom Context, Participants, and Methods

Embedded in Arvid's claim "Mathematics is bad for society" lies the idea that mathematics acts in society and that it is not value-free, as Skovsmose (2007)

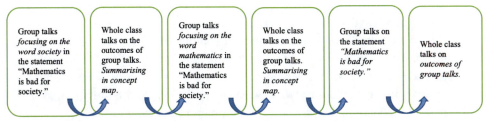

FIGURE 7.1 Flow chart of lesson orchestration

points out. Therefore, this very statement was taken as a starting point for group and whole class explorative talks (Mercer et al., 2004). In groups of four or five, students were asked to talk and reason about the statement. The outcome of each group discussion was elaborated on in whole class talk orchestrated by Ulrika. She drew a concept map on the board to summarise the students' findings. The orchestration of this discussion in one 40-minute lesson plus one 20-minute lesson,[3] organised by Ulrika, is shown in the flow chart in Figure 7.1.

The whole class talks were inspired by interactive, talk-based teaching (Hufferd-Ackles et al., 2004) in which the practices of explorative talks are characterised in a way that:
– all relevant information is shared;
– all members of the group are invited to contribute to the discussion;
– opinions and ideas are respected and considered;
– everyone is asked to make their reasons clear;
– challenges and alternatives are made explicit and are negotiated;
– the group seeks to reach agreement before taking a decision or acting (Mercer et al., 2004, p. 362).

The lesson orchestration was designed to provide good opportunities for students to make, question, use, and interconnect each other's claims while synthesising knowledge bases to unpack the meaning of "Mathematics is bad for society."

Arvid's classroom is situated in the south of Sweden in a suburban community close to two cities, to which most residents commute for work. The school districts of the municipality incorporate both middle class and socio-economically deprived areas. In this particular Grade 5 class,[4] some students travel to school from homes located in the deprived areas, a choice made by their parents to avoid as one student said, "the rowdy local schools." Most students are Swedish-only speakers but over a third of them (8) claim to have various degrees of access to languages other than Swedish, including Albanian, Arabic, Bosnian, Hebrew, Kurdish, Norwegian, Persian, Polish, and Serbian.

The formal language of teaching and learning is Swedish. Despite the fact that about 20% of the students at the school have one or two parents born abroad, the Swedish-only-discourse (Norén, 2010; Norén & Andersson, 2016; Skog & Andersson, 2014) is strongly operating. For instance, there are no signs or books in languages other than Swedish and languages other than Swedish are seldom heard in the corridors, classrooms, or schoolyard.

Two students, *Samir* and *Elsa* exemplify how several of the students in Arvid's class have cultural, social, and linguistic backgrounds that are complex and blurred. Samir speaks Arabic, Hebrew, and sometimes Kurdish at home. His parents are well-educated refugees who arrived from the Palestine about 2.5 years ago. Elsa, a girl with divorced parents, alters on a weekly basis between living with her well-off CEO father, who speaks Serbian and came to Sweden during the Balkan war, and her Swedish working-class mother, who lives in a socio-economically deprived area. The students were used to group and whole class talks during mathematics class, since that is part of their usual teacher's pedagogy. However, from individual interviews, Ulrika learned that they were not used to talking critically about mathematics.

To grapple with the students' reasoning about critical interconnections between mathematics and society, we attended to *what* they inferred from "mathematics" and "society" in the claim "Mathematics is bad for society." We also analysed inferential interconnections, which were used to articulate critical aspects of mathematics in society. Critical instances chosen for analysis were when students made explicit aspects of mathematics in society following from "Mathematics is bad for society." Analysis of the critical instances pivoted around the following questions:

– What inferential interconnections are discerned when the students play the GoGAR about the statement, "Mathematics is bad for society"?
  – How are these inferential interconnections used as premises and consequences in claims about mathematics in society?
  – How do these interconnections articulate critical aspects about mathematics in society?

Moreover, we analysed interaction that illustrates *how* the students expressed, treated, and (dis)acknowledged claims as they reasoned in the language diverse classroom, to address the following questions:

– How are attempts to play the GoGAR well made; e.g., (how) do students help each other out with discerning what follows implicitly from statements by normatively assessing and using each other's claims?
  – What are the outcomes of these attempts?

In the following section, we present the results of our analysis.

4   Reasoning about "Mathematics in Society"

When Ulrika wrote, "Mathematics is bad for society" on the board there was a little surprised and curious fuss as the students were not used to talking about mathematics as something bad. However, the students quickly engaged in the group and whole class talks with curious interest.

4.1   *Students' Inferential Interconnections between Mathematics and Society*

In this section, we elaborate on how the students reasoned about society and mathematics and how they located mathematics within their reasoning about society and vice versa. Figure 7.2 shows an image of the concept map that summarises the students' reasoning. This concept map provided the empirical material for our analysis.

To make explicit what follows implicitly from using the concept "society" in the statement, the students discerned inferential connections focusing on their environment; "school, house, trees, where we live, pollution." They positioned "society" as inferentially related to humans as social beings: "us," "humans shape it," "where we live"; and to humans' power distributing actions: "we change it together," "what we do," "we affect society with our pollution."

When reasoning about "mathematics" as used in "Mathematics is bad for society," the students discerned connections to do with mathematics as actions:

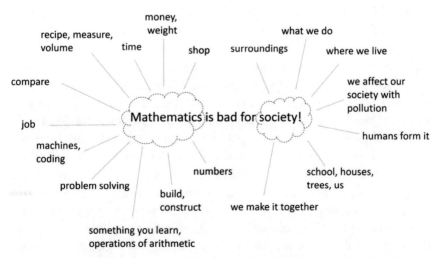

FIGURE 7.2   Image of the concept map showing the inferential interconnections that the students made

"problem-solving," "measure," "learning," "comparing," "coding," "building"; and as conceptual constructs: "time," "money," "weight," "volume," "numbers." They also located mathematics in physical objects: "workplaces," "shops," "machines," "recipes."

The students' inferential interconnections, as written on the whiteboard, revealed a stereotypical middle-class discourse of society as something that an undefined "we" (the students?) participate in, have the agency to impact, and are obliged to care for environmentally. Students made inferential interconnections showing that mathematics operates as a tool for the working, consuming, and problem-solving citizen in such a society. Hence, their reasoning reflected and reproduced functional mathematical literacy, but lacked critical aspects of mathematics in society. This is precisely why Arvid's claim "Mathematics is bad for society" is crucial for the students to elaborate on while it troubles mathematics as merely functional.

Further, the students articulated prevailing ideas about society and mathematics that did not appear to accommodate their linguistic, cultural, and social diversity; instead, diversity seemed to be silenced. One of Ulrika's hopes when designing the mini-project was that talking about "mathematics as bad for society" might disrupt and trouble stereotyped images and allow for complexity and plurality to emerge in the students' talk, as suggested by Chronaki et al. (2015). The mind map on the board did not show conflicting ideas or culturally diverse images speaking about different worlds using various "accents" (Radford, 2012).

There could be several reasons for this lack of diversity. Small group talks preceded the whole class discussion. From these group talks, a group spokesperson summarised their group's contribution to the mind map. In the small group talks, ways of applying concepts, in this case society and mathematics, were normatively assessed by the students. It is likely that the Swedish-only-discourse excluded linguistic and cultural troubling, while the students assessed them as normatively inappropriate in the group talks. Hence, the group spokesperson did not report them in the whole class talk. Language, social, and cultural diversity did not appear to be norms that regulated the talks. The fact that Ulrika is a middle-class native Swedish speaker and a former mathematics teacher with many years of teaching experience shapes the "accent" she used to understand and account for the students' summaries, which adds to the complexity of interpreting the concept mapmaking. The episode below illustrates some of the complexity that emerged in the classroom as Ulrika grappled with making the concept map.

5 Attempts to Play the GoGAR Well—Episode 1: Overbridging Different "Accents"

Episode 1 illustrates how Ulrika struggled to grasp what Aldrin, a speaker of Persian and Swedish, wanted her to add to the map about the concept "mathematics." Darko, who speaks Serbian and Swedish, assisted their conversation by using Ulrika's formal Swedish mathematical "accent" (turn 3; "equations," turn 10; "assignments." turn 13; "problem-solving") to interconnect or overbridge Aldrin's claims and Ulrika's grasping of them. With the help of Darko, the three interlocutors formed a team that managed to play the GoGAR so that they, at least seemed to discern enough of what follows from Aldrin's claim in turn one for Ulrika to grasp it, namely the fact that we have numbers at all is due to mathematics.

While this interaction was in progress, Ulrika found herself in a dilemma. On the one hand, to grasp Aldrin's claim, which she thought might be unclear, not only to herself but to other students in the classroom as well, she needed to find reasons for it. Specifically in turns 2, 9, 11, and 17 she implicitly tried to elicit what reasons Aldrin had for his initial claim (turn 1). On the other hand, while doing so she realised that she was assessing the inferential interconnections Aldrin brought forward using her own middle-class mathematics teacher "accent," such as, for example, when she claimed not to have understood what Aldrin meant in turns 9 and 17.

When Ulrika asked the students for reasons for their statements, in order to grasp them, her assessment of the claims shaped what was included in the concept map. This resulted in Ulrika acting in a way that was quite the opposite of her aspiration of allowing the students to disrupt and trouble stereotyped images about mathematics and society and to let complexity and plurality emerge. Hence, teachers' good intentions concerning students' diverse "accents" or personal ways of knowing and talking about mathematics (Radford, 2012) and society appears to be a complex matter. However, students' interruptions in solidarity with one another, such as Darko's overbridging actions, can underpin these good intentions.

5.1 Students' Derived Inferences from "Mathematics Is Bad for Society"

In this section, we show how four students discerned what could follow implicitly from the statement "Mathematics is bad for society" to articulate critical aspects of mathematics as a power distributor in society.
- *Felix's claim:* Felix said "Man kan ha programmerat fel på trafikljusen så att det blir (OHÖRBART) krsch" ["Someone could have made a coding mistake with the traffic lights so it gets (UNINTELLIGIBLE) krsch"]. Felix used

EPISODE 1   Overbridging different "accents"

1	Aldrin:	Ja ett tal med ett tal det är lika med någonting. Det är matematik.	Yes one number together with another number equals something. That is mathematics.
2	Ulrika:	Räknesätt menar du?	An operation of arithmetic you mean?
3	Darko [INTERRUPTS]:	Ja det är ekvationer.	Yes it is equations.
4	Aldrin:	Räknesätt är ju plus minus och sådant.	Operations of arithmetic are plus and minus and such stuff.
5	Ulrika:	Ja, det var det du menade?	Yes is that what you meant?
6	Aldrin:	Att man tar ett tal och ett annat tal ... ja typ som ett räknesätt	That you take one number and another number ... yes well kind of like operations.
7	Ulrika:	Eller är det inte det du menar?	Or is that not what you meant?
8	Aldrin [hesitant]:	Ja ...	Yes ...
9	Ulrika:	Nu förstår jag inte riktigt vad du menar.	Now I do not quite understand what you mean.
11	Ulrika [to Aldrin]:	Du löser uppgifter ...?	You do assignments ...?
12	Aldrin:	Det är som det ...	It is that which it ...
13	Darko:	Problemlösning	Problem-solving
14	Aldrin:	Det som ... (OHÖRBART)	That which ... (UNINTELLIGIBLE)
15	Ulrika:	Var det det du menade?	Is that what you meant?
16	Aldrin:	Typ	Kind of
17	Ulrika:	Typ fast inte riktigt. Det är jag som inte fattar vad du menar. Säg en gång till så ska jag försöka se om jag förstår hur du menar.	Kind of but not quite. It is I who do not get what you mean. Say it once more and I will try to see if I can get what you mean.
18	Aldrin:	Typ att man tar ett tal med ett annat tal så lägger man ihop det och så ...	Kind of that you take one number and add it to another number and then ...
19	Ulrika:	Alltså *att* det finns tal som man kan använda och lägga ihop och så?	That there *are* numbers which we can use and add and so on?
20	Aldrin:	Ja!	Yes!

inferential interconnections, conceptualised as humans in action driving cars, and mathematics as actions materialised as coding located in physical objects i.e. traffic lights. In making these interconnections, Felix showed an awareness of the mathematical algorithms operating behind the switching traffic lights. Algorithms are designed by constructors who intentionally command the traffic and, therefore, hold power over people's lives. Thus, Felix made inferential interconnections between the statement "Mathematics is bad for society" and critical aspects of black boxed mathematics (Gellert & Jablonka, 2009).

- *Edin's claim:* Edin said "Man kan räkna ut något fel och då kan det bli dåligt för samhället" ["You can make a calculus mistake and then it can be bad for society"]. As premises for his claim, Edin used inferences interconnected to humans as social beings whose actions affect each other. Mathematics in his claim is related to systems of thought, such as calculus.
- *Elsa's claim:* Elsa said "på sjukhusen finns maskiner och om de blir felprogrammerade då så kanske de gör något som är farligt för människorna eller typ skadar dem" ["At the hospitals there are machines and if they get wrongly programmed they might do something which is hazardous to people or kind of hurt them"]. We interpret Elsa's claim as meaning that erroneous input data ("wrongly programmed") put into the hospital machines by operators that causes the harm, and not the algorithms themselves (as in the case with the traffic light). Elsa recognised that operators put information into machines and from that information, the machine "makes decisions." Thus, there is human action on two levels (constructors and operators) involved in the decisions of the machines. Elsa used inferences interconnected to society as physical places (hospitals) and human actions (giving care). She related mathematics as inferentially located in physical objects (machines) and conceptual constructs (data to be put into the machines).
- *Aldrin's claim:* Aldrin said, "Jag tänker så här att om man kör bil och sen så 20 (OHÖRBART) 20 på den där vägen och så får man köra 70 då måste man kunna matte" [I think like this that if you drive a car and then 20 (UNINTELLIGIBLE) 20 on that road the speed limit is 20 and you may drive 70 you need to know maths"]. Aldrin's claim places mathematics inferentially interconnected to regulatory power that shapes citizen behaviour. He recognised that mathematics is "useful" for conforming to the speed limit. Mathematics is helpful to regulate ourselves within societal norms and rules. Precisely how his claim is given as a reason for "mathematics being bad for society" is unclear. Perhaps he would prefer no speed limits. If so, his claim could be interpreted as an objection to the regulatory powers of mathematics. He inferentially interconnected mathematics to conceptual constructs related to time and distance or, in other words, speed.

Our analysis reveals how students provided reasons for why "mathematics is bad for society" by articulating inferential interconnections which showed how mathematics acts and is made to act in society. For instance, in Felix's and Aldrin's claims, mathematics operates as a regulating power in people's lives. In Edin's and Elsa's claims, mathematics was made to act when hospital employees use machines or when calculus is used in general. Edin's and Elsa's claims also showed that mathematics in society can distribute responsibility. It was implicit in Elsa's claim that hospital machines make decisions rather than humans, and hence that the machines will be held responsible in case of an accident. Edin's claim showed that humans rely on mathematics to tell the "truth"; that is, unless a calculus mistake has been made. In Edin's case, mathematics was a trusted "truth" teller (who is responsible) when things go right. Should things go wrong, i.e. should mathematics not tell the "truth," then it is a human calculator who is responsible for the "mistake."

The students used their own observations of the world to reason about mathematics in society, in contrast to teachers providing students with *their* observations of the world for the students to reason about. We argue that critical mathematics education not only means that students discuss social issues formulated as mathematical problems or approach these issues mathematically with the help of their teachers (see for example, Andersson, 2011; Barwell, 2013; Frankenstein, 1990; Gutstein, 2006, 2016). We think that critical mathematics education also means providing classroom activities where students put to the fore their own observations about the world and reason about them as a matter of interconnecting them to knowledge on mathematics in action in society. Moreover, as shown in the students' claims discussed above, such activities provide opportunities for students to disrupt discourses in and about mathematics as a value-free functional tool. At the same time, such activities may highlight students' individual "accents," shaping and sharing ways of talking and thinking about critical aspects of mathematics in society.

6 Attempts to Play the GoGAR Well—Episode 2: Peers Struggling to Grasp Each Other's Claims

As the students started the group talks focusing on "society" in the statement "mathematics is bad for society," Samir, an emergent Swedish speaker, claimed, "I know what society is. It is my brother's school." None of the three other students in the group responded to Samir's claim or used their own claims. For a while, Samir was silent. Then he re-entered the group talk telling the other students that he does not understand what "society" is. Episode 2 shows how the group talk proceeded thereafter.

REASONING ABOUT MATHEMATICS AS PART OF SOCIETY

EPISODE 2   Samir and his peers struggling to grasp each other's claims

9	Samir:	Jag fattar inte vad samhälle är.	I don't get what society is
10	Darko	Samhälle det är Fältvidda ... det är ett samhälle ... samhälle är som en ort.	Society it is Fältvidda [the community where the school is located] ... that is a samhälle [in Swedish the same word, samhälle, is used both for society and community] ... samhälle is a place.
11	Greta:	Jag tycker att det är människorna runt omkring en som innebär ett samhälle.	I think that it is the people around you that means a society.
12	Alla/All	Ja, ja.	Yes, yes.
13	Samir:	Kan ni förklara för mig?	Can you explain to me?
14	Greta:	Samhälle det är alltså typ så här jag tänker att det är människorna runtomkring en som bildar ett samhälle som är en del av samhället.	Society it is kind of I picture it as the people around you together make a society which is part of the society.
15	Samir:	Jag tycker samhälle är en skola som min bror går.	I think that society is a school that my brother attends.
16	Greta:	Ok [SLÅR UT MED HÄNDERNA] Tror du att det där är samhälle?	Ok [PUTS HER HANDS OUT] Do you think that is society?
17	Darko:	[SKAKAR PÅ HUVUDET]	[SHAKES HIS HEAD]
18	Samir:	Det är gymnasiet.	It is upper secondary school.
19	Darko:	Solajmon [SLANG?] TYSTNAD	Solajmon [SLANG?] SILENCE
20	Oscar:	Ja men ja det Greta sa.	Yes, but yes that what Greta said.
21	Samir:	Vad sa du? [TITTAR PÅ GRETA]	What did you say? [LOOKING AT GRETA]
22	Greta:	Att människorna är ... [BLIR DISTRAHERAD AV DARKO]	That the people are ... [GETS DISTRACTED BY DARKO]
23	Samir:	Människorna är ...?	The people are ...?
24	Greta:	Det är människorna runt omkring en som bildar ett samhälle.	It is the people around you who form a society.
25	Samir:	Jag fattar inte.	I don't get it.
26	Darko:	Samir Samir du ser de husen där borta?	Samir Samir do you see the houses over there?
27	Samir:	Jepp, jepp.	Yeah, yeah.
28	Darko:	Det är samhället ... Fältvidda är ett samhälle.	That is society/community ... Fältvidda is a society/community
29	Greta:	För det är människor i Fältvidda så bildar de ett samhälle.	Because there are people in Fältvidda they form a society.
30	Samir:	Fältvidda är ett samhälle. [HOPPAR SITTANDE UPP OCH NER PÅ SIN STOL]	Fältvidda is a society. [JUMPS UP AND DOWN IN HIS CHAIR]

We find in this episode an attempt to play the GoGAR well, so that Samir and his peers can discern what follows implicitly from each other's claims in order to grasp them.

In lines 9, 13, 21, 23, and 25, Samir urged his classmates to give reasons for their claims and in lines 10, 11, 14, 24, 26, and 28 they try to do so. The problem is that they did not manage to use Samir's claim about his brother's school as premises or conclusions in their own claims and vice versa. Samir's claim is inferentially related to the upper secondary programme that Samir's brother attends, which is called "Samhällsprogrammet" [Social science programme]. Literally, this translates as "Society programme," which is how Samir attempted to inferentially interconnect his brother's school programme with his peers' claims about "society." However, the other group members did not find it appropriate to make inferential interconnections between somebody's school programme and what can be inferred from "society," according to their previously played GoGARs. Samir, on the other hand, does not appear to assess the other group members' claims as appropriate. In line 30, Samir said "Fältvidda is a society" which could indicate that he had assessed Darko's claims in lines 10 and 28 as appropriate. However, Samir jumps up and down in his chair uttering the words in a chanting style, indicating that he is simply repeating Darko's words.

The missing inferential interconnections, the inferences from claims in lines 10, 11, 14, 24, 26, and 28 to Samir's claim about his brother's school were not made explicit. This meant that the group was unable to provide Samir with inferential interconnections which would have been useful for him in order to position his own, and his peers' claims as interconnected to each other and vice versa. For the students to play the GoGAR well, in this case to make explicit the interconnections between society and the upper secondary school programme "Samhällsprogrammet" [Social science programme] someone who can make the interconnection needs to enter the conversation. Such a GoGAR player could provide the missing inference to overbridge Darko and Greta's claims about what society is with Samir's claims about his brother's school. In the previous episode, Darko's "accent" comprised the inferences needed to overbridge Aldrin's and Ulrika's claims. In this episode, such an "accent" is missing, which could be a reason for the unsuccessful outcome of the GoGAR.

7 Attempts to Play the GoGAR Well—Episode 3: A Peer Gives Reasons for an Emergent Swedish-Speaker's Claim

In line with the notion of explorative talk (Mercer et al., 2004), Ulrika invited the students to challenge each other's claims. Samir disagreed with a peer who

EPISODE 3 Samir makes a claim and gets entitlements to it through support from a peer

1	Ulrika:	Jag frågar om det är någon som vill protestera jag frågar vad ni tycker.	I ask you if somebody would like to object I ask what you think.
2	Samir:	Det här som vi sa jag tycker inte att alls det är så.	This what we said. I do not think that is how it is.
3	Darko:	Affär för där har man ju en dator som räknar ut åt en man räknar ju ut på en dator man scannar ju så får man talet där så plussar man så så har man ju en dator som räknar ut det istället	Shops, because there you have a computer that counts for you. You count on the computer. You scan and you get the number and you add so so you have a computer to do that for you instead.
4	Ulrika:	Och då är det inte matematik menar du eller?	And then that is not mathematics you mean?
5	Darko:	Ja.	Yes.

claimed that cashiers who operate tills use mathematics. Darko, sitting next to Samir in the classroom, entered the whole-class talk right after Samir's objection. In the video recording, it is possible to hear the two of them engaging quietly in an intense conversation right before Samir makes his objection. What they say is unfortunately inaudible in the recording. It is likely that they were discussing reasons for Samir's objection.

Darko, who knew more Swedish than Samir, immediately gave reasons for Samir's claim using previously articulated inferential interconnections between mathematics and shops and computers. While doing so, Darko acted as a carrier of reasons for Samir's claim and as such he made it possible for Samir to provide good reasons for his initial claim. If Darko had refrained from giving reasons for Samir's claim, it could have been questioned and Samir would have risked not being able to give good reasons for it (in Swedish). Furthermore, the GoGAR would not have been played well, since the inferential interconnections revealed by Samir would have been left unarticulated. As it turned out, Samir's claim, the reasons for which were articulated by Darko, was questioned by other students. As a result, even more reasons for it were given, and additional inferential interconnections between Samir's and other students' claims were discerned.

In this episode, students discerned conflicting reasons for locating mathematics either in people's head or in machines. Finally, they were able to discern good reasons for claiming both locations. The analysis shows attempts to play the GoGAR well when a peer acted as a carrier of reasons, which to some extent overbridged the skewed access to language caused by the "Swedish only" discourse (Norén, 2010; Norén & Andersson, 2016; Skog & Andersson, 2014).

8 Closing Remarks

Of course, the small-scale project analysed in this chapter does not equip the students with all means necessary to fully establish the interconnections between knowledge bases that Gutstein (2016) discusses. However, we find that it did allow the students to see mathematics and society as interconnected and to grasp the political role of mathematics in society, i.e. to be critically mathematical literate. If students cannot see mathematics and society as interconnected, teachers' efforts to engage students with critical mathematics activities risk becoming just another mathematics assignment to students. For the students in Arvid's classroom to make inferences connecting mathematics and society, they had not only to unpack implicit meanings of mathematics in society, but also to make displacements from prevailing discourses about mathematics as being neutral or beneficial in society towards disturbing these same discourses. It requires courage, confidence, and language proficiency to articulate and unpack such ideas—a complex challenge, particularly in a language diverse classroom. In our study, Darko appeared to be aware of this challenge as he displayed a meta-understanding of language diversity and acted accordingly, by for instance, overbridging Ulrika's and Aldrin's "accents" and by giving reasons for Samir's claim.

As students and teachers grapple with unpacking critical aspects of mathematics in society in a language diverse but monolingual classroom, their reciprocal assessment of claims based on their "accents" of knowing and talking about mathematics and society shape both their actions and the outcome of their efforts. Hence, the critical aspects of mathematics in society that come to the fore in a language diverse mathematics classroom are intertwined with students' and teachers' (lack of) meta-understanding of language diversity and attempts to make their ideas explicit in order to put forward and grasp each other's claims. As normative assessments guide the outcome of these attempts, power is present in the reasoning. In other words, the semantic *whats* are dialectically entangled with the social, power-related *hows* in the complexity of addressing and enhancing critical mathematical literacy in a language diverse yet monolingual classroom. Further research to address this complexity is needed in order to deepen and widen the understanding of how critical mathematical literacy can be established in classrooms like Arvid's.

Notes

1. A version of this chapter appears in Ulrika Ryan's doctoral dissertation (Ryan, 2019).
2. In this chapter we use the word "acknowledge" with its colloquial meaning.

3   The lessons were video recorded using a Lessonbox©, i.e. a set of three cameras and three microphones. Unfortunately, one of the Lessonbox© cameras did not function. Therefore, a handheld camera was used in addition.
4   For ethical reasons school location and students' names in the chapter are pseudonyms.

References

Andersson, A. (2011). A "curling teacher" in mathematics education: Teacher identities and pedagogy development. *Mathematics Education Research Journal, 23*(4), 437–454. https://doi.org/10.1007/s13394-011-0025-0

Andersson, A., & Wagner, D. (2017). Numbers for truth and reconciliation: Mathematical choices in ethically rich texts. *Journal of Mathematics and Culture, 11*(3), 18–35.

Barwell, R. (2013). The mathematical formatting of climate change: Critical mathematics education and post-normal science. *Research in Mathematics Education, 15*(1), 1–16. https://doi.org/10.1080/14794802.2012.756633

Brandom, R. B. (1998). *Making it explicit: Reasoning, representing, and discursive commitment*. Harvard University Press.

Brandom, R. B. (2001). *Articulating reasons: An introduction to inferentialism*. Harvard University Press.

Bransen, J. (2002). Normativity as the key to objectivity: An exploration of Robert Brandom's articulating reasons. *Inquiry, 45*(3), 373–391. https://doi.org/10.1080/002017402760258204

Chronaki, A. (2010). Revisiting mathemacy: A process-reading of critical mathematics education. In H. Alrø, O. Ravn, & P. Valero (Eds.), *Critical mathematics education: Past, present and future* (pp. 31–49). Sense. https://doi.org/10.1163/9789460911644_005

Chronaki, A., Moutzouri, G., & Magos, K. (2015). "Number in cultures" as a playful outdoor activity: Making space for critical mathematics education in the early years. In U. Gellert, J. Giménez Rodríguez, C. Hahn, & S. Kafoussi (Eds.), *Educational paths to mathematics: A C.I.E.A.E.M. Sourcebook* (pp. 143–159). Springer. https://doi.org/10.1007/978-3-319-15410-7_8

Derry, J. (2013). Can inferentialism contribute to social epistemology? *Journal of Philosophy of Education, 47*(2), 222–235. https://doi.org/10.1111/1467-9752.12032

Frankenstein, M. (1983). Critical mathematics education: An application of Paulo Freire's epistemology. *Journal of Education, 165*(4), 315–339. https://doi.org/10.1177/002205748316500403

Frankenstein, M. (1990). Incorporating race, gender, and class issues into a critical mathematical literacy curriculum. *The Journal of Negro Education, 59*(3), 336–347. https://doi.org/10.2307/2295568

Frankenstein, M. (2014). A different third R: Radical math. *Radical Teacher, 100*, 77–82. https://doi.org/10.5195/rt.2014.160

Gellert, U., & Jablonka, E. (2009). The demathematising effect of technology: Calling for critical competence. In P. Ernest, B. Greer, & B. Sriraman (Eds.), *Critical issues in mathematics education* (pp. 19–24). Information Age.

González, N., Andrade, R., Civil, M., & Moll, L. (2001). Bridging funds of distributed knowledge: Creating zones of practice in mathematics. *Journal of Education of Students Placed at Risk, 6*(1–2), 115–132. https://doi.org/10.1207/S15327671ESPR0601-2_7

Gutstein, E. (2006). *Reading and writing the world with mathematics: Toward a pedagogy for social justice.* Routledge. https://doi.org/10.4324/9780203112946

Gutstein, E. (2016). "Our issues, our people—Math as our weapon": Critical mathematics in a Chicago neighborhood high school. *Journal for Research in Mathematics Education, 47*(5), 454–504. https://doi.org/10.5951/jresematheduc.47.5.0454

Hauge, K. H., & Barwell, R. (2017). Post-normal science and mathematics education in uncertain times: Educating future citizens for extended peer communities. *Futures, 91*, 25–34. https://doi.org/10.1016/j.futures.2016.11.013

Hufferd-Ackles, K., Fuson, K. C., & Sherin, M. G. (2004). Describing levels and components of a math-talk learning community. *Journal for Research in Mathematics Education, 35*(2), 81–116. https://doi.org/10.2307/30034933

Jablonka, E. (2003). Mathematical Literacy. In A. J. Bishop, M. A. Clements, C. Keitel, J. Kilpatrick, & F. K. S. Leung (Eds.), *Second international handbook of mathematics education* (pp. 75–102). Springer. https://doi.org/10.1007/978-94-010-0273-8_4

Kollosche, D. (2014). Mathematics and power: An alliance in the foundations of mathematics and its teaching. *ZDM Mathematics Education, 46*(7), 1061–1072. https://doi.org/10.1007/s11858-014-0584-0

Mercer, N., Dawes, L., Wegerif, R., & Sams, C. (2004). Reasoning as a scientist: Ways of helping children to use language to learn science. *British Educational Research Journal, 30*(3), 359–377. https://doi.org/10.1080/01411920410001689689

Norén, E. (2010). *Flerspråkiga matematikklassrum: Diskurser i grundskolans matematikundervisning* [*Multilingual mathematics classrooms: Discourses in compulsory school in Sweden*] (Doctoral dissertation). Stockholms universitet.

Norén, E., & Andersson, A. (2016). Multilingual students' agency in mathematics classrooms. In A. Halai & P. Clarkson (Eds.), *Teaching and learning mathematics in multilingual classrooms: Issues for policy, practice and teacher education* (pp. 109–124). Sense. https://doi.org/10.1007/978-94-6300-229-5_8

Radford, L. (2012). Commentary on the chapter by Richard Barwell, "Heteroglossia in multilingual mathematics classrooms." In H. Forgasz & F. Rivera (Eds.), *Towards equity in mathematics education: Advances in mathematics education* (pp. 339–342). Springer. https://doi.org/10.1007/978-3-642-27702-3_30

Ryan, U. (2019). *Mathematics classroom talk in a migrating world: Synthesizing epistemological dimensions* (Doctoral dissertation). Malmö University.

Schindler, M., Hußmann, S., Nilsson, P., & Bakker, A. (2017). Sixth-grade students' reasoning on the order relation of integers as influenced by prior experience: An inferentialist analysis. *Mathematics Education Research Journal, 29*(4), 471–492. https://doi.org/10.1007/s13394-017-0202-x

Skog, K., & Andersson, A. (2014). Exploring positioning as an analytical tool for understanding becoming mathematics teachers' identities. *Mathematics Education Research Journal, 27*(1), 65–82. https://doi.org/10.1007/s13394-014-0124-9

Skovsmose, O. (1994). *Towards a philosophy of critical mathematics education*. Kluwer.

Skovsmose, O. (2007). Mathematical literacy and globalisation. In B. Atweh, A. C. Barton, M. C. Borba, N. Gough, C. Keitel, C. Vistro-Yu, & R. Vithal (Eds.), *Internationalisation and globalisation in mathematics and science education* (pp. 3–18). Springer. https://doi.org/10.1007/978-1-4020-5908-7_1

Skovsmose, O., & Borba, M. (2004). Research methodology and critical mathematics education. In P. Valero & R. Zevenbergen (Eds.), *Researching the socio-political dimensions of mathematics education: Issues of power in theory and methodology* (pp. 207–226). Kluwer. https://doi.org/10.1007/1-4020-7914-1_17

CHAPTER 8

A Critical Mathematics Education for Climate Change

A Post-Normal Approach

Richard Barwell and Kjellrun Hiis Hauge

Abstract

Climate change is an urgent global challenge. Responding to climate change requires significant critical mathematical understanding on the part of all citizens. In this chapter, we consider what a critical mathematics education for climate change might look like. We draw on ideas from Skovsmose's work, including the notion of formatting, as well as the body of work known as post-normal science. As a starting point for pedagogical reflection, we propose twelve principles, operating within landscapes of investigation, and organised into three groups relating to: forms of authenticity; forms of participation; and reflection on and with mathematics. We illustrate these ideas with an example of a possible landscape of investigation relating to historical temperature change.

Keywords

critical mathematics education – post-normal science – climate change – formatting – landscape of investigation

∙ ∙ ∙

In January 2019, Greta Thunberg, then a 16-year-old school student from Sweden, addressed the World Economic Forum in Davos, Switzerland. She told the assembled leaders of industry, nations, and billionaires, "I want you to panic." Her speech[1] made headlines around the world. She was speaking about climate change:

> Either we prevent 1.5°C of warming or we don't. Either we avoid setting off that irreversible chain reaction beyond human control or we don't. Either we choose to go on as a civilisation or we don't. That is as black or white as it gets. There are no grey areas when it comes to survival.

The moral force of her speech was one of the reasons it went round the world. She challenged powerful people for thinking too much about money and growth, and not enough about survival. She challenged them to act. Her speech and the crisis that prompted it raise many questions. What should we, as mathematics educators, be doing about this crisis? How can we prepare today's young people to act? How can we ensure that citizens understand supposedly simple ideas like "1.5°C of warming" or a carbon budget?

Critical mathematics education research has mostly focused on questions of social justice, with little attention to questions of environmental sustainability, such as the threat of climate change.[2] Our planet faces an array of complex, challenging environmental problems, including mass extinctions, pollution, habitat loss, and climate change. Moreover, mathematics plays a key role, both in understanding such problems *and* in making possible the technologies that contribute to them (Barwell, 2018). Critical mathematics education, in combination with a perspective on complex environmental problems called postnormal science (see below), offers a valuable framework with which to think about the role of mathematics and of mathematics education in response to these problems (Hauge & Barwell, 2017). In particular, we have worked on the question of how mathematics educators can prepare teachers to educate future citizens to participate in the democratic debates these problems will engender. In this chapter, we focus on the specific issue of climate change. Our purpose is to explore what this theoretical work might mean for mathematics classroom practice. To do so, we first review some of the relevant context in relation to climate change and, in the next section, summarise some key theoretical ideas. We then propose a set of principles derived from our theoretical position and designed to inform classroom practice. Our aim is to prompt more thinking on what a mathematics pedagogy for the climate might look like. The principles we propose are therefore offered as a starting point, which we illustrate with an example of a possible activity.

1 Our Changing Climate

Climate change is undoubtedly one of the most serious problems faced by humans, since it is likely to radically modify our planetary weather systems and ecosystem in possibly dangerous ways. There is strong evidence that the emission of greenhouse gases like carbon dioxide and methane, largely as a result of human activity, is affecting the equilibrium of the climate system (Intergovernmental Panel on Climate Change [IPCC], 2018). Hence, the atmosphere, the oceans, and the cryosphere (glaciers and polar ice caps) are becoming warmer. This warming affects weather patterns in unpredictable ways, with consequential impacts on a wide range of ecosystems, as well as on humans. Documented effects include changes in the spread of insect-borne diseases, increased drought or flooding, increased intensity of hurricanes, increases in damage caused by forest fires, reduced polar ice cover, migration of species towards the poles, coral bleaching, to name just a few (IPCC, 2018). In 1980, the United Nations created the Intergovernmental Panel on Climate Change (IPCC) to review the known science on this topic and produce regular reports. The most recent report concluded:

> Human activities are estimated to have caused approximately 1.0°C of global warming above pre-industrial levels, with a likely range of 0.8°C to 1.2°C. Global warming is likely to reach 1.5°C between 2030 and 2052 if it continues to increase at the current rate. (IPCC, 2018, p. 6)

The reference to 1.5°C is significant: in December 2015, governments from around the world signed the Paris Agreement, committing themselves to take steps to limit warming to this amount.[3]

Climate change is a complex scientific problem, but addressing climate change also leads to many social and political tensions. For example, the most straightforward measure to minimise climate change would be to immediately halt the extraction of fossil fuels, as well as their consumption in transportation, power generation, and other large-scale processes. Unfortunately, of course, such a measure would drastically affect the way of life of most people on the planet. As Greta Thunberg pointed out, there are many reasons relating to money and growth why such measures are difficult to put in place. Deciding what to do about climate change has therefore become a highly politicised issue, involving multiple lobbying groups, some overt, others covert, all attempting to influence national and international policies. Climate change is increasingly an issue in elections, and its impacts can destabilise societies (e.g., through drought or crop failures) around the world. Tackling climate change has therefore become a space of fierce debate, where sceptical voices have a presence out of proportion with their number. Media outlets give space to sceptics, often in an effort to be "fair and balanced," despite overwhelming scientific consensus on the nature and causes of climate change, and the increasing acceptance of the population at large in many countries. In an era of fake news, however, it can sometimes be difficult to know whom to believe.

The role of mathematics in all of this is substantial. Mathematics is involved in describing, predicting, and communicating climate change (Barwell, 2013). It is used as a tool to describe and understand the changes that are happening, as well as the nature of the climate system. Mathematics is used to develop powerful models to make predictions about the future evolution of the climate globally, regionally, and increasingly, locally. Mathematics is also used to communicate the nature and impacts of climate change among scientists, as well as for policymakers, politicians, the media, and the general public. Mathematics, then, is important for the scientists researching climate change, but it is also important for the people developing plans to reduce the severity of future climate change and to mitigate its effects. Mathematics is also important for citizens engaging with the debates about climate change. The claims of many climate sceptics, for example, draw on mathematical arguments. Citizens need a critical awareness of how mathematics is used in arguments in order to develop an informed understanding of the issues, make reasoned decisions, and participate in democratic debate. They also need an informed understanding of how mathematics cannot provide precise assessments or solutions because of uncertainty inherent in such complex situations. Finally, citizens need an awareness of the (often overlooked) role of values in relation to the mathematics and science of climate change. In the next section, we develop these points, drawing on ideas from critical mathematics education and post-normal science.

2   Critical Mathematics Education and Post-Normal Science

In our previous work, we have developed the position that for mathematics education to adequately address issues like climate change, ideas from critical mathematics education need to be supplemented with a theorisation of the nature of science and its role in society in the context of complex environmental problems (see Barwell, 2013; Hauge & Barwell, 2017). For this latter theorisation, we draw on the philosophy of post-normal science (Funtowicz & Ravetz, 1993), which specifically conceptualises the nature of problems like climate change. It characterises such problems needing post-normal science in the search for solutions. This term indicates that such problems cannot be solved through "normal" science (in the sense of Thomas Kuhn) in which scientists choose a scientific problem that is solvable in accordance with peer-reviewed theories and methodologies. Normal science problems are usually clearly defined within closed systems, often with a high level of predictability. Post-normal situations, in contrast, have three important features: a high level of conflict, a high level of uncertainty, and a high level of urgent risks. These features are apparent in the case of climate change. The associated stakes are conflicting so that decisions on how to respond to climate change, or indecision, affect people around the world differently. The climate system and the evolution of climate change over time are complex, involving interactions throughout the planetary ecosystem. The effects of greenhouse gas emissions, for example, are not restricted to the location of the emissions: they can contribute to changes in oceans, polar ice caps, or rainfall many thousands of miles from their source. This means there is also a high degree of uncertainty: a perfect description of the climate system is impossible, there are many factors that science does not include, and the multiple interactions of the system mean that future states cannot be predicted with certainty. The IPCC reports (e.g., 2018, p. 8), for example, present a range of scenarios with associated probabilities, rather than a specific prediction for future climate change. Finally, climate change involves a high degree of risk if no action is taken or whatever course of action is taken. Business as usual is expected to lead to catastrophic climate change impacts, but the proposed interventions may also have unforeseen consequences on the ecosystem or on human society or both.

A central feature of post-normal situations is the importance of values. Deciding which measures to take in the light of climate change is not simply a question of (normal) science. Climate change is too closely interwoven with human society and its collective and individual choices. To give one example, climate change is reducing the summer extent of arctic sea ice, meaning that commercial shipping and oil exploration are becoming possible in the arctic ocean (IPCC, 2018). Whether to exploit these opportunities is not really a scientific question: such decisions depend on values, such as the relative importance we ascribe to protecting the arctic wilderness versus exploiting new economic opportunities. There is no purely scientific way to make this choice.

From the perspective of post-normal science, these features of post-normal situations mean that citizens need to be more involved in the scientific process. If the problem is completely interwoven with human society, then the weighing of evidence and the development of responses must involve members of society beyond the scientific community. Funtowicz and Ravetz (1993) refer to this idea as an "extended peer community," to allow for the values dimension of problems like climate change to be debated and discussed, in the light of values, complexity, uncertainty, and risk. More broadly, citizens need to be involved in the political debates around proposed measures, many of which will have a direct impact (not always negative) on their lives.

Given the strong mathematical component in climate science and all of the associated debates, if citizens are to participate in the extended peer community, we must ask what kind of preparation they need (Hauge & Barwell, 2017). In particular, what kind of mathematics education could prepare them to contribute to democratic processes around climate change? To respond to this question, we draw on critical mathematics education and, specifically, on Skovsmose's concepts of formatting and realised abstraction. Formatting refers to the embedded role of mathematics in contemporary technologically mediated society. While mathematics is ubiquitous, particularly through the use of models and algorithms, its role is often invisible. The idea of formatting is that this human-designed mathematics has real social effects: our lives are organised by mathematics. This mathematics makes possible activities that risk exacerbating climate change. For example, consumer society is organised by mathematical systems that make possible a highly internationalised process of production and delivery, which results in cheaper mass-produced products, but with high levels of production-related and transport-related emissions.

Skovsmose refers to the way in which mathematics becomes part of social reality as *realised abstraction*. Mathematics, particularly in the process of modelling, is used to describe different aspects of reality. These descriptions, however, can become prescriptions, dictating how people should behave. Systems of taxation, for example, are based on economic models that describe flows of income and revenue within the economy and project government revenues according to whatever general principles a government considers as fair and wishes to implement. These mathematical models are realised abstractions: they have real effects in the lives of people. Climate change can also be thought of as a realised abstraction (Barwell, 2013). Our understanding of climate change is largely based on mathematical models, whether to provide broad descriptions of the changing climate or develop predictions of future changes. These models form the basis of government policy, commercial choices, and individual decisions. Climate models thus become part of social reality. Students, as future citizens, therefore need opportunities to develop a "reflective" knowing (Skovsmose, 1994) of the mathematics of climate change that includes awareness of the role of mathematics in causing climate change and in understanding climate change (Barwell, 2013).

In this section, we have summarised some key ideas with which we can think about mathematics education and climate change. Mathematics is a central part of climate science, and the debates about how to respond to climate change. As a post-normal situation, these debates need the wide involvement of citizens in various forms of democratic processes, including as contributors to an extended peer community connected with the science-policy process. These debates involve a range of values, and must address the complexity, uncertainty, and risks associated with climate change. Science alone cannot determine how to respond. For citizens to participate in these debates, they need to be able to engage at some level with the mathematics of climate science and they also need an understanding of the formatting role of mathematics in a technological society. The question now arises of what mathematics teaching for climate change (or for any post-normal situation) might look like. In the next section, we propose some principles to guide mathematics teaching in the context of climate change.

3 Mathematics Teaching and Climate Change

The following principles are derived from the theoretical ideas in the previous section and are informed by our earlier work developing mathematics classroom tasks (Coles et al., 2013; Hauge, 2016a; Hauge et al., 2015), classroom observations, and a survey of teachers in Norway and Canada (Abtahi et al., 2017). Our principles are organised into three groups: *forms of authenticity, forms of participation*, and *reflecting on and with mathematics*. We see these principles as a starting point for thinking about mathematics teaching in relation to climate change, rather than as a definitive set of empirically validated standards. How they are interpreted, applied, or modified will vary greatly from place to place and from one classroom to another. The principles are summarised in Table 8.1. For clarity, we present them as normative principles, setting out how, for us, based on our previous work, mathematics education for climate change could look. As such, we assume that they will be challenged and contested. Ultimately, our goal is to prompt the reader to consider what principles they would propose or adopt. Our principles are illustrated in the final section by an extended example.

3.1 *Forms of Authenticity*

We propose four principles relating to forms of authenticity. Post-normal situations such as climate change affect all our lives, but they can seem rather abstract or dispersed: as a realised abstraction, it is difficult for individuals to "see" climate change (which is one reason why mathematics is an important tool in understanding it). It is therefore important for students to engage with climate change authentically, so that they understand its concrete impact in their own current or future lives. Moreover, the development of reflective knowing in relation to climate change is likely to be more effective if students have a direct, authentic connection with the tasks and activities they encounter in the mathematics classroom.

The first principle relating to authenticity is to *use problems about climate change that students find relevant in their lives*. In many cases, relevant problems may be based on local climate concerns and issues, focusing on, for example, exploring changes in local climate, local greenhouse gas emissions, or local climate change impacts, such as on flooding, local biodiversity, or commercial interests. In other cases, however, students may identify problems arising from their own interests and engagement with related topics such as international development, human rights, business, or politics. An interest in animal welfare, for example, might lead to a focus on arctic ice cover in relation to projected extinction of polar bear populations. By working on relevant problems, students are more likely to perceive and consider the complexity of these problems (Appelbaum, 2009; English & Gainsburg, 2015; Kaiser & Schwarz, 2010).

Second, *students should work with real data* as much as possible. Real data, as opposed to made-up data, can be collected or generated by students through observation or surveys, or can be obtained from publicly available datasets. In many countries, for example, climate data is available online, and much other data can be located on greenhouse gas emissions and many other topics. One role of teachers, in relation to the use of real data, is to support students to access and filter the data: large online datasets may be unwieldy and teachers may need to make some initial selections or help students to make such selections. The use of real data can allow students to appreciate the often-messy nature of climate data or emissions data and discuss aspects of uncertainty, such as how to deal with missing data, changes in measurement protocols, or unmeasurable phenomena (e.g., English & Watson, 2018).

Third, *students' own ideas and values should have a central role*. Mathematics is a human activity, and investigating topics like climate change should enable students to understand the nature and effect of human mathematising. Students could, for example, discuss what data to collect or which variables to include in a model. They could also consider what important aspects of their problem are difficult to mathematise, such as psychological or aesthetic impacts. This kind of approach can provide some insight into the role of values in climate science and can lead to some awareness of how values shape the choices of others, such as politicians or scientists.

Fourth, *students should have the opportunity to engage in meaningful debate* relating to climate change, based on their mathematical investigations. We do not propose that teachers should impose a particular agenda about climate change, other than that it is a pressing global problem. Through thoughtful use of mathematics, students can develop a deeper, critical understanding of the issues and more clearly thought-out responses (Appelbaum, 2009; Hauge & Barwell, 2017).

An example of an activity that displays authenticity can be found in Coles et al. (2013). The activity, which is from the U.K. context, involves collecting publicly available data about flood risk and intersecting it with data about property values for the area in which students live. The activity involves important mathematics, notably about probability, the formal calculation of risk, as well as data handling. By focusing on the local contexts, questions and discussion are likely to be meaningful for students. The activity leads to questions about where to invest resources to mitigate climate change in relation to property values.

3.2 Forms of Participation

The second group of principles relates to forms of participation. These principles arise, in part, from the need to prepare students to contribute to extended peer communities. They therefore need to be exposed to the communication of mathematical ideas and the use of mathematics in debate and deliberation. These principles also relate to aspects of critical mathematics education that emphasise the importance of dialogue in the development of critical awareness.

The first principle is simply that *students should participate in mathematics*. We mean here that the role of students should be an active one, in which they do much more than solve problems provided by the teacher. Rather, they should be participants in the selection of problems, the mathematising of problems, the selection of data, the selection of mathematical tools, the construction of models, among other things. This principle is not, of course, specific to climate change, but is widely proposed in different forms in relation to a problem-solving approach to mathematics teaching (see, for example, Barbosa, 2007). Active participation in mathematics is a key principle that permits students to reflect on mathematics, as discussed in the final set of principles.

Second, *students should actively participate in their classrooms*. Participation in mathematics could be an individual activity, but we wish to emphasise the collective nature of classroom participation. Students may work together in small groups, share their work with classmates, discuss and critique each other's work, and reflect on each other's findings. If students are not familiar with this kind of group working, teachers may need to structure their participation in order to cultivate productive collaboration.

Third, *students should actively participate in their communities*. These communities could include their school, the communities in which they live, or mathematical communities. Investigating climate change is not simply an interesting context for learning mathematics: the results of students' work can inform many aspects of school life and that of the surrounding community, such as in relation to energy consumption, traffic patterns, or local political action. Students could collect data from community members, such as asking local elders about their experience of climate changes, or conducting a survey about recycling. The results of students' investigations could lead to presentations to local politicians or municipal representatives, letters to local newspapers or proposals to school leaders (for examples of community participation in mathematics teaching, see Appelbaum, 2009).

Fourth, *students should actively engage with and participate in public debate*. Public media, for example, can provide many starting points for mathematical activities, including television or newspaper reports, opinion pieces, blogs, and government statements and policies. Students can also present their findings as responses to positions noted in public debate, supporting, refuting, or critiquing different opinions. Again, this work could lead to communication with local or national politicians or newspapers.

The following example illustrates some of these forms of participation (although it does not directly concern climate change). The project concerned traffic safety and was conducted by a class of high school students in Norway (Hauge, 2016b; Hauge & Barwell, 2017). Close to the students' school, there was a stretch of road which the school bus passed every day, and where cars had driven off the road and into the sea. A person had died the year before the project. The road barriers had been too low to prevent these accidents. With protection from the police, the students measured traffic and the heights of the barriers. The local newspaper covered the story. The teacher's aim was to use statistical concepts found in the curriculum, and to show how mathematics can make a difference as a useful tool in argumentation. She developed and discussed the project together with her students. Through this project, the students participated to make sense of data, information, and arguments. They participated in discussion and debate within their student body, as members of the community, and they considered possible responses and contributions to a public debate. Two months after the data collection, the measured barriers had been replaced by new and taller ones.

In another project more closely connected to climate change, high school students were invited to discuss and debate the possibility of opening up the offshore area near their town to oil exploitation (Hauge & Barwell, 2017). The students were asked to provide argumentation based on their own opinions. After a session with related group tasks, they discussed oil exploitation in a plenary session. The debate reflected the complexity of the issue at hand and included consideration of economic opportunities, the development of their home town, and possible impacts on fish stocks, fisheries and tourism. Although the students disagreed on the matter, they explored each other's arguments with respect. This is an example that shows that controversial issues in classrooms can be fruitful as they may be engaging for students.

3.3 Reflecting on and with Mathematics

Our final set of four principles concerns reflecting on and with mathematics. These principles are particularly derived from the critical mathematics education idea that students need to understand the role of mathematics in shaping their society and their lives, as well as the role of mathematics in understanding problems like climate change. These principles also tackle the potential role of students in all forms of participation, and particularly in public debate, promoting the development of a critical awareness of how mathematics is used (or misused) to communicate information, advance positions, serve interests, and undermine opponents.

The first reflection principle is that *students should have opportunities to reflect on how mathematics is useful*. By working on authentic tasks and engaging in various forms of participation, students should develop some valuable sense of what mathematics can make possible. For example, mathematics can clarify an underlying warming trend in messy temperature data that would otherwise be difficult to observe, and certainly difficult to physically experience in many places. This principle is coupled with the second: that *students should have opportunities to reflect on the limits of mathematics*. Again, having worked on authentic tasks, students should have a sense of what mathematics cannot do. Mathematics cannot calculate what level of emissions is acceptable, since "acceptable" is a value-laden term. Mathematics cannot easily model emotions such as what it feels like when your house is flooded. Mathematics cannot easily model the significance of disappearance, such as the extinction of species of fish or insects that result from warming oceans or changes in seasons. Mathematics can, to some extent, model fish or insect populations, but it cannot capture the tragedy of extinction: the loss of a creature, of its place in an ecosystem, of its missing beauty (Barbosa, 2007; Barwell, 2018; Hauge & Barwell, 2017).

The third reflection principle is that *students should consider the role of values in mathematics*. In particular, students should think about how values shape their choice of project, their choice of data, and their interpretation of their findings. For example, in a project on climate impacts on local farms, some students might be motivated by economic considerations, such as loss of income for farmers, while others might be motivated by a concern for biodiversity. Their choice of which data to collect could be influenced by these motivations. The interpretations of their findings would emphasise their preferred interests and downplay other considerations. By engaging in participation in the classroom, and in the community, students would have the opportunity to reflect on how their mathematical activity is shaped by values relevant to the situation (see Pratt et al., 2011).

The final reflection principle is that *students should have opportunities to reflect on uncertainty* and consider different ways to deal with it. Through their authentic activities, students are likely to encounter various kinds of uncertainty, including an inherent level of imprecision in their data, the absence of some kinds of data, and the possibility of unrecognised factors influencing a situation. For some students, such discussions could be an opportunity to explore statistical techniques for managing imperfect data or evaluating different sorts of uncertainties (see Hauge & Barwell, 2017). For others, the discussion is a chance to understand the role of uncertainty in shaping thinking about climate change and the decisions that are made as a result of mathematical analyses.

TABLE 8.1   Principles for teaching mathematics in the context of climate change

Forms of authenticity
- relevant problems
- real data
- students' own ideas and values
- in classroom discussion

Forms of participation
- in mathematics
- in classrooms
- in community
- in public debate

Reflecting on and with mathematics
- on how mathematics is useful
- on limits of mathematics
- on values of mathematics
- on uncertainty

In the rest of this chapter, we exemplify the principles we have proposed through an example of a possible mathematics classroom project. We see the project as offering a "landscape of investigation" (Skovsmose, 2011) in which students can explore climate-related topics and related mathematics. Skovsmose (2011) defines a landscape of investigation as an activity where students explore mathematical characteristics through asking questions such as "What if …?" The teacher invites the students into the landscape, but in order to call it a landscape of investigation, the invitation must be accepted. This means that the task is open in the sense that exploring can take students in different directions, where there might be no correct or wrong answers, and where the landscape is appealing to the students so that they wish to explore it through posing their own "what if" questions. Some aspects of our approach are also similar to Appelbaum's (2009) notion of "taking action," in which explorations akin to a landscape of exploration extend into engagement with real-world, community-based problems. The traffic survey is a good example of taking action. The project involved a degree of student direction and their work was taken up in their community.

In adopting this kind of approach, it is clear that we have made some assumptions about the role of learners and teachers in this process. We assume, for example, that at some level, students are concerned about environmental sustainability. While we know many students have these concerns, we realise not all students will see the relevance. Indeed, we do not wish to impose a particular environmental ideology on students through mathematics teaching. We see the idea of a landscape of investigation as helpful in addressing this implicit tension. The metaphor of exploring a landscape suggests that teaching should follow students' interests, rather than dictating the direction of the work. This position in turn assumes particular demands on the teacher: to be open to students' interests and willing to follow and support them. In the example about oil exploration, for instance, students' level of participation varied, with some more actively engaged than others. Not all students were motivated by environmental considerations; some were more concerned about the jobs and economic development that they assumed oil extraction would bring. The point is, the exploration of a particular landscape allowed for an exploration of different ideas and perspectives. In the following, we sketch a task that may develop into a landscape of investigation.

4 Investigation: What Was the Temperature on Your Birthday?

In many countries, extensive historical weather data is available online. In Norway, for example, the Norwegian Broadcasting Corporation together with the Norwegian Meteorological Institute keeps track of weather data, which is accessible online for anyone.[4] In one online service, you can choose a certain date in a certain year and check what the weather was at a chosen place in Norway. For a few cities, the measurements go back to 1902, but there are still data for the weather further back in time. The data provided, depending on how far back in time it goes, consist of temperature, wind strength, and a symbol showing whether it was a rainy or sunny day. Similar datasets are available in the other countries, including the United Kingdom, Canada, the United States, and Australia. In some cases, schools might even have their own datasets.

The premise of this investigation is that students look up temperature data (or other weather data) on the date of their birth, and in the location of their birth (or their current place of residence), for each year of their life, and going back in time. Depending on the age of the students, support may be needed to access and extract the relevant data. A balance needs to be struck between providing a "clean" dataset and struggling with complex, messy databases. In many cases, extracted data may contain gaps or corrections, such as when, for example, measuring equipment is upgraded. It is important for students to consider how to deal with such situations.

Having extracted the data, students should consider how to explore it. Calculating averages and making a graph of temperatures over time are obvious possibilities. These are tasks in which students can work with real data, and with individual time series, including all their flaws. Students can discuss what temperature data to include in a graph: the mean temperature, the temperature at a certain time of the day, or other. Similarly, students can consider and discuss whether to work with averages such as mean daily temperature, mean decadal temperature, or mean temperature anomalies. The aim of such activities is to discuss global warming and consider whether there is a trend towards warmer temperatures. The students' graphs will not all be the same, and each graph is likely to show significant variation. With young students, it may be sufficient to draw on their experiences to discuss variation in weather, what influences the weather, what a trend is, and the difference between weather and climate. Older students can develop moving averages, where they can explore what happens when they exchange data points with averages of three, four, or more data points, to see what it reveals with respect to possible trends. In addition, students can use software to produce linear regressions. Students can also explore questions about how the temperature on their birthday may evolve in future years.

Will students' data and analyses demonstrate the occurrence of global warming? This question can initiate a discussion that covers all four elements of reflecting on and with mathematics. Students can reflect on the usefulness of the data and the ways that mathematics was applied to show various pictures of how the temperature has changed over time. At the same time, students can reflect on the ways in which mathematics does not provide clear answers. Uncertainty is apparent, both in the form of natural variation and lack of knowledge, which may involve indeterminate aspects in the data or in mathematics. How to deal with such uncertainties is a key question in policymaking. Students could go on to explore the 1.5°C target set out in the Paris Agreement by searching for information online. In light of their investigations into the temperatures on their birthdays (see Figures 8.1 and 8.2), students

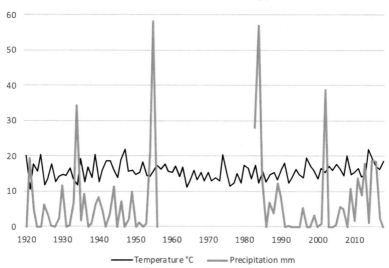

FIGURE 8.1   Temperature and rain in Bergen, Norway, August 31st since 1920 (www.yr.no). Relevant topics to explore include: Describe the weather illustrated in the graph. The temperature is taken at alternately 1 and 2 a.m. Do you think this matters? What do you think the graph looks like in the years where rain was not measured? What is the difference between climate and weather? Does the graph show that the climate has changed over time? What other data could give better information on climate change?

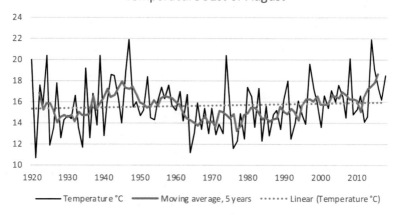

FIGURE 8.2   Temperature in Bergen, Norway, August 31st since 1920 (www.yr.no) together with moving average of 5 years and a linear regression. Relevant topics to explore include: Describe the trends in temperature over the years. How do you perceive this presentation compared to Figure 8.1? Does the graph show that the climate has changed over time? What other data could give better information on climate change?

could discuss how one might know whether the target is reached. Indeed, students can reflect on what it means to reach this threshold – does it refer to temperature on one day, in one year, or in one decade? This issue is also an opportunity to discuss whether mathematics is an objective enterprise or whether values can be hidden in mathematics or promoted through mathematics.

Our proposed investigation is a potential starting point for a more developed landscape of investigation. Having completed the initial opening tasks we have suggested, students can be prompted to generate questions for further investigation individually or in groups. For example, students might: compare temperature trends on the birthdays of two or more students; investigate how temperatures have changed or not further back in time; discuss the quality of older data; explore other data, such as for wind, precipitation, snow cover, frost, and so on; explore data for other locations, regions, or the globe; examine web sites to see how mathematics is used in argumentation; and discuss possible values hidden in the mathematics.

The landscape of investigation we have outlined illustrates the principles for a mathematics education of climate change that we have proposed in this chapter. The activity involves four forms of authenticity. Students are invited to examine weather data for their own community, for which the impacts of climate change are likely to be very relevant. It involves working with real data. It allows students to introduce their own ideas and values, such as through selecting data, making decisions about data gaps and errors, and choosing how to interrogate the data and report their work. In addition, the activity assumes that students will engage in meaningful discussion of their work: that is, they are not expected simply to find the answer to a standard question; rather, they are expected to think authentically with mathematics as it relates to their community and their lives.

The investigation also involves four forms of participation. Students are participating in mathematics by making decisions about the questions, choice of data, treatment of data, analysis, and presentation of their work. Students are not simply asked to apply a pre-prepared process or algorithm. Students are participating in their classroom, through discussing their work with peers, with their teachers, and in whole class discussion. These discussions should encourage critique of each other's ideas, as a way to explore the limits and values embedded in the mathematical processes. The investigation prompts participation in students' communities outside of school. Students should consider what their findings mean for their community and the surrounding ecosystem, and they can be encouraged to explore these findings with community representatives, such as parents, school administrators, local counsellors, and others. Finally, the investigation prompts participation in public debate, through, for example, participation in public discussions in school, in the media, in the town hall, or at their parliament.

Finally, the investigation creates possibilities for reflection. Students may reflect on the mathematical methods and concepts they use. For example, they can, depending on their age, develop deeper understanding of concepts of mean, moving average, modelling, and linear regression. Further, however, the investigation is an opportunity to reflect on how these concepts and techniques are useful in understanding climate change, as well as the limits of these concepts and techniques. For example, techniques like moving averages are useful in discerning underlying trends, but are limited in focusing on a narrow measure of climate. Students can also reflect on the role of values by thinking about, for example, how information and data is selected for their investigation, in relation to what mathematical techniques can include. Finally, students have opportunities to think about different forms of uncertainty, such as in the treatment of missing data, the treatment of variation, and the limitations of different sources of data. In considering possible future trends, students encounter even more starkly the uncertainty inherent in projecting future climate.

5   Concluding Remarks

Climate change is a global problem that is becoming increasingly urgent. As mathematics educators, we are concerned that this situation is not being sufficiently addressed in mathematics classes, mathematics curriculum, and mathematics education research. In this chapter, we have reviewed the recent synthesis of ideas of critical mathematics education and post-normal science and have used these ideas to propose a set of pedagogical principles for the development and organisation of mathematics classroom activities related to climate change. By proposing activities that involve students in different forms of authenticity, different forms of participation, and in different reflections on and with mathematics, we believe that students will develop a critical understanding of the nature of climate change as well as of the role of mathematics in relation to climate change. This role includes the use of mathematics to study climate change, but also the role of mathematics in the organisation of the consumer society that is driving climate change. Students may also appreciate the role of mathematics in critiquing this society. As mathematics educators, we contribute to treating students as citizens in the present and in their preparation to be the citizens of tomorrow; the citizens who will be called on to deal with the unsolved problem of climate change and its consequences. We believe that we must prepare these future citizens to have a critical understanding of the role of mathematics and its limitations in relation to the difficult decisions they will need to take.

Notes

1 https://www.theguardian.com/environment/2019/jan/25/our-house-is-on-fire-greta-thunberg16-urges-leaders-to-act-on-climate
2 Of course, environmental sustainability is intimately related to issues of social justice, as reflected in the current UN sustainable development goals. It is therefore surprising to us that there has not been more critical mathematics education work on environmental issues.
3 https://unfccc.int/process-and-meetings/the-paris-agreement/what-is-the-paris-agreement
4 https://www.yr.no/klima/

References

Abtahi, Y., Gøtze, P., Steffensen, L., Hauge, K. H., & Barwell, R. (2017). Teaching climate change in mathematics classrooms: An ethical responsibility. *Philosophy of Mathematics Education Journal, 32*.

Appelbaum, P. (2009). Taking action: Mathematics curricular organization for effective teaching and learning. *For the Learning of Mathematics, 29*(2), 39–44.

Barbosa, J. C. (2007). Teacher-student interactions in mathematical modelling. In C. Haines, P. Galbraith, W. Blum, & S. Khan (Eds.), *Mathematical modelling: Education, engineering and economics (ICTMA 12)* (pp. 232–240). Woodhead. https://doi.org/10.1533/9780857099419.5.232

Barwell, R. (2013). The mathematical formatting of climate change: Critical mathematics education and post-normal science. *Research in Mathematics Education, 15*(1), 1–16. https://doi.org/10.1080/14794802.2012.756633

Barwell, R. (2018). Some thoughts on a mathematics education for environmental sustainability. In P. Ernest (Ed.), *The philosophy of mathematics education today* (pp. 145–160). Springer. https://doi.org/10.1007/978-3-319-77760-3_9

Coles, A., Barwell, R., Cotton, T., Winter, J., & Brown, L. (2013). *Teaching secondary mathematics as if the planet matters*. Routledge. https://doi.org/10.4324/9780203357286

English, L. D., & Gainsburg, J. (2015). Problem solving in a 21st-century mathematics curriculum. In L. D. English & D. Kirshner (Eds.), *Handbook of international research in mathematics education* (3rd ed., pp. 313–335). Routledge. https://doi.org/10.4324/9780203448946-21

English, L. D., & Watson, J. (2018). Modelling with authentic data in sixth grade. *ZDM Mathematics Education, 50*(1–2), 103–115. https://doi.org/10.1007/s11858-017-0896-y

Funtowicz, S. O., & Ravetz, J. R. (1993). Science for the post-normal age. *Futures, 25*(7), 739–755. https://doi.org/10.1016/0016-3287(93)90022-L

Hauge, K. H. (2016a). Usikkerhet i temperaturprognoser [Uncertainty in temperature prognoses]. In T. E. Rangnes & H. Alrø (Eds.), *Matematikklæring for framtida – Festskrift til Marit Johnsen-Høines* (pp. 217–240). Caspar Forlag AS.

Hauge, K. H. (2016b). Matematikksamtaler om risiko [Mathematical conversations about risk]. In R. Herheim & M. Johnsen-Høines (Eds.), *Matematikksamtaler – Undervisning og læring – analytiske perspektiv* (91–106). Caspar Forlag AS.

Hauge, K. H., & Barwell, R. (2017). Post-normal science and mathematics education in uncertain times: Educating future citizens for extended peer communities. *Futures, 91*, 25–34. https://doi.org/10.1016/j.futures.2016.11.013

Hauge, K. H., Sørngård, M. A., Vethe, T. I., Bringeland, T. A., Hagen, A. A., & Sumstad, M. S. (2015). Critical reflections on temperature change. In K. Krainer & N. Vondrová (Eds.), *Proceedings of the Ninth Conference of the European Society for Research in Mathematics Education* (pp. 1577–1583). Charles University in Prague, Faculty of Education and ERME.

Intergovernmental Panel on Climate Change [IPCC]. (2018, October). *Global warming of 1.5°C*. https://www.ipcc.ch/sr15/

Kaiser, G., & Schwarz, B. (2010). Authentic modelling problems in mathematics education: Examples and experiences. *Journal für Mathematik-Didaktik, 31*(1), 51–76. https://doi.org/10.1007/s13138-010-0001-3

Pratt, D., Ainley, J., Kent, P., Levinson, R., Yogui, C., & Kapadia, R. (2011). Role of context in risk-based reasoning. *Mathematical Thinking and Learning, 13*(4), 322–345. https://doi.org/10.1080/10986065.2011.608346

Skovsmose, O. (1994). Towards a critical mathematics education. *Educational Studies in Mathematics, 27*(1), 35–57. https://doi.org/10.1007/bf01284527

Skovsmose, O. (2011). *An invitation to critical mathematics education*. Sense. https://doi.org/10.1007/978-94-6091-442-3

CHAPTER 9

The Mathematical Formatting of How Climate Change Is Perceived

Teachers' Reflection and Practice

Lisa Steffensen, Rune Herheim and Toril Eskeland Rangnes

Abstract

This chapter concerns how three teachers in lower secondary school include climate change in school mathematics. Data was collected over a one-year period, where the teachers organised several teaching activities such as fieldwork, posters, contribution to an exhibition, and dialogue and debates, to facilitate students' critical mathematics competences through working with climate change. We apply a teacher perspective and focus on the role mathematics can play in formatting the understanding of climate change. A formatting power of mathematics is identified at three levels: (1) in teachers' meta-reflections, (2) when the teachers use mathematics to format students' understanding, and (3) when teachers facilitate students' awareness of the formatting power of mathematics. The findings suggest that a complex issue like climate change brings forth an awareness of the formatting powers of mathematics.

Keywords

teachers' reflection and practice – mathematical formatting – climate change – uncertainty – research partnership

⋯

Climate change can be regarded as one of our society's greatest challenges, with profound consequences and a high degree of complexity.[1] The Intergovernmental Panel on Climate Change (IPCC) (2018b) stated in a press release that "limiting global warming to 1.5°C would require rapid, far-reaching and unprecedented changes in all aspects of society" (p. 1). These changes, or the consequences of not making them, can potentially have a huge impact on citizens' everyday lives. The IPPC report concerning global warming of 1.5°C (2018a) was written by experts from different fields, in which 91 lead authors

© LISA STEFFENSEN, RUNE HERHEIM AND TORIL ESKELAND RANGNES, 2021
DOI: 10.1163/9789004465800_009
This is an open access chapter distributed under the terms of the CC BY 4.0 License.

and 133 contributing authors accessed more than 6,000 scientific publications. The IPCC reports over the years have been influential (e.g., on the Paris agreement) and have received much public attention. Some have disputed the science provided by the IPCC, such as by The Nongovernmental International Panel on Climate Change (NIPCC). The NIPCC[2] argued that the IPCC is "politically motivated, and predisposed to believing that climate change is a problem in need of a UN solution."

An understanding of climate change depends largely on scientific and mathematical knowledge. For instance, our understanding of future climate scenarios is to a large extent based on mathematical climate models. Thus, mathematics, or the ways that mathematics is used, contributes to the formatting of how future climate change is understood. Considering mathematics as a formatting power in society is in line with Skovsmose's (1994) argument that "mathematics has an important social influence; it follows that to understand this formatting power becomes an essential aspect of critical mathematics education" (p. 207).

Lloyd and Winsberg (2018) underlined that it is vital to understand the conceptual and philosophical foundations of climate models in order to make well-informed judgments on how to act towards climate change. They discussed an example in which Christy (2016), an expert on satellite climate data, showed a graphical discrepancy between global mid-tropospheric temperature models and measurements done by satellites and weather balloons. Christy gave testimony to the United States Congress where he highlighted this discrepancy by using different graphs. His graphs are widely used by media and political and scientific communities (Lloyd & Winsberg, 2018). Nuccitelli (2016) referred to Christy's graphs as the Republicans' favourite climate charts, and the graphs appear on several climate sceptic websites, such as in a blog post by Hamlin (2016). However, several researchers (e.g., Santer et al., 2008), have discredited Christy's discrepancy between models and observations by using statistical argumentation. For instance, Schmidt (2016), a climate modeller at NASA, argued in a blog post that the graph presented by Christy was misleading due to "incomplete model spread, inconsistent smoothing, no structural uncertainty in the satellite observations, weird baseline." These are all arguments that concern the methodological and mathematical choices made when making the graphical representation. Schmidt presented a graph that showed how the climate model projections are trustworthy, by using satellite observations and a different analysis.

The graphs from Christy (2016) and Schmidt (2016) offer two different representations of reality, based on mathematical choices and methodology. The question is then, which representation do policy-makers and citizens use to develop their understanding of climate change, and subsequently, to take action? Lloyd (2018) highlighted how data and observations can be "laden with assumptions and theory" (p. 138). With reference to Christy's (2016) example, Lloyd (2018) argued that "it now appears that the models were mostly right and the early data were mostly wrong, and therein lies an interesting story about data and their relations to scientists, models, and reality" (p. 138).

Kingan (2005) argued that incorporating social advocacy in mathematics education could include involvement in pressing real-world issues like climate change. She exemplified this idea by using three graphs that showed the amount of CO_2 in the atmosphere (the Keeling curve), a comparison of CO_2 and temperature, and a reconstruction of surface temperature over the last 1,000 years. The latter graph is named "the hockey stick graph" due to its resemblance in shape to a hockey stick, and played an important role in an IPCC report (2001) about global warming and abrupt temperature rise. Kingan (2005) suggested that an understanding of functions, graphs, and scientific methods could "motivate students to study mathematics and understand, and potentially act upon, some of the controversial issues in the news" (p. 242).

Climate change involves competencies from several scientific fields, political and economic expertise, and skills in making value and judgment calls. Nordén (2018) underlined that some researchers on education for sustainable development focus on a transdisciplinary approach rather than a subject-oriented approach, in order "to support holistic learning of complex issues" (p. 663). Teachers in her study considered transdisciplinary approaches challenging, and Nordén argued that a better understanding of how teachers and students can work with complex and challenging issues in the classroom would help develop competencies in decision-making on these urgent issues.

Barwell (2013, 2018) highlighted that mathematics is involved and intertwined in many aspects of climate change. Mathematics provides technology that can affect the climate, and it is important in order to understand, describe, and predict future climate changes. Communication about climate change is to a large extent done with numbers and graphs. Barwell therefore argued that mathematics educators need to be engaged in climate change because of the extensive use of mathematics, and that students need to learn to reflect on the role that mathematics can play in climate change. He suggested Critical Mathematics Education (CME) as a theoretical perspective, as a way of engaging students as critical citizens. Furthermore, Barwell (2018) argued, in line with Skovsmose (1994), that to identify what shapes our society is an important part of being critical citizens. Barwell particularly highlighted the importance of identifying what shapes our understanding of climate change, to identify the mathematical formatting *of* climate change.

How can mathematics education facilitate students' abilities to identify the role mathematics plays in the world? Inspired by this question, we investigated three lower secondary school teachers' choices and arguments for when they include climate change issues in their mathematics and natural science teaching. We focus on identifying the potential for facilitating students' awareness and understanding of the formatting power of mathematics.

1   Theoretical Perspective: Critical Mathematics Education

Teaching mathematics in the context of climate change brings challenges and possibilities beyond teaching statistics and functions without a real-life context, and hence also a different theoretical perspective. Barwell (2018) argued that "critical mathematics education can offer a perspective with which to conceptualise how mathematics teaching and learning might educate future citizens" (p. 145) when discussing mathematics education for environmental sustainability. In this chapter, CME constitutes the main theoretical perspective for analysing and discussing the data. First, we introduce CME. Then, we present three key concepts within critical mathematics education, namely the formatting power of mathematics, uncertainty, and being critical citizens.

Several mathematics education researchers have explored different directions within CME, such as ethnomathematics (D'Ambrosio, 2007), pedagogy for dialogue and conflict (Vithal, 2003), and social justice (Gutstein, 2012). Of particular interest for this chapter is the work of Skovsmose (1994), who promoted a critical mathematics education in which students reflect on how mathematics can format their life. He described critical mathematics education in terms of a concern: "To address social exclusion and suppression, to work for social justice in whatever form possible, to try open new possibilities for students, and to address critically mathematics in all its forms and application" (2014, p. 116). The use of mathematics in climate change issues concerns social justice, both directly and indirectly. Climate change is a global challenge, but affects people and nations differently. The consequences of climate change are not always distributed fairly. It is not socially just when farmers lose their livelihood and people have to move from their homes, while CO_2 polluters can carry on doing business as usual. As Barwell (2018) highlighted, mathematics is a crucial part of how we understand, describe, predict, and communicate about climate change, and it is therefore important to consider mathematics as an integrated part of challenges such as the economic impact worldwide, and the ethically and socially unjust situations connected to climate change. Addressing mathematics critically, as described by Skovsmose (2014), within a climate change context, can affect how people understand and act towards climate change.

1.1 The Formatting Power of Mathematics

Skovsmose (1994) introduced the notion of the formatting power of mathematics as a power that can shape our society. He asked: "Could a science like mathematics (formal or not) become not only interpretative but also formative?" (p. 42). Can mathematics format our understanding of climate change and our behaviour towards it? Can mathematically based choices made by professionals such as climate modellers, mathematicians, graphical designers, journalists, or teachers format our understanding and behaviour? By the formatting powers of mathematics, we understand how mathematics can format our society, and how people's intentional and unintentional use of mathematics can format our understanding and behaviour. Hauge and Barwell (2017) argued that when models of weather systems are "built into the fabric of society ... the mathematical models that drive them no longer describe reality, they become part of reality – they become prescriptive" (p. 28). Barwell (2013) used the expression "the mathematical formatting of climate change" with reference to Skovsmose's (1994) concept of the formatting power of mathematics. Barwell argued that climate change is operationalised through science, mathematics, technology, and by climate model projections in particular. Without mathematically based climate models, it would be difficult to identify and become aware of future challenges, because most qualified predictions and forecasts somehow involve mathematics. Furthermore, people's actions toward predicted scenarios are also being formatted, such as by choosing to eat less or not eat meat, commuting by public transport, or by reducing flights. Similarly, mathematics can format the understanding of climate change, how it is perceived, and what actions are taken towards it. Skovsmose (1994) discussed the process when mathematics goes from being descriptive to becoming prescriptive, by arguing that mathematics not only provides descriptions; it also provides "models for changed behaviour. We not only 'see' according to mathematics, we also 'do' according to mathematics" (p. 55).

1.2 Uncertainty

The Organisation for Economic Co-operation and Development (OECD) (2016) highlighted uncertainty as "a phenomenon at the heart of the mathematical analysis of many problem situations" (p. 72) in their Programme for International Student Assessment (PISA) 2015 report. Funtowicz and Ravetz (2008) argued that when "facts are uncertain, values in dispute, stakes high and decisions urgent" (p. 365), there is a need for what they call post-normal science.

They regard climate change as such a challenge, and suggest an approach that goes beyond the traditional expert-policy regime in which experts provide solutions and politicians act according to their advice. Funtowicz and Ravetz discuss how climate change could involve an extended peer community consisting of ordinary citizens, such as representatives from interest-based organisations. An important part of such involvement will often include values and uncertainty. Hauge and Barwell (2017) reflected on how mathematics education can prepare students to contribute in these extended peer communities. They highlight three kinds of uncertainties from post-normal science: technological, methodological, and epistemic uncertainty. While the first two types of uncertainty can be addressed by applying mathematical and/or technological skills, Hauge and Barwell emphasise that epistemic uncertainty arises "from lack of knowledge, information or suitable methods, or the lack of awareness of some features of the situation" (p. 29).

With regard to climate change, there is still much to learn. In the IPCC report about global warming of 1.5°C (IPCC, 2018a), they emphasised the knowledge gap and included detailed descriptions of methodologies and key uncertainties. Although the IPCC recognises and communicates uncertainties, these reports have a huge formatting power and impact on society. The reports provide scientific information that nations use when developing climate policies that, in turn, affect people's everyday life. It is therefore imperative to critique the content of these reports, and the subsequent political actions. However, such critique has to be informed and well-founded. If not, it amounts to little more than dismissing science. In public and political debates, uncertainty is often connected to lack of knowledge, a subject poorly understood, as a weakness, and that scientists "do not know *anything* about a topic, just because they do not know *everything* about it" (Corner et al., 2012, p. 464). It can therefore be argued that one has to wait for more certainty before acting. In that sense, uncertainty becomes a formatting power on its own. It is therefore crucial that citizens learn about uncertainties in order to be able to reflect on different types of uncertainty as well as other aspects like precautionary principles. Hauge and Barwell (2017) connected epistemic uncertainty to Skovsmose's concept of reflective knowing, and argued that this is an important competency for citizens in an extended peer community. Skovsmose (1994) defined the notion of reflective knowing as "the competence needed to be able to take a justified stand in a discussion of technological questions" (p. 101). He underlined how mere mathematical or technological skills are insufficient, and emphasised that other aspects, such as sociological and ethical considerations, norms and values, need to be a part of how students reflect. Dealing with the challenges of climate change requires citizens to not only consider scientific knowledge, but to understand this as integrated with ethical and economic aspects. Skovsmose emphasised that reflective knowing is crucial for acting as a critical citizen, which brings us to our last key concept.

1.3 Being Critical Citizens

In today's society, where citizens are surrounded by a massive amount of information on complex matters, there is a need for citizens to be critical and reflective. With regard to climate change, much of this information involves scientific literacy. The OECD (2016) defined scientific literacy as the ability "to engage with science-related issues [...] as a reflective citizen" (p. 13), with competencies to explain phenomena, evaluate and design scientific enquiry, and interpret data and evidence scientifically.

Presenting and understanding climate change information also requires mathematical literacy: "an individual's capacity to formulate, employ, and interpret mathematics in a variety of contexts" (Organisation for Economic Cooperation and Development, 2016, p. 13). Mathematical literacy goes beyond mastering certain algorithms or procedural knowledge, and entails an emphasis on mathematics within a context. Furthermore, the OECD (2016) highlighted how an important part of mathematical literacy is to "assist individuals to recognise the role that mathematics plays in the world and to make the well-founded judgments and decisions needed by constructive, engaged and reflective citizens" (p. 13). The OECD's specifications on mathematical literacy connect with Skovsmose's (1994) formatting power of mathematics through the recognition of the role mathematics plays in society. However, neither of the definitions explicitly emphasise the role of being critical. Barwell (2013) problematised parts of the perspective on mathematical literacy presented by the OECD by arguing that "the general orientation is to the use of mathematics to interpret information and solve problems, rather than for critique" (p. 6).

When discussing scientific literacy in the PISA 2015 framework, the OECD (2016), highlighted that new curriculum models do not focus "on producing individuals who will be 'producers' of scientific knowledge, i.e. the future scientists; rather, it is on educating all young people to become informed, critical users of scientific knowledge" (p. 18). Similar considerations apply for mathematics curricula. Very few students will become mathematicians who produce climate models, but all of them will need the skills to understand and critically assess such models in different ways. The recent focus in the media on "fake news" can be expected to generate increased interest in education on the importance of students being critical. The OECD (2015) underlined that although there seems to be a consensus on promoting critical thinking as a twenty-first century skill, "it is not clear how these skills can be made visible and tangible and articulated by teachers, students, and policy makers, especially as part of the curriculum" (p. 3) . For instance, what does it really mean to enable students' critical thinking within mathematics education, and, in particular, in the context of climate change? In science, there is a tradition of acknowledging the importance of a critical perspective for research, including the generation of hypotheses and theories. In the climate change debate, it is often highlighted as important to think critically about claims and arguments. Interestingly, being critical is also important for proponents of views that differ from the scientific consensus on climate change, such as those who reject the human impact on climate change.

From a mathematical perspective, it should be underlined that being critical does not mean rejecting scientific results. On the contrary, being critical can strengthen science by enabling students to recognise that uncertainties involved in climate models or climate observations are a natural part of mathematics and science. Similarly, emphasising that students (and teachers) learn to recognise and identify the role mathematics can play in formatting our society does not mean that the formatting power of mathematics is something that should be rejected, or in other ways be diminished (although that might be the case in some situations). Rather, it is about raising an awareness of the formatting power of mathematics – as Skovsmose (1994) puts it: "Mathematics has an important social influence; it follows that to understand this formatting power becomes an essential aspect of critical mathematics education" (p. 207).

2   Methods: Facilitating Critical Mathematics Competencies

Three teachers (Kim, Max, and Tim) and a researcher (Steffensen) established a research partnership to explore ways to facilitate students' critical mathematics competencies. In this chapter, we look, in line with Skovsmose (1994), at an awareness and understanding of the formatting power of mathematics as a key part of critical mathematics competency. The research partnership lasted for about a year, and consisted of seven partnership meetings, 42 lessons, a fieldwork activity, and participation in an energy exhibition. The research partnership meetings were a collaborative space for planning and reflecting on how the lessons could be done and had been done. These meetings were audio recorded while the lessons were both video and audio recorded. Kim and Tim had one grade ten class each, Max had two grade ten classes, and there were approximately 30 students in each class. The teachers were experienced mathematics and natural science teachers, and they taught the students in both subjects, but the observation only took place in the mathematics lessons. The teachers' written notes such as PowerPoint slides and handouts to the students served as additional material.

In order to identify the potential for facilitating students' awareness and understanding of the formatting power of mathematics, we investigate examples from three contexts: (1) the teachers' introductions to climate change and mathematics, (2) the teachers' meta-reflections when planning the fieldwork activity, and (3) the teachers' choices regarding a quiz made for the energy exhibition.

In their introductions, the teachers presented the topic of climate change and relevant mathematics to the students by sharing some of their own thoughts on the topic, as well as engaging the students to share their thoughts. We discuss an example from Max's introduction that serves as an example of how the teachers connected climate change issues to the curriculum.

In the examples from the research partnership meetings, the teachers are planning a fieldwork activity in which the students should measure climate-relevant data (such as CO_2 and temperature of seawater) and do a fieldwork report. We have chosen to discuss some of Kim's utterances because they provide interesting insights into the teachers' reasoning and reflections underlying the fieldwork activity.

The energy exhibition was a gathering in which teachers and students from four different schools attended and presented energy-related topics to the public and to the local business community. The teachers and students made posters and a quiz as their contributions to the exhibition. We focus on the quiz, because the differences between the teachers' quiz questions illustrate well some of the choices the teachers had to make, such as choosing between different climate graphs. Although the researcher had a participatory role in the research partnership meetings, the teachers designed the lessons and activities, both collaboratively and individually.

The teachers' choices and utterances are our units of analysis. The choices and utterances presented in this section are selected because they represent distinct examples of how students' understanding of the formatting power of mathematics can be facilitated in a climate change context and they illustrate well some of the challenges teachers face in this respect. The data were transcribed, coded, and categorised by using NVivo. The coding resulted in four main categories, two of which were relevant for identifying the potential for facilitating students' awareness and understanding of the formatting power of mathematics: climate change related utterances (e.g., discussing CO_2 and its impact on climate change), and critical mathematics competency utterances. Utterances associated with the formatting power of mathematics were identified in the meetings, lessons, and activities, and emerged as one of the sub-categories of critical mathematics competency. As a part of identifying how students' awareness and understanding about the formatting power of mathematics can be facilitated, we analysed utterances where the teachers and students reflected on how graphs, numbers, and models could affect people's perception of reality. Questions like, "How does understanding of climate change come about?," "What is hidden?" and "What is taken for granted?" were used as support in the analysis process.

3 Critical Mathematics Education and Climate Change in the Three Classes

In the following, we first discuss an example when Max introduced the project to the students. We then focus on teachers' meta-reflections by discussing two of Kim's utterances regarding the fieldwork planning, and finally, we discuss Max's and Kim's choices for the quiz.

3.1 *The Teachers' Introductions to Climate Change and Mathematics*

In their introductions, the three teachers expressed several goals for the lesson, such as introducing the topic of climate change and mathematics, inviting the students to contribute their ideas to what climate change in the mathematics classroom can look like, and introducing some basic climate change concepts like the difference between climate and weather. The teachers expressed concerns regarding the abstractness of climate change and mathematics. Max therefore decided to make some slides as an introduction, to point out links between mathematics and climate change.

In the first slide, Max argued for the purpose of mathematics as described in the curriculum by writing: "Active democracy requires citizens who are able to study, understand, and critically assess quantitative information, statistical analyses, and economic prognoses. Hence, mathematical competence is required to understand and influence processes in society." This utterance is a direct quotation from the mathematics curriculum (Ministry of Education and Research, 2013), and both the terms "understand" and "critically assess" are explicitly stated. The emphasis on not only understanding but also on critically assessing is highlighted as important in the curriculum and something that Max explicitly displayed to her students. The curriculum quote was accompanied by a picture of a polar bear clinging to a small piece of melting ice (see Figure 9.1).

A polar bear and melting ice has, for many, become a symbol of climate change (Born, 2019), and the picture that Max used drew the students' attention

FIGURE 9.1
The picture on Max's first slide
(photograph by Arne Naevra)

towards climate change challenges. When Max used this symbol of climate change, she positioned the mathematics with a clear connection to the active democratic purpose of mathematics. Such positioning can be interpreted as an action to motivate students to engage and influence processes in society by saving the polar bears from extinction due to climate change.

One of the other slides required participation from students, with the headline "Reflections." It contained the following questions: "What do you know about climate and challenges related to this? Take two minutes to think individually, and then discuss with a learning partner." The students provided written answers, and there was a plenary discussion at the end. One group provided the following written statement:

> The climate is getting hotter because of increased CO_2 emissions in the atmosphere. The increased heat leads to the risk of melting the polar ice, which will cause massive floods and climate change. There is therefore an international goal that the average temperature should not rise by more than 2°C. It is therefore relevant to discuss the question whether we should open a new oil field or not.

The students based their arguments on scientific and mathematical knowledge such as "increased CO_2 emissions" and "increased heat leads to the risk of melting the polar ice." They went on by arguing that as a consequence of the 2°C temperature target, the Norwegian government should "discuss the question whether we should open a new oil field or not." However, they did not provide any written discussion concerning the claim that the temperature should not rise by more than 2°C, and did not show that they could "critically assess quantitative information" (which was stressed in the first slide). Although Max emphasised evaluating arguments and evidence in a mathematical way, it was not documented that any of the students explicitly did this in this first lesson. The 2°C target appears to be taken for granted and the formatting power of numbers and mathematics is not identified, discussed, or reflected upon by the students. As Skovsmose (1994) and Hauge and Barwell (2017) argued, the global 2°C temperature target becomes a number built into the fabric of society and no longer just describes reality; it prescribes reality.

Frisch (2018) highlighted that the 2°C target is based on precautionary principles and political consensus, more than on strictly scientific knowledge. For instance, he referred to an interview where John Broome, a philosopher and climate change author, who said that the 2°C target "has just been pulled out of the air" (Frisch, 2018, p. 415). Although the students did not critique the 2°C target, one might say that the students are taking a stand on social justice matter through mathematics, in line with Skovsmose's (2014) definition of CME, by critically engaging in what the Norwegian society should look like. Although there are political forces working towards stopping further oil and gas exploitation, the present situation in Norway is that the government continues with opening new search fields for oil and gas. By raising the controversial political question of whether to open new oil and gas fields, the students are reflecting on and challenging the present Norwegian policy. It is a big question to raise, taking into consideration that the Norwegian economy is largely dependent on income from oil and gas, and a reduction in income would generate major consequences for the students and for Norwegian society. The 2°C target then has a formatting power when the students prescribe which actions the government should take (see Skovsmose, 1994).

3.2 *The Teachers' Meta-Reflections When Planning a Fieldwork Activity*

During the partnership meetings, the teachers discussed a wide variety of issues, including which topics that might be relevant to include in the lessons and how politicians make decisions on climate change-related issues. When reflecting on historical temperatures, on statistics, and on techniques used to measure the Earth's temperature, Kim said the following (… = 1–3 seconds pause):

> Measuring uncertainty is also a bit interesting, if we can focus on that. Because ... they have measurement stations round about. There are discussions on where they are located. For instance, near big cities, do urban areas affect the temperature, for example? Then, the temperatures have to be adjusted by a machine with regard to this. Is it most relevant to use this [ground measurements close to cities], or is it more relevant to use the temperatures in balloons that you send into the atmosphere ... and then measure the temperature? What gives the best picture? And how many measurement stations do you have in that area and how many do you have in that area? Take Antarctica. There are not many measurement stations there ... and that is a huge area. And elsewhere as well. This could be interesting to discuss, in terms of uncertainty, and what affects the results.

Kim expressed an interest in uncertainty related to measurement. He asked "if we can focus on that," which can be regarded as a proposal to the other participants that measuring uncertainty is a relevant topic to explore. All the teachers later included Kim's proposal in the fieldwork activity. When Kim designed the fieldwork activity, he deliberately aimed for bringing about differences between the students' measurement results by asking the students to measure several times and with multiple instruments (see Figure 9.2). He included several questions in order to make the students reflect, discuss, justify their measurements, and help them decide which temperature was the most representative and should thus be included in their report. Kim's last question in Figure 9.2 extended the students' attention from their seawater measurements to the more general measurements of the Earth. The focus on measurement differences can be considered as a part of enabling students to deal with uncertainty, as a preparation to participate in an extended peer community by learning to cope with uncertainty (Hauge & Barwell, 2017).

Kim continued by saying "there are discussions" regarding the location of measurement stations. The discussions Kim refers to can be linked to some of the controversies connected to temperature changes and climate change. He points to stations "near big cities," and asks if "urban areas affect the temperature." The heat island effect is sometimes used as an argument in the climate change debate (e.g., Sherrington, 2018). The IPCC (2013) described and discussed this phenomenon and the uncertainty related to this, and concluded that these urban affected temperatures are not likely to have a significant impact on global land warming trends. Similarly, Oreskes (2018) emphasised that the Berkeley Earth Surface Temperature Group found that "the observed warming cannot be explained away this way" (p. 46) (referring to the heat island effect).

SEAWATER				
	Measurements			
Method	1	2	3	Average
Digital				
Analogue				

- Why do you think you should take three measurements and calculate the average?
- What are possible sources of error?
- How accurate do you consider your measurement results to be? Justify the answer.
- Discuss how you think the global average temperature of the Earth is measured.

FIGURE 9.2   Kim's measurement table and four of the questions

However, Oreskes argued that this potential source of error is emphasised by some opponents. Kim's suggestion to include measurement uncertainties in teaching could serve as an opportunity for the students to explore potential sources of error in, for example, statistics, graphs, and models.

Kim then problematised that "the temperatures have to be adjusted by a machine." The machine reference can be interpreted as pointing to the black box problem where some input magically is transformed into some output, where computers handle mathematical calculations and models by themselves. Skovsmose (1994) emphasised situations where human-made decisions were hidden behind technology as important for identifying formatting powers. When these students decided on the most representative temperature measurement, they knew that other measurements could be just as relevant, and such knowledge is potentially transferable to other situations as well.

Kim compared two measurement techniques by asking if "it is most relevant to use this [ground measurement closes to cities], or is it more relevant to use the temperatures in balloons that you send into the atmosphere?" The temperatures from different methods can differ, and give a different perceived reality to the public. Lloyd (2018) highlighted that in Christy's (2016) report, the measured satellite data was treated "as windows on the world, as reflections of reality, without any art, theory, or construction interfering with that reflection" (p. 143). Kim then asked, "What gives the best picture?" When scientists describe reality, it will always be a chosen representation. Different representations can give different impressions. Therefore, it becomes important to discuss how representations can (re)present different connections to reality, often depending on choices of a statistical or practical nature, such as when Kim designed the field report, asking for multiple measurements of the same quantity. He facilitated students' reflective knowing, as emphasised by Skovsmose (1994). When mathematical decisions and choices are involved in describing reality, the mathematics can take on a formatting role of how climate change is understood and perceived.

Kim continued to focus on measurement issues by questioning the number of measurement stations in different areas around the world: "Take Antarctica, there are not many measurement stations there ... and that is a huge area." There is a high density of ground measurements in populated areas, and few in more remote areas (Hijmans et al., 2010). Kim pointed out that the location of measurements influences the models and the extent to which the temperatures are regarded as high or low. Such choices influence the models, and the models influence how people understand the world. By emphasising how choices and models can influence people's perception of climate change, Kim provides an argument for the formatting power of mathematics.

Later on, the teachers discussed climate models. The researcher asked whether the students' attention was directed towards how mathematics could be used to influence them. Kim responded by referring to how politicians could be influenced:

> Then they [the politicians] think that this is how it is ... they are told that it is like this. They really have no qualifications to say this or that. They just have to trust what the advisers and others say to them ... and then they must decide that this is the reality. [...] So, those who decide what society we are going to have, they are influenced by others who have decided that this is the way it is.

Kim started by pointing out that politicians "think that this is how it is," and emphasised that politicians' perceptions of reality are based on climate models. He continued by stating, "they are told that it is like this." Kim positioned politicians as passive recipients. Initially, he does not explicitly say how or by whom the politicians are told this, but later he refers to "advisers and others." In climate change issues, advisers typically are experts on climate change models and data. Kim's reference to such advisers can be regarded as an example of what Funtowicz and Ravetz (2003) referred to as an expert-regime. Kim then added, "they really have no qualifications to say this or that." Even though politicians are not experts on topics such as climate change, they still have to make decisions. When Kim claimed that "they just have to trust what the advisers and others say to them," he again referred to the hidden power of the experts and their models. Using the word "trust" suggests an emphasis on the power relations between politicians/decision makers and the experts/models. One side must rely on the other to make good decisions. This interpretation is strengthened by Kim's next utterance: "and then they must decide that this is the reality." Linking advisers, experts and their models, to how politicians perceive reality is another way of highlighting the hidden powers through which mathematics can format the society.

Kim finished his arguments by emphasising even more the hidden powers that scientists and mathematicians potentially can have, by saying: "So, those who decide what society we are going to have, they are influenced by others who have decided that this is the way it is." This is in line with Skovsmose's (1994) argument that we not only see according to mathematics, we also do according to mathematics. In climate change issues, experts act according to numbers and models, and in turn, decision-makers act according to experts' arguments on the climate and the economy. Mathematics can therefore format both understanding and action about climate change. When the researcher asked Kim about students' awareness of the formatting powers of mathematics, he referred to how politicians are influenced by experts. By pointing to how politicians can be influenced, Kim put in perspective how challenging it can be to facilitate students' understanding and awareness of the formatting power of mathematics.

3.3 The Teachers' Choices Regarding a Quiz Made for an Energy Exhibition

In this section, we provide examples of how the teachers' mathematical choices and their highlighting of certain topics relating to climate change potentially can format students' understanding of climate change. The examples come from the energy exhibition. The teachers had made a multiple-choice quiz, and the students asked participants at the exhibition to answer five quiz questions. The teachers had agreed in the partnership meeting that it could be interesting to ask questions that could surprise the participants. They said they wanted to generate engagement and discussions.

The teachers had three identical questions (Q1, Q2, and Q5), but they chose to differ in two of the questions (Q3 and Q4). Figure 9.3 shows Kim's quiz with correct answers indicated. Max chose to replace two of Kim's questions. Her argument for doing this was that although the questions and answers were sort of correct, they could give an incorrect impression of climate models and an increase in temperature.

Kim asked in the third question whether climate models correlate well with measured temperatures over the last 20 years. The focus is on the imprecision of climate models, and the correct answer according to the quiz was "very poorly." A graph that backed up this answer was shown on the back of the quiz. The graph appeared in Christy's (2016) United States Senate testimony and shows temperature changes predicted by 102 different climate models, and compares these with observed temperature changes measured by satellites and balloons. Lloyd (2018) explained how this graph was used to support the claim that climate models and observed data have discrepancies, and thus climate models

> Q1: Which greenhouse gas affects the temperature on the Earth the most?
>
> a) ☐ Carbon dioxide, CO_2 b) ☒ Water vapour, H_2O c) ☐ Methane, CH_4 d) ☐ Ozone, O_3
>
> Q2: How many temperature stations on the Earth measure temperatures used to calculate the atmospheric average temperature?
>
> a) ☒ about 6 000   b) ☐ about 50 000   c) ☐ about 400 000   d) ☐ about 1 000 000
>
> Kim's Q3: How well do the climate models' temperature scenarios correlate with measured temperatures over the last 20 years?
>
> a) ☐ Very well   b) ☒ Very poorly
>
> Kim's Q4: How much has the Earth's average temperature increased since 1998?
>
> a) ☒ Almost nothing b) ☐ approximately 1°C c) ☐ approximately 2°C d) ☐ approximately 4°C
>
> Q5: If power stations running on gas on Norwegian platforms are replaced by stations running on electricity via power cables from land, will that lead to less CO_2 emissions from Norwegian gas?
>
> a) ☐ Yes   b) ☒ No

FIGURE 9.3   Kim's quiz

are not trustworthy. To compare climate models with real observations is both important and a relevant part of scientific work. Kim's choice to focus on the uncertainties of climate models by focusing on the discrepancy displayed by this particular graph, could contribute to formatting students' (and quiz participants') opinions on climate change, by suggesting that projections from climate models are not trustworthy. This was also one of Max's arguments for replacing this question on her quiz. It is imperative to keep in mind that mathematical models can never be exact replications of reality; neither can the observations represent reality in a precise manner. Such discrepancies are important to acknowledge when comparing models with observations. As Corner et al. (2012) argued, just because scientists "do not know everything" about a topic does not mean they "do not know anything" about it (p. 464).

Kim could have chosen another graph, such as the graph made by Schmidt (2016) in Figure 9.4. Schmidt compared satellite observations with projections from climate models, and displayed a quite different picture from that implied by Christy's graph. In Schmidt's graph, the differences between the observed data and model projections diminish. Kim's claim in the quiz, that climate models correspond "very poorly" with measured temperatures, is erroneous according to this graph, because most of the observed data are within the extremities of the projections. Furthermore, by focusing on the comparison of measurements done by satellites (and weather balloons) in the mid-troposphere, Kim highlighted measurements that show the most discrepancy with the climate models. Several other climate model projections are more in compliance with measured data. For instance, as summarised in an article

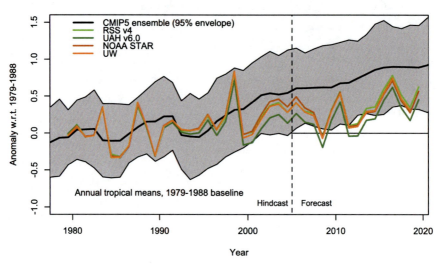

FIGURE 9.4 Schmidt's graph (2020, personal communication) – climate model projections versus satellite observation (for an older version of this graph, see Schmidt, 2016)

by Nuccitelli (2016), the temperature on the Earth's surface (see, for example, Mann et al., 2016), sea level rise (see e.g., Intergovernmental Panel on Climate Change, 2013), Arctic sea ice (Stroeve et al., 2012), and ocean heating (Cheng et al., 2015) are all examples where there is little discrepancy between measured observations and projections.

In the fourth question, Kim asked about the magnitude of the Earth's average temperature increase over the last 20 years. The correct answer was "almost nothing." The answer was justified by the graph in Figure 9.5. The graph emphasises small temperature changes over the last 20 years, without displaying any ordinate axis nor temperature levels. A similar focus can be seen in the framing of the question, by the choice of a relatively short timeline, the choice of distractors, the correct answer situated at one end of the scale, and the wording "almost nothing." Together, these two questions and graphs can influence the understanding of climate change in the sense that there is no increase in temperature and that climate models are not trustworthy. The mathematical-based choices of measurements, and graphs, can contribute to format society.

Max chose to replace Kim's third and fourth question with her own questions (see Figure 9.6). Max's questions concerned the Arctic sea ice level and sea level changes. The correct answer on the third question, -36%, was different from the distractors because it stood out by being considerably bigger

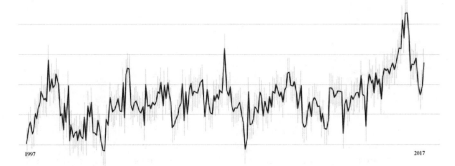

FIGURE 9.5 The temperature graph from the quiz, recreated from a graph in Watts (2017) (Source: Met Office)

Max Q3: How much sea ice was in the Arctic in 2016 compared to a normal level?

  a) ☐ + 10%   b) ☐ equal   c) ☐ -10%   d) ☒ -36%

Max Q4: Satellite data indicate that the sea level had changed. How much has the sea increased in recent years?

  a) ☐ approximately 5 nanometers   b) ☒ approximately 3.4 mm
  c) ☐ approximately 5.7 cm   d) ☐ approximately 1.2 m

FIGURE 9.6 The two questions Max used to replace two of Kim's questions (a normal level is the arithmetic average of recorded levels from 1961–1990)

and was not a multiple of 10. Max confirmed in a partnership meeting that she chose the distractors consciously in order to accentuate the severity of ice melting, in line with how she used the picture of the polar bear in one of her slides in the introduction to the students. By highlighting the correct answer in this way, Max could potentially influence the students' understanding of climate change in a way that focused on the big ice melting in Arctic.

The fourth question focused on sea level changes, and this question also contained big differences between the distractors (from nanometres to metres). However, the correct answer was in the middle (3.4 mm), and did not stand out to the same extent as the correct answer to the third question. Like Kim, Max chose to focus on one particular measurement method, the satellite data. These data have a timeline that starts in 1993. However, if Max had chosen another measurement method, such as coastal tide gauge records, the answer would have shown a smaller sea level increase (1.8 mm instead of 3.4 mm per year[3]). Both methods do, however, illustrate a similar and increasing trend (see Figure 9.7).

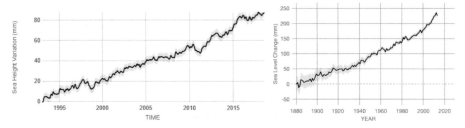

FIGURE 9.7   The graph to the left shows data from satellites with an annual increase of 3.2 mm, while the graph on the right shows coastal tide records with an annual increase of 1.8 mm (Source: NASA, https://climate.nasa.gov/vital-signs/sea-level/, accessed 2018)

In line with Kingan (2005), Kim and Max incorporated a real-world issue like climate change in mathematics education. While Kim highlighted the uncertainties in climate models and the small increase in temperature, Max emphasised the large ice-melting and the increase in sea level. Their choice of numbers, distractors, and the focus of their questions, suggest that Max and Kim emphasised different perspectives on climate change. These choices can be more or less deliberate. A discussion between Max and Kim in a partnership meeting showed that Max did try, to some extent, to influence the quiz participants' views on climate change by deliberately leaving Antarctic out of the ice melting statistics (Steffensen et al., 2018). If teachers include climate change in their mathematics teaching, choices like this, whether they are deliberate or not, are worth reflecting on for the teachers themselves, as well as together with their students. Such discussions offer a fruitful arena for facilitating students' development of an awareness and understanding of the formatting power of mathematics.

4   Concluding Comments

In order to develop teachers' and students' competencies to identify the mathematical formatting powers of climate change, we need more knowledge about the existing awareness of the formatting power of mathematics in teachers' and students' work with climate change. Formatting powers of mathematics are identified in three contexts in the data: the teachers' introductions, their meta-reflections when planning a fieldwork activity, their choices regarding a quiz to an energy exhibition. In the first example, the teacher emphasised to the students the importance of being critical in order to understand and influence society. This is in line with the focus in the national curriculum on being able to critically assess quantitative information. Although the students were encouraged to critically assess quantitative information, it was not observed in the chosen example that the 2°C target was questioned. It could seem like they took it for granted.

In the second example, when the teachers planned the fieldwork activity, they discussed how the global temperature is measured, the different choices involved in such measurements, and the uncertainty connected to these methods. For instance, deciding whether to choose ground or atmospheric measurements is a human choice that could, from the teachers' perspective, shape how reality is perceived. Similarly, politicians' perceptions of reality and the foundation for making decisions rely on experts' models. In the third example, the teachers, more or less intentionally, used mathematics to influence the students' and the participants' understanding of climate change. They did this through their choices in making the quiz and through the way they used particular numbers and graphs to highlight different topics and perspectives regarding climate change. Society consists of individuals. Without individuals being influenced or using mathematics to influence others, one can argue that society will not be formatted. In this text, we have extended the formatting power of mathematics to include how mathematics can format individuals and how individuals can use mathematics as a tool to format others' understanding of reality, which consequently can impact society.

Regarding the measurement of the temperature of the Earth, new technology will make it possible to do measurements all across the world. However, there will still be choices to be made that involve scientific, technological, and mathematical questions, and complete "certainty" can never be achieved. These choices include deciding on an appropriate number of measurement stations; whether to use ground measurement or atmospheric measurements; deciding on the size of the heat island effect; or whether or not to include the ocean temperatures. The numbers and graphs showing global temperatures might seem appealingly easy for the public to conceive, but behind the mathematics, there are a number of choices not particularly visible or easily accessible for the public sphere.

Numbers and graphs are often used in public debates on climate change. Such data can be based on observations as well as predicted data from climate models, and both situations can contain different levels of uncertainty. However, if public debates make people think that the observed and predicted data cannot be trusted because of the element of uncertainty, then the element of uncertainty could lead to disengagement in climate change and distrust in mathematics, as well as format how climate change is perceived. Therefore, researchers, such as Hauge and Barwell (2017), have underlined that educating students to deal with different types of uncertainty can provide a greater understanding of how to deal with uncertainties of climate change. Furthermore, such uncertainties are not necessarily flaws that have to be corrected, but rather to be included as a natural part of scientific processes.

So, how can students' competencies to identify the formatting power of mathematics in a climate change context be facilitated? We identified challenges at different levels. Teachers need to develop an awareness about how mathematics is used in argumentation, as the teachers in this study did. They also need an awareness of how they themselves make use of the formatting power of mathematics in their teaching and facilitation for critical learning. Developing students' understanding and awareness of the formatting power of mathematics is anything but straightforward. Students need time and opportunities to experience how to be critical in constructive ways. There is a need for teachers and researchers to design research together, to explore possible teaching methods that can develop students' abilities to be critical and to recognise the formatting powers of mathematics. Working with measurements, modelling, or other mathematical topics connected to climate change is one possibility. The complexity of climate change can generate problems other than those found in more traditional mathematical tasks – problems that are more relevant for the real-life problems of society. Discussing uncertainty and evaluating argumentation can be a fruitful approach for students to learn how to use mathematics in their own argumentation, as well as to be critical about others' use of mathematics. The aim of being critical is not to make students reject mathematically based results from science. Rather, by recognising and discussing uncertainty in their own projects and in climate research, we believe the credibility of research can be increased through a more nuanced understanding, which is necessary if we are going to make changes for a sustainable future.

Notes

1 This chapter is an extended version of Steffensen, Herheim, and Rangnes (2018). A version of the chapter appears in Lisa Steffensen's (2021) doctoral dissertation.
2 http://climatechangereconsidered.org
3 The observed measurements are retrieved from Kartverket, the same source that Max used in the quiz question (https://kartverket.no/til-sjos/se-havniva/havniva/slik-maler-vi-havnivaet).

References

Barwell, R. (2013). The mathematical formatting of climate change: Critical mathematics education and post-normal science. *Research in Mathematics Education, 15*(1), 1–16. https://doi.org/10.1080/14794802.2012.756633

Barwell, R. (2018). Some thoughts on a mathematics education for environmental sustainability. In P. Ernest (Ed.), *The philosophy of mathematics education today* (pp. 145–160). Springer. https://doi.org/10.1007/978-3-319-77760-3_9

Born, D. (2019). Bearing witness? Polar bears as icons for climate change communication in National Geographic. *Environmental Communication, 13*(5), 649–663. https://doi.org/10.1080/17524032.2018.1435557

Cheng, L.-J., Zhu, J., & Abraham, J. (2015). Global upper ocean heat content estimation: Recent progress and the remaining challenges. *Atmospheric and Oceanic Science Letters, 8*(6), 333–338. https://doi.org/10.3878/AOSL20150031

Christy, J. R. (2016). *U. S. House Committee on Science, Space and Technology: Testimony of John R. Christy*. https://docs.house.gov/meetings/SY/SY00/20160202/104399/HHRG-114-SY00-Wstate-ChristyJ-20160202.pdf

Corner, A., Whitmarsh, L., & Xenias, D. (2012). Uncertainty, scepticism and attitudes towards climate change: Biased assimilation and attitude polarisation. *Climatic Change, 114*(3), 463–478. https://doi.org/10.1007/s10584-012-0424-6

D'Ambrosio, U. (2007). Peace, social justice, and ethnomathematics. In B. Sriraman (Ed.), *International perspectives on social justice in mathematics education* (pp. 37–50). Information Age.

Frisch, M. (2018). Modeling climate policies: The social cost of carbon and uncertainties in climate predictions. In E. A. Lloyd & E. Winsberg (Eds.), *Climate modelling: Philosophical and conceptual issues* (pp. 413–448). Springer. https://doi.org/10.1007/978-3-319-65058-6_14

Funtowicz, S., & Ravetz, J. (2003, February). Post-normal science. In *Internet encyclopedia of ecological economics*. International Society for Ecological Economics. http://isecoeco.org/pdf/pstnormsc.pdf

Funtowicz, S., & Ravetz, J. (2008). Values and uncertainties. In G. H. Hadorn, H. Hoffmann-Riem, S. Biber-Klemm, W. Grossenbacher-Mansuy, D. Joye, C. Pohl, U. Wiesmann, & E. Zemp (Eds.), *Handbook of transdisciplinary research* (pp. 361–368). Springer. https://doi.org/10.1007/978-1-4020-6699-3_23

Gutstein, E. (2012). *Reading and writing the world with mathematics: Toward a pedagogy for social justice*. Routledge. https://doi.org/10.4324/9780203112946

Hamlin, L. (2016, May 25). Climate models don't work. Watts Up With That? https://wattsupwiththat.com/2016/05/25/climate-models-dont-work/

Hauge, K. H., & Barwell, R. (2017). Post-normal science and mathematics education in uncertain times: Educating future citizens for extended peer communities. *Futures, 91*, 25–34. https://doi.org/10.1016/j.futures.2016.11.013

Hijmans, R. J., Cameron, S., Parra, J., Jones, P., Jarvis, A., & Richardson, K. (2010, May 8). *WorldClim: Global weather stations*. Data Basin. https://databasin.org/datasets/15a31dec689b4c958ee491ff30fcce75

Intergovernmental Panel on Climate Change. (2001). *Climate change 2001: The scientific basis*. Cambridge University Press. https://www.ipcc.ch/site/assets/uploads/2018/07/WG1_TAR_FM.pdf

Intergovernmental Panel on Climate Change. (2013). *Climate change 2013: The physical science basis*. Cambridge University Press. http://www.climatechange2013.org/images/report/WG1AR5_ALL_FINAL.pdf

Intergovernmental Panel on Climate Change. (2018a). *Global warming of 1.5 °C*. https://www.ipcc.ch/sr15/

Intergovernmental Panel on Climate Change. (2018b, October 8). *Summary for policymakers of IPCC special report on global warming of 1.5 °C approved by governments*. https://www.ipcc.ch/2018/10/08/summary-for-policymakers-of-ipcc-special-report-on-global-warming-of-1-5c-approved-by-governments/

Kingan, S. (2005). Rethinking and connecting algebra to real-world issues. In E. Gutstein & B. Peterson (Eds.), *Rethinking mathematics: Teaching social justice by the numbers* (pp. 238–242). Rethinking Schools.

Lloyd, E. A. (2018). The role of "complex" empiricism in the debates about satellite data and climate models. In E. A. Lloyd & E. Winsberg (Eds.), *Climate modelling: Philosophical and conceptual issues* (pp. 137–173). Springer. https://doi.org/10.1007/978-3-319-65058-6_6

Lloyd, E. A., & Winsberg, E. (2018). Introduction. In E. A. Lloyd & E. Winsberg (Eds.), *Climate modelling: Philosophical and conceptual issues* (pp. 1–28). Springer. https://doi.org/10.1007/978-3-319-65058-6_1

Mann, M. E., Rahmstorf, S., Steinman, B. A., Tingley, M., & Miller, S. K. (2016). The likelihood of recent record warmth. *Scientific Reports, 6*, 1–7. https://doi.org/10.1038/srep19831

Ministry of Education and Research. (2013, June 21). *Curriculum for the common core subject of mathematics*. http://data.udir.no/kl06/MAT1-04.pdf?lang= http://data.udir.no/kl06/eng

Nordén, B. (2018). Transdisciplinary teaching for sustainable development in a whole school project. *Environmental Education Research, 24*(5), 663–677. https://doi.org/10.1080/13504622.2016.1266302

Nuccitelli, D. (2016, February 19). Republicans' favorite climate chart has some serious problems. *The Guardian*. https://www.theguardian.com/environment/climate-consensus-97-per-cent/2016/feb/19/republicans-favorite-climate-chart-has-some-serious-problems

Organisation for Economic Co-operation and Development. (2015). *Intervention and research protocol for OECD project on assessing progression in creative and critical thinking skills in education*. http://www.oecd.org/education/ceri/EDU-CERI-CD-2015-12-REV1.pdf

Organisation for Economic Co-operation and Development. (2016). *PISA 2015 assessment and analytical framework: Science, reading, mathematic and financial literacy*. https://doi.org/10.1787/9789264255425-en

Oreskes, N. (2018). The scientific consensus on climate change: How do we know we're not wrong? In E. A. Lloyd & E. Winsberg (Eds.), *Climate modelling: Philosophical and conceptual issues* (pp. 31–64). Springer. https://doi.org/10.1007/978-3-319-65058-6_2

Santer, B. D., Thorne, P. W., Haimberger, L., Taylor, K. E., Wigley, T. M. L., Lanzante, J. R., Solomon, S., Free, M., Gleckler, P. J., Jones, P. D., Karl, T. R., Klein, S. A., Mears, C., Nychka, D., Schmidt, G. A., Sherwood, S. C., & Wentz, F. J. (2008). Consistency of modelled and observed temperature trends in the tropical troposphere. *International Journal of Climatology, 28*(13), 1703–1722. https://doi.org/10.1002/joc.1756

Schmidt, G. (2016, May 7). *Comparing models to the satellite datasets*. Real Climate. http://www.realclimate.org/index.php/archives/2016/05/comparing-models-to-the-satellite-datasets/#more-18943

Sherrington, G. H. (2018, December 20). *The climate sciences use of the urban heat island effect is pathetic and misleading*. Watts Up With That? https://wattsupwiththat.com/2018/12/20/the-science-of-the-urban-heat-island-effect-is-pathetic-and-misleading/

Skovsmose, O. (1994). *Towards a philosophy of critical mathematics education*. Kluwer. https://doi.org/10.1007/978-94-017-3556-8

Skovsmose, O. (2014). Critical Mathematics Education. In S. Lerman (Ed.), *Encyclopedia of mathematics education* (pp. 116–120). Springer. https://doi.org/10.1007/978-94-007-4978-8

Steffensen, L. (2021). *Critical mathematics education and climate change. A teaching and research partnership in lower-secondary school* (Doctoral dissertation). Western Norway University of Applied Sciences.

Steffensen, L., Herheim, R., & Rangnes, T. E. (2018). Wicked problems in school mathematics. In E. Bergqvist, M. Österholm, C. Granberg, & L. Sumpter (Eds.), *Proceedings of the 42nd Conference of the International Group for the Psychology of Mathematics Education* (Vol. 4, pp. 227–234). PME.

Stroeve, J. C., Kattsov, V., Barrett, A., Serreze, M., Pavlova, T., Holland, M., & Meier, W. N. (2012). Trends in Arctic sea ice extent from CMIP5, CMIP3 and observations. *Geophysical Research Letters, 39*(16), 1–7. https://doi.org/10.1029/2012GL052676

Vithal, R. (2003). *In search of a pedagogy of conflict and dialogue for mathematics education*. Springer. https://doi.org/10.1007/978-94-010-0086-4

Watts, A. (2017). *Global temperatures plunge in April – "The pause" returns*. Watts Up With That? https://wattsupwiththat.com/2017/05/01/global-temperatures-plunge-in-april-the-pause-returns/

CHAPTER 10

The Mathematical Formatting of Obesity in Public Health Discourse

Jennifer Hall and Richard Barwell

Abstract

Rising rates of obesity are of widespread public concern and are targeted by public health policies around the world. In this chapter, we examine the origins of the most common definition of obesity, which is based on the Body Mass Index (BMI). We draw on Skovsmose's concept of formatting, combined with an examination of the origins of the BMI, to show how obesity is a form of realised abstraction. In particular, we show how, while the BMI originated as a statistical descriptor of specific populations, it is now used as a prescriptive construct applied to all individuals across the general population. We discuss how mathematics is therefore used to format or define obesity in a particular way, indicate some of the consequences of the particular way that this occurs through the BMI, and suggest some possibilities for mathematics teaching arising from this work. Our analysis is an example of how critical mathematics education provides a productive perspective with which to examine topics of widespread social concern, and thus inform both public education and mathematics education in schools.

Keywords

mathematical formatting – Body Mass Index (BMI) – obesity – public health discourse – critical mathematics education

∙ ∙ ∙

Obesity rates have been widely reported to be increasing in both children and adults, leading to higher rates of mortality and diseases like heart disease and diabetes. Societal effects include a less healthy population and increased pressure on health care systems. In response, governments around the world have developed public health policies, including school-based and public education programmes. For example, in the United Kingdom, Public Health England emphasises the negative effects of obesity on children and promotes various policies including school health plans, healthy diets, and physical activity for children.[1] In Ontario, Canada, meanwhile, the government has set a goal of reducing childhood obesity by 20% over five years.[2] Public and educational discourses tend to focus on the negative effects of obesity, contrasted with the positive effects of exercise and a healthy diet. In schools, obesity, diet, and fitness are typically addressed in health and physical education curricula. The construction of obesity is, however, partially based on mathematics.

We see mathematics education as extending beyond classrooms to include wider public and educational discourses in which mathematics plays a role. In particular, we draw on Skovsmose's (1994) idea that mathematics shapes reality, known as *formatting*. We see a role for critical mathematics education in conducting analyses of formatting in different domains, in order to uncover the often-hidden ways that mathematics shapes contemporary human experience. In this chapter, we offer an example of such an analysis focussed on a standard measure of obesity: the Body Mass Index (BMI). We examine the history and recent use of this measure to show how mathematics has effects on the wider experience of weight, obesity, and, by extension, body image. In our analysis, we reveal some problematic issues. We argue that such analyses provide an opportunity for students and citizens to participate critically in the production and consumption of public health information. To give a sense of public discourse about obesity, we begin with a brief overview of claims made in public health policy and research.

1   The "Obesity Epidemic"

The discourse of an "obesity epidemic" has infiltrated the collective cultural consciousness. For example, in a recent US poll, Allen (2014) found that childhood obesity was the most common childhood health concern reported by the adult participants, with 55% of participants selecting this option, compared to 52% for bullying (which may be weight-related in some cases[3]) and 49% for drug abuse. In Canada, the overall prevalence of obesity increased from 9% to 21% over a 25-year period (Elgar & Stewart, 2008). More specifically, in the 2013 edition of the Canadian Community Health Survey (CCHS), which uses self-reported height and weight data, it was found that 18.8% of adults were obese (Statistics Canada, 2014). When considering men and women separately,[4] marked sex differences were seen: 62% of men and 45% of women were considered to be either overweight or obese. Although the proportion of overweight or obese women has remained stable since the 2010 edition of the CCHS, the combined rate of overweight/obesity in men had a statistically significant increase from the 2012 edition of the CCHS (Statistics Canada, 2014). While increases in the percentage of the US population in the "obese" category, as measured by the BMI, were seen from 1976 to 2000, this percentage has stabilised in recent years: Flegal et al. (2012), using nationally-representative data from over 5,000 U.S. adults, found that there was no statistically significant difference in the proportion of men or women who were "obese" between 2003 and 2008.

Similar trends have been seen with regard to obesity in children and adolescents: substantial increases in the proportion of obese young people in the 1980s and 1990s, followed by a plateau in the 2000s (Ogden et al., 2012). Using a nationally representative sample of over 4,000 US children and adolescents, Ogden et al. (2012) found no statistically significant difference in the proportion of obese young people between 2007–2008 and 2009–2010. However, when considering this dataset from 1999–2000 to 2009–2010, statistically significant increases in the proportion of obese children and adolescents (ages 2 to 19) were seen for boys, but not for girls. In contrast, in a study involving adolescents in Ontario, Canada, McCrindle et al. (2010) found a statistically significant increase each year from 2002 to 2008 in the proportion of adolescents, both girls and boys, who were obese. In the most recent edition of the CCHS, it was found that levels of overweight/obesity in Canadian youths aged 12 to 17 are stabilising: 20.7% of participants were found to be overweight or obese in the 2013 survey, which is similar to the percentage reported in the 2008 survey, although an increase over the percentage (18.7%) reported in the 2007 survey (Statistics Canada, 2014). The self-reported levels of physical activity in the 2013 survey were not statistically significantly different between the "normal" weight participants and the overweight/obese participants.

As this overview suggests, public discourse is highly mathematical, with widespread reference to statistical findings, measures, and trends. We should not take this mathematical presentation of obesity at face value. In the rest of this chapter, we examine this mathematised version of obesity in more depth.

2 BMI in the Media

BMI is a frequently discussed topic in public media. Using a sample of the top US and Canadian newspapers by circulation (Cision Canada, 2017; Cision US, 2017), we investigated the discourse surrounding the BMI in popular media. For instance, in *USA Today*, the US newspaper with the top circulation, a search for "BMI" yielded 12 relevant articles and videos. While some of these articles and videos provided critiques of BMI due to its focus on weight rather than body composition, using phrases such as "a controversial way of measuring obesity" (Buzz60, 2013) and "an oversimplified number calculation" (Nickel, 2016), the BMI was also mentioned without being critiqued in other articles (e.g., discussing links between drinking different types of milk and childhood obesity). Furthermore, inaccurate information was provided in the articles and videos, such as descriptions of BMI as "a measurement of body fat based on height and weight" (Saker, 2015) and "a way of determining obesity by standardising weight for people of different heights" (Macklin, 2014). While the latter description is more accurate than the former, it still equates a BMI value to an indicator of obesity.

In *The Globe and Mail*, the top Canadian newspaper by circulation, a search for BMI yielded 326 relevant results, so only the first 12 were considered, as a point of comparison to the *USA Today* sample. In some of the articles, no definition was given for the BMI. In others, an accurate but vague definition was provided, such as "a measure of weight relative to height" (Kennedy, 2017). In these instances, no critiques of the BMI were provided. Furthermore, as with the aforementioned example (Macklin, 2014), obesity and high BMI values were equated in articles (e.g., Hutchinson, 2015). As we explain later in this chapter, it is possible to have a high BMI value and not be obese, so drawing such a parallel is problematic.

3 A Critical Mathematics Education Perspective

Understandings of obesity are heavily influenced by medical and epidemiological research, as well as by health-care systems. These influences are based, in part, on mathematical foundations. Mathematics is not, however, a neutral tool in these endeavours. For Skovsmose (1994), mathematics in operation formats society – in this case, public health discourse – through being embedded in the technological systems that organise contemporary society. Skovsmose explains how formatting works in terms of a distinction between thinking abstractions and realised abstractions. Applying mathematics to the world involves thinking abstractions – that is, it involves using mathematical concepts and, in particular, mathematical models to approximate aspects of the natural or social world. For example, climate models, epidemiological models, and quantum mechanics involve using mathematics to describe the behaviour of the climate, diseases, or subatomic particles, respectively. These models are, however, abstractions in the sense that those who create them select some features and omit others in describing reality, depending on the purpose of the mathematical model. Skovsmose contrasts thinking abstractions with realised abstractions. With realised abstractions, what comes to be experienced as reality derives from mathematical models or systems: The models become, in some sense, real. Examples of realised abstractions mentioned by Skovsmose include money, taxation, and internet search results (see, for example, Skovsmose, 2001). In the case of the latter, for example, search results are obtained through the application of sophisticated algorithms, which use information from the internet, as well as information about the searcher, to produce a specific ordered list of websites. These results could determine where users go on holidays, the house they buy, for whom they vote, or many other significant or insignificant choices. This example illustrates how mathematical models have real social effects: they are realised abstractions.

Mathematical formatting occurs when realised abstractions are embedded in technological systems. Internet search engines are entirely electronic, and users do not need to understand or even be aware of the algorithms when using the system. The algorithms, and hence the search results, are mathematical human creations, involving deliberate choices, including choices based on commercial interests (e.g., in relation to advertising). For the most part, however, users of search engines do not give much thought to the algorithms or their human designers, and simply make use of the first page or so of search results. Instead, they adjust their behaviour to fit the system. Hence, in Skovsmose's (1994) conception, "Mathematics intervenes in reality by creating a 'second nature' around us, by giving not only descriptions of phenomena, but also by giving models for changed behaviour. We not only 'see' according to mathematics, we also 'do' according to mathematics" (p. 55).

The idea of mathematical formatting can be used to understand the treatment of obesity through the BMI. Mathematics is used as a tool to understand obesity: or rather, mathematics contributes to the creation of obesity as a concept and as a problem, and thus shapes people's experiences of obesity and of themselves. This idea is similar to discourse theories that emphasise how language is not simply a means of describing the world or of transmitting thoughts between people; language influences what it is possible to say and to see, providing categories, structures, and ways of organising experience. Moreover, both discourse in general and mathematics in particular are not simply tools; their use reflects the interests of those who use them (e.g., Edwards & Potter, 1992). They contribute to and reflect prevailing ways of understanding the world to the extent that they become largely invisible.

Realised abstractions arise, of course, through historical processes. As Skovsmose (1994) suggests:

> Every society and every culture has developed a realm of realised abstractions. But from what sources? They must be brought into existence by

some creative act. We may, for instance, be able to trace some realised abstractions back to ideological structures or to metaphysical systems. However, as realised abstractions they have attained the status of laws and principles for the formation of certain social entities. They have to be taken into consideration as part of reality. They are not any longer just models for our thinking ... the concepts come to life. (p. 52)

This observation suggests a method with which to examine the role of mathematics in the production of realised abstractions in society. In the case of obesity, a concept that is now widely used to organise public, education, and health policies, we can trace the origins of its definition, paying attention to the ways that mathematics has shaped its development and implantation in public discourse. We can also, through this process, uncover the interests at stake and the social effects of the particular ways that the concept of obesity has been realised.

4 What Is the BMI?

The BMI is calculated using the formula[5]

$$BMI = weight/(height)^2$$

According to the Centers for Disease Control and Prevention (2014a), BMI values fall into four categories: underweight (BMI < 18.5), normal weight (18.5 ≤ BMI ≤ 24.9), overweight (25.0 ≤ BMI ≤ 29.9), and obese (BMI > 30.0). For example, an individual who is 1.63 m tall would need to weigh less than 49 kg to be considered underweight, 49 to 66 kg to be considered normal weight, 66 to 79 kg to be considered overweight, and more than 79 kg to be considered obese. For children (ages 2 to 19), the BMI formula is used in a different way than it is used for adults, due to children's rapidly changing growth patterns, and sex differences in body fat percentage (which, oddly, the BMI does not consider for adults). A child's BMI is calculated using the standard formula, and then the BMI and age are plotted on a graph (one for boys and one for girls) that shows percentiles (Centers for Disease Control and Prevention, 2014b). Children are considered underweight if their BMI/age data are less than the 5th percentile, normal weight if their BMI/age data range from the 5th to less than the 85th percentile, overweight if their BMI/age data range from the 85th to less than the 95th percentile, and obese if their BMI/age data are greater than or equal to the 95th percentile (Centers for Disease Control and Prevention, 2014b).

It is apparent that the definition of obesity, based on the BMI, involves a number of assumptions, including the selection of weight and height as variables, the ratio weight / height^2, and the cut off points for the different BMI categories. On what, then, are these assumptions based? Next, we review the history of the development of the BMI and similar indices. In the section after that, we examine some of the assumptions that emerge from this account.

4.1 History of the BMI Formula

The Body Mass Index (BMI) formula was formerly known as the Quetelet Index, in deference to Adolphe Quetelet (1796–1874), the Belgian statistician who derived the formula. Quetelet was a polymath, with a strong interest and talent in both the arts and sciences, and he made significant contributions to a variety of fields, including statistics, meteorology, visual arts, mathematics, and astronomy (Eknoyan, 2008). In 1835, he published *Physique Sociale, ou Essai sur le Development des Facultés de L'Homme* (published in 1842 in English as *A Treatise on Man and the Development of his Faculties*), in which he sought to describe l'homme moyen (the average man – note the gender), in terms of a variety of social and physical characteristics (Eknoyan, 2008; Faerstein & Winkelstein, 2012). Quetelet used population census data from men from the Netherlands as the basis for his statistical work, creating formulas to fit the existing data (Eknoyan, 2008). He struggled to fit the relationship between weight and height data using a Gaussian (bell) curve, a pattern followed by many of the other variables he examined. Quetelet (1842) noted the following:

> If man increased equally in all his dimensions, his weight at different ages would be as the cube of his height. Now, this is not what we really observe. The increase of weight is slower, except during the first year after birth; then the proportion which we have just pointed out is pretty regularly observed. But after this period, and until near the age of puberty, weight increases nearly as the square of the height. The development of the weight again becomes very rapid at the time of puberty, and almost stops after the twenty-fifth year. In general, we do not err much when we assume that, *during development, the squares of the weight at different ages are as the fifth powers of the height*; which naturally leads to this conclusion, in supporting the specific gravity constant, that the transverse growth of man is less than the vertical. (p. 66, emphasis in original)

Due to his recognition of this relationship, Quetelet's Index was derived as the formula now known as the BMI. Despite the index's recent, widespread use as an indicator of obesity, "In developing his index, Quetelet had no interest in obesity. His concern was defining the characteristics of 'normal man' and fitting the distribution around the norm" (Eknoyan, 2008, p. 49). Notably, Quetelet's "normal man" was based on data from men in the Netherlands in the 1800s, a rather homogeneous White European population. As a result, the widespread use of this index to describe obesity in both men and women in a worldwide population is problematic, since men and women have different physiological characteristics and variation exists between populations in different parts of the world.

Quetelet's Index was not well-known by the general public for more than a century after its publication. Indeed, obesity was not a major societal concern until the 20th century, when the relationship between obesity and ill health became a focus, particularly by the insurance industry (Eknoyan, 2008). In 1943, Louis Dublin, a statistician and vice-president of the Metropolitan Life Insurance Company, developed tables of "ideal weights" for men and women based on height and weight data from insurance clients (Jarrett, 1986). These tables were formed using data from individuals aged 25 to 29, as they tended to have the lowest mortality rates (Wildman & Medeiros, 1999). Presuming that this low mortality rate was linked to body weight is flawed statistical reasoning. Arguably, lower rates of disease and age-related ill health (most of which are unrelated to being overweight or obese) are a more likely explanation for young adults' low mortality rates. As with the dataset upon which Quetelet's Index was based, the Metropolitan Life tables were based on a rather homogeneous dataset comprised mostly of White European individuals (Pekar, 2011). Data were included from people who were wearing clothing and shoes during the measurements, and 20% of the data were self-reported (Jarrett, 1986); both of these factors decrease confidence in any claims derived from the dataset.

The Metropolitan Life tables were separated by frame size, with the acceptable weight for each height being divided into thirds, relative to small, medium, and large frame sizes. Problematically, these divisions were not based on any measurements of bone structure; rather, Dublin noticed that "healthy" weights (i.e., those associated with low mortality) encompassed a range of up to 40 pounds, and then, in order to account for this range, he divided it arbitrarily into thirds, based on his explanatory notion of bone structure (Gaesser, 2002; Pekar, 2011). Weights falling into the lowest 20–25% and highest 30% for a height were considered undesirable with regard to insurance purposes (Eknoyan, 2008). Similar to the use of the BMI as a measurement of obesity, the Metropolitan Life tables were used out of context: these tables were initially intended for use as an actuarial tool. However, Dublin did promote the link between excess weight and early mortality (Oliver, 2006). The widespread adoption of the Metropolitan Life tables has been cited as the impetus for a dieting frenzy that began in the 1940s and continues to this day, as people – mostly women – sought to match the "ideal" weights promoted by the tables (Crossen, 2003). The tables were revised in subsequent decades using more recent actuarial data from Metropolitan Life clients, and actual measurements of body frame (elbow breadth) were incorporated, but many of the aforementioned problems remained, including the lack of consideration of age or ethnic background (Crossen, 2003; Gaesser, 2002; Himes & Bouchard, 1985).

Dublin's tables remained in common use well into the 1970s, when a study by Keys et al. (1972) shifted the focus of the obesity measurement conversation, by confirming the validity of Quetelet's Index. In so doing, these researchers challenged many of the assumptions underpinning the Metropolitan Life tables. For example, they argued that the sample used as the basis of the tables was not random and thus should not have been generalised, since "persons examined in connection with application for life insurance are far from being a random sample of the population" (p. 330). Other ratios, such as weight/height, $(weight)^{1/3}$/height (ponderal index), and weight/height^3 (Rohrer index), were considered in this study, but Quetelet's Index best fit existing weight and height data. Keys and colleagues suggested referring to this index as the Body Mass Index, the first known use of this term. To examine this index, these researchers used data from nearly 7,500 men in Japan, South Africa, the United States, and several European countries. As with Quetelet's original dataset on which his index was based, Keys and colleagues' dataset also only included men, a major oversight since the BMI is now applied to both women and men. The men in this study were subjected to skinfold measurements (to show subcutaneous fat) and density measurements (to show body composition). When comparing these precise measurements to the aforementioned ratios, Keys and colleagues found that "the body mass index seems preferable over other indices of relative weight" (p. 341), and noted that it was simple in its application.

This simplicity in application arguably underpinned the promotion of the BMI as a tool for measuring (or at least estimating) a person's "fatness." The World Health Organization has been using the BMI to calculate worldwide obesity statistics since the early 1980s (Marchand, 2010), while the U.S. National Institutes of Health (NIH) began using the BMI in 1985 (Singer-Vine, 2009). At this point, the NIH defined overweight individuals as those who were in the 85th percentile of BMI by sex: 27.8 for men and 27.3 for women (Singer-Vine, 2009). However, in 1998, the NIH changed their BMI "cut-off" points to 25 for overweight and 30 for obese individuals, with men and women now grouped together despite their differences in body fat (Singer-Vine, 2009); as Cohen and McDermott (1998) reported, 25 million Americans who were not considered overweight previously were suddenly placed in that category, simply due to the NIH's new cut-off points for the BMI measurement. Cohen and McDermott pointed out a few of the key problems with the BMI: lack of consideration of body composition, sex, and frame size. These issues, and others, will be considered in the next section.

5 Critically Interrogating Obesity and the BMI

It is apparent from our brief historical account of the BMI that a number of assumptions, generalisations, and simplifications were included in the development of the formula and its application. We summarise the most significant issues and highlight some of their implications.

First, there are a number of mathematical over-simplifications. The BMI does not take into account body composition (Cohen & McDermott, 1998). Fat, bone, and muscle all have different densities (fat = 0.9 g/mL, muscle = 1.06 g/mL, and bone = 1.85 g/mL), but these differences are not measured by the BMI (Devlin, 2009). Consequently, individuals may have the same BMI, but very different body compositions and thus, different health risks. A bodybuilder, athlete, or other highly muscular person (who has a low percentage of body fat) would have the same BMI as a same-height individual with a far higher percentage of body fat, as long as they weigh the same amount. Arguably, the former person is the less "overweight" with regard to obesity-related health concerns, but both individuals would have the same BMI and thus would be considered equally "overweight." Notably, on the Centers for Disease Control and Prevention (n.d.) website, which has a wealth of resources related to the BMI under a section entitled "Assessing Your Weight," the following claims are made: "A high BMI can be an indicator of high body fatness. BMI can be used to screen for weight categories that may lead to health problems but it is not diagnostic of the body fatness or health of an individual." Thus, even though the BMI is promoted by the Centers for Disease Control and Prevention as a tool to assess one's weight (and, presumably, related health risks), these caveats are also provided. Indeed, recent findings (Statistics Canada, 2017) from the Canadian Health Measures Survey indicate that "health risks associated with being overweight or obese (as determined by body mass index, or BMI) were offset by high levels of aerobic fitness." Thus, rather than using a simple ratio of height and weight as the basis for judging a person's health risks based on being "obese" or "overweight," other, more meaningful measurements (e.g., aerobic fitness, blood pressure, blood sugar) should be taken to determine health risks.

Furthermore, Quetelet's formulation of the BMI, as well as subsequent verification (Keys et al., 1972), was based on measurements of White European men living in the early 19th century. As such, the BMI has been generalised from one category of person to apply to all sexes and racial backgrounds. In similar fashion, the Metropolitan Life tables were based on White men and women in their twenties (who applied for life insurance), but were applied to the population as a whole. Again, these data were used to make generalisations about a more diverse population, including people of all ages.

In addition, the formula for BMI (weight/height^2) overestimates "fatness" in tall people and underestimates "fatness" in short adults (as well as in children) (MacKay, 2010; Marchand, 2010). That is, for a given weight, BMI is inversely proportional to height^2. Since the BMI formula is used for people of all heights, these issues with scaling imply that for a given body shape, a taller person is less healthy (i.e., more obese) than a shorter person (MacKay, 2010), simply because they are taller.

The origins of the BMI go deeper, however, for which we must look more carefully at the purpose of Quetelet's work. The *Treatise on Man* (Quetelet, 1842) contributed to a significant moment in the emergence of statistics. Quetelet's goal was not to define obesity or any other physical characteristics of individuals, but to describe a population. Hacking (1990) describes how, up until the time that the *Treatise on Man* was published, a burgeoning body of statistical data had been established. European governments began to organise more careful collection of such data, which encompassed everything from prison populations to forms of suicide to the physical characteristics of soldiers. At the point at which the *Treatise on Man* was published, however, such data were largely provided in tables. Many attempts were made to identify patterns and much excitement was generated by the discovery of social "laws" that appeared to demonstrate constant rates of infant mortality or disease, for example. The key step taken by Quetelet was to move from the description of individuals to the description, and hence definition, of a population. Hacking (1990) summarises the significance of this step:

> Up to here the monograph considered quantities that exist in nature. Here we pass from a real physical unknown, the height of one person, to a postulated reality, an objective property of a population at a time, its mean height or longevity or whatever. This postulated truth ... was thought of not as an arithmetical abstract of real heights, but as itself a number that objectively describes the population. (p. 109)

The important point here is that the very idea of standard, "normal" heights, weights, and other characteristics had not previously been conceived. The formula now known as the BMI was not simply descriptive – It created the idea of a normal weight.

Quetelet's work therefore influenced another important development in nineteenth century thought: a new ideology of normal (Hacking, 1990). Quetelet derived normal characteristics of populations, including national characteristics, such as the heights of men from Scotland. The idea that a population, or a people, could be in some sense defined by such averages, was new. Over time, however, "normal" came to mean more than "typical"; individuals who were far from the normal became constructed as being abnormal or pathological. Normal then came to be seen as a desirable state, and as desirable *for* the state. Hacking (1990) summarises these developments as encapsulating "two kinds of progress":

> The normal stands indifferently for what is typical, the unenthusiastic objective average, but it also stands for what has been, good health, and for what shall be, our chosen destiny. That is why the benign and sterile-sounding word 'normal' has become one of the most powerful ideological tools of the twentieth century. (p. 169)

Into the twenty-first century, one only has to think of the pressure on women, and increasingly men, to conform to certain normalised conceptions of appearance, beauty, and health. Quetelet, then, was central to the story of the emergence of the idea of an average representing not simply a group of individuals, but a population, and hence to the emergence of averages as realised abstractions used to define and control people.

As indices like the BMI or the Metropolitan Life tables became widely used (facilitated by information technology, mass communication, and mass health care systems), they became realised abstractions, and as such were part of the new ideology of "normal." These norms are used to define what people *should* weigh and, indirectly, what they should look like. Mathematics formats obesity through these realised abstractions and accompanying ideology, embedded in the technology of public health-care systems. For this interpretation, we consider technology to be more than specific information technology systems; we see the public health-care system as a whole as a complex human-made technology through which conditions like obesity are defined, identified, and treated, whether through specific medical interventions or more diffuse public health campaigns. Such systems are vectors for the ideology of normal; indeed, health-care systems now depend fundamentally on the Quetelian man[6] as an implicit reference point. Mathematics is embedded in the system, with doctors, health workers, health policy workers, and citizens all making decisions based on a relatively poorly interrogated realised mathematical abstraction.

Our summary of the problems with defining obesity comes from the health literature, so it is clear that health researchers are well aware of the mathematical limitations of the BMI. The literature shows that other indices have also been considered, so there is no sense that BMI is *the* definitive measure. Nevertheless, when the mathematical force of the BMI as the "preferred" index, partly due to its simplicity, is implanted into health care systems and public health and education policy, these kinds of subtleties tend to be smoothed off, leaving only a definitive (i.e., it defines people) formula, with various cut-offs based on statistical analyses for what constitutes obese, overweight, normal, or underweight. The ideological basis for the application of the BMI is, however, less easily challenged. The BMI, moreover, is not simply a technical tool; it has real consequences for real people. For example, the implementation of "BMI report cards" for students in elementary and secondary schools has been reported in the United States, the United Kingdom, and Malaysia (Flaherty, 2013). Such interventions illustrate the logical conclusion of the ideological construction of normal as chosen destiny, in which the state chooses the desired destination and uses statistics, in essence, as a means of control.

Our point, then, is not that obesity does not exist or that obesity is not associated with health risks. Our point is that the certainty of science, through the use of mathematics, turns a fuzzy and complex phenomenon into a normative, prescriptive, and ideological abstraction, which in turn leads to concrete interventions (i.e., control), in the form of advice, medication, and penalties, such as, in some cases, exclusion from school. This normativity, in turn, is likely to feed into wider discourses relating to such topics as body image, femininity, masculinity, identity, and race. It is worth noting that in addition to contributing to the development of the new field of statistics, Quetelet's work was taken up by the founders of eugenics (Hacking, 1990).

We must ask who benefits from this mathematical formatting of obesity. It seems clear that there is much profit to be made from the weight loss industry, which requires individuals to be identified as obese or overweight in order to ensure a market for their products. Similarly, various medical interventions, including surgery, have become widespread in response to the obesity epidemic. Our account of the history of obesity indices also highlights the connection with life insurance providers, who have an interest in identifying low-risk clients and excluding high-risk ones. In particular, life insurance providers would seem likely to have an interest in exaggerating or over-weighting possible risks in order to protect their business. The state, too, may have reasons to seek to control the weight of the population, reasons that may, for example, relate to the need for a healthy workforce.

5.1 Implications for Mathematics Education

An internet search for mathematics lessons or activities about BMI yielded several examples of lesson plans in which students are charged with calculating BMI values (and often graphing the data), using height and weight data from celebrities, fictitious individuals, personal contacts (e.g., family members, neighbours), and, problematically, themselves. Several popular media articles chronicle issues that may arise when students are required to be weighed in school,[7] such as bullying, self-esteem issues, and eating disorders (e.g., Deardorff, 2013; Kilen, 2014; Steuter-Martin, 2017), but few of the lessons that we found provided any sort of warning regarding such potential problems. In one particularly troubling lesson (Gill, n.d.), students are required to measure their heights and weights in small groups and then calculate their BMI values. Then, as an assessment, students must write "a take home essay determining why you think you have a particular BMI index. If your score is over the normal amount explain why, if your score is under the normal amount explain why?" (p. 2). Notably, students whose BMI values are in the "normal" range are not expected to explain their BMI values, which is a very troubling message to send to students.

Beyond the weight-related social and emotional issues that such lessons may raise, very few of the lessons provide any critique of the BMI, instead using it as though it is a benign formula. For instance, in a lesson that featured in a recent article (Yanik & Memis, 2016) in *Teaching Children Mathematics*, students calculated the BMI values for fictional children, decided how much weight the children needed to lose or gain to be "healthy," and then created diet plans for the children. At no point in this lesson is the BMI formula (or the issues with equating weight and health) ever challenged. Problematically, the article ended with a section entitled "Using Math to Make Informed Decisions," wherein the authors made erroneous claims regarding "healthy BMI" values and "healthy weights." One notable counter-example (Mathalicious, n.d.) to such troubling lessons explicitly focuses on challenging the BMI as a measurement of "health" through the use of height and weight data from celebrities such as Arnold Schwarzenegger to show how the BMI is flawed.

The learning and teaching of mathematics in school can address the role of mathematics in society (Skovsmose, 1994). In the case of obesity, for example, students could study the history that we have recounted in this chapter, test different indices using data that they have collected themselves, and discuss the validity of their findings. This kind of work relates to curriculum goals for statistics, algebra, and other mathematical topics. Such explorations could also be developed as cross-curricular topics, so that, for example, health education and mathematics education are combined. In this way, the role of mathematics in defining health can be discussed.

We do not see mathematics education as something confined to schools and curricula. In an increasingly information-rich society, there is scope for a stronger form of public mathematics education. Citizens must engage with information about health in general and about themselves in particular, in order to make decisions about their lives, their families, and their communities. Public mathematics education would not presume that citizens are incapable of using information effectively; rather, it would prompt them to look "beyond the data" rather than accepting the prescribed role of passive consumers of health information.

6   Concluding Remarks

In public health discourse, obesity is constructed as a significant challenge. We have not had space to enter into its complex discursive construction, which involves the intersection of identities, genders, sexualisation of body image, advertising, fashion, health, fitness, and other discourses. We have, however, shown how obesity is mathematically formatted, through an analysis of the historical development of measures of body mass. In this analysis, we have also highlighted the problematic nature of this formatting, such as its basis in narrow subsets of the population, and more generally the shift from descriptive to prescriptive models and its association with the ideology of normal.

Broadly, this work demonstrates the value of such analyses. A great deal of everyday, taken-for-granted aspects of contemporary society are mathematically formatted through the use of models and other mathematical tools, embedded in some form of technology – either IT systems or broader technologies of public sector administrative systems. We contend that the kind of critical mathematics education analysis that we have presented in this chapter offers a valuable method by which to uncover and critically interrogate these forms of mathematical formatting. Such analyses, in turn, create opportunities to engage citizens and school students in examining the society in which they live. Indeed, we believe that conducting such analyses can form a valuable part of mathematics education in school, thus contributing to the preparation of students to participate in democratic life.

Notes

1   See https://www.gov.uk/government/publications/childhood-obesity-a-plan-for-action/childhood-obesity-a-plan-for-action
2   See www.health.gov.on.ca/en/public/programs/obesity/

3   Although the term weight is widely used, technically, and as indicated in the name of the index, the issue is one of mass. Here, we use "weight" to reflect the common discourse around the topic of the BMI.
4   BMI is always calculated based on a sex binary, thus ignoring intersex individuals.
5   An alternate formula, using the Imperial measurement system (pounds and inches), is: BMI = weight/(height)^2 × 703, with 703 being a conversion factor. Consequently, the units for the BMI are either kg/m^2 or lb/in^2, although these units are rarely cited with a BMI value.
6   Unfortunately, medicine and healthcare are still often based on male-normed research.
7   There are guidelines from the Centers for Disease Control and Prevention for collecting weight/height data in schools: https://www.cdc.gov/healthyschools/obesity/BMI/BMI_measurement_schools.htm
    These guidelines advise, among other things, students weighing themselves in private. There is no clear evidence that being weighed helps children with weight loss.

References

Allen, J. (2014, August 13). *U-M study finds obesity, bullying and gun-related violence among top childhood health concerns.* M Live. https://www.mlive.com/news/ann-arbor/2014/08/u-m_study_finds_obesity_bullyi.html

Buzz60. (2013, July 29). Man told he's too fat for work visa [Video]. *USA Today.* https://www.usatoday.com/videos/news/world/2013/07/29/2596847/

Centers for Disease Control and Prevention. (2014a). *About BMI for adults.* https://www.cdc.gov/healthyweight/assessing/bmi/adult_bmi/index.html

Centers for Disease Control and Prevention. (2014b). *About BMI for children and teens.* https://www.cdc.gov/healthyweight/assessing/bmi/childrens_bmi/about_childrens_bmi.html

Centers for Disease Control and Prevention. (n.d.). *Assessing your weight.* https://www.cdc.gov/healthyweight/assessing/bmi/index.html

Cision Canada. (2017). *Canada's top 20 daily newspapers.* https://www.cision.ca/trends/canadas-top-20-daily-newspapers/

Cision US. (2017). *Top 10 US daily newspapers.* https://www.cision.com/us/2014/06/top-10-us-daily-newspapers/

Cohen, E., & McDermott, A. (1998, June 17). *Who's fat? New definition adopted.* CNN Interactive. http://www.cnn.com/HEALTH/9806/17/weight.guidelines/

Crossen, C. (2003, July 16). Americans are gaining weight, but the 'ideal' size keeps shrinking. *The Wall Street Journal.* https://www.wsj.com/articles/SB105830232931443000

Deardorff, J. (2013, May 17). BMI measuring in schools proves weighty issue. *Chicago Tribune.* https://www.chicagotribune.com/lifestyles/ct-xpm-2013-05-17-ct-met-bmi-backlash-20130517-story.html

Devlin, K. (2009, May). *Do you believe in fairies, unicorns, or the BMI?* Mathematical Association of America. https://www.maa.org/external_archive/devlin/devlin_05_09.html

Edwards, D., & Potter, J. (1992). *Discursive psychology*. Sage.

Eknoyan, G. (2008). Adolphe Quetelet (1796–1974) – The average man and indices of obesity. *Nephrology Dialysis Transplantation, 23*(1), 47–51. https://doi.org/10.1093/ndt/gfm517

Elgar, F. J., & Stewart, J. M. (2008). Validity of self-report screening for overweight andobesity: Evidence from the Canadian Community Health Survey. *Canadian Journal of Public Health, 99*(5), 423–427. https://doi.org/10.1007/BF03405254

Faerstein, E., & Winkelstein Jr., W. (2012). Adolphe Quetelet: Statistician and more. *Epidemiology, 23*(5), 762–763. https://doi.org/10.1097/EDE.0b013e318261c86f

Flaherty, M. R. (2013). "Fat letters" in public schools: Public health versus pride. *Pediatrics, 132*(3), 403–405. https://doi.org/10.1542/peds.2013-0926

Flegal, K. M., Carroll, M. D., Kit, B. K., & Ogden, C. L. (2012). Prevalence of obesity and trends in the distribution of body mass index among US adults, 1999–2010. *Journal of the American Medical Association, 307*(5), 491–497. https://doi.org/10.1001/jama.2012.39

Gaesser, G. A. (2002). *Big fat lies: The truth about your weight and your health*. Gürze Books.

Gill, E. (n.d.). Health lesson plan. *Scribd*. https://www.scribd.com/document/406321936/Erin-Health-Lesson-Plan-1-doc

Hacking, I. (1990). *The taming of chance*. Cambridge University Press. https://doi.org/10.1017/cbo9780511819766

Himes, J. H., & Bouchard, C. (1985). Do the new Metropolitan Life Insurance weight-height tables correctly assess body frame and body fat relationships? *American Journal of Public Health, 75*(9), 1076–1079. https://doi.org/10.2105/AJPH.75.9.1076

Hutchinson, A. (2015, February 1). What your genes can tell you about your health. *The Globe and Mail*. https://www.theglobeandmail.com/life/health-and-fitness/fitness/what-our-genes-tell-us-about-our-health/article22724898/

Jarrett, R. J. (1986). Is there an ideal body weight? *British Medical Journal, 293*(6545), 493–495. https://doi.org/10.1136/bmj.293.6545.493

Kennedy, M. (2017, June 16). Sleeping-in on weekends linked to lower body weight. *Reuters*. https://www.reuters.com/article/us-health-sleep-body-weight/sleeping-in-on-weekends-linked-to-lower-body-weight-idUSKBN1972EJ

Keys, A., Fidanza, F., Karvonen, M. J., Kimura, N., & Taylor, H. L. (1972). Indices of relative weight and obesity. *Journal of Chronic Diseases, 25*(6–7), 329–343. https://doi.org/10.1016/0021-9681(72)90027-6

Kilen, M. (2014, November 13). Student's protest sparks debate over weighing at school. *USA Today*. https://www.usatoday.com/story/news/nation/2014/11/13/students-protest-sparks-debate-over-weighing-at-school/19006167/

MacKay, N. J. (2010). Scaling of human body mass with height: The body mass index revisited. *Journal of Biomechanics, 43*(4), 764–766. https://doi.org/10.1016/j.jbiomech.2009.10.038

Macklin, T. (2014, July 1). BMI not a total picture of health. *The Roanoke Times.* https://www.roanoke.com/archive/bmi-not-a-total-picture-of-health/article_6db5572e-f662-5ecc-91a3-afb575ca9c7b.html

Marchand, V. (2010). Author's response: Letter to the editor. *Paediatrics & Child Health, 15*(5), 258. https://dx.doi.org/10.1093%2Fpch%2F15.5.258

Mathalicious. (n.d.). *Hi, BMI: What's a healthy weight?* https://www.mathalicious.com/lessons/hi-bmi

McCrindle, B. W., Manlhiot, C., Millar, K., Gibson, D., Stearne, K., Kilty, H., Prentice, D., Wong, H., Chahal, N., & Dobbin, S. W. (2010). Population trends toward increasing cardiovascular risk factors in Canadian adolescents. *The Journal of Pediatrics, 157*(5), 837–843. https://doi.org/10.1016/j.jpeds.2010.05.014

Nickel, L. (2016, June 13). Packers: Forget BMI, now it's all about body composition. *Milwaukee Journal Sentinel.* https://www.jsonline.com/story/sports/nfl/packers/2016/06/13/packers-forget-bmi-now-its-all-about-body-composition/85857580/

Ogden, C. L., Carroll, M. D., Kit, B. K., & Flegal, K. M. (2012). Prevalence of obesity and trends in body mass index among US children and adolescents, 1999–2010. *Journal of the American Medical Association, 307*(5), 483–490. https://doi.org/10.1001/jama.2012.40

Oliver, J. E. (2006). *Fat politics: The real story behind America's obesity epidemic.* Oxford University Press.

Pekar, T. (2011, Summer). Body mass index. *IMS Magazine,* 21–22. https://issuu.com/imsmagazine/docs/imssummer2011/22

Quetelet, M. A. (1842). *A treatise on man and the development of his faculties.* William and Robert Chambers.

Saker, A. (2015, February 17). Super obese won't get longer life from bariatric surgery. *USA Today.* https://www.usatoday.com/story/news/nation/2015/02/17/bariatric-surgery-obesity/23555329/

Singer-Vine, J. (2009, July 20). Beyond BMI: Why doctors won't stop using an outdated measure for obesity. *Slate.* https://slate.com/technology/2009/07/why-are-doctors-still-measuring-obesity-with-the-body-mass-index.html

Skovsmose, O. (1994). *Towards a philosophy of critical mathematics education.* Kluwer. https://doi.org/10.1007/978-94-017-3556-8

Skovsmose, O. (2001). Mathematics in action: A challenge for social theorising. In E. Simmt & B. Davis (Eds.), *Proceedings of the 2001 annual meeting of the Canadian Mathematics Education Study Group* (pp. 3–17). CMESG.

Statistics Canada. (2014, June 12). *Canadian Community Health Survey, 2013.* https://www150.statcan.gc.ca/n1/daily-quotidien/140612/dq140612b-eng.htm

Statistics Canada. (2017, March 28). *Study: Aerobic fitness, body mass index and health-related risk factors.* https://www150.statcan.gc.ca/n1/daily-quotidien/170328/dq170328a-eng.htm

Steuter-Martin, M. (2017, January 26). 'A humiliating experience': Quebec debates weighing students in school. *CBC News*. https://www.cbc.ca/news/canada/montreal/national-assembly-weigh-students-quebec-1.3953078

Wildman, R. E. C., & Medeiros, D. M. (1999). *Advanced human nutrition*. CRC Press.

Yanik, H. B., & Memis, Y. (2016). What is your body mass index? *Teaching Children Mathematics, 22*(7), 442–446. https://doi.org/10.5951/teacchilmath.22.7.0442

Epilogues

CHAPTER 11

From the Present towards Hope for the Future

Ulrika Ryan and Lisa Steffensen

Abstract

In this epilogue we elaborate on and synthesise what we have learnt from reading this book. We start by considering what the word "apply" in Applying Critical Mathematics Education might mean. Apply connotes to put into action, but it is also related to the following ideas: to work hard at, to pay close attention to, to have relevance for and to request something. In the context of our readings we think of being relational and dedicated as a matter of enhancing situated critical awareness, addressing relevant issues as a matter of highlighting complex global and local challenges and making demands as a matter of agency and power. To us, these themes together synthesise the insights on critical mathematics education in action that the authors of this book offer; namely, propositions on how to illuminate and execute social justice and heterogenous subjectification by critically entangling local and global knowledges in contextually situated educational enactments that hold the potential to address complex challenges. We close by sharing our ideas on how the contribution of this book gives us hope for the future in these times of crises and complex challenges.

Keywords

critical mathematics education – hope – complex challenges – critical awareness – subjectification

∙ ∙ ∙

The title of this volume is *Applying Critical Mathematics Education*. Initially, we thought of applying as "putting into action." We considered the notion of action and its connectedness to hope for the future. If there is no future, there is no notion of action: we act because we have hopes for tomorrow. The relationship between hope and action raises questions about what kinds of acts and, perhaps, hopes the word "apply" connotes. As emergent writers and speakers of academic English, we sometimes turn to thesauri to grasp embedded meanings in English words. We looked up the word "apply" and learned that apart from "putting into action," it is also related to the following ideas: to work hard at, to pay close attention to, to have relevance for and to request something (Cambridge Dictionary Online, n.d.). Hence, applying critical mathematics education may imply acting by being relational and dedicated, by addressing relevant issues and by making demands. Drawing on our understanding of the meaning of "apply," therefore, we think of being relational and dedicated as a matter of enhancing *situated critical awareness*. We think of addressing relevant issues as a matter of highlighting *complex global and local challenges*. We think of making demands as a matter of *agency and power*. Hence, we have organised our text in three main parts according to this logic. In doing so, we connect the ideas and concepts brought forward in the book to unpack the lessons we learned from our reading and the hopes that our reading gave us. In the last part of this epilogue, we direct our gaze at future concerns for critical mathematics education in the context of issues that we, Ulrika and Lisa, have at heart. We follow Andersson and Wagner (this volume) who suggested synthesising critical mathematics education and ethnomathematics. Hence, when we write critical mathematics education, we refer to their synthesised meaning.

1 Situated Critical Awareness

A culturally situated critical mathematics education rejects the myth of mathematics as culture-free and neutral and contributes to fostering active participation in societal and political life. Situated critical awareness emphasises students' local contexts, power relations in the classroom, and mathematics as social and cultural activities that may serve as tools for or objects of critique (Andersson & Wagner, this volume). In other words, situated critical awareness enmeshes the critical use of mathematics with critique of mathematics, while simultaneously recognising that the two activities are contextual.

1.1 *To Apply: Acting by Being Dedicated to the Critical Means to Care about Justice*

To understand what it means to use mathematics critically in different situations students must learn how to "walk the walk and talk the talk." But they must also learn how to be critical of how the walk operates: what mathematics does or does not influence and in what way it is influential. And they must learn to be critical of what the talk lets you know or not know or experience in different situations. This can mean giving underprivileged groups of students access to successful participation in dominant mathematics and mathematics education practices. Access to dominant mathematics is a prerequisite for understanding how mathematics is used in the argumentation of dominant societal structures. Hence, access to dominant mathematics is needed to develop critical awareness (Barwell & Hauge, this volume).

However, mere access to dominant mathematics does not necessarily foster critical awareness (Ryan, Andersson & Chronaki, this volume; Steffensen, Herheim & Rangnes, this volume). It is, therefore, urgent to act by facilitating opportunities for students to challenge how dominant mathematics operates in their lives, in their communities and in society in general. Such challenges are not only about the facts of, for example, the unjust distribution of resources or of climate change, but also involve critically recognising and problematising personal affective and embodied experiences with mathematics (Lunney Borden, this volume; le Roux & Rughubar-Reddy, this volume).

1.2 To Apply: Acting by Being Dedicated to the Relational Means for Dealing with Dominant Eurocentric Mathematics Values

A culturally situated mathematics education has the potential to decolonise education and transform researchers' approaches. For instance, learning about and with community knowledge can result in displacements in pedagogical approaches from Eurocentric values and beliefs towards more culturally situated approaches (Lunney Borden, this volume). Furthermore, a decolonising stand is not a matter of either/or knowledge and values, but encompasses both/and views that shape conceptual interconnections (Ryan & Parra, 2019). Adopting such educational approaches involves "a complex interplay of the categories inside/outside (of Indigenous social, cultural and political spaces), that are not conceived of as mutually excluding but as nested and in implicated in a continuous, mutual reshaping" (Parra & Valero, this volume). Decolonising pedagogical stances need not be a matter of replacing one hegemony with another. Instead, by adopting educational approaches that strengthen cultural identity and authority over education, and that value both community and dominant mathematics, universalised de-rooted subjectification may be escaped. Adopting such an approach addresses concerns that go beyond Indigenous contexts, as, for example, Le Roux and Rughubar-Reddy (this volume) have demonstrated.

2 Complex Global and Local Challenges

Climate change and obesity as a global pandemic are complex or "wicked" problems. They are characterised by the urgent need for action, a vague problem-formulation, a lack of well-described solutions involving uncertainty and disagreements, and with no central authorities (Rittel & Webber, 1973). Both challenges already exist in society and students face them in and out of school. There are many other global and local complex challenges such as, for example, the global Covid-19 pandemic.

2.1 To Apply: Acting by Addressing Relevant Issues Means Emotional Labour

Climate change, as well as obesity, can create feelings in students and teachers, such as confusion, resignation, or motivation to act (see Abtahi, Gøtze, Steffensen, Hauge, & Barwell, 2017; Steffensen & Hansen, 2019). In terms of climate change, Thunberg (2018) articulated her feelings in her speech at the World Economic Forum in Davos. She used words like "hope," "panic," "fear," "act," and "crisis" to push for urgent action on a broad personal and societal scale, rather than for us to put our hope in experts or technological solutions. She clearly stated that she does not want hope, but rather wishes for people to panic and experience fear, as shown by her statement "I want you to act." That is, she is not calling for a retreat from the problem or for passive despair. In the same vein, obesity is a complex problem that often includes despair, retreat and an attempt to assign blame (Finegood, Merth, & Rutter, 2010). Thus, we identify similar feelings of fear in issues concerning obesity to those expressed by Thunberg.

Discourses on climate change and obesity are highly mathematical. Mathematics is involved in describing, predicting and communicating climate change, and references to statistical findings, measures and trends are also connected to obesity (Barwell & Hauge, this volume; Steffensen et al., this volume; Hall and Barwell, this volume). The highly mathematical discourses that are used to articulate these problems mean that mathematics education needs to be involved. Introducing such challenges in the classroom can lead teachers to question whether such topics are too complex, too controversial, or cause negative feelings such as fear and despair (Abtahi et al., 2017; Steffensen & Hansen, 2019). However, complex problems need not be an all-or-nothing matter. In empirical research by Steffensen (e.g., 2021; Steffensen, Herheim, & Rangnes, 2018; Steffensen & Rangnes, 2019), two teachers emphasised that they wanted to communicate to students that even small changes mattered, which we interpreted as meaning that teachers provide hope for students' actions. We argue that although complex problems can involve controversies or cause emotional labour, citizens and society need to address them, and mathematics education has a responsibility to enable students to deal with such problems.

2.2 To Apply: Acting by Addressing Relevant Issues Means Dealing with Uncertainty and the Formatting Power of Mathematics

To deal with complex problems in the classroom is not a straightforward task. Teachers might need to reconsider how they look at problems when including climate change in the mathematics class. Normally when society encounters scientific problems, groups of experts are relied upon to solve the problem. They are expected to suggest the best solution so that decision-makers can take satisfactory measures. However, in complex problems, the experts may arrive from a range of scientific fields, and the decision-makers from multiple countries representing a variety of standpoints on what actions should be taken. Climate change also involves uncertainty, risks, values, and conflicts. At the same time, the urgency of the problem calls for action. When dealing with complex problems, one could involve students in decision-making where dialogue is an essential keyword. An applied critical mathematics education can emphasise teaching about these uncertainties and values (Hauge & Barwell, 2017). For instance, in this book, Steffensen et al. reflected on an example where the teachers had facilitated students to reflect on uncertainty: their own measurement differences and the uncertainties involved in calculating the global average temperature of the Earth. Mathematics can also format society, in connection, for instance, to obesity. Hall and Barwell (this volume) critically scrutinised the Body Mass Index (BMI) as an example of a mathematically based model that becomes a part of categorising and defining people as "normal" or "obese." Mathematics is used for more than just describing the problem; it becomes prescriptive of (un)desired bodies.

3   Agency and Power

Collaboration between researchers and teachers who are willing to learn to cooperate in respectful ways and minority communities may provide opportunities for agency to address complex challenges such as educational decolonisation (e.g., Lunney Borden, this volume; Parra & Valero, this volume). Such collaboration requires that dominant societies, ideologies and institutions treat minoritised groups in respectful ways and acknowledge their ways of knowing, being, speaking and feeling (Hand et al., this volume; Ryan, 2019a) and that the privileged make way for the underprivileged.

3.1   *To Apply: Empowering by Enhancing Political and Mathematical Understanding and Knowledge ...*

Enabling students to have agency and power to act on socio-political issues requires an environment of reflective knowing and critique (Barwell & Hauge, this volume; Steffensen et al., this volume), through, for example, fostering an understanding of the formatting power of mathematics. However, Steffensen et al. (this volume) showed that dealing with the formatting power of mathematics in classroom contexts is a multifaceted matter. On the one hand, education can support students to engage in critical scrutiny of mathematical models. On the other hand, from such scrutiny, the uncertainty captured in the models becomes apparent, a disclosure that may jeopardise students' trust in science. Mathematics education must, therefore, necessarily include dealing with different levels of uncertainty.

Sustaining institutional structures in the light of resisting colonisation can be shaped both mathematically and politically. Mathematics education has the potential to provide interfaces where local community ways of knowing mathematics encounter Western academic mathematics in a mutually beneficial way (Andersson & Wagner; le Roux & Rughubar-Reddy; Lunney Borden; Parra, & Valero, this volume). To advance such interfaces means to interpret and situate mathematics education in each specific context. Such actions allow for moves that articulate local responses to homogenisation and globalisation, since it is a mathematics education from and for the people. Le Roux and Rughubar-Reddy (this volume) demonstrates how mathematics education scholars can act agentically in an intermediate space that need not dichotomise, for example, Western and non-Western approaches. Instead, by entangling theories and locality, concepts may be reworked and subsequently enrich the complexity of mathematics and mathematics education.

3.2   ... Is Not Always an Easy Matter

Good intentions to sustain actions and structures that allow the underprivileged to speak sometimes fall short, as some of the chapters show (e.g., Hand et al., this volume; Ryan et al., this volume). That does not, of course, mean that we should not continue to struggle, but that we must humbly accept and remind our (privileged) selves of our own ignorance. To educate privileged ignorance can mean to get to know the knowledge and experiences of the Other in respectful ways that do not put an extra burden on the underprivileged. An extra burden may be put on the underprivileged when more privileged groups demand that the underprivileged explains or shares their experiences. To avoid this, Hand et al. (this volume) followed Patel (2015) when they suggested pausing in such situations. Pausing means to stop and make space to seek together to critically understand injustice in social and institutional relations and its origins, in order to find ways to undertake joint work under respectful and just circumstances.

4   Actions and Hopes for the Future

So far in this epilogue, we have tried to capture what actions we found embedded in the chapters of this book with respect to the concept "applying." We found three overarching interconnected themes (situated critical awareness, complex global and local challenges, and agency and power). These themes together synthesise what the contributors to this book hope to bring about by applying critical mathematics education: namely, to promote social justice and heterogenous subjectification by critically entangling local and global knowledges in contextually situated educational enactments that hold the potential to address complex challenges. We share this hope in these times of crises and complex challenges.

Some complex challenges are highly visible in our (Ulrika's and Lisa's often privileged) Scandinavian contexts, while some are less visible to us. We want to highlight that the underprivileged may suffer daily from the consequences of complex challenges that may be ignored or "forgotten" by hegemonic societies (Swanson, 2017). We want to contribute to illuminating the "forgotten." Grasping "forgotten" complex challenges may be overwhelming and impose a sense of despair upon us (Steffensen et al., this volume). hooks (2003) has highlighted that "despair is the greatest threat. When despair prevails, we cannot create life-sustaining communities of resistance" (p. 12). As teachers, we might feel conflicted about introducing challenges that could cause despair among our students. However, the word "apply" suggests acting. Relatedly, Swanson (2017) has written:

> Perhaps it is time for us to remember what the intentions of mathematics education should be, to live well with mathematics education in order to live well with others; to live and research well with mathematics education in order to make possible futures of radical hope. (Swanson, 2017, p. 13)

To have radical hope is to hope for future goodness that is not yet imagined. A future for which we lack the appropriate concepts to conceptualise it (Lear, 2006). In this book, the contributors grapple with providing concepts and ideas that may allow us to live well, or at least better with mathematics education and research and with each other, which we conceive of as hope for the future.

To conclude, we turn to future concerns that we, Lisa and Ulrika, will engage with, from the point of view we synthesised in the sentence above – because that will give us hope.

From the perspective of neoliberal consumerism, Lisa regards a socially just production and distribution of resources such as food, energy, clean air and water as needing to be addressed. The privileged, knowledgeable student needs to be positioned not only as a consumer or a problem solver, but also as a part of the problem. Engaging in complex problems, with the intention to live well with each other cannot merely be a matter of solving problems; it is also an affective matter of performing solidarity. Challenges such as climate change or the recent coronavirus pandemic affect people differently. However, those who suffer the most should not be "forgotten"; and consequently, mathematics education should remember its role and empower students with hope and give them the agency to act.

From the perspective of heterogeneous subjectivity, Ulrika struggles to have radical hope (Lear, 2006) in the context of the rapidly increasing digitalised and globalised world. In some sense digitalisation and globalisation bring people closer. At the same time, it makes way for global homogenisation and thereby jeopardises heterogeneous subjectification and recognition of and respect for the Other. Critical mathematics education has the potential to provide power and agency to address and resist homogenisation by enacting and fostering situated critical awareness. In a migrating world, this is a matter of solidarity that becomes actualised in mathematics classroom talk, in which language is not merely a matter of communication. Language is also an epistemological matter of what counts as (mathematical) knowledge and who counts as mathematically knowledgeable (Ryan, 2019a, 2019b; Ryan & Parra, 2019; Ryan, Andersson, & Chronaki, this volume). By excluding some ways of talking about and knowing mathematics, some subjectivities will become excluded and heterogeneity thereby jeopardised. Those subjectivities must not be "forgotten"; to live well with mathematics, we mathematics educators and researchers must remember our role as safeguarders of heterogeneous ways of experiencing, knowing and doing mathematics.

We are inspired by the aspects of action and hope that the contributors to this book express. We look forward to applying critical mathematics education in our future research, embarking on familiar and unfamiliar areas and, at the same time, bringing action and hope for the future. As early career female Scandinavian researchers, we hope we will honour the meaning of apply. That is, we will try to enact situated critical awareness, to address complex challenges and to highlight issues of agency and power. Although this is our ambition, at times we will fail. But we will keep on trying. And bring with us our hopes for the future.

References

Abtahi, Y., Gøtze, P., Steffensen, L., Hauge, K. H., & Barwell, R. (2017). Teaching climate change in mathematics classroom: An ethical responsibility. *Philosophy of Mathematics Education Journal, 32*.

Finegood, D. T., Merth, T. D. N., & Rutter, H. (2010). Implications of the foresight obesity system map for solutions to childhood obesity. *Obesity, 18*(S1), S13–S16. doi:10.1038/oby.2009.426

Hauge, K. H., & Barwell, R. (2017). Post-normal science and mathematics education in uncertain times: Educating future citizens for extended peer communities. *Futures, 91*, 25–34. doi:10.1016/j.futures.2016.11.013

hooks, b. (2003). *Teaching community: A pedagogy of hope*. Routledge. https://doi.org/10.4324/9780203957769

Lear, J. (2006). *Radical hope: Ethics in the face of cultural devastation*. Harvard University Press.

Patel, L. (2015). *Decolonizing educational research: From ownership to answerability*. Routledge. https://doi.org/10.4324/9781315658551

Rittel, H. W. J., & Webber, M. M. (1973). Dilemmas in a general theory of planning. *Policy Sciences, 4*(2), 155–169. doi:10.1007/BF01405730

Ryan, U. (2019a). *Mathematics classroom talk in a migrating world: Synthesizing epistemological dimensions* (Doctoral dissertation). Malmö University.

Ryan, U. (2019b). Mathematical preciseness and epistemological sanctions. *For the Learning of Mathematics, 39*(2), 25–29.

Ryan, U., & Parra, A. (2019). Epistemological aspects of multilingualism in mathematics education: An inferentialist approach. *Research in Mathematics Education, 21*(2), 152–167. https://doi.org/10.1080/14794802.2019.1608290

Steffensen, L. (2021). *Critical mathematics education and climate change. A teaching and research partnership in lower-secondary school* (Doctoral dissertation). Western Norway University of Applied Sciences.

Steffensen, L., & Hansen, R. (2019). Klimaendring i matematikkundervisning – lærerperspektiver [Climate change in mathematics education – Teachers' perspectives]. In T. E. Rangnes & K. M. R. Breivega (Eds.), *Demokratisk danning i skolen. Tverrfaglige empiriske studier* [Democratic bildung in school. Interdisciplinary empirical studies] (pp. 203–226). Universitetsforlaget.

Steffensen, L., Herheim, R., & Rangnes, T. E. (2018). Wicked problems in school mathematics. In E. Bergqvist, M. Österholm, C. Granberg, & L. Sumpter (Eds.), *Proceedings of the 42nd Conference of the International Group for the Psychology of Mathematics Education* (Vol. 4, pp. 227–234). PME.

Steffensen, L., & Rangnes, T. E. (2019). Climate change controversies in the mathematics classroom. In J. Subramanian (Ed.), *Proceedings of the Tenth International Mathematics Education and Society Conference* (pp. 814–823). MES10. https://www.mescommunity.info/proceedings/MES10.pdf

Swanson, D. M. (2017). Mathematics education and the problem of political forgetting: In search of research methodologies for global crisis. *Journal of Urban Mathematics Education, 10*(1), 7–15.

Thunberg, G. (2018, September 20). Our house is on fire [Video file]. *World Economic Forum*. https://www.youtube.com/watch?v=U72xkMz6Pxk

CHAPTER 12

Critical Mathematics Education Imaginaries
Culturally Situated, Situating, Transformative, Decolonising, and More

Anita Rampal

Abstract

Reflections on how critical mathematics education can offer a diverse and expanding arena to address several themes, without necessarily needing to synthesise it or blur its contours with respect to ethnomathematics. Using the perspective of "righting our world," inspired by Freire's sense of "writing the world," the focus is on transforming and decolonising mathematical knowledge.

Keywords

critical mathematics education – righting our world – textbooks – decolonising – indigenous and civilisational knowledge

• • •

The wide range of explorations found in this book reflect the possible imaginaries of how critical mathematics educators view themselves and the field. Drawing on and extending the unsettling questions for scientists asked by the anthropologist G. E. Marcus (1995), we could ask ourselves: What is it like to be doing critical mathematics education in the twenty-first century? How have shifts in power affected our practices to address difficult moral and professional issues at this juncture of global change and discontent? What imaginaries of hope and solidarity can critical mathematics education help us to forge?

The chapters in this book look at diverse situations, such as equity-oriented action research for teacher development, quantitative literacy in the professional development of medical doctors, climate change in mathematics classrooms, and reconciliation and renewed relationships between Indigenous and non-Indigenous Canadians. I was particularly interested in the contributions on the decolonisation of education through the stance of critical mathematics education to contest typical dichotomies in ethnomathematics (old vs. new, indigenous vs. western, academic vs. vocational, local vs. universal, etc.).

Andersson and Wagner (this volume) draw upon their review of the research literature of critical mathematics education and ethnomathematics to propose a *synthesised* "culturally situated critical mathematics education" framework, that encompasses both perspectives and brings the strengths of each to the other. It is interesting to note the relationships between the two fields, the demographics of where and which research gets conducted, and how some studies in one of the traditions implicitly invoke elements from the other. An attempt to forge a synthesis deserves serious reconsideration. In response, this epilogue presents some reflections on the way critical mathematics education offers a diverse and expanding arena to address several kinds of initiatives without necessarily enveloping or blurring its contours with respect to ethnomathematics.

Through work with my colleagues over the last many decades, I have come to look at critical mathematics education in the Freirian sense of "reading and *righting* our world" with mathematics, inspired by Freire's "writing the world". In the 1990s during India's National Literacy Campaigns, we critiqued traditional mathematics lessons and worked on a critical numeracy curriculum for adult learners (Rampal, 2003; Rampal, Ramanujam, & Saraswathi, 1999), drawing upon their indigenous[1] knowledge of everyday mathematics, within a critical pedagogy framework (Rampal, 2015). A similar framework, with a focus on social constructivist theories of learning, had helped restructure our national primary school curriculum and textbooks (NCERT, 2006–2008). It was around then that we saw our reframed mathematics to be aligned with critical mathematics education, since it invoked indigenous and "everyday" knowledge as a socio-cultural or even political construct. These initiatives had not necessarily required either a formal delineation of, or a conscious "border crossing" between, or even a synthesis of the enabling frameworks of critical pedagogy, critical mathematics education, indigenous knowledge, everyday mathematics, ethnomathematics, etc.

For some contexts it might help to focus specifically on any one of these areas, such as, say ethnomathematics. Even there, scholars may deal with aboriginal knowledge, rather than the wider arena of indigenous knowledge as, say, may be done in diverse rural non-aboriginal contexts. However, in its broadest sense, critical mathematics education does allow us to address all of the four "concerns" listed by Andersson and Wagner, namely: (i) analysing community features; (ii) focusing on acting persons; (iii) reflecting on mathematics (which is not only a tool but also an object of critique); and (iv) reflecting on education. The need to synthesise critical mathematics education with ethnomathematics should not arise, more so when a study of the latter may need a specific niche, not necessarily aiming to address all of the four "concerns" listed above. For instance, asserting the need for a niche for Critical Mathematical Inquiry a recent call for papers for a special issue of a journal (Greenstein & Russo, 2019) stated that applied mathematics has generally been used to identify and challenge injustice, for instance, through statistics or the solving of practical problems. In contrast, it suggests that the mathematics of Critical Mathematical Inquiry could be pure and independent of application, just for the sake of doing mathematics, as long as the pedagogy was critical. The engagement of Critical Mathematical Inquiry for the context of pure mathematics was invoked to address injustices and inequities, not in the world outside, but inside the classroom, where the formal curriculum is a cause of alienation or disenfranchisement. The critical in Critical Mathematical Inquiry is thus emphasised, quoting from Wager and Stinson (2012), to move beyond teaching mathematics about and for social justice, to teaching mathematics *with* social justice, through pedagogical practices that co-create a classroom culture to ensure equal participation and status. The critical mathematics education "list of concerns" may well subsume Critical Mathematical Inquiry in its larger fold, yet that may not warrant folding up the niche itself, in an attempt to create a synthesis.

1 Critical Mathematics Education, Cultural Engagement and Decolonisation

The authors of the different chapters refer to culture and cultural situatedness in diverse ways. Andersson and Wagner state that most papers in the MES proceedings deal with cultural issues, highlighting its importance in socio-cultural and socio-political research, even when this work is not ethnomathematical. For them, a significant difference between critical mathematics education and ethnomathematics is that critical mathematics education engages students to do mathematics in a cultural situation, while traditional ethnomathematics observes and documents mathematics done in a cultural situation. However, we need to look beyond "cultural situations," for the process of cultural engagement is the premise of critical mathematics education, related to the "reading of the world," and the making of meaning.

Lunney Borden (this volume) speaks of cultural engagement for decolonising mathematics as restoring "the ways of knowing, being, and doing that are a central part of community languages and worldviews and use these to engage in learning mathematics in new ways." Parra and Valero (this volume), writing of "educacion propia" as a tool for decolonisation, quote the anthropologist Joan Rappaport, who says that "culture is not an existing constellation of practices and meanings located on the 'inside' but a projection of how future life-ways should look, driven by a process in which elements of the inside are revitalized through the incorporation of ideas from outside; that is, culture necessarily straddles the frontier ... While ethnographers engage in cultural description with an eye to analyzing it, indigenous autoethnographers study culture to act upon it" (Rappaport, 2008, pp. 20–21).

This dichotomy of the inside-outside locations of knowledge is reminiscent of the historic debate (Bhattacharya, 1997) on culture and decolonisation, between two major Indian thinkers, Gandhi and Tagore, whose respect for each other refined their differences and influenced national ideas on culture, nationalism, development, education, language, etc. Gandhi led a movement of "non-cooperation" against the British colonisers, and supported the "swadeshi"[2] (indigenous) movement by boycotting British goods, including their schools. Tagore ran his own indigenous school, but strongly critiqued narrow nationalism as "cannibalistic," although he also wrote the poem that is the national anthem of India. He advocated for civilisational "humanism," and a collective internationalism, warning that the "struggle to alienate our heart and mind from those of the West is an attempt at spiritual suicide ... [as indeed] for a long time we have been out of touch with our own culture" (p. 62). Gandhi respected Tagore's stance, and explained the need to be culturally rooted while learning from other cultures: "It is unbearable for me that the vernaculars should be crushed and starved as they have been ... I want the cultures of all the lands to be blown about my house as freely as possible. But I refuse to be blown off my feet by any" (p. 64).

This historic debate reconnects with several contemporary educational debates. The curriculum manifests as an ongoing "complicated conversation" and a "social and subjective reconstruction," that allows an analysis of "one's experience of the past and fantasies of the future in order to understand more fully, with more complexity and subtlety, one's submergence in the present" (Pinar, 2004, p. 4).

Reflecting on the modernisation-indigenisation dilemma, I recall an interaction in South Africa while I was collaborating on a rural schools project with the Nelson Mandela Foundation (2005). Inadvertently I had stirred a hornet's nest, by wondering why plastic tables and chairs were attributed such a high priority in primary schools, even at the cost of more pressing requirements for better learning. In South Africa and India most children sat on the floor as part of their home culture. Black educators had expressed indignation, declaring that things they had earlier been deprived of in schools should now be "rightfully" theirs, asking "How can children write otherwise?" and asserting that it was demeaning and inhuman for children to sit on the floor and write. An interesting debate ensued and I was moved to demonstrate how we sat on the floor, even in prestigious political or musical gatherings, in a cross-legged posture westerners paid substantial sums to emulate through yoga classes! "Culture" or "identity" used as signifiers of race and colour continue to bear problematic and painful connotations of colonial pasts and apartheid. Was this not ironic that Africa, the Cradle of Writing, with its ingenious use of papyrus and quill, now found it demeaning to write without plastic tables and chairs? (Rampal, 2009).

2   Righting Our Knowledge

An often recalled Zimbabwean proverb (Brock-Utne, 2002) reminds us of the need for a historical righting of knowledge: "Stories of the hunt will be stories of glory until the day when animals have their own historians." The modernisation-indigenisation dichotomy continues to appear in some form in several countries, around differently nuanced categories of power and hierarchy, including the material-cultural politics of identity, economic developmental vs. the ecological crisis, "rational" vs. "moral" values, "local" vs. "universal," "academic" vs. "everyday" knowledge, "mind" vs. "body," "intellectual" vs. "manual" work, and "English" vs. "mother tongue." Moreover, attempts to incorporate cultural or civilisational resources in education have been part of major political contestations, especially in multicultural countries with rich and complex colonial histories.

Indeed, an indigenous discourse on education calls for new metaphors for the notion of a "national" or "multicultural identity." One metaphor for the diverse and dynamic society sought in post-apartheid South Africa is the "Garieb" (The Great River), proposed by Alexander (2002, p. 107). In this metaphor, the mainstream is composed of a confluence of all the contributing currents, which in their ever-changing forms continue to constitute and reconstitute the river, such that no single current dominates, and there is no "main stream." Could this metaphor also allow us to think of critical mathematics education, not as a synthesised or homogenising mainstream, but as a dynamic confluence of its significant currents?

Movements for decolonisation have called for an audit of the "ecological debt" of colonising countries, whose exploitation over centuries of mineral and other natural resources of the South have caused its deep economic debt. There is, I have felt in our work, a need to reassert and claim a similar acknowledgement of their "cognitive debt" to the indigenous knowledge of the oldest civilisations. The development of modern science and mathematics was based on several knowledge traditions (which included material resources, techniques, devices, specimens, data, etc.) of the cultures that came in contact with the voyages of discovery, or those that were part of the colonies of Europe. In the course of the development of modern science and mathematics, these other traditions were either delegitimised or even "cognitively lost." In their call to dethrone such hegemonic and violent regimes of knowledge that continue to sustain the modernist project, Parra and Valero (this volume) quote from (Stavrou & Miller, 2017) who asserted that: "Applying decolonizing strategies to mathematics will make visible that it is a subject developed in time and place, and will expose the imperialistic operation that deprives mathematics of its historical roots and human construction" (p. 106). Indeed critical mathematics education and ethnomathematics provide potential decolonising frameworks, contrary to the fear expressed by Andersson and Wagner (this volume), of ethnomathematics serving as yet another form of colonial "mining."

In my response to Rochelle Gutiérrez's plenary lecture at the MES10 conference (Rampal, 2019), I indicated that by acknowledging that knowledge in the past was constructed and nurtured by active cross-transmission between civilisations, critical mathematics education can devise creative decolonising strategies to collaboratively mine civilisational knowledge (Goonatilake, 1998). Moreover, critical mathematics education must further extend its domain to focus on theories of situated learning, which, unlike traditional cognitive theories that isolate and distance the "mind" from its experience, do not separate thought, action and feelings. Traditionally, knowledge is thought to be imported from the "outside" to the "inside" of the head of a person. However, the use of "activity" as the unit of analysis in theories of situated learning now allows a reformulation of the relation between the head, heart and hand, and also between the individual and the socio-cultural environment (Rogoff, 1995). An "activity" is not an ephemeral one-off event, but is shaped by the active contributions of individuals, their social partners, historical traditions, the materials used and also their transformations. People participate in activities and learn to handle subsequent activities based on their involvement in previous events. As a person acts on the basis of previous experience, the past is present in the participation, and contributes to the event by having prepared the ground for it. The present event is therefore transformational, different from what it would have been if the previous events had not occurred. Such theories of learning and doing mathematics are based on critical transformations and afford critical cultural engagement for reading and *righting* our world.

Notes

1 In this chapter, indigenous is used in its general sense of a word for something belonging to a place.
2 *Swadeshi* means "made or belonging to one's country" and was mostly used in the context of products at that time, so goods produced in Britain were boycotted.

References

Alexander, N. (2002). *An ordinary country: Issues in transition from apartheid to democracy in South Africa*. University of Natal Press.
Bhattacharya, S. (Ed.). (1997). *The Mahatma and the poet: Letters and debates between Gandhi and Tagore 1915–1949*. National Book Trust.
Brock-Utne, B. (2002). Stories of the hunt – Who is writing them? In C. A. Odora Hoppers (Ed.), *Indigenous knowledge and the integration of knowledge systems: Towards a philosophy of articulation* (pp. 237–256). New Africa Education.
Goonatilake, S. (1998). *Toward a global science: Mining civilizational knowledge*. Indiana University Press.
Greenstein, S., & Russo, M. (2019). Teaching for social justice through Critical Mathematical Inquiry. *Bank Street Occasional Paper Series, 41*, 4–14. https://educate.bankstreet.edu/occasional-paper-series/vol2019/iss41/11
Marcus, G. E. (Ed.). (1995). *Technoscientific imaginaries: Conversations, profiles, and memoirs*. University of Chicago Press.
NCERT. (2006–2008). *Math-magic* (Textbooks for primary mathematics). National Council for Educational Research and Training.
Nelson Mandela Foundation. (2005). *Emerging voices: A report on education in South African rural communities*. HSRC Press.
Pinar, W. F. (2004). *What is curriculum theory?* Lawrence Erlbaum.
Rampal, A. (2003). Counting on everyday mathematics. In T. S. Saraswathi (Ed.), *Cross-cultural perspectives in human development: Theory, research and applications* (pp. 326–353). Sage.
Rampal, A. (2009). An indigenous discourse to cradle our cognitive heritage and script our aspirations. In R. Cowen & A. M. Kazamias (Eds.), *International handbook of comparative education* (pp. 739–753). Springer. https://doi.org/10.1007/978-1-4020-6403-6_48
Rampal, A. (2015). Curriculum and critical agency: Mediating everyday mathematics. In S. Mukhopadhyay & B. Greer (Eds.), *Proceedings of the 8th International Mathematics Education and Society Conference* (Vol. 1, pp. 83–110) Ooligan Press.

Rampal, A. (2019). Crafting new dispositions in mathematics: Challenging dispossession: A response to Rochelle Gutiérrez's plenary. In J. Subramanian (Ed.), *Proceedings of the Tenth International Mathematics Education and Society Conference* (pp. 148–153). MES10.

Rampal, A., Ramanujam, R., & Saraswathi, L. S. (1999). *Numeracy counts!* National Literacy Resource Centre/LBS National Academy of Administration.

Rappaport, J. (2008). Beyond participant observation: Collaborative ethnography as theoretical innovation. *Collaborative Anthropologies, 1*(1), 1–31. https://doi.org/10.1353/cla.0.0014

Rogoff, B. (1995). Observing sociocultural activity on three planes: Participatory appropriation, guided participation, and apprenticeship. In J. V. Wertsch, P. D. Rio, & A. Alvarez (Eds.), *Sociocultural studies of mind* (pp. 139–164). Cambridge University Press. https://doi.org/10.1017/CBO9781139174299.008

Stavrou, S. G., & Miller, D. (2017). Miscalculations: Decolonizing and anti-oppressive discourses in Indigenous mathematics education. *Canadian Journal of Education/ Revue canadienne de l'éducation, 40*(3), 92–122.

Wager, A. A., & Stinson, D. W. (2012). *Teaching mathematics for social justice: Conversations with educators.* National Council of Teachers of Mathematics.

CHAPTER 13

Pessimism of the Intellect, Optimism of the Will

Swapna Mukhopadhyay and Brian Greer

Abstract

In this time of environmental, political, and pandemic global crises, we invoke Gramsci's "optimism of the will" to express our conviction that, as critical mathematics educators, we have no choice but to continue the struggle to advance the conscientisation of those working in our field. We reflect on the emergence of the critical mathematics movement, the complementarity of reflection and action, and the centrality of the concept of Otherness, and we suggest some challenges for the coming generation of scholar-activists.

Keywords

global crises – humanising mathematics education – reflection and action – Otherness – optimism of the will

∴

Arundhati Roy (2019) described the global situation thus:

> As the ice caps melt, as oceans heat up, and water tables plunge, as we rip through the delicate web of interdependence that sustains life on earth, as our formidable intelligence leads us to breach the boundaries between humans and machines, and our even more formidable hubris undermines our ability to connect the survival of our planet to our survival as a species, as we replace art with algorithms and stare into a future in which most human beings may not be needed to participate in (or be remunerated for) economic activity – at just such a time we have the steady hands of white supremacists in the White House, new imperialists in China, neo-Nazis once again massing on the streets of Europe, Hindu nationalists in India, and a host of butcher-princes and lesser dictators in other countries to guide us into the Unknown.

This quotation eloquently expresses what Gramsci, in his prison notebooks, called "pessimism of the intellect" by which he meant "a realistic description of the status quo" (Antonini, 2019, p. 2). Faced with this brutal reality, how can critical mathematics educators, collectively and individually, act? Some answers are provided in the preceding chapters. In this epilogue, we begin by taking stock of progress made within our movement. Then we consider how it stands in relation to the field of mathematics education as a whole, to current geopolitical circumstances, and to contemporary culture. We offer suggestions for challenges to be taken up by the younger generation, reaffirming Gramsci's appeal to "optimism of the will," namely "a genuine commitment to the possibility of transforming reality" (Antonini, 2019, p. 2).

1 Emergence of a Critical Mass within Mathematics Education

There is now a relatively coherent network of scholar-activists who self-identify as *critical* mathematics educators, including the "Mathematics Education and Society" community, represented by the contributors to this book.[1] For historical reviews, we refer the reader to the first chapter of Vithal (2003), and to Greer and Skovsmose (2012); here we simply identify a few major early developments:

- Important early European writings in the 1970s were written in languages other than English (Vithal, 2003, p. 43, note iii). (We may comment, in passing, that the dominance of that language in the literature is an issue that deserves more attention.)
- At the fifth International Congress on Mathematical Education in 1984, Ubiratan D'Ambrosio brought Ethnomathematics to prominence in a plenary talk during the extra day that was added to address "Mathematics, Education, and Society" (see Greer & Skovsmose, 2012).
- A similar Special Programme was included in the sixth International Congress on Mathematical Education in 1988 (see Powell, 2012).

The biennial Mathematics Education and Society (MES) meetings began in 1998 in Nottingham, having been proceeded by three conferences on "Political Dimensions of Mathematics Education." Of the first six MES meetings, five were in Europe, the other in Australia, but more recent meetings have been more geographically diverse: MES7 was in South Africa, MES8 in the Americas (as we, as the organisers, strove to frame it), and MES10 in India.

As it has developed, then, Critical Mathematics Education, insofar as it can be considered a coherent movement, reflects a philosophical/political/ethical position, among the family resemblances of which are the following:

- Skepticism about the view that mathematics and mathematics education are inherently benevolent (Valero, 2004; Skovsmose, 2016). The possibility that "mathematics is bad for society" (Ryan, Andersson, & Chronaki, this volume) needs to be debated in school classrooms, as everywhere else.
- Rejection of the view that mathematics and mathematics education can be carried on as if they are politically and ethically neutral, and of the image of mathematics as a pure and innocent intellectual activity. While this may be true of some aspects of what counts as doing mathematics (compare playing chess) it is not tenable once any application involving people is attempted. Mathematical modeling of the physical universe is inextricably implicated in an ideology of control and exploitation that has contributed greatly to our current circumstances.
- Celebration of diversity "in all its human forms, specifically in relation to mathematics and mathematics education: culture, ethnicity, gender, forms of life, worldviews, cognition, language, value systems, perceptions of what mathematics education is for" (Greer, Mukhopadhyay, & Roth, 2012, p. 1).

The overarching theme is *humanising* mathematics and mathematics education and this has been extended to the philosophy of mathematics. At the start of his book *What is mathematics, really?* Reuben Hersh argued as follows:

> I show that *from the viewpoint of philosophy* mathematics must be understood as a human activity, a social phenomenon, part of human culture, historically evolved, and intelligible only in a social context. I call this viewpoint "humanist." (Hersh, 1997, p. xi, italics in original)

In alignment with this position, Ravn and Skovsmose (2019) presented a reinterpretation of the philosophy of mathematics that transcends the traditional preoccupation with epistemology and ontology by proposing two additional dimensions, the social and the ethical (and, as they acknowledge, others could be added, including the aesthetic).

2   The Other

The essence of humanising lies in the relationships with the Other, individually and collectively. We focus on those that we consider most germane to this discussion.

Consider the methodological problems inherent in attempts to understand the Other that occur in multiple contexts: therapist and patient, developmental psychologist and child, anthropologist and person of another culture. A criticism often leveled against ethnomathematicians is that they are interpreting the Other through their own cultural lens. In a related historical context, Høyrup (2010) describes the hard work he puts into interpreting Old Babylonian mathematical texts, including principles of close reading and structural analysis inspired by the study of literature. In a clinical analysis, he points out how certain commentators not working with the original texts either reframed the geometrical procedures used to solve certain problems in terms of modern algebra or concluded that those procedures did not really count as mathematics. In either case, "the implied message (probably resulting because it is the implicit starting point ...) is [that] there *is* only one kind of mathematics: ours" (p. 4).

Racism and coloniality: As a preliminary, we briefly and selectively address the problematic aspects of relations with the Other, namely the many forms of prejudice that are as prevalent in mathematics education as in society in general, and manifest themselves even more strongly in specific ways. Here we restrict ourselves to Eurocentrism, and further restrict our attention to Africa (LeRoux & Rughubar-Reddy, this volume). In an attempt to convey, albeit in sketchy fashion, the complexity of the issues (Greer, 2013; Vithal & Skovsmose, 1997), we summarise a series of interchanges at a conference (described in more detail in Atweh & Clarkson, 2001, pp. 86–87). In response to mathematics educators promoting the idea of culturally situated mathematics education, the president of the African Mathematical Union (Kuku, 1995, p. 407) "warned against the overemphasis on culturally oriented curriculum for developing countries that act against their ability to progress and compete in an increasingly globalized world." That it is not just a question of traditional culturally-based mathematics versus academic mathematics is illustrated by the experience of the young Bruno Latour in the Ivory Coast, where he volunteered to work on a study commissioned by the French government. As reported by Kofman (2018) in the *New York Times*:

> In the French-run engineering schools, black students were taught abstract theories without receiving any practical exposure to the actual machinery they were expected to use. When they were subsequently unable to understand technical drawings, they were accused of having "premodern," "African" minds. "It was clearly a racist situation," he said, "which was hidden behind cognitive, pseudohistorical, and cultural explanations."

Somewhat earlier, the cultural psychologist Michael Cole experienced a similar epiphany in Liberia (Cole, Gay, Slick, & Sharp, 1971).

Decolonising research in mathematics education: The beginnings of this struggle may be located in the ongoing freeing of anthropology from its racist/colonial roots, specifically in the deconstruction of the Eurocentric narrative about the development of mathematics. Within Critical Mathematics Education, we may trace an evolution towards a decolonised perspective. We begin (like Stavrou & Miller, 2017) with a brief description of our own backgrounds, Indian and Irish respectively. Swapna grew up in Kolkata in West Bengal, part of the state divided by the English, the other part becoming East Pakistan and subsequently Bangladesh, and her first language is Bengali. Brian grew up in both parts of Ireland (likewise partitioned by the English), and his first language is English, with minimal learning of Irish, a language rendered close to extinction by the English over centuries (in passing, note how this illustrates that the blanket use of the word "European" is itself problematic).

We sketch a progression towards equality which begins with serious attempts to understand the Other, as discussed above. A stronger version takes the form of working within a community over an extended period of time, as exemplified by the work of Lunney Borden (this volume); other examples include the long-term program of research by Lipka and his colleagues among the Yupik people (e.g., Lipka, Yanez, Andrew-Ihrke, & Adam, 2009) and Urton's (1997) analysis of Quechuan mathematics. Such extended commitment often goes with becoming a political ally and advocate (e.g., Ferreira, 2015; Knijnik & Wanderer, 2012). Stavrou and Miller (2017) argue forcefully that all such efforts need to be grounded in explicit recognition of the historically racialised context of the work.

Beyond such more or less enlightened positions by researchers within the field, Others speak for themselves (e.g., Smith, 1999). For example, Martin and Gholson (2012) have documented their experiences as Black researchers. As described by Gutstein (2012), his students chose topics to analyse in mathematics class reflecting sociopolitical issues of importance in their lives, and made community and conference presentations of their findings. This work could be considered an example of Youth Participatory Action Research (Raygoza, 2016).

In a critique of ethnomathematics, Parra-Sanchez (2017) argues for "noncolonialist interactions among stakeholders, recognizing their different interests, their different ways to conceptualize and their interdependence" (p. 89). In this spirit, the biennial Tlingit Clan Conference in Juneau, Alaska, which we frequently attend, juxtaposes cultural events and academic papers under the title "Sharing our Knowledge."

3 Reflection and Action

What is signified by inserting "applied" in front of "critical mathematics education"? (Andersson & Barwell, this volume). Paolo Freire, the relevance of whose work to mathematics education was argued in a seminal paper by Frankenstein (1983), made clear that "reflection without action is sheer verbalism, 'armchair revolution,' whereas action without reflection is 'pure activism,' that is action for action's sake" (Freire, 1972, p. 41). The title of Gutstein's (2006) book, *Reading and Writing the World with Mathematics*, underlines this by emphasising Freire's call to go beyond understanding (reading) the social and political environment in which one lives to taking action (writing) to change it.

In our view, writing, such as the contributions to this volume, may legitimately be regarded as a form of action, insofar as it represents an attempt to radicalise the field of mathematics education. We believe we are not merely "publishing whilst others perish" (Zinn, 1997). Then there is the teaching many of us do, of school students and teachers-to-be. Gutstein's (2006) teaching stands as an example of the goal that "students need to be prepared through their mathematics education to investigate and critique injustice, and to challenge, in words and actions, oppressive structures and acts" (p. 4).

As scholar-activists, we can be engaged in political struggles beyond schools in which mathematics and mathematics education are implicated. The most urgent is the climate justice crisis (Barwell & Hauge, this volume; Steffensen, Herheim, and Rangnes, this volume), in response to which, led by Greta Thunberg, children in many countries have taken part in demonstrations, including in our own city. The Portland group of the grassroots teacher organisation, Rethinking Schools,[2] produced a volume of curricular materials (Bigelow & Swinehart, 2014) that has been adopted by Portland Public Schools, which in 2019 appointed a Climate Change and Climate Justice Programs Manager (the first such appointment in the United States) to co-ordinate teaching of the topic in science and social studies classes.

4 Digging Where We Stand

In this section, we begin by offering some general thoughts on the relationship of Critical Mathematics Education to Mathematics Education as a whole. Moving, as we tend to do, within circles of scholars with whom we are philosophically and politically aligned, we may get a perception that we have penetrated, and, to some extent, impacted the field. However, and absent a systematic enquiry to attempt to quantify how warranted such a belief is, we state our perception that the field remains largely unchanged, and deploys powerful mechanisms to absorb and neutralise any impact.

By way of example, consider the book edited by Fried and Dreyfus (2014), a festschrift for the mathematician and mathematics educator Theodore Eisenberg. In our opinion, it provides a good overview of the psychological research and theory on understanding how people learn mathematics and how to teach it. However, a theme that recurs throughout the book is that there is a crisis in the relationship between mathematicians and mathematics educators, that Critical Mathematics Education is a major culprit in this regard, and that political issues should not be a major consideration for mathematicians or mathematics educators. In Eisenberg's (2014) chapter "Some of my pet-peeves with mathematics education" the very title seeks to belittle what are serious ideological differences. He comments that "what is strikingly absent these days in mathematics education research journals is the presence of mathematics itself" (p. 36). This strikes us as hyperbole easily dismissed by scanning the contents of current issues of leading journals. Particularly telling is his complaint that mathematics educators "have moved away from our historical roots of being a subcategory of mathematics" (p. 36), echoing a nostalgic lament from Fried (2014) in the same volume for the time in the past when "asking about the distinction between mathematics and mathematics education would have been like asking about the distinction between mathematics and geometry" (p. 4). Fried goes on to state that "even [critical mathematics educators] would have to admit that there is something accidental about mathematics' place in the political superstructure" (p. 9). No, we do not admit that – we see deep reasons why uses of mathematics are implicated in structures of power and oppression. Further "once one puts on the glasses of critical mathematics education, every mathematical notion becomes suspect and must be examined for its socio-political function: every mathematical idea has an ulterior meaning" (p. 9). We accept this characterisation with a caveat that takes us to the heart of the matter, namely that the socio-political functions and ulterior meanings are *constructions of human actors*. Likewise, it is the *uses* of mathematics, not some disembodied Platonic entities, that pervade the political superstructure.

An outstanding ongoing example of a sustained challenge to the mainstream establishment in mathematics education is the work of Danny Martin in critiquing the rhetoric and policies of the National Council for Teachers of Mathematics in the United States on issues relating to race (e.g., Martin, 2003, 2013, 2015, 2019). The position of the NCTM has been predominantly framed in terms of access and equity, for example under the slogan "Mathematics for all" (Martin, 2003). However, as Martin argues (2019), "the forms of inclusion offered up in equity-oriented discourses and reforms have typically involved two trajectories: (1) inclusion accompanied by marginalization; and (2) assimilation into the existing cultures of mathematics education, thereby sustaining the fundamental character of the domain" (p. 461). He positions his argument within "a broader antagonistic relationship between blackness and (the possibility of) humanity" in relation to which we would argue a direct link between the narrative of mathematics as a purely White European achievement and the continuing "taken-for-granted racial hierarchy within the domain" (p. 460). In relation to the supposed deficiencies of Black children entering school, he argues as follows:

> within contemporary research contexts, a number of studies have been conducted to show that poor (Black) children enter school with only pre-mathematical knowledge, and lack the capacity to mathematize their experiences, engage in abstraction and elaboration, and use mathematical ideas and symbols to create models of their everyday lives ... In such discursive dehumanization, little inclination is expressed for questioning why these processes best represent mathematical thinking. (p. 463)

5 Geopolitical Contexts

We next turn to discussion of powerful global forces framing the background against which we work. These forces emanate from a bewildering complexity of organisational actors striving to shape mathematics education (for a remarkable effort to illuminate this complexity within the United States, see Wolfmeyer, 2014). Key issues, as we see them, include the following:

– *What might be termed "the unreasonable political effectiveness of 'mathematics'"* (the quotation marks are to indicate that what we mean is discourse using the word). Across all developed countries, the urge for "mathematics for all" has become a "naturalized truth" (Valero, 2004, p. 119). More generally, political rhetoric proclaims that excellence in science, technology, engineering, and mathematics (STEM) education is essential to economic competitiveness in the global market-place (for a contrary position, see Greer, 2019). This discourse is typically nationalistic and often militaristic, and does not sit well with the image of mathematics projected by mathematicians as universal, politically neutral, and so on.

– *Homogenisation through globalisation.* In his analysis of the globalisation of education, Spring (2015) advances a number of concepts. By "economisation of education" he means "the increasing influence of economists on educational research and judging school outcomes in economic terms" (p. xiii).

"Corporatisation of education" refers to "multinational corporations influencing global school policies to educate and shape human behaviors for the corporate workplace." And what he terms "the audit state" refers to "the use of performance standards to assess government programs, including the use of standardized assessments to evaluate educational performance" (2015, p. xiv). All of these forces contribute to homogenisation in mathematics education in terms of curriculum (mutual global "benchmarking" against other curricula in a convergent process), and international assessments, about which Keitel and Kilpatrick (1999) concluded "The studies rest on the shakiest of foundations – they assume that the mantel of science can cover all weaknesses in design, incongruous data and errors of interpretation. They not only compare the incomparable, they rationalize the irrational" (p. 254).

Lindblad, Pettersson, and Popkewitz (2015) document the dominance of such assessments (in which mathematics has a preeminent place) in shaping educational policymaking on a global scale. More profoundly, they present arguments about the harmful effects of uncritical obeisance to the authority of numbers, and about the use of numbers, and associated statistical and modelling techniques, in furthering the rise of neoliberal hegemony in education.

– *The formatting power of mathematics.* For decades, Skovsmose has been drawing attention to what he terms "formatting" as a specific aspect of "mathematics in action" (e.g., Skovsmose, 2005). This concept refers to the way in which many aspects of our lives are controlled by algorithms and computerised models that are outside our control, not accessible to inspection, and with harmful consequences (e.g., O'Neil, 2016). And the phenomenon is escalating (e.g., Zuboff, 2019).

We finish this section with some comments on contemporary culture. Paris and Alim (2017) point out that "contemporary linguistic, pedagogical, and cultural research has pushed against the tendency of researchers and practitioners to assume static relationships between race, ethnicity, language, and cultural ways of being" (p. 7). Here we confine our discussion to arguably the most obvious and pervasive aspect of contemporary culture, namely the ubiquity of electronic devices. While there is a great deal of concern about the adverse effects of this reality and the need to develop technoscepticism (Greer, 2019), electronic tools obviously have great potential for good as well; at the risk of stating the obvious, the writing of this chapter has been greatly facilitated by the use of a word processor and access to the Internet to gather information, download publications, and so on. Rubel, whose work is discussed in Andersson and Wagner (this volume), has developed the concept of "spatial justice" and, in particular, how students can use technology to access information helpful in addressing sociopolitical issues in their environments – in the example under discussion, in relation to a lottery (see Nobre, 1989). Parra's project among the Nasa people, described in Parra and Valero (this volume), also integrates local toponymical knowledge with applications of technology for collecting and recording stories about seven locations. And Ochigame and Holston (2016) document how activists engaged in land struggles in Brazil (see, for example, Knijnik & Wanderer, 2012) have developed IT-savvy strategies to circumvent exclusion of their messaging.

There are of course very many ways to integrate technology in mathematics classes. A particularly interesting approach is the concept of Ethnocomputing,[3] in particular as developed by Eglash (e.g., Davis, Lachney, Zatz, Babbitt, & Eglash, 2019).

6 Choosing the Best Future: Optimism of the Will

Critical Mathematics Educators have no choice but to continue the struggle. Against the background of the pessimism of the intellect, there are reasons for hope. People are in the streets in countries across the world. Indigenous peoples around the world are forging solidarity. Young people worldwide are protesting against the existential crisis posed by climate catastrophe. The deleterious effects of social media on society are being exposed; at the same time, activists are finding creative and subversive ways to use them.

We might also take solace in Stein's Law, which states with stark simplicity: "If something cannot go on for ever, it will stop." The implications in relation to our physical environment, and the consequent urgency of a total reorientation, have been forcefully argued by, amongst others, Latour (2018) and Klein (2014). The implications in relation to ideologically driven human constructions of markets, profits, labor, and capital have been examined in great historical detail by Piketty (2020). Something has to change.

There is no shortage of questions and issues for us and the next generation of critical mathematics educators to address, and we offer a few for consideration (the reader can certainly extend the list):
– *Overcoming the apparent inaudibility of brute facts about the world.* As we observe our society, it strikes us that there is an inexplicable ability to choose to ignore brute facts, most notably about climate change and wealth inequality. It is legitimate to complain that mathematics education does a poor job of helping people to evaluate statistical information critically and intelligently. Yet how much understanding of mathematics is required to

react to the information that the 2,153 billionaires in the world control as much wealth as the 4,600,000,000 people in the bottom 60% of humanity (Lawson et al., 2020)? (And see the World Inequality Database[4] with which Piketty (2020) is associated).

- *Tracing the effects of mathematics education in forming individual and collective world-views.* Such a program is admittedly very ambitious and complex. Here, we restrict ourselves to briefly outlining conjectures about illustrative core elements of the standard mathematics curriculum and their possible implications.
    - In many systems of mathematics education, considerable emphasis is given to procedural fluency and the rigid application of algorithms. We conjecture that this contributes to a disposition to follow rules and thereby abdicate responsibility for making judgments.
    - There are multifarious manifestations of teaching children to simplistically map real-world situations onto mathematical models, including a considerable literature on how this happens through learning the rules of the "word problem game."
    - More generally, we assert that the complex nature of mathematical modelling is poorly conveyed in mathematics education, failing to nurture a critical attitude that takes into account the motivations of those carrying out and/or paying for the exercise, the modeling tools available, the complexities of interpretation, and the nuances of communicating conclusions. The history of measurements of intelligence and how they have been misused affords a clear example.
- *Examining language traps in the discourse around mathematics and mathematics education.* The question "What is mathematics?" would be disallowed in a court of law as a leading question, since its formulation implies that the answer is some kind of thing that, moreover, is both singular and timeless. An example from mathematics education discussed above is the slogan "mathematics for all" that falls apart under any serious analysis. Hacking (2006) cites Nietzche's aphorism that "unspeakably more depends on what things are called than on what they are ... Creating new names and assessments and apparent truths is enough to create new 'things'" (and see Hacking, 2002).
- *The complicity of mathematicians in the military-industrial-academic complex.* As stated by D'Ambrosio (2010):

> It is clear that mathematics provides the foundation of the technological, industrial, military, economic and political systems and that in turn mathematics relies on these systems for the material bases of its

continuing progress. It is important to question the role of mathematics and mathematics education in arriving at the present global predicaments of humankind. (p. 51)

Addressing such a statement is part of the general challenge to persuade mathematicians first to accept that they have ethical responsibilities, then to act upon them. Can we envisage a situation where such a discussion is integral to every university mathematics program?

In a recent talk, the mathematician Chandler Davis (2015), reviewed attempts by himself and other mathematicians to critique the policies formulated during the Cold War period, partly on the basis of abstract mathematics such as game theory. He finished by posing a challenge to the next generation:

> in this great jeopardy, when you must rouse yourselves to better efforts than we managed just to have any future, I implore you: have the wisdom and the strength not merely to survive but to survive proudly and happily. To choose the best future.

Notes

1 See MEScommunity.info, which includes proceedings from the MES conferences.
2 rethinkingschools.org
3 https://en.wikipedia.org/wiki/Ethnocomputing
4 http://WID.world

References

Antonini, F. (2019). Pessimism of the intellect, optimism of the will: Gramsci's political thought in the last miscellaneous notebooks. *Rethinking Marxism*, *31*(1), 42–57. https://doi.org/10.1080/08935696.2019.1577616

Atweh, B., & Clarkson, P. (2001). Internationalization and globalization of mathematics education: Toward an agenda for research/action. In B. Atweh, H. Forgasz, & B. Nebres (Eds.), *Sociocultural research on mathematics education: An international perspective* (pp. 77–94). Lawrence Erlbaum.

Bigelow, B., & Swinehart, T. (Eds.). (2014). *A people's curriculum for the Earth*. Rethinking Schools.

Cole, M., Gay, J., Glick, J. A., & Sharp, D. W. (1971). *The cultural context of learning and thinking: An exploration in experimental anthropology*. Basic Books.

D'Ambrosio, U. (2010). Mathematics education and survival with dignity. In H. Alrø, O. Ravn, & P. Valero (Eds.), *Critical mathematics education: Past, present and future* (pp. 51–63). Sense. https://doi.org/10.1163/9789460911644_006

Davis, C. (2015). *Choosing our future*. Pakula Lecture given at the University of Toronto. www.youtube.com/watch?v=HeA-0OV1RZ8

Davis, J., Lachney, M., Zatz, Z., Babbitt, W., & Eglash, R. (2019). A cultural computing curriculum. In E. K. Hawthorne & M. A. Pérez-Quiñones (Eds.), *SIGCSE'19: Proceedings of the 50th ACM Technical Symposium on Computer Science Education* (pp. 1171–1175). Association for Computing Machinery. https://doi.org/10.1145/3287324.3287439

Eisenberg, T. (2014). Some of my pet-peeves with mathematics education. In M. N. Fried & T. Dreyfus (Eds.), *Mathematics and mathematics education: Searching for common ground* (pp. 35–44). Springer. https://doi.org/10.1007/978-94-007-7473-5_3

Ferreira, M. K. L. (2015). *Mapping time, space and the body: Indigenous knowledge and mathematical thinking in Brazil*. Sense. https://doi.org/10.1007/978-94-6209-866-4

Frankenstein, M. (1983). Critical mathematics education: An application of Paulo Freire's epistemology. *Journal of Education, 165*(4), 315–339. https://doi.org/10.1177/002205748316500403

Freire, P. (1972). *Pedagogy of the oppressed*. Penguin.

Fried, M. N. (2014). Mathematics & mathematics education: Searching for common ground. In M. N. Fried & T. Dreyfus (Eds.), *Mathematics and mathematics education: Searching for common ground* (pp. 31–22). Springer. https://doi.org/10.1007/978-94-007-7473-5_1

Fried, M. N., & Dreyfus, T. (Eds.). (2014). *Mathematics and mathematics education: Searching for common ground*. Springer. https://doi.org/10.1007/978-94-007-7473-5

Greer, B. (2013). Teaching through ethnomathematics: Possibilities and dilemmas. In M. Berger, K. Brodie, V. Frith, & K. le Roux (Eds.), *Proceedings of the Seventh International Mathematics Education and Society Conference* (Vol. 2, pp. 282–290). MES7. https://www.mescommunity.info/mes7b.pdf

Greer, B. (2019). STEM and the race between education and catastrophe. In J. Subramanian (Ed.), *Proceedings of the Tenth International Mathematics Education and Society Conference* (pp. 144–147). MES10. https://www.mescommunity.info/proceedings/MES10.pdf

Greer, B., Mukhopadhyay, S., & Roth, W.-M. (2012). Celebrating diversity, realizing alternatives. In S. Mukhopadhyay & W.-M. Roth (Eds.), *Alternative forms of knowing (in) mathematics: Celebrations of diversity of mathematical practices* (pp. 1–8). Sense. https://doi.org/10.1007/978-94-6091-921-3_1

Greer, B., & Skovsmose, O. (2012). Introduction: Seeing the cage? The emergence of critical mathematics education. In O. Skovsmose & B. Greer (Eds.), *Opening the cage: Critique and politics of mathematics education* (pp. 1–19). Sense. https://doi.org/10.1007/978-94-6091-808-7_1

Gutstein, E. (2006). *Reading and writing the world with mathematics: Toward a pedagogy for social justice*. Routledge. https://doi.org/10.4324/9780203112946

Gutstein, E. (2012). Mathematics as a weapon in the struggle. In O. Skovsmose & B. Greer (Eds.), *Opening the cage: Critique and politics of mathematics education* (pp. 23–48). Sense. https://doi.org/10.1007/978-94-6091-808-7_2

Hacking, I. (2002). *Historical ontology*. Harvard University Press.

Hacking, I. (2006). Making up people. *London Review of Books, 28*(16). https://www.lrb.co.uk/the-paper/v28/n16/ian-hacking/making-up-people

Hersh, R. (1997). *What is mathematics, really?* Oxford University Press.

Høyrup, J. (2010, August). *Old Babylonian "Algebra," and what it teaches us about possible types of mathematics*. Paper presented at the ICM satellite conference Mathematics in Ancient Times.

Keitel, C., & Kilpatrick, J. (1999). The rationality and irrationality of international comparative studies. In G. Kaiser, E. Luna, & I. Huntley (Eds.), *International comparisons in mathematics education* (pp. 241–255). Routledge.

Klein, N. (2014). *This changes everything: Capitalism vs the climate*. Simon & Schuster.

Knijnik, G., & Wanderer, F. (2012). Genealogy of mathematics education in two Brazilian rural forms of life. In O. Skovsmose & B. Greer (Eds.), *Opening the cage: Critique and politics of mathematics education* (pp. 187–202). Sense. https://doi.org/10.1007/978-94-6091-808-7_9

Kofman, A. (2018, October 25). Bruno Latour, the post-truth philosopher, mounts a defense of science. *New York Times Magazine*. www.nytimes.com/2018/10/25/magazine/bruno-latour-post-truth-philosopher-science.html

Kuku, A. (1995). Mathematics education in Africa in relation to other countries. In R. Hunting, G. Fitzsimons, P. Clarkson, & A. Bishop (Eds.), *Regional collaboration in mathematics education* (pp. 403–423). Monash University.

Latour, B. (2018). *Down to earth: Politics in the new climatic regime*. Polity.

Lawson, M., Butt, A. P., Harvey, R., Sarosi, D., Coffey, C., Piaget, K., & Thekkudan, J. (2020). *Time to care: Unpaid and underpaid care work and the global inequality crisis*. Oxfam GB/Oxfam International.

Lindblad, S., Pettersson, D., & Popkewitz, T. S. (2015). *International comparisons of school results: A systematic review of research on large scale assessments in education*. Vetenskapsrådet.

Lipka, J., Yanez, E., Andrew-Ihrke, D., & Adam, S. (2009). A two-way process for developing effective culturally based math: Examples from math in a cultural context. In B. Greer, S. Mukhopadhyay, A. P. Powell, & S. Nelson-Barber (Eds.), *Culturally responsive mathematics education* (pp. 257–280). Routledge. https://doi.org/10.4324/9780203879948

Martin, D. B. (2003). Hidden assumptions and unaddressed questions in Mathematics for All rhetoric. *The Mathematics Educator, 13*(2), 7–21.

Martin, D. B. (2013). Race, racial projects, and mathematics education. *Journal for Research in Mathematics Education, 44*(1), 316–333. https://doi.org/10.5951/jresematheduc.44.1.0316

Martin, D. B. (2015). The collective Black and "principles to actions." *Journal of Urban Mathematics Education, 8*(1), 17–23.

Martin, D. B. (2019). Equity, inclusion, and antiblackness in mathematics education. *Race Ethnicity and Education, 22*(4), 459–478. https://doi.org/10.1080/13613324.2019.1592833

Martin, D. B., & Gholson, M. (2012). On becoming and being a critical Black scholar in mathematics education: The politics of race and identity. In O. Skovsmose & B. Greer (Eds.), *Opening the cage: Critique and politics of mathematics education* (pp. 203–222). Sense. https://doi.org/10.1007/978-94-6091-808-7_10

Nobre, S. R. (1989). The ethnomathematics of the most popular lottery in Brazil: The "Animal Lottery." In C. Keitel, P. Damerow, A. Bishop, & P. Gerdes (Eds.), *Mathematics, education, and society: Reports and papers presented in the Fifth Day Special Programme on "Mathematics, Education, and Society" at the 6th International Congress on Mathematical Education* (pp. 175–177). UNESCO.

Ochigame, R., & Holston, J. (2016). Filtering dissent: Social media and land struggles in Brazil. *New Left Review, 99*, 85–110.

O'Neil, C. (2016). *Weapons of math destruction: How big data increases inequality and threatens democracy.* Crown.

Paris, D., & Alim, H. S. (Eds.). (2017). *Culturally sustaining pedagogies: Teaching and learning for justice in a changing world.* Teachers College Press.

Parra-Sanchez, A. (2017). Ethnomathematical barters. In H. Straehler-Pohl, N. Bohlmann, & A. Pais (Eds.), *The disorder of mathematics education: Challenging the sociopolitical dimensions of research* (pp. 89–105). Springer. https://doi.org/10.1007/978-3-319-34006-7_6

Piketty, T. (2020). *Capital and ideology* (A. Goldhammer, Trans.). Harvard University Press.

Powell, A. B. (2012). The historical development of criticalmathematics education. In A. A. Wager & D. W. Stinson (Eds.), *Teaching mathematics for social justice: Conversations with educators* (pp. 21–34). National Council for Teachers of Mathematics.

Ravn, O., & Skovsmose, O. (2019). *Connecting humans to equations: A reinterpretation of the philosophy of mathematics.* Springer. https://doi.org/10.1007/978-3-030-01337-0

Raygoza, M. C. (2016). Striving toward transformational resistance: Youth participatory action research in the mathematics classroom. *Journal of Urban Mathematics Education, 9*(2), 122–152.

Roy, A. (2019). *Literature provides shelter: That's why we need it.* Arthur Miller Freedom to Write Lecture, PEN America. https://www.theguardian.com/commentisfree/2019/may/13/arundhati-roy-literature-shelter-pen-america

Skovsmose, O. (2005). *Travelling through education: Uncertainty, mathematics, responsibility*. Sense. https://doi.org/10.1163/9789087903626

Skovsmose, O. (2016). Mathematics: A critical rationality? In P. Ernest, B. Sriraman & N. Ernest (Eds.), *Critical mathematics education: Theory, praxis, and reality* (pp. 1–22). Information Age.

Smith, L. T. (1999). *Decolonizing methodologies: Research and Indigenous peoples*. Zed Books.

Spring, J. (2015). *Globalization of education: An introduction* (2nd ed.). Routledge. https://doi.org/10.4324/9781315795843

Stavrou, S. G., & Miller, D. (2017). Miscalculations: Decolonizing and anti-oppressive discourses in Indigenous mathematics education. *Canadian Journal of Education, 40*(3), 92–122.

Urton, G. (1997). *The social life of numbers: A Quechua ontology of numbers and philosophy of arithmetic*. University of Texas Press.

Valero, P. (2004). Socio-political perspectives on mathematics education. In P. Valero & R. Zevenbergen (Eds.), *Researching the socio-political dimensions of mathematics education: Issues of power in theory and methodology* (pp. 5–23). Kluwer. https://doi.org/10.1007/1-4020-7914-1_2

Vithal, R. (2003). *In search of a pedagogy of conflict and dialogue for mathematics education*. Kluwer. https://doi.org/10.1007/978-94-010-0086-4

Vithal, R., & Skovsmose, O. (1997). The end of innocence: A critique of "ethnomathematics." *Educational Studies in Mathematics, 34*(2), 131–157. https://doi.org/10.1023/a:1002971922833

Wolfmeyer, M. (2014). *Math education for America? Policy networks, big business, and pedagogy wars*. Routledge. https://doi.org/10.4324/9781315883564

Zinn, H. (1997). The uses of scholarship. In *The Zinn reader: Writings on disobedience and democracy* (pp. 499–507). Seven Stories Press.

Zuboff, S. (2019). *The age of surveillance capitalism: The fight for a human future at the new frontier of power*. PublicAffairs.

Index

Aboriginal 48, 49, 52, 61, 241
abstraction 18, 27, 29, 30, 32–34, 194, 213, 220, 222, 251, 255, 259; *see also* realised abstraction
Abtahi, Y. 172, 234
Abya-yala 72
academic mathematics 27–30, 44, 51, 236, 241, 251
accent 109, 150, 154–156, 158, 160, 162
access 3, 14, 15, 38, 75, 84, 100, 102, 109–118, 138, 140, 151, 161, 173, 178, 179, 205, 232, 233, 254, 256, 257
achievement gap 86, 92; *see also* gap instinct
achievement/performance 80, 85, 86, 91, 92, 107, 111, 116, 256
action 2, 9, 14, 19, 35, 39, 40, 47, 48, 55, 61, 62, 65, 72, 75, 83, 89, 90, 94, 101, 110, 112, 113, 115, 130, 133–135, 144, 153, 155, 157, 162, 170, 174, 178, 187, 189, 190, 195, 196, 200, 231, 233–236, 238, 245, 248, 253; *see also* calls to action, mathematics in action
action research 32, 36, 83, 125, 240, 252
activism 2, 19, 20, 87, 88, 92, 248, 249, 253, 257
actuarial 217, 218
acultural 51
Adam, S. 51, 252
Adams, B. 84
addition (mathematical operation) 62, 78
admission 15, 106–108, 111, 112, 116, 117, 129
Africa 15, 30, 83, 102, 103, 107, 115, 124, 244, 251
Africa-centred Critical Mathematics Education 100, 102, 104, 115, 116, 118
Africa-centred theory 100, 102–104
agency/agentive 38, 39, 42, 43, 103, 104, 110, 112, 115, 117, 123, 127, 129, 132, 133, 140, 154, 231, 232, 235, 237, 238
Aikenhead, G. S. 51, 56
Alaska 252
Albania 144
Albanian 151
Alexander, N. 244
Alexander, R. 105, 111, 117
algorithm 5–7, 16, 157, 171, 181, 191, 214, 248, 256, 258

alienation 28, 242, 243
Alim, H. S. 256
Allen, J. 211
ally 127, 140, 252
Alrø, H. 101, 102, 116
Americas 9, 32, 38, 72, 249
Amidon, J. 140
Andersson, A. 13, 17, 25–27, 32, 34, 37, 42, 145, 147, 152, 158, 161, 232, 233, 236, 238, 241, 242, 245, 250, 253, 256
Andes mountains 14, 72
Andrade, R. 148
Andrew-Ihrke, D. 252
Antarctic 204
Antarctica 197, 198
anthropology 25, 27, 88, 240, 243, 251, 252
anti-oppressive education 86
anti-racist 127, 135, 136, 138, 139
Antonini, F. 249
Anzaldúa, G. 131, 138
Aotearoa/New Zealand 89, 90
Apartheid 26, 101, 102, 244
Appelbaum, P. 11, 173, 175, 178
applied/applying mathematics 2, 4, 9, 11, 14, 19, 52, 60, 146, 179, 188, 190, 213, 242, 250
appropriation 55, 71, 74, 75, 81, 82, 86, 88, 90, 91, 93, 103
Arabic 151, 152
Arctic sea ice 170, 173, 202
Arctic, the 203
argumentation 6, 18, 169, 175, 181, 186, 192, 196, 200, 206, 233
artefact 14, 25, 52, 60, 78, 147
Ascher, M. 27
Ashcroft, B. 103
Asian 125, 132
assessment 3, 7, 43, 74, 75, 77, 79, 80, 84–86, 91, 105, 108, 109, 111–116, 144, 149, 150, 152, 154, 155, 160, 162, 169, 191, 194, 196, 205, 219, 223, 256, 258
assimilation 48, 71, 72, 87, 255
assumptions 4, 6, 9, 10, 15, 30, 31, 52, 88, 91, 94, 115, 124, 172, 178, 181, 187, 216, 218, 219, 256
Atlantic Canada 14
atmosphere 167, 187, 195, 197, 198, 201, 205

Atweh, B.   7, 101, 251,
audience   110, 112, 115, 127, 136, 138
audit state   256
Australia   178, 249
authentic tasks   172, 176, 177
authenticity   17, 166, 172, 173, 177, 181, 182
authority   42, 43, 72, 74, 77, 79, 103, 233, 256
autoethnography   88, 243
autonomy   74, 81, 87, 89, 94
average   5, 6, 179, 180, 182, 195, 198, 201, 202, 203, 216, 221, 235
awareness   4, 5, 7, 18, 26, 39, 42, 50, 62, 75, 79, 85, 91, 92, 147, 157, 162, 169, 171, 173, 174, 176, 185, 188–190, 192–194, 200, 204, 206, 214, 222, 231–233, 236, 238; *see also* self-aware

Babbitt, W.   257
background   12, 37, 76, 105–107, 114, 125, 132, 144–146, 150, 152, 218, 220, 252, 255, 257
Ball, D. L.   125
Balto, A. M.   44
Bang, M.   128
Bangladesh   252
Barbosa, J. C.   174, 176
Bartell, T. G.   16, 140
Barthes, R.   27, 43
Barton, B.   13, 27, 61, 90
Barwell, R.   17, 18, 145, 147, 158, 167–171, 173, 175–177, 187–191, 196, 197, 206, 233–235, 253
Bassier, I.   113
Battey, D.   53, 124
Battiste, M.   50, 52, 58
Bayesian statistics   4
Behari-Leak, K.   109, 114
Belgium   216
belonging   71, 75, 81, 83, 88, 90, 92–94, 108, 112, 117, 118, 145, 246
Bengali   252
Bergen   17, 180
best practices   92
Bhan, G.   103
Bhattacharya, S.   243
bias   4–7, 21
big data   20
Bigelow, B.   253
bilingual   73, 74, 81, 84, 85, 125
binary   6, 103, 118, 225
biodiversity   173, 176

Bishop, A. J.   56
Black Lives Matter   3
blackbox   147, 157, 198
Blackfoot   54
Blanco-Álvarez, H.   84
blind spot   6, 7
Body Mass Index (BMI)   18, 210, 211, 216, 218, 219, 235
Bolaños, G.   94
Booysen, S.   108
Bopape, M.   101
Borba, M.   28–30, 148
Born, D.   194
Bosnian   151
Bouchard, C.   218
Bourdieu, P.   110
Boyer, P.   84
Brandom, R. B.   17, 146, 148, 149
Bransen, J.   149
Brantlinger, A.   32
Brazil   80, 90, 257
Britain   243, 246
Britzman, D. P.   128
Brock-Utne, B.   244
Broome, J.   196
Brown, W.   91
Bullock, E. C.   124, 125, 132
Buzz60   213
Byun, S.   16, 140

cabildo   75, 94
Caicedo, N.   82
calculation   11, 64, 106, 108, 113, 115, 174, 176, 179, 198, 201, 213, 215, 218, 223, 225, 235
calculus   157, 158
calls to action   47, 49, 50, 65, 235
Canada   14, 32, 47–49, 57, 61, 65, 66, 172, 178, 211, 212
capital   91, 124, 257; *see also* human capital
capitalism   8, 116, 124, 129, 131
Cappon, P.   58
carbon dioxide   2, 167, 187, 188, 193, 195, 196, 201
Carson, R.   28, 29, 52
caste   19
Castillo, E.   83, 84
Cauca   72–74, 81, 89
Centers for Disease Control and Prevention   215, 219, 225
certainty   80, 170, 190, 222

INDEX

Cheng, L.-J.   202
Chicago   9
China   28, 248
Christy, J. R.   186, 187, 198, 200, 201
Chronaki, A.   17, 147, 150, 154, 233, 238, 250
circle   36, 56
Cision Canada   212
Cision US   212
citizens   4, 18, 30, 33, 34, 102, 147, 154, 157, 166, 167, 169–171, 182, 183, 185–188, 190, 191, 194, 211, 222, 224, 234
citizenship   18, 30, 31, 34
civil rights movement   124
Civil, M.   148
Clarke, D.   37
Clarkson, P.   101, 251
classification   87, 91, 118
climate change   1–3, 6, 17–20, 166–177, 180–182, 185–206, 233–235, 237, 240, 253, 257
climate justice   2, 253
CO_2 see carbon dioxide
Cobb, P.   125
Coburn, C. E.   125
cognitive imperialism   50
Cohen, D. K.   125
Cohen, E.   218, 219
Cole, M.   252
Coles, A.   172, 173
collaboration   15, 16, 36, 37, 54, 65, 83, 113, 128, 132, 174, 192, 193, 235, 243, 245
collective   52, 55, 74, 77, 82, 83, 85, 89, 92, 94, 108, 135, 170, 174, 211, 243, 249, 250, 258
Colombia   14, 32, 71–75, 83, 94
colonialism   29, 30, 48, 50, 51, 65, 103
coloniality   11, 20, 48, 50–52, 59, 60, 65, 71, 86, 87, 101, 112, 116, 244, 245, 251, 252
colonisation   26, 30, 37, 40, 42, 50, 51, 58, 61, 72, 87, 90, 137, 236, 243, 244
commitment   15, 40, 75, 103, 110, 149, 249, 252
communication of mathematical ideas   7, 113, 168, 174, 187, 188, 234
communitarian   84, 85, 91
community   9, 12, 14, 20, 33–35, 37–41, 44, 47–49, 51–60, 63–66, 71, 72, 74–77, 79–91, 93, 94, 107, 109, 110, 112, 118, 128, 135, 139, 151, 159, 170, 171, 174–178, 181, 186, 190, 193, 197, 211, 224, 233, 235–237, 241, 249, 252
commutativity   65
complex challenges   231–233, 235, 237, 238

complex problems   3, 5, 167–169, 234, 235, 237
complex questions   1–3, 7
complexity   6, 15, 20, 37, 55, 63, 88, 90, 92, 103, 104, 116, 118, 126, 133, 146, 148, 152, 154, 155, 162, 169–171, 173, 175, 179, 185, 187, 191, 206, 221, 222, 224, 233–236, 243, 244, 251, 255, 258
conflict   14, 17, 31, 34, 40, 61, 74, 78, 154, 161, 169, 188, 235, 237
Connell, R.   102, 103
consciousness   8, 108, 211
Consejo Regional Indígena del Cauca (CRIC)   72–74, 81, 84, 91
CONTCEPI   74
control   2, 10, 18, 50, 74, 79, 84, 113, 166, 221, 222, 250, 256, 258
conversation   6, 17, 24, 53–58, 60, 61, 63, 65, 118, 126, 127, 129, 132–135, 138, 148, 155, 160, 161, 218, 243
conversion   78, 225
Cooper, B.   103
Copenhagen   149
Corner, A.   190, 201
corporatisation of education   256
Cosby M. D.   140
counter discourse/act   57, 86, 87, 124, 223
counters (manipulative)   64
courage   162
COVID-19 pandemic   3, 5, 20, 234
creativity   20, 36, 101, 102, 110, 115, 117, 215, 245, 257
Cree   58
Crenshaw, K.   132, 133
Criado Perez, C.   4, 5
CRIC see Consejo Regional Indígena del Cauca
crisis   7, 101, 167, 234, 244, 253, 254, 257
critical awareness   169, 174, 176, 231–233, 236, 238
critical citizens   187, 188, 191
critical literacy   15, 18, 100, 102, 104, 109, 110, 115, 145, 147, 148, 162
critical mathematical inquiry   242
critical mathematics education   1, 3–21, 24–26, 30–38, 40, 42–44, 47, 50, 53, 71, 80, 94, 100, 101, 144, 145, 147, 158, 166, 167, 169, 174, 176, 182, 183, 186, 187, 188, 192, 194, 210, 211, 213, 224, 231, 232, 235, 237, 238, 240–242, 244, 245, 248, 249, 252–254, 257

critical race feminism   133
critical race theory   15, 124, 134
critical understanding   18, 166, 173, 182, 183
critical Whiteness   123, 124, 126, 127, 129, 131, 135, 137, 139
critique   3, 4, 6, 7, 9–11, 14, 24, 26, 28, 30, 31, 33, 34, 41, 42, 53, 56, 72, 80, 83, 86, 89, 101, 116, 127, 130, 132, 145, 149, 174, 181, 190, 191, 196, 212, 213, 223, 232, 235, 241, 243, 252, 253, 259
Cross, M.   102
Crossen, C.   218
cube   62, 216
cuisenaire rods   63
culturally situated critical mathematics education   24, 25, 32–34, 37, 43, 232, 241
culture   7, 9, 10, 12, 14, 15, 17, 21, 24–44, 47–54, 56–60, 64, 65, 72–76, 80–86, 88–94, 103–104, 108, 110, 136, 149, 150, 152, 154, 211, 214, 232, 233, 240–245, 249–252, 255, 256
curriculum   3, 4, 7, 8, 12, 15, 20, 28, 33, 36, 39, 41, 42, 50, 52, 61, 62, 73, 74, 79, 80, 84, 85, 90, 93, 101, 110, 117, 146, 147, 175, 182, 191–194, 205, 211, 223, 224, 241–243, 251, 253, 256, 258

D'Ambrosio, U.   27, 51, 101, 188, 249, 258
Davis, C.   259
Davis, J.   15, 257
Davos   166, 234
de Freitas, E.   25
Deardorff, J.   223
debate   3, 71, 74, 101, 112, 114, 118, 167–171, 173–177, 182, 185, 190, 192, 197, 205, 243, 244, 250
decimal system   78
decoloniality   71, 87–89
decolonisation   12–14, 20, 40, 42, 47, 50–53, 65, 66, 90, 112, 235, 240, 242–244
decolonising   11, 14, 32, 40, 41, 43, 47, 50–55, 60, 61, 64, 65, 71, 72, 83, 86, 87, 89, 233, 240, 242, 245
decolonising research   252
DeCuir, J. T.   124
dehumanisation   134, 136, 138
Dei, G. J. S.   71
democracy   1, 3, 7, 11, 13, 14, 17–19, 101, 102, 114, 118, 129, 147, 167, 169–171, 194, 195, 224

Denmark   31
Derrickson, G. C. R. M.   58
Derry, J.   146
desconocimiento (refuse to know)   131
design   5, 15, 36, 37, 39, 42, 77, 100, 105, 110–112, 115–118, 123, 125, 126, 129, 147, 191, 206, 256
Devlin, K.   219
DeVries, E.   86
dialectically entangled   162
dialogue   11, 12, 28, 86, 125, 129, 139, 146, 148, 174, 185, 188, 235
DiAngelo, R.   136
dichotomy   6, 87, 236, 241, 243, 244
differential power   128, 137
dignity   49, 82, 101, 102, 112, 118
discourse   4, 9–11, 17–19, 27, 42, 65, 83, 86, 88, 92, 94, 102, 108, 114, 116, 123, 125, 126, 128–130, 133–138, 152, 154, 158, 161, 162, 210–215, 222, 224, 225, 234, 244, 254, 255, 258
discrimination   31, 40
displacements from prevailing discourses about mathematics   86, 142, 233
distributive property   64, 78
diverse classrooms   17, 107, 117, 144–146, 148, 150, 152, 162
diversity   10, 12, 14, 15, 18, 28, 30, 33, 74, 80–84, 86, 87, 100, 104, 105, 110, 111, 113, 114, 116–118, 123, 144, 145, 154, 155, 162, 220, 240–242, 244, 249, 250
division (mathematical operation)   62
Dixson, A. D.   124
domination/dominance   7, 10, 15, 16, 42, 48, 51, 52, 62, 72, 81, 83, 84, 87, 92, 100, 103, 108, 110–112, 114, 116–118, 124, 126, 128, 130–134, 138, 232, 233, 235, 244, 249, 256
Donald, D.   58
Doolittle, E.   52
Dowling, P.   30
dreams   1, 40, 89, 107
Dreyfus, T.   254
Duarte, E. M.   127
Dublin, L.   217, 218

East Pakistan (former state)   252
ecological debt   244
economy   1, 3–5, 7, 10–12, 14, 52, 71, 84, 90, 91, 93, 101, 103, 104, 108, 124, 147, 152, 170, 171, 175, 176, 178, 187–189, 191, 194, 196, 200, 244, 248, 255, 258

ecosystem   1, 167, 168, 170, 176, 181
edges   62
educación propia   71, 72, 74–76, 80, 82–85, 88, 89, 91–94
Edwards, D.   214
Eglash, R.   257
Eiland, M.   140
Eisenberg, T.   254
Eknoyan, G.   216, 217
Elders   14, 54–57, 59–61, 63, 76, 77, 79, 81, 174
Elgar, F. J.   211
emancipation   8, 30, 36, 38, 42, 43
emissions   2, 167, 170–173, 176, 195, 196, 201
empower   8, 9, 13, 20, 36, 38–40, 42, 101, 235, 238
engaged   1, 3, 7, 13, 15
English language   61, 62, 104, 107, 109, 112, 114, 216, 231, 244, 249, 252
English, L. D.   173
environmental sustainability   12, 147, 167, 178, 183, 188
equations   19, 155, 156
equitable system   16, 125
equity   2, 38, 53, 66, 81, 102, 104, 118, 123, 125, 127–129, 137, 138, 240, 254
Ernest, P.   101
ethical/ethics   38, 42, 43, 52, 107. 113, 163, 188, 190, 191, 249, 250, 259
ethno-education   74, 76, 84
ethnocomputing   257, 259
ethnography   88, 243
ethnomathematics   1, 11–13, 20, 24–33, 35–39, 41–44, 47, 51, 53, 54, 56, 58, 59, 64, 71, 80, 92, 188, 232, 240–242, 245, 249
   critiques of   26–30, 41–44, 52, 251, 252
eugenics   222
Eurocentrism   19, 50, 51, 52, 56, 58, 103, 233, 251, 252
Europe   91, 245, 248, 249
European   13, 30, 42, 51, 57, 58, 61, 101, 217–220, 249, 252, 255
exclusion   52, 58, 88, 103, 107–109, 154, 188, 222, 233, 238, 257
exoticism   26
exploitation   124, 170, 175, 196, 244, 250
explorative talk   151, 160
explore   3, 9, 13, 14, 16–18, 24, 28, 47, 51, 52, 54, 57, 58, 60, 62, 71, 72, 76, 81, 85, 90, 93, 105, 106, 111, 113, 116–118, 124, 125, 128, 129, 135, 144–146, 167, 170, 172, 175, 177–181, 188, 192, 197, 198, 206, 223, 240
exponents   20
extended peer community   170, 171, 174, 190, 197
extinction   1, 173, 176, 195, 252

fabric of society   6, 128, 189, 196
faces (of a shape)   62
Faculty of Health Sciences (University of Cape Town)   104, 108
Faerstein, E.   216
failure   16, 37, 123, 125, 128, 129, 132, 134, 136, 138, 168
Fairclough, N.   110
fairness   109, 113
fake news   3, 168, 191
Fallism movement   108, 109, 112
Fanon, F.   53
feedback loops   2
Ferreira, M. K. L.   252
financial access   100, 109, 111, 116
Fine, M.   128
Finegood, D. T.   234
First Nations   14, 47, 57, 58
Flaherty, M. R.   222
Flegal, K. M.   212
Foote, M. Q.   140
foreground   60
Forgasz, H.   7
formal mathematics   28, 113, 174, 189
formatting power of mathematics   16, 18, 166, 171, 185–194, 196, 198–201, 204–206, 210, 211, 213, 214, 222, 224, 234, 235, 256
forms of participation   17, 166, 172, 174–177, 181, 182
formula (mathematical)   18, 215, 216, 219–223, 225
Foucault, M.   1, 7, 9–11, 13, 15, 18
fragmentation   59
France   28, 251
François, K.   13
Frankenstein, M.   8, 9, 11, 32, 38, 51, 145, 147, 148, 158, 253
Freire, P.   1, 7–9, 15, 32, 83, 110, 111, 145, 240, 241, 253
Fried, M. N.   254
Frisch, M.   196
Frith, V.   105
functionalism   29

functions (mathematical)   62, 187
funding   105, 107, 108, 112, 113, 125, 128, 129, 138, 148
Funtowicz, S. O.   169, 170, 189, 190, 199

Gaesser, G. A.   217, 218
Gainsburg, J.   173
Gandhi   243
gap instinct   6
García, G.   87, 92
Gaspé Region   66
gatekeeping   16, 38, 44, 139
Gaussian (bell) curve   216
Gay, J.   252
Geertz, C.   27
Gellert, U.   147, 157
gender   3–6, 10, 11, 18, 103, 109, 132, 216, 224, 250
geometry   4, 28, 251, 254
geopolitics of knowledge   87, 103
Gerdes, P.   27, 30
ghettoisation   26, 114
Gholson, M. L.   252
Gill, E.   223
Giroux, H.   126
global change   240
global warming   168, 179, 185, 187, 190
GoGAR *see* language game of giving and asking for reasons
González, N.   148
good intentions   16, 123, 128, 129, 137, 138, 139, 155, 236, 237
Google   5, 79, 82
Goonatilake, S.   245
Gøtze, P.   234
Government of Canada   48, 57
Goyer, K. C.   106
Gramsci, A.   248, 249
graphs   20, 62, 63, 179, 180, 186, 187, 193, 194, 198, 200–205, 215, 223
grass-root movements   84
Greece   28, 51, 55, 56
Green, L.   113, 118
Greene, M.   138
Greenstein, S.   242
Greer, B.   19, 53, 249–251, 255, 256
Grosfoguel, R.   86, 94
grounded theory   36
Guido Guevara, S. P.   75
Gutiérrez, K. D.   128

Gutiérrez, R.   7, 11, 50, 53, 55, 56, 72, 110, 114, 129, 131, 245
Gutstein, E.   9, 32, 38, 53, 110–113, 145–148, 158, 162, 188, 252, 253

Hacking, I.   10, 220–222, 258
Hall, J.   18, 234, 235
Hamlin, L.   186
Hand, V.   16, 123, 125, 140, 235, 236
Hansen, R.   234
Harding, S.   89, 94
harm   123, 127–130, 132, 135–139, 149, 157, 256
Harper, F.   140
Harris, C. I.   124
Harro, B.   136
Hartman, N.   104
Hauge, K. H.   17, 147, 167, 169, 170, 172, 173, 175–177, 189, 190, 196, 197, 206, 233–235, 253
Haviland, V. S.   126
Hebrew   151, 152
hegemony   8, 9, 51, 83, 84, 86, 87, 93, 94, 103, 133, 233, 237, 245, 256
Henderson, J. Y.   58, 61
Herbel-Eisenmann, B.   16, 26, 140
Herheim, R.   17, 206, 233, 234, 253
Hersh, R.   250
heterogeneous subjectivity   231, 237, 238
hidden curriculum   7
Hijmans, R. J.   199
Himes, J. H.   218
HIV pandemic   103, 118
Hodes, R.   103, 115
holistic   58, 59, 62, 82, 187
Holston, J.   257
hooks, b.   134, 138, 237
hope   1, 20, 41, 44, 65, 82, 108, 138, 139, 154, 231, 232, 234, 236, 237, 238, 240, 257
Høyrup, J.   251
Hufferd-Ackles, K.   151
human capital   91
humanising mathematics education   248, 250
Hutchinson, A.   213

identity   49, 51, 54, 71, 72, 74, 75, 80, 82, 86, 88–90, 110, 125, 126, 128, 129, 132, 133, 136, 222, 224, 233, 244
ideology   8, 10, 18, 51, 52, 108, 110, 115, 116, 123, 124, 129–131, 136, 137, 178, 215, 221, 222, 224, 235, 250, 254, 257

imaginaries   92, 240
imperialism   50, 61, 87, 108, 245, 248
in classroom discussion   177
in(ex)clusion   71, 72, 103, 109
inclusion   52, 84, 94, 254, 255
India   243, 248, 249, 252
India's National Literacy Campaign   241
Indian residential schools (Canada)   48–50, 66
Indigenous   1, 11, 13, 14, 20, 21, 25, 32, 35–41, 47–52, 54, 55, 58–62, 65, 66, 71–76, 79–90, 93, 94, 233, 240, 241, 243–246, 257
indigenous discourse   244
Indigenous identities   71, 75, 82, 88, 90
Indigenous knowing   12, 13, 47, 36, 38, 50–52, 58–60, 83–86, 241, 245
Indigenous mathematics   14, 41, 71, 72
Indigenous perspectives   1, 86
inequality   4, 5, 9, 20, 31, 33, 34, 41, 86, 257, 258
inequity   3–5, 14, 19, 32–34, 47, 49, 50, 102, 103, 111, 113, 116, 242
inferential interconnections   146, 149, 152–155, 157, 158, 160, 161
Inglis, S.   54
injustice   3, 4, 9, 11, 13, 20, 37, 52, 125, 236, 242, 253
inquiry-based education   83, 85
inside/outside   88, 92, 233, 243, 245
intercept   62
interculturality   37, 74, 81, 82, 84–86, 92
interdisciplinary   1, 3, 7, 11
Intergovernmental Panel on Climate Change (IPCC)   2, 167, 168, 185, 202
International Congress on Mathematical Education (ICME)   249
interrogate   3, 11, 12, 129, 131, 135, 181, 219, 222, 224,
intersectionality   108, 123, 132, 133
involves critique   1, 3, 7
Inzá   75, 76
IPCC *see* Intergovernmental Panel on Climate Change
Ireland   252
Irish   252
Ivory Coast   251

Jablonka, E.   146, 147, 157
Jackson, B.   140
Jackson, K.   125

Janks, H.   15, 100, 102, 110, 111, 114, 116, 117
Japan   218
Jarrett, R. J.   217
Jett, C. C.   15
Johnson, S.   140
Jones, D.   140
Joseph, G. G.   50, 51, 56
Juneau   252
Jung, M.-K.   124
Jurdak, M.   27
Jurow, A. S.   128

Kaiser, G.   173
Keeling curve   187
Keitel, C.   256
Kempf, A.   71
Kennedy, M.   213
Keys, A.   218, 219
Khuzwayo, H.   102
Kilen, M.   223
Kilpatrick, J.   256
Kingan, S.   187, 204
Kirkness, V. J.   58
Klein, N.   257
Knijnik, G.   11, 33, 51, 80, 90, 252, 257
knowledge bases   144–146, 148, 151, 162
knowledge keepers   54, 60, 65
knowledge-production   103
Koestler, C.   140
Kofman, A.   251
Kolkata   252
Kollosche, D.   147
Kovach, M.   50, 55, 58
Kress, R.   8
Kuhn, T.   169
Kuku, A.   251
Kurdish   151, 152

L'nui'ta'simk   47, 60–62, 64
Labrador   66
Lachney, M.   257
Ladson-Billings, G.   85
Laenui, P.   40
Lake, T.   8
land   30, 48, 49, 52, 72, 75, 82, 90, 91, 126, 137, 197, 201, 257
land-based education   82, 84
Landless People's Movement (Movimento Sem Terra)   80, 91

landscape of investigation   18, 166, 177, 178, 181
language as a resource   103
language game   17, 146, 148
language game of giving and asking for reasons (GoGAR)   17, 146, 148–150, 152, 155, 158, 160, 161
language register   25
language revitalisation   14, 57
Larnell, G.   140
Lasky, S.   37
Latin America   87, 91, 94
Latour, B.   251, 257
Lawson, M.   258
le Roux, K.   15, 16, 103, 233, 236
Lear, J.   237, 238
Leonardo, Z.   124, 126
Lester, N. A.   136
Levalle, S.   87, 89
Leyva, L. A.   53, 124, 133
Liberia   252
Lindblad, S.   256
linear regression   179, 180, 182
Lipka, J.   52, 60, 84, 252
literacy   8, 15, 32, 100, 102, 104, 105, 109–112, 115, 145–148, 154, 162, 191, 240, 241
Little Bear, L.   54, 61
lived experiences   103, 108, 138
Lloyd, E. A.   186, 187, 198, 200
local   12, 16, 20, 31, 33–40, 43, 52, 54, 77, 80, 82–85, 87, 89, 93, 94, 103, 104, 118, 135, 151, 169, 172–176, 181, 193, 231–234, 236, 237, 241, 244, 257
locus of enunciation   86, 87, 90
Lomitas   14, 15, 75–80, 82, 88
López Leiva, C.   140
Lunney Borden, L.   14, 15, 32, 33, 51, 52, 55–57, 59–63, 233, 235, 236, 242, 252

MacKay, N. J.   220
Macklin, T.   213
Maine   66
Makoni, S.   84
Malagon, M. C.   133
Malaysia   222
Mann, M. E.   202
Manuel, A.   58
Māori   51, 89, 90
Marchand, V.   218, 220
Marcus, G. E.   240

marginalisation   8, 52, 83, 116, 128, 129, 134, 147, 255
market   147, 222, 255, 257
marketisation   108, 115
Martin, D. B.   15, 53, 123, 124, 126, 129, 132, 138, 252, 254
Marx, K.   8, 11
Mathalicious   223
MathEdCollective   129
Mathematics Education and Society conference (MES)   25, 26, 30, 32, 138, 242, 249, 259
mathematics educators   7, 17, 21, 35, 51, 72, 145, 167, 182, 187, 238, 240, 248, 249, 251, 254, 257
mathematics for all slogan   254, 255, 258
mathematics in action   80, 158, 256
mathematise   10, 173, 174, 212
Matias, C. E.   124
mawikinutimatimk   54, 55, 60, 63
Mbembe, A. J.   103
McCrindle, B. W.   212
McDermott, A.   218, 219
MacDonald, Sir J. A.   48
McKenna, S.   108, 113
McMurchy-Pilkington, C.   90
mean value   6, 179, 182, 220
Meaney, T.   44, 90
measurement   40, 77, 78, 173, 178, 186, 197–199, 201–203, 205, 206, 213, 217–219, 223, 225, 235, 258
Medeiros, D. M.   217
medical programme   15, 100, 102, 104–107, 109, 111–118
Mellin-Olsen, S.   10, 17, 31
Memis, Y.   223
Mendick, H.   11
Mercer, N.   151, 160
Merth, T. D. N.   234
meta-understanding of language diversity   144, 162
Mi'kma'ki   66
Mi'kmaq   61, 62, 63, 66
Mi'kmaw   14, 15, 47, 48, 50, 51, 53–64, 66
Mignolo, W. D.   87, 94
migration   12, 168, 238
military-industrial-academic complex   258
Miller, D.   86, 87, 245, 252
Ministerio de Educacion Nacional de Colombia   75

Ministry of Education and Research (Norway)   194
models/modelling (mathematical)   5, 10, 16, 18, 20, 62, 64, 65, 171, 173, 174, 176, 182, 186, 187, 189, 191, 192, 194, 198–202, 204–206, 213–215, 224, 235, 236, 250, 255, 256, 258
modernity   10, 51, 87, 103
Molina Bedoya, V. A.   86, 92
Moll, L.   148
moral   43, 167, 240, 244
Morrell, R.   103, 115
Morrow, W.   118
mother tongue   12, 73, 82, 144, 145, 244
Mozambique   30
Mpofu-Walsh, S.   108
Mukhopadhyay, S.   19, 250
multiculturalism   17, 37, 83–86, 89, 150, 244
multilingualism   17, 103, 104
multiplication   62, 64, 65, 78, 132
Muntingh, L.   106
myth   26, 27, 29, 30, 41, 43, 50, 51, 53, 56, 232

Nasa People   71, 72, 75–77, 79, 81, 82, 87–91, 93, 94, 257
Nasayuwe   76, 77, 79, 89
National Council for Teachers of Mathematics (NCTM)   254
National Council for Educational Research and Training (NCERT)   241
Ndelu, S.   109
Ndofirepi, A.   102
Nebres, B.   7
Nelson Mandela Foundation   243
neoliberalism   84–86, 103, 237, 256
neoliberal multiculturalism   84–86
nepantla   131
Netherlands   216, 217
neutrality   7, 17, 51, 80, 103, 104, 110, 113, 129, 162, 213, 232, 250, 254, 255
New Brunswick   66
New York City   2, 9, 19
New Zealand *see* Aotearoa
Newfoundland   66
Ngcukana, L.   106
Nickel, L.   213
Nicol, C.   83, 85
Nicolson, M.   124
Nielsen, L.   11, 31, 33–35, 38, 43
Nigeria   125
Noble, S. U.   5, 6

Nobre, S. R.   257
nominalisation   62
non-cooperation movement   243
Nordén, B.   187
Nordic School   1, 7, 10, 11; *see also* Scandinavian tradition
Norén, E.   152, 161
norm   5, 27–29, 217
normalisation   10, 53, 84, 93, 113, 212, 215, 217, 220–224, 235
North   103, 104
North America   8, 13, 25, 30, 32, 35, 86
northern epistemologies   15
Norway   31, 172, 175, 178, 180, 196, 201
Norwegian   151
Nottingham   249
Nova Scotia   47, 48, 66
Nuccitelli, D.   186, 202
number line   64
Nutti, Y. J.   13, 25, 35–43

O'Neil, C.   5, 6, 16, 256
obesity   12, 18–20, 210–225, 233–235, 238
objectivity   5, 8, 51, 80, 87, 127, 130, 181, 220, 221
Ochigame, R.   257
Ogden, C. L.   212
oil   87, 170, 175, 178, 195, 196
Old Babylonia   251
Oliver, J. E.   217
Oluo, I.   136
Omar, Y.   108
Ontario   211, 212
operations (in mathematics)   62, 63, 156
oppressed   8
oppression   5, 7, 8, 9, 11, 13, 14, 16, 32, 58, 86, 125, 127–132, 134, 135, 145, 253, 254
optimism of the will   248, 249, 257
Oreskes, N.   197, 198
Organisation for Economic Co-operation and Development (OECD)   189, 191
Osibodu, O.   140
Other, the   83, 128, 236, 238, 250, 251, 252

Pais, A.   101, 123, 125, 128, 129
Palestine   152
pan-Africanism   108
Paris Agreement   2, 168, 179, 186
Paris, D.   256
Parra, A.   11, 14, 15, 29, 30, 32, 33, 75, 84, 90, 94, 233, 235, 236, 238, 242, 245, 252, 257

participation 3, 17, 154, 166, 172, 174, 176, 178, 182, 192, 245, 248
 in classrooms 85, 110–112, 150, 174–177, 181, 195, 242
 in community 57, 82, 131, 135, 136, 150, 174–177, 181
 in mathematics 42, 110, 174, 175, 177, 181, 232
 in public debate 11, 102, 147, 167, 169–171, 175–177, 182, 197, 211, 224, 232
 in research activities 14, 59, 63, 83, 125, 133, 138–140, 193, 252
Pascal's triangle 28
Patel, L. 125, 128, 137, 139, 236
patriarchy 108, 131
patterns (mathematical) 28, 29, 58, 62, 63, 215, 216, 220
pausing 125, 137, 139, 236
Programa de Educación Bilingüe Intercultural (PEBI) 81
pedagogy 8, 9, 11, 13, 17, 20, 24, 36, 40, 52, 71, 75, 80, 82, 84, 89, 92, 101, 115, 145, 148, 152, 166, 167, 182, 188, 233, 241, 242, 256
Pekar, T. 217
Pennycook, A. 84
People for Education Conference 66
People's Maths for People's Power 101
percentiles 215, 218
Perez, G. 4, 5
performativity 29, 72, 89, 94
Persian 151, 155
Perú 85
pessimism of the intellect 248, 249, 257
Pettersson, D. 256
philosophy of mathematics 250
physical access 111, 112, 113, 115, 116
pi 50, 55, 56
Piaget, J. 10
Picower, B. 124, 126
Piketty, T. 257, 258
Pinar, W. F. 243
Pinxten, R. 13
PISA see Programme for International Student Assessment
Pithouse, R. 102, 108, 115
Pityana, B. 109, 117
place 11, 15, 25, 39–42, 48, 58, 75–80, 83, 87, 103, 110, 116, 118, 125, 127–129, 131, 138, 172, 176, 245, 246
place-based education 36, 38, 40, 82, 84

polar bear 173, 194, 195, 203
Polish 151
political 4, 6, 9, 11, 19, 51–54, 71, 72, 75, 80–82, 87–93, 101, 103, 110, 117, 124, 145–147, 150, 162, 168, 170, 186, 187, 190, 196, 232, 236, 244, 248, 249, 252–255, 257, 258
 political dimension 3, 10, 43, 44
 political engagement 13, 15, 18, 74, 80
 political institutions 49, 94
 political questions/concerns 32, 44, 71, 80, 94, 196
 political research 43, 71, 72, 89, 91, 92, 94, 242
 political role 17
 political struggle 14, 71, 72, 80, 94, 253
 political superstructure 254
 politically active 1, 3, 7, 31, 33–35, 174, 190
 political neutrality 250, 255
 political space 51, 80, 88, 233
politicians 6, 12, 39, 169, 173, 175, 190, 196, 199, 200, 205, 235, 236, 241
politicised trust 123, 137, 138
politics of knowledge 33
politics of mathematics education 10
Popkewitz, T. S. 256
Portland 253
positionality 139
post-normal science 17, 19, 166, 167, 169–172, 182, 189, 190
post-political 91
Potter, J. 214
poverty 6, 19, 41, 42, 91, 102, 115, 255
Powell, A. B. 11, 51, 249
power 11, 15, 18, 30, 31, 33, 34, 39, 41–43, 51, 74, 80, 81, 86, 87, 92, 100–104, 109–111, 113, 115–117, 123, 127, 128, 131, 132, 134, 137, 139, 147, 153, 155, 157, 158, 162, 168, 185, 186, 188–194, 196, 199, 200, 204–206, 231, 232, 234, 235, 237, 238, 240, 244, 254, 256
Pratt, D. 176
Prince Edward Island 66
Prince, R. 105
prism 62
Prison Overcrowding and Health (Prisons) 105, 106, 112–115
privilege 16, 20, 30, 51, 86, 107, 124, 129, 131, 235, 236, 237
probability 2, 4, 41, 58, 170, 174
problem-based education 83

INDEX

problem-solving   5, 27, 105, 154–156, 174
product (mathematical)   62
prospective medical doctors *see* medical programme
Programme for International Student Assessment (PISA)   189, 191
propio   14, 71, 72, 74, 75, 80–83, 86–94
protest   2, 3, 15, 74, 78, 102, 106, 108, 109, 112–118, 257
Proyecto Educativo Comunitario (PEC)   74,75
public debate   175–177, 182, 205
Public Health Care Directorate (South Africa)   104
pyramid   62
Pythagorean theorem   28, 50

quantitative literacy   105, 240
quantity   63, 198, 220
Quebec   66
Quechua   94, 252
Quetelet Index   216–218
Quetelet, M. A.   216–222
Quijano Valencia, O.   93
quotient   62

race   1, 5, 12, 15, 18, 20, 41, 107, 109, 111–113, 117, 123–126, 128, 129, 132–134, 136, 137, 140, 220, 222, 244, 254, 256
racial hierarchy   3, 6, 16, 86, 108, 117, 124, 125, 131, 133, 255
racial justice   12, 15, 16, 132
racialisation   102, 123, 125, 130, 132, 133, 252
racism   1, 5, 15, 20, 86, 114, 123, 124, 127, 130, 132, 135, 136, 138, 139, 251, 252
Radford, L.   150, 154, 155
radical hope   237, 238
Ramanujam, R.   241
Rampal, A.   19, 241, 244, 245
Rangnes, T. E.   17, 206, 233, 234, 253
Rappaport, J.   88, 243
rate   14, 57, 105, 106, 108, 113, 168, 210, 212, 217, 220
ratio   105, 216, 218, 219
rationality   9, 10
Ravetz, J. R.   169, 170, 189, 190, 199
Ravn, O.   250
Raygoza, M. C.   252
reading (and writing) the world   8, 9, 11, 32, 33, 53, 110, 112, 113, 115, 241, 242, 245, 253

real data   173, 177, 179, 181
realised abstraction   171, 172, 210, 213–215, 221, 222
reflecting on and with mathematics   17, 33, 34, 40–42, 44, 131, 166, 172, 174, 176, 177, 179, 181, 182, 187, 188, 190, 196, 197, 235, 241
reflection of a graph   62
reflexivity   1, 3, 7, 12, 13–16, 101–103
regime of truth   91, 92
relations (mathematical)   10, 56, 63, 216, 217
relationships   9, 12, 24, 27, 39, 40, 42, 48, 49, 52, 55, 57, 59, 61, 65, 72, 81, 82, 85, 89, 127, 132, 137, 138, 145, 240, 241, 250, 251, 253, 254
relevance   4, 10, 12, 13, 14, 16, 19, 36, 37, 57–60, 71, 73, 77, 80, 84, 86, 87, 90, 93, 104, 108, 151, 167, 178, 181, 195–198, 201, 231, 232, 234, 253
relevant problems   172, 173, 177, 180, 206
reproduction (power relations)   31, 33, 34, 41, 86, 92, 124
Rethinking Schools organisation   253
righteous anger   138
righting our world   240, 241, 244, 245
rights   32, 106, 108, 112–114, 124, 173
Rigney, L. I.   55
risk   2, 5, 17, 52, 80, 85, 92, 103, 117, 130, 131, 161, 162, 169–171, 173, 174, 195, 196, 219, 222, 235, 256
Rittel, H. W. J.   233
Roberts, T.   140
Rogoff, B.   245
Rojas, A.   83, 84
role of values in mathematics   169, 173, 176, 182
Rosling Rönnlund, A.   6
Rosling, H.   6
Rosling, O.   6
Roth, W.-M.   250
Rotorua   90
Rowlands, S.   28, 29, 52
Roy, A.   248
Rubel, L. H.   13, 25, 35–42, 256
Rughubar-Reddy, S.   15, 16, 233, 236, 251
Russo, M.   242
Rutter, H.   234
Ryan, U.   17, 19, 162, 233, 235, 236, 238, 250

Saker, A.   213
Sámi   24, 35–43

San Andres de Pisimbalá 75
Santer, B. D 186
Santibañez, L. 84, 86
Sápmi 13, 25, 42
Saraswathi, L. S. 241
Scandinavian tradition 30, 31; *see also* Nordic school
Scandiuzzi, P. P. 81
Schindler, M. 149
Schleppegrell, M. J. 62
Schmidt, G. A. 186, 201, 202
Schwarz, B. 173
Schwarzenegger, A. 223
Scotland 221
Scroggins, A. 140
self-aware 1, 3, 7
Sepedi 107
Serbian 151, 152, 155
settler colonialism 48, 51
Shackville TRC 108, 109
Sharp, D. W. 252
Sharp, F. 84
Sharp, N. 84
Sherrington, G. H. 197
Show Me Your Math programme 53, 54, 56–60
Shubenacadie 48
Sichra, I. 75
Silver, N. 4
Singer-Vine, J. 218
Sistema Educativo Indígena Propio (SEIP) 74, 80
skepticism 250
Skog, K. 152, 161
Skovsmose, O. 1, 10, 11, 16, 31, 33–35, 38, 43, 44, 50, 52, 53, 60, 80, 101, 102, 110, 116, 147, 148, 150, 166, 171, 177, 186–192, 196, 198, 200, 210, 211, 213, 214, 223, 249–251, 256
slope 63
small-scale project 17, 145, 146, 148, 162
Smith, L. T. 50, 51, 54, 83, 252
Smith, S. 127
Sobel, D. 83, 85
social access 100, 112, 114, 116
social justice 9, 14, 19, 36, 37, 39–41, 43, 57, 101, 102, 105, 110, 113, 118, 167, 183, 188, 196, 231, 237, 242
societal issues 1, 11, 19, 32m 145, 147, 210, 217

society 3–13, 16–18, 20, 31, 34, 37, 40, 48, 49, 54, 75, 83, 84, 92, 93, 100–102, 104, 106, 108, 110, 114, 116–118, 129, 144–155, 157–160, 162, 168–172, 176, 182, 185–187, 189–192, 194–196, 199, 200, 202, 205, 206, 213–215, 223, 224, 232–235, 237, 244, 250, 251, 257
solidarity 123, 155, 237, 238, 240, 257
Sotho group of languages 106
South 103, 244
South Africa 15, 20, 26, 100–106, 108–111, 114–118, 218, 243, 244, 249
South America 32, 72
Southern Theory 102
sovereignty 48, 75, 77
Spanish 72, 74, 76, 79, 81, 94
spatial justice 35, 37, 39, 41, 42
Spring, J. 255
square colour tiles 65
standard deviation 6
statistics 4, 10, 43, 108, 113–115, 175, 177, 186, 188, 194, 196, 198, 204, 210, 212, 216–220, 222, 223, 234, 242, 256, 257
Statistics Canada 211, 212, 219
Stavrou, S. G. 86, 87, 245, 252
Steffensen, L. 17, 19, 192, 204, 206, 233, 234, 235, 237, 253
STEM education 255
stereotype 6, 14, 47, 49, 52, 113, 114, 116, 117, 154, 155
Steuter-Martin, M. 223
Stewart, J. M. 211
Stinson, D. W. 53, 242
Stockholm 149
Street, B. 110
stretch of a graph 62
Stroeve, J. C. 202
structuralism 29, 30
student debate 114, 145, 146, 151, 152, 155, 158, 160, 161, 173, 175, 177
student ideas 40–43, 57, 59, 60, 62, 65, 77–79, 81, 113, 114, 144, 146, 148–155, 158, 162, 173, 175, 177, 193, 196, 198
student values 64, 108–109, 113, 114, 145, 158, 173, 176–178
subaltern 83, 84, 87
subjectification 92, 231, 233, 237, 238
subjectivation 74, 75, 92
subjectivity 91–93, 238, 243, 245
subtraction 62
sum 62, 78

INDEX

Swanson, D. M.   83, 237
Sweden   2, 17, 144, 151, 152, 166
Swedish   17, 146, 151, 152, 154, 155, 158–161
Swinehart, T.   253
Switzerland   166

Tabares Fernández, J. F.   86, 92
Tagore   243
talk and reason   151
Tattay, L.   71, 75, 81, 84, 88, 92
Tatum, B. D.   136
Te Aho Matua   89
Te Kura o Te Koutu   90
Te Reo Māori   90
technoscepticism   256
temperature   2, 166, 176, 178–181, 186, 187, 193, 195–205, 235
ten frames   64
tensions   16, 28, 29, 50, 91, 123, 124, 126–132, 134–136, 138, 139, 168, 178
textbook   36, 39, 42, 57, 240, 241
theory   8, 10, 11, 15, 17, 20, 24, 36, 52, 100–104, 109, 117, 118, 124, 134, 148, 149, 187, 198, 254, 259
Thesen, L.   103
Thunberg, G.   2, 3, 9, 19, 20, 166, 168, 234, 253
Tierradentro   14, 75, 77
tipping points   2
Tlingit Clan Conference   252
Topkok, A.   60
transforming   8, 18, 31, 33, 34, 36, 38, 39, 49, 50, 53, 55, 61, 62, 66, 71, 72, 75, 82, 83, 91, 94, 112, 114, 128, 139, 149, 198, 233, 240, 245, 249
translation of a graph   62
triangle   62
Trinick, T.   90
trust   55, 123, 130, 135–139, 199, 236
truth   28, 29, 158, 220, 255, 258
Truth and Reconciliation Commission of Canada (TRC)   14, 47–51, 56, 59, 65
Tuck, E.   48, 50, 53
Turkey   125

Ubuntu   83
UK *see* United Kingdom
uncertainty   17, 53, 126, 169–171, 173, 177, 179, 182, 185, 186, 188–190, 192, 197, 198, 201, 204–206, 233–236
United Kingdom (UK)   132, 173, 178, 210, 222

United States (USA)   5, 15, 16, 24, 38, 91, 124, 125, 129, 132, 140, 178, 186, 200, 212, 218, 222, 253–255
universality   28, 51, 74, 83, 84, 87, 88, 92, 103, 233, 241, 244, 255
University of Cape Town   15, 104, 105
unreasonable political effectiveness of "mathematics"   255
urgency   1–3, 6, 7, 17–19, 50, 166, 169, 182, 187, 189, 233–235, 253, 257
Urton, G.   252
useful mathematics   108, 157, 176, 177, 179, 182

Vakil, S.   123, 137
Valero, P.   7, 14, 15, 32, 33, 72, 87, 91, 92, 101, 233, 235, 236, 242, 245, 250, 255, 257
value-laden space   2, 8, 11, 17, 20, 27, 29, 30, 43, 49, 51, 54, 59, 61, 63, 80, 81, 100–102, 110, 115, 128, 145, 147, 149, 150, 158, 169–171, 173, 174, 176, 177, 181, 182, 187, 189, 190, 233, 235, 244, 250
variable   173, 216
verbifying   47, 62–65
vertices   62
violence   87, 109, 113
Vithal, R.   11, 52, 102, 188, 249, 251
voice   14, 15, 19, 37, 47, 49, 51, 52, 55, 64, 72, 104, 106, 112, 114, 117, 118, 134, 168
Volmink, J.   102

Wager, A. A.   140, 242
Wagner, D.   13, 25–27, 32, 34, 51, 55–57, 59, 147, 232, 236, 241, 242, 245, 256
Walkerdine, V.   10
Walsh, C.   84, 108
waltes   57, 58, 63
Wanderer, F.   90, 252, 257
Warren, E.   86
Watson, J.   173
Watts, A.   203
We'koqma'q   47, 48, 54, 66
Webber, M. M.   233
West Bengal   252
Western knowledge   51, 59, 65, 86, 101, 103, 241
western mathematics   28, 36, 37, 40, 42, 44, 52, 72, 90, 92, 236
white institutional space   16, 126, 132, 138
white supremacy   86, 124, 127–131, 133, 248

whiteness (the centering of)   16, 53, 123–135, 137–139
Wildman, R. E. C.   217
Wing, A. K.   133
Winkelstein Jr., W.   216
Winsberg, E.   186
Wiseman, D.   51, 52, 59
Wittgenstein, L.   17, 148
Wolfmeyer, M.   136, 255
workers   3, 5, 102, 108, 112–117, 222
working class   8, 152
working conditions   109, 112, 113
World Economic Forum   166, 234
World Health Organization   218
worldview   6, 47, 59, 61, 64, 65, 74, 242, 250

xenophobia   102

Yanez, E.   252
Yang, K. W.   48, 50, 53
Yanik, H. B.   223
Yasukawa, K.   110
Yolcu, A.   140
Yup'ik   60, 252

Zatz, Z.   257
Zavala, M.   83
Zevenbergen, R.   7
Zimbabwe   244
Zinn, H.   253
Zolkower, B.   25
Zuboff, S.   256

Printed in the United States
by Baker & Taylor Publisher Services